D1018024

*The National Archives*

Colonel House and Woodrow Wilson in 1917

# WOODROW WILSON
## *AND*
# COLONEL HOUSE

## *A Personality Study*

ALEXANDER L. GEORGE

*and*

JULIETTE L. GEORGE

DOVER PUBLICATIONS, INC.

NEW YORK

*For our son*
*and for Dr. Marjorie S. Braude*

Copyright © 1956 by Alexander L. George and Juliette L. George
Copyright © 1964 by Alexander L. George and Juliette L. George
All rights reserved under Pan American and International Copyright Conventions.

Published in Canada by General Publishing Company, Ltd., 30 Lesmill Road, Don Mills, Toronto, Ontario.
Published in the United Kingdom by Constable and Company, Ltd., 10 Orange Street, London WC 2.

This Dover edition, first published in 1964, is an unabridged and corrected republication of the work first published by The John Day Company in 1956. A new preface has been written by the authors especially for this Dover edition.

***Standard Book Number: 486-21144-4***
***Library of Congress Catalog Card Number: 64-18850***

Manufactured in the United States of America
Dover Publications, Inc.
31 East 2nd Street
Mineola, N.Y. 11501

# PREFACE TO DOVER EDITION

We welcome the opportunity afforded by publication of this new edition of our effort to study the life of Woodrow Wilson in the light of psychoanalytic theory to set down a few thoughts on the general problem of the relevance of psychoanalysis to the biographer's work.*

It has often been noted that there exists a gap, which can never be bridged, between the range of data available to the psychoanalyst and that available to the biographer. For this reason, some have concluded that biographers cannot make effective use of psychoanalysis.

The analyst has the opportunity of learning in detail from the patient himself the unconscious feelings, wishes and fantasies which are the wellspring of his behavior. He has the object of his inquiry on his couch, providing the necessary material in the form of descriptions of his life experience, transference reactions, dreams and free associations.

The biographer, on the other hand, has no such access to his subject's intimate thoughts through personal contact. In those rare cases in which his subject is alive and willing to provide him information, the biographer who ventured to ask for the sort of personal revelation which the analyst routinely requires of his patient doubtless, and understandably, would be given short shrift indeed. Almost always even when his subject is alive and always when he is dead, the biographer is at the mercy of a finite and distressingly incomplete body of information.

The force of this argument cannot be denied. It must be admitted that no biographer can "psychoanalyze" his subject because he is not in possession of that data pertaining to the subject's unconscious without which psychoanalysis in the classical sense is not possible.

* The following pages are part of a study on psychoanalysis and biography which we are preparing. Our work has been aided by a grant from the Foundations' Fund for Research in Psychiatry.

However, those who rely on this obvious point to substantiate the argument that psychoanalysis is therefore of no use in the biographer's enterprise overlook two important facts. They overlook, first, that "psychoanalysis" refers not only to a therapy for personality disorders: it also denotes a theoretical system of psychology, based on empirical clinical observation, which accounts for the structure, functioning and development of human personality. They overlook, second, that there is a crucial difference in the respective tasks of the psychoanalyst and the biographer, a difference which makes it possible for the biographer to work effectively on the basis of data which would not suffice for the purposes of the psychoanalyst.

The psychoanalyst is bent upon a therapeutic result with his patient, upon a reawakening in the analytic situation of unresolved conflicts with a view to providing the patient an opportunity to achieve more satisfactory solutions than those he originally adopted. The biographer, on the other hand, is spared the difficult task of attempting to alter his subject's personality. He wishes only to comprehend it and to transmit his comprehension to an audience of readers by means of a written narrative. These two facts are of paramount importance in the controversy about the feasibility of applying psychoanalytic theory to biographical material.

Psychoanalytic psychology comprehends individual human behavior in terms of the history and development and the past and present relationships of the id, the ego and the superego which, it claims, comprise the human psyche. By now, psychoanalysts have studied these complex relationships in thousands of cases in which patients have provided data about their unconscious processes and in which the psychoanalytic procedure has served as a method of research as well as a method of cure.

Certain types of readily observable behavior have been related to certain causal factors and varieties of conflict. Adequate understanding of analytic theory and experience sensitizes the biographer (as well as the analyst in *his* task) to the types of material to watch for as he examines the data available to him. The large body of published clinical data gathered by psychoanalysts over the past few generations puts at the biographer's disposal clues as to the possible significance of certain patterns of behavior or habits or traits of character of which he might otherwise take no notice.

The biographer's need is satisfied by this access to diagnostic hypotheses. The therapist's task, however, only begins with diagnosis, for he has the job of helping his patient achieve a more satisfactory distribution of his instinctual energies, one which will eliminate the need to invest so large a proportion of his emotional capital in maintaining repressions and struggling, consciously or unconsciously, to realize unrealizable infantile fantasies. To achieve this goal, he embarks with his patient upon an exploration of the patient's unconscious. If the therapeutic collaboration is successful, the patient will become aware of his repressed impulses and will learn to deal with them more expeditiously, consciously. The analyst's relentless pursuit of his patient's unconscious fantasies is necessitated by the fact that in order to renounce the unattainable infantile pleasures around which are woven the fantasies which hold him in thrall, the patient must confront his past and his deepest impulses with courage and feeling.

For his part, the analyst has in most instances long since known what ails his patient. Their intensive work together is not primarily to provide material for the analyst's diagnosis—although undoubtedly his diagnosis becomes more exact as the material unfolds—but to enable the patient to grow and change.

Indeed, psychoanalysts are usually able to perceive the essential dynamics of the patient's personality and the general nature of his problems very early in the treatment situation, even before the patient has produced the dreams, free associations and transference reactions which reveal in detail the contents of his unconscious.

Freud once remarked that, try as he may, a person cannot conceal what is motivating him—all manner of surface behavior expresses the basic constellation of unconscious impulses. Again, in a paper on analytic technique, Freud noted that "it is not difficult for a skilled analyst to read the patient's hidden wishes plainly between the lines of his complaints and the story of his illness." Some contemporary training analysts—e.g., Franz Alexander and Leon Saul—hold that the analyst can and should discern the patient's central conflict and the basic outlines of his personality in the very first interview or, at the most, in the first few interviews, which usually consist largely in the patient's account of his difficulties and an initial narrative of significant life experiences.

For the analyst, then, to "read" the patient's unconscious and to understand what his problems are is apparently the least onerous part of his task. The real challenge is to induce the patient to change, and it is in connection with that part of the analytic endeavor that the patient must come to know the contents of his unconscious. (Some analysts claim that even for therapeutic purposes, it is often unnecessary to reconstruct the patient's unconscious infantile past; that, however, is strictly a point of therapeutic technique and not of concern in this context.)

A biographer, unless he is singularly unfortunate (in which case even a conventional biography will prove difficult), usually has considerable data about the way his subject feels and reacts to the problems of life, and he has even more detailed knowledge about his subject's actions in various situations. Indeed, he has available to him material which the analyst customarily does not have relating to the actual impact of his subject on other people, and he has more accurate evidence of how his subject actually interacts with others in reality since his materials include not only his subject's impressions of certain sequences of events but those of other people as well. In short, he often has at his disposal considerable data of a character which is meaningful in terms of psychoanalytic hypotheses, and these can be an invaluable aid to interpretation.

To argue the possibility of the fruitful application of psychoanalytic theory to biography is by no means to suggest that all biographers can or should attempt it. To master psychoanalytic theory takes many years of study. To apply it to biographical materials in a useful fashion is an extraordinarily difficult task which makes many demands upon the biographer not only as a scholar but as a human being.

The biographer's raw material customarily is locked up in books and files. There will usually be letters to and from the great man—the scrawl of the schoolboy writing to his parents, the ardent letters of the young man to his wife-to-be or perhaps to a friend in whom he confides his views of the world and his notion of his own place in it, the workaday correspondence with those associated with him in the conduct of his business. There will be newspaper accounts of his activities, memoranda by contemporaries, both friend and foe, telling the story of their association with the great man. If the political figure be of the mid-twentieth century or later, the biographer will be able to see and hear him at first hand by means of recordings and films, to study his gestures, his facial expressions, and personally to experience the impact of his public "style." Perhaps there are books written by the subject, or diaries revealing secret hopes and preoccupations. There will be official records—transcripts of meetings in which the great man participated and of speeches he made. There will be books of reminiscences by people who stood in various relationships to the biographical subject—adviser, wife, political rival, political supporter, journalist, friend. Each may have encountered a different facet of the great man so that he emerges in many different lights, and there is the further complication that each account will be colored by the idiosyncrasies of its author and also by his motives for undertaking to write it.

All this mass of material the biographer lets flow freely into him. He is the medium through whom the chaotic raw data is digested, ultimately to be rendered back in an orderly verbal re-creation of an intelligible human being, his individuality revealed. Insofar as the biographer correctly perceives and succeeds in expressing the logical connections among disparate facts, the subject of his biography will achieve a new life, vouchsafed to any who care to read about it. Only the biographer who has been able to filter the data through his own personality without in the end distorting it in consequence of its tortuous passage can perform this creative task.

It is, indeed, an extraordinary function that the biographer sets out to fulfill in relation to his subject. To perform it satisfactorily, he must possess, in addition to that devotion to diligent scholarship the need for which has been abundantly discussed in works of historiography, qualities of mind and spirit which have been less thoroughly explicated. Certainly biographers have been told often enough that they ought to be "unbiased" and that they ought to aim at presenting the "truth." The actual processes involved, however, the vicissitudes of the data between the time the biographer first encounters it and the time he finally transmutes it into a synthesized account, generally have been left untackled on the theory that these are manifestations of artistic creativity and that the essence of artistic creativity defies analysis. In short, the most vital aspect of the biographer's enterprise, the nature of the processes involved in his perception and digestion of the data, has been neglected.

The biographer wishes to *understand* the man whose life he is studying. In order to grasp why his subject behaved as he did in various situations, the biographer wishes to know him emotionally, to be able to experience vicariously the feelings which his subject experienced at various junctures of his life. He wishes to be able to participate in his subject's emotional experience sufficiently to comprehend it, but not to become so intensely involved that he is unable to stand back and dispassionately evaluate that experience in the full context of reality. In order to achieve his objective of conveying some truth about the human being he is studying, the biographer, as the psychoanalyst, must have the capacity for both involvement with and detachment from his subject. He must be involved in order to gain understanding of his subject's reactions; he must be detached in order to evaluate and analyze.

As the data flows into him, the biographer gradually builds a picture of what kind of person his subject was, what his characteristic attitudes and defenses were and how they developed, what made him anxious, what gratified him, what goals and values he adopted, how he went about pursuing them and so on.

At first, the biographer's picture of his subject is vague and sketchy, but as he becomes steeped in the data, more and more details are limned in, providing increasing points of reference. Then when he comes upon a situation in which the subject's behavior is somewhat puzzling, he pauses and attempts to project himself into his subject via the personality picture of him he has formed: how would a given situation or problem—perhaps it is some sort of political challenge or provocation—*feel* to the subject? The biographer, having saturated himself in knowledge of the times in which his subject lived and the external realities of his situation, now "listens" to the data from the inside, as it were, from the point of view of the interior reactions of his subject. If his image of the subject's personality has been well and sensitively derived and his insight into the nature of the problem at hand is accurate, the biographer is likely to achieve an understanding of how the subject experienced the external problem. The behavior, perhaps previously unfathomable, will then seem logical in terms of the inner psychological reality which produced it.

By empathizing, the biographer reaches his subject's feelings in a given situation. Giving free rein to his faculties, both conscious and unconscious, he next tries to grasp the logical connections between the emotions thus perceived and the subject's whole life history. Now he must subject the inferences which his intuition has yielded to strict, rational scrutiny in an attempt to evaluate their validity.

If his data is sufficient and he has functioned well in empathizing, in intuiting and finally in rigorously examining his conclusions, the biographer is now in a position to interpret the bit of historical evidence to which he has been addressing himself. The interpretation will be consonant with all that he knows about his subject, and it, and all the insights which contributed to its formulation, will enable him to develop and refine his mental image of his subject. That, in turn, will improve his ability to cope with the next problem of interpretation, for he will face it with an enriched awareness of his subject.

This is an iterative process. The biographer is constantly re-examining and revising his earlier interpretations of his subject's behavior with improved hypotheses gained from his expanding familiarity with and understanding of the data. His view of his subject gradually achieves an internal consistency as he works and reworks the material.

The foregoing account of the way in which the biographer goes about his work applies also to the way the psychoanalyst works—this aspect of his functioning has been fully described in psychoanalytic literature.* Many historians, however, undoubtedly would consider it merely word juggling: of course the biographer must empathize and intuit, they might reply. The real question is, how do you do it? What, since erudition alone obviously is not the answer, makes some people good at it and others inept? It is all very well to say that the biographer has in mind a picture of his subject's personality and that if this picture has been sensitively derived he will be able to project his own consciousness into his subject's feelings. The riddle lies precisely in what has been glossed over in the phrase, "if this picture has been sensitively derived": what, indeed, contributes and what detracts from the biographer's ability to be sensitive?

In this area, psychoanalysis has much to offer the historian which is novel to his accustomed way of thinking. Everything which psychoanalysts have discovered about what impairs or facilitates an analyst's ability to "see" his patient—all the phenomena of what is known in psychoanalytic theory as countertransference—holds also for what impairs or facilitates a biographer's ability to "see" his subject truly and fully.

* An excellent exposition, to which we are greatly indebted, is Dr. Ralph Greenson's paper "Empathy and Its Vicissitudes," read at the 1959 meeting of the International Psycho-Analytical Association and published in the *International Journal of Psycho-Analysis,* Vol. 41, July-October, 1960.

In order to understand his subject, the biographer must maintain that same attitude of freely hovering attention that Freud prescribed for analysts vis-à-vis their patients. If an analyst's capacity to maintain that attitude is impaired by anxious, hostile or guilty reactions to the patient deriving from unresolved problems of his own life experience, his understanding of the patient is impeded by his countertransference reactions. So too is the biographer's understanding of his subject reduced when the materials at hand elicit irrational irruptions from his own past. If that happens he is likely to produce that familiar phenomenon—the biography more revealing of its author than of its subject.

Analyst and biographer both must be able to participate without inhibition in the feelings of their subjects and this ability depends upon the range and quality of their emotional resonance as well as upon their rational equipment. Non- or even anti-psychoanalytically oriented biographers perforce also use their emotional endowment but, being unaware of that fact or denying it, they are in a poorer position to engage in full self-scrutiny for the purpose of eliminating distortions of perception and interpretation arising out of their own idiosyncrasies.

The psychoanalytic theory of human development is widely recognized as a rich source of hypotheses concerning human behavior. Within the past few generations, the fields of education, sociology, psychology and anthropology have been transformed by the impact of analytic conceptions. It would seem natural, then, that the historian and biographer, who wish not merely to describe but to account for the behavior of people individually and collectively, would seek to absorb and make use of this new body of knowledge. Some half century after Freud's formulation of the basic tenets of psychoanalytic theory, however, it must be conceded that there have been few noteworthy psychoanalytically oriented biographies. Why is this so?

For one thing, there are few first-rate psychoanalysts with the time and interest to do full-length biographical studies (Erik Erikson, who wrote an excellent biography of Luther, is one of the notable few); and there are few first-rate biographers with the time, interest and capacity to master analytic theory. Psychoanalytic theory cannot be used successfully by analysts as a short cut which reduces the need for painstaking historical research and the most scrupulous attention to the social setting in which the biographical subject lived. Nor can biographers inadequately grounded in psychoanalytic theory successfully appropriate bits and pieces of it to "explain" their protagonists. Numerous biographical atrocities committed particularly during the 1920's and 1930's, and quite properly dismissed by serious scholars as mockeries of the biographer's art, testify to this fact.

Another impediment to the development of a fruitful union between psychoanalytic theory and biographical research is the persistence of mutual suspicion between many psychoanalysts and many historians. A serious biographer, seeking to obtain research training in psychoanalytic theory with a view not to becoming a therapist but to applying analytic concepts to historical materials, will find the doors of the major psychoanalytic institutes closed to him. Nonmedical "outsiders" are rarely accepted as students for intensive training. To social scientists desiring to gain the technical competence required for the responsible use of analytic theory in their own disciplines, this bar to the privilege of formal instruction seems unreasonable.

Similarly, historians, as a group, regard psychoanalysis with an attitude of hostile skepticism. In 1957, the distinguished diplomatic historian, Professor William Langer of Harvard, then president of the American Historical Association, called attention to this fact in his presidential address to the Association. Professor Langer's talk was entitled "The Next Assignment," and this he identified as the exploitation by historians of the concepts and findings of psychoanalysis. He urged his colleagues to abandon their "almost completely negative attitude toward the teachings of psychoanalysis" and open their minds to analytic theory as the most promising key to further progress in historical study. It is hardly surprising that few historians to date have chosen to run the gantlet of their fraternity's scorn and possibly even to jeopardize their careers by attempting interdisciplinary work along lines so unsympathetically regarded.

These barriers to communication, however, are already giving way under the pressure of the quest for truth, and there are many hopeful beginnings of cooperative effort between psychoanalysts and social scientists. The psychoanalytically oriented biographer is likely to gain for his work today a fairer hearing than he could ever have hoped for in the past. His task remains difficult, but the promise of a deeper understanding of his subject is an irresistible lure and any success he achieves in this direction is a reward justifying his best effort.

A. L. G.
J. L. G.

*Los Angeles, California*
*January, 1964*

# AUTHORS' NOTE

Many people have helped us in our work either by giving us the benefit of their stimulating ideas, by giving us access to important manuscript collections or by applying their skills to our text.

We are indebted to Mrs. Woodrow Wilson for permission to consult the papers of Woodrow Wilson at the Library of Congress and to quote from certain of Wilson's writings; to Dr. Charles Seymour, for permission to examine and quote from the papers of Edward M. House at the Yale University Library; and to Miss Katharine E. Brand for permission to consult the papers of Ray Stannard Baker at the Library of Congress and to quote certain statements from them. Since 1949, the staff of the Library of Congress has accorded us many courtesies for which we should like to express our gratitude.

It is a pleasure for the senior author to acknowledge his long-standing indebtedness to Dr. Nathan Leites, whose course on personality in politics in 1941 at the University of Chicago started him on the study of Woodrow Wilson, and to Dr. Harold D. Lasswell, whose writings on power and personality have provided some of the central ideas we have attempted to apply in this study.

Our manuscript profited greatly from the discerning editorial attention it received from Elise F. Kendrick, who also prepared the index. Lucille M. Goldsen and Rosalie Fonoroff processed the manuscript with precision and good judgment.

Finally, we welcome the opportunity to record our thanks to Mary O. Lombard of the John Day Company, whose unflagging interest in our research over a period of several years has been a spur to our efforts.

A. L. G.
J. L. G.

# ACKNOWLEDGMENTS

The authors wish to thank Mrs. Harris E. Kirk for permission to quote a statement about Wilson prepared by her late husband for Ray Stannard Baker; Henry Cabot Lodge, Jr., for permission to quote from Senator Lodge's *The Senate and the League of Nations* (Charles Scribner's Sons, 1925) and also from certain of Senator Lodge's letters; Mrs. Charles E. Merriam for permission to quote from Charles E. Merriam's *Four American Party Leaders* (The Macmillan Company, 1926); Edmund Wilson for permission to quote from *Shores of Light* (Farrar, Straus and Young, Inc., 1952).

They also wish to thank the following publishers for permission to quote from books issued by them, as follows:

APPLETON-CENTURY-CROFTS, INC.: James Kerney, *The Political Education of Woodrow Wilson.* Copyright, 1926, Century Company. Quoted by permission of Appleton-Century-Crofts, Inc.

BEAVERBROOK NEWSPAPERS, LTD.: David Lloyd George, *Memoirs of the Peace Conference* (Yale University Press, 1939).

THE BOBBS-MERRILL COMPANY, INC.: James E. Watson, *As I Knew Them* (Copyright © 1936), used by special permission of the publishers; Edith Bolling Wilson, *My Memoir* (Copyright © 1938), used by special permission of the publishers.

COLUMBIA UNIVERSITY PRESS: Woodrow Wilson, *Constitutional Government in the United States* (1908).

DOUBLEDAY & COMPANY, INC.: Ray Stannard Baker, *What Wilson Did at Paris* (1919), *Woodrow Wilson: Life and Letters* (8 volumes), *Woodrow Wilson and World Settlement* (3 volumes)—all quoted by permission of Doubleday & Company, Inc.; Herbert C. F. Bell, *Woodrow Wilson and the People* (Doubleday, Doran and Company, Inc., 1945); Stephen Bonsal, *Unfinished Business* (1944), quoted by permission of Doubleday & Company, Inc.; Carter Glass, *An Adventure in Constructive Finance* (Doubleday, Page & Company, 1927); A. D. H. Smith, *The Real Colonel House* (George H. Doran Company, 1918); Joseph P. Tumulty, *Woodrow Wilson As I Know Him* (1921), quoted by permission of Doubleday & Company, Inc.

GERALD DUCKWORTH & COMPANY, LTD., for the British rights to: George S. Viereck, *The Strangest Friendship in History* (Liveright, Inc., 1932).
FARRAR, STRAUS & CUDAHY, INC.: William S. Hillman, *Mr. President.* Copyright 1952 by William Hillman and Alfred Wagg. Published by Farrar, Straus & Cudahy, Inc. Quoted by permission of the publisher.
VICTOR GOLLANCZ, LTD., for British rights to: George A. R. Riddell, *Lord Riddell's Intimate Diary of the Peace Conference and After, 1918–1923* (1933).
HARCOURT, BRACE AND COMPANY, INC.: George A. R. Riddell, *Lord Riddell's Intimate Diary of the Peace Conference and After, 1918–1923* (Victor Gollancz, Ltd., 1933).
HARPER & BROTHERS: Allan Nevins, *Henry White: Thirty Years of American Diplomacy* (1930).
HOUGHTON MIFFLIN COMPANY: Robert Lansing, *The Peace Negotiations* (1921); William Lawrence, *Henry Cabot Lodge* (1925); Henry Cabot Lodge, *War Addresses, 1915–1917* (1917); Charles Seymour, *The Intimate Papers of Colonel House* (1930); William Allen White, *Woodrow Wilson* (1924); Woodrow Wilson, *Congressional Government* (15th edition).
B. W. HUEBSCH, INC.: William B. Hale, *The Story of a Style* (1920).
INDIANA UNIVERSITY PRESS: Edward H. Buehrig, *Woodrow Wilson and the Balance of Power* (1955).
LIVERIGHT PUBLISHING CORPORATION: George S. Viereck, *The Strangest Friendship in History* (1932).
THE MACMILLAN COMPANY: Thomas A. Bailey, *Woodrow Wilson and the Great Betrayal* (1945), and James T. Shotwell, *At the Paris Peace Conference* (1937), both quoted by permission of The Macmillan Company.
NEW YORK UNIVERSITY PRESS: Edward S. Corwin, *The President, Office and Powers, 1787–1948* (1948).
OVERSEAS PRESS CLUB OF AMERICA, INC.: George S. Viereck, "Behind the House-Wilson Break," in *The Inside Story* (Prentice-Hall, Inc., 1940).
OXFORD UNIVERSITY PRESS, INC.: Edith G. Reid, *Woodrow Wilson* (1934).
PRINCETON UNIVERSITY PRESS: Arthur S. Link, *Wilson: The Road to the White House* (1947).
G. P. PUTNAM'S SONS: D. F. Fleming, *The United States and the League of Nations, 1918–1920* (1932); Mary Allen Hulbert, *The Story of Mrs. Peck* (Minton, Balch & Co., 1933); David Hunter Miller, *The Drafting of the Covenant* (1928).
THE UNIVERSITY OF CHICAGO PRESS: Robert E. Osgood, *Ideals and Self-Interest in America's Foreign Relations* (Copyright 1953 by the University of Chicago).

# CONTENTS

# INTRODUCTION

At the turn of the century, Woodrow Wilson and Edward Mandell House were entering early middle age seemingly well settled in careers at some remove from the national political scene. Both men, to all outer appearances, were highly successful. House, in Austin, Texas, had been chief adviser to four Texas governors and was eagerly sought after to continue in that capacity. Wilson was a distinguished professor at one of the nation's great universities, Princeton, and was soon to be chosen its president. Yet both men suffered from a sense of failure. For House had long cherished dreams of guiding events on a national scale: he wanted to be a *President's* adviser. And Wilson, from childhood on, had wanted to be a statesman. They were both apparently firmly committed to other paths of activity at a stage of life at which most men tend to feel permanently settled in their vocations. Yet, eleven years later when they met, each helped the other to achieve the ambition of his life. House helped Wilson to become President of the United States. Wilson accepted House as adviser and close personal friend.

House lived to play a role which the New York *Times* truly characterized, the day after his death, as "unique in history." Except during the Paris Peace Conference and, during the war, on special missions to Europe to confer with Allied leaders, he had occupied no official position. He had been neither elected nor appointed to any office. He was, simply, President Wilson's personal friend and adviser. A President's relations with his personal adviser are prescribed neither by law nor custom and they are legally delimited only in that the adviser cannot formally exercise the powers of the President.

Wilson chose to give House unprecedented scope for his activities. He sought and accepted House's advice on a wide variety of problems, both public and personal. The President's reliance on him elevated House to a position of great power. The Colonel, whose health was poor, disliked traveling to Washington, especially in hot weather; so the President often journeyed to New York to consult him. House suggested seven of the ten members of Wilson's first Cabinet. Although there was, as usual, a Secretary of State, many diplomats paid scant attention to him except, of course, socially. Instead, they too journeyed to New York or sometimes to Magnolia, Massachusetts, House's summer retreat, to present their most important requests. For they had learned that this mild-mannered man, although just a private citizen, exercised a powerful influence on United States foreign policy, and could be of considerable help to them whatever their problem might be.

House was shy and self-effacing. The public interest in his activities seemed genuinely to disconcert him. He preferred to work out of the limelight. So tactful and adroit was he that it was said that he could walk over dry leaves and make no sound, or walk over dough and leave no footprints. The mystery of his influence inspired millions of words of speculation on the part of journalists and historians all over the world. The celebrated "break" between House and Wilson at the Paris Peace Conference touched off a flood of conjecture.

The House-Wilson story is a fascinating one and well worth the telling for its own sake. The authors have had the privilege of consulting the papers of Colonel House at Yale University, and are able to present relevant information, as yet unpublished, which throws new light on the collaboration between the two men and permits a more detailed examination of the basis upon which it rested.

Many writers, after considering the facts of the House-Wilson relationship, conclude that it is yet another manifestation of Wilson's "enigmatic" and complex personality. It is a striking characteristic of the myriad evaluations of Wilson that he is so regularly depicted as a man beset by great inner conflict which somehow led to self-defeat.

Shortly before his death in 1924, Wilson selected Ray Stannard Baker as custodian of his private papers. Baker embarked upon a monumental biographical study, in the course of which he solicited the reminiscences of hundreds of people who had known Wilson—his boyhood friends, teachers, classmates, relatives, friends, business associates. These fascinating memoranda are preserved in the Baker Papers in the Library of Congress, where the authors examined them. One after another, they testify to the existence in Wilson of some consuming inner difficulty for which he paid a terrible price. By common consent, he contributed heavily to the ruinous imbroglio in which he became involved as President of Princeton University. As President of the United States, his provocative behavior all but invited the catastrophic defeat he suffered when the Senate refused to ratify the Versailles Peace Treaty with the League of Nations in it. And one by one, in anguish, he cast away the cherished friends who might have helped him, if only he would let them. Of these, Colonel House was the most celebrated. One can dip into these Baker memoranda almost at random and come upon comments like the following.

"If I were going to write a biography of Mr. Wilson," wrote Harris E. Kirk, a Presbyterian minister who had known Wilson both at Princeton and later, in Washington, "I should explain his policies and career chiefly in terms of his personality; finding the key to them all in his, shall I venture to say, divided nature."

Thomas F. Woodlock wrote Baker: "The nemesis that Woodrow Wilson vainly fought was within himself, but it was as unchangeable, as inexorable as the Greek Fates. In the last few years of his life there was something Promethean about him. The eagle's beak and claws were in his vitals as he lay bound and helpless on his rock of sickness, but he was grimly enduring and coldly defiant to the last. In the lonely citadel of his soul, proud in the conviction that his cause was wholly just, utterly intolerant of criticism, utterly ruthless to opposition, he could not compromise with his daemon. Tragedy if it be not noble is not tragedy, and no one will deny to Woodrow Wilson the elements of nobility. Yet it must be said that the world suffers when Prometheus suffers, and that the very essence of statesmanship lies not in the grim endurance of foreordained defeat, but rather in the wisdom to know when to take occasion by the hand and by yielding the shadow to gain the substance. To deny to Woodrow Wilson the quality of supreme statesmanship is only to say that he followed his daemon to the last. And his is a tragedy that Sophocles might well have imagined."

Lindley M. Garrison, at one time Wilson's Secretary of War, confessed his perplexity to Baker: "I was never able to understand Mr. Wilson and with due deference I doubt if you or anybody else can. He was the most extraordinary and complex character I ever encountered."

After long immersion in the Wilson materials, Baker wrote that "the dictum of Edward Gibbon, long ago set down in his memoirs, that 'the most essential and important' part of the biographer's task lies in discovering and presenting the 'private life' of his subject, applies with a peculiar force in the case of Woodrow Wilson."

In his biography of Wilson, William Allen White writes: ". . . One who follows the Wilson story feels like clamoring wildly, like a gallery god in a melodrama, for a brawl, for a bitter contest, for someone to come and release the festering rage in our hero's underconsciousness, by a whacking blow, spiritual, or even physical, to give his soul relief and to restore wholesome circulation of his moral blood."

Wilson himself was aware of a disturbing inner turbulence. He once told his wife that he felt as though he were carrying a volcano about with him. On another occasion he confessed to her that he had constantly to "guard my emotions from painful overflow." A few hours after news of his nomination for the Presidency reached him, he remarked to his private secretary, "You know, Tumulty, there are two natures combined in me that every day fight for supremacy and control. On the one side, there is the Irish in me, quick, generous, impulsive, passionate, anxious always to help and to sympathize with those in distress. And like the Irishman at the Donnybrook Fair, always willin' to raise me shillalah and to hit any head which stands firninst me. Then, on the other side, there is the Scotch—canny, tenacious, cold and perhaps a little exclusive. I tell you, my dear friend, that when these two fellows get to quarreling among themselves, it is hard to act as umpire between them."

Wilson has been denounced by some biographers and extolled by others. A few, notably A. S. Link, have set down the facts of his career impartially and discerningly. A generation after his death, the task of telling what Wilson did is well under way. The task of gaining insight into *why* and *how* he made important decisions and *why* he was attracted to the type of leadership tactics which were at the root of both his successes and failures, lags far behind. (See Research Note, p. 317 *ff.*)

In his relationship with House, many facets of Wilson's personality were thrown into bold relief. If we can truly comprehend this remarkable political collaboration in all its complexity, we will be a long step closer to understanding Wilson's behavior as a whole. We have tried to tell the House-Wilson story in a way which, we hope, will replace some of the "enigma" and "mystery" with a delineation of the characteristics of both men which make their behavior comprehensible.

This book, then, essays a portrait of Wilson's career in terms of those aspects of it which reveal the personality factors which entered into his political actions. We do not attempt to touch upon all the important events of his career, or to analyze the policies and measures which he sponsored, except as they bear upon our theme.

Another word of caution: while an understanding of relevant personality factors is requisite to an understanding of any man's political action, it is important always to bear in mind the situational context in which the individual operates. Personality traits of leaders, in short, do not alone "determine" events. They are a part—frequently an important part—of the causal picture. A leader's personal values, motives and dispositions shape his perception of the situations which confront him, and his definition and evaluation of the choices of action open to him.

The external situation in which a political leader functions, however, necessarily defines and delimits the field upon which his individual traits can gain expression. As Wilson himself once very truly observed: ". . . no reform may succeed for which the major thought of the nation is not prepared. . . . The legislative leader must perceive the direction of the nation's permanent forces and must feel the speed of their operation. There is initiative here, but not novelty. . . . Practical leadership may not beckon to the slow masses of men from beyond some dim, unexplored space or some intervening chasm: it must daily feel the road that leads to the goal proposed. . . ." So with all aspects of leadership: it must express some vital force within the body politic else, in a democracy, it will be repudiated.

The theoretical concepts which we found most useful as guides to the selection and organization of data belong to dynamic psychology. It is by relating Wilson's overt behavior, which sometimes seems naïve or unreasonable, to some of his emotional needs, which were given their particular hue by his upbringing as a child, that the inner logic of his actions becomes clear. We can at least understand much of his behavior, even if we must still regret some of it.

Much has been written in the past decade about the desirability of applying the insights developed by psychologists to historical materials. This study is an attempt in that direction.

# WOODROW WILSON AND COLONEL HOUSE

*A Personality Study*

Tragedy . . . is an imitation . . . of incidents arousing pity and fear. . . . Pity is occasioned by undeserved misfortune, and fear by that of one like ourselves. . . . The change in the hero's fortunes must be . . . from happiness to misery; and the cause of it must lie not in any depravity, but in some great error in his part. . . .

ARISTOTLE, *Poetics*

## CHAPTER I

# WILSON'S BOYHOOD

A boy never gets over his boyhood, and never can change those subtle influences which have become a part of him, that were bred in him when he was a child.

Woodrow Wilson [1]

ONE DAY when Woodrow Wilson was sixteen years old, his younger cousin, Jessie Bones, came up to him as he sat at his desk practicing shorthand. On the wall where he could see it every time he glanced up hung the portrait of an austere-looking man. Jessie inquired who it was. "That is Gladstone, the greatest statesman that ever lived," the boy answered reverently. "I intend to be a statesman, too." [2]

There is, of course, nothing remarkable in this avowal. Countless adolescents boldly proclaim their intention of becoming statesmen, military heroes, incomparable surgeons or, in this atomic age, explorers of outer space. What is remarkable in this instance is that the young dreamer succeeded in converting his high-flown fantasy into reality. The traits of character which enabled him to do so were forged in his childhood, as such traits usually are. So too were those compulsive tendencies which caused him to be perpetually dissatisfied with himself, his very great accomplishments notwithstanding, and drove him to ruinously self-defeating behavior when the supreme goal of his life—ratification of the League of Nations Covenant—was at stake. It is to Wilson's early years, then, that we must look for the origins of his superb strength and of his truly classical tragic weakness.

Thomas Woodrow Wilson was born on December 28, 1856, in

Staunton, Virginia. His mother, Jessie Woodrow Wilson, came of a learned, religious Scottish family, distinguished through many generations for its scholars and Presbyterian ministers. His father, Joseph Ruggles Wilson, was a Presbyterian minister of Scotch-Irish extraction.

For many generations back Wilson's forebears on both sides were for the most part ministers, elders, professors of theology, or their dutiful wives or children. All, including those who were attracted to other occupations, were deeply religious. Their religion was the very core of their existence. It was a stern Calvinistic doctrine they believed, according to which man is innately depraved, a corrupt sinner who deserves eternal punishment. His only chance for salvation lies in being elected by God to a state of grace and eternal life.

It is not surprising that true subscribers to this dogma are greatly preoccupied with the problem of their state of grace and engage in anxious, sometimes terrified, self-examination for signs that they are or are not among the elect. The tension is heightened by the fact that, strictly speaking, there are no such reliable signs: God, according to His inscrutable will, has preordained each individual's fate and nothing the individual does on this earth can alter the decision as to his eternal destiny. Through the years, however, this severe concept has been mitigated by widespread acceptance of the notion that good works and pure thoughts are signs of election, whereas sinful behavior is a sign of one's doom. It therefore becomes a matter of momentous consequence for the believer to be able to deduce from his examination of his conduct and thoughts that he is among the elect. There is great pressure to do good works and to resist all forms of temptation—indeed, to conquer even the feeling that he is tempted.

It is painful to accept the notion that all men (all infants, even) share a heinous guilt, and to struggle against impulses which are part of the nature of the human animal. Those who succeed in persuading themselves that they may indeed be subjects of God's electing grace are sometimes rewarded with a thrilling sense of freedom from human authority. For such a man is convinced that nothing can separate him from the love of God, that in doing what he conceives to be God's works he is guided and protected by divine strength. Small matter what other men think. No matter, even, if it be necessary to fly in the face of temporal authority. A man's only real responsibility is, through his conscience, to his Lord and Maker.

Such a creed produces men of conviction, who find it possible to cling to their principles no matter what the opposition. Young Tommy heard many tales of the courage of his ancestors. In his youth, he witnessed an example of this variety of tenacity on the part of his uncle, Dr. James Woodrow, a professor of science at the Columbia Theological Seminary. Dr. Woodrow became convinced of the validity of Darwin's theory of evolution, and taught it, at a time when it was anathema to the orthodox. After a long controversy, during which he refused to repudiate his opinion, he was ousted from his position. Wilson's parents admired Dr. Woodrow for his steadfastness. So did Wilson.

The boy Wilson was steeped in a tradition which extolled moral achievement above all else. His family unanimously accepted Calvinistic doctrine and their faith was firmly knitted to the same faith of generations of their forebears. Religion must have appeared to the boy an overwhelming, immutable component of everyday existence. There is ample evidence that this was the case and, further, that it remained so throughout his life. He never permitted himself to question the basic tenets of his church. "So far as religion is concerned," he once remarked, "argument is adjourned." [3] He prayed, on his knees, daily; read the Bible daily; said grace before every meal; attended church regularly. These were the outer expressions of a faith which penetrated to his innermost being.

The Wilsons neither had nor coveted wealth. They did not lack for the necessities, but they were among the genteel poor. In later years, Wilson loved to relate how one day his father met a member of his congregation on the street. The minister's horse and trap were drawn up to the curb. "Your horse looks very well, Mr. Wilson. Much better than you do," said the parishioner. "Yes," Dr. Wilson retorted. "You see I keep my horse, but I am kept by my congregation!" [4]

Wilson's mother was a rather plain, serious woman, extremely reserved, greatly devoted to her family. There is little in the historical record on the boy's relationship with his mother. He was his parents' third child, their first son. His sister Marion was six years old when he was born; his sister Anne was two. We know from contemporary letters that he was a placid infant—"a fine healthy fellow," "just as fat as he can be," "*beautiful*" and "just as *good* as he can be," according to one description written by Wilson's mother when he was four months old.[5]

". . . I remember how I clung to her (a laughed-at 'mama's boy') till I was a great big fellow," Wilson wrote of his mother many years later in a letter to his wife. "But love of the best womanhood came to me and entered my heart through those apron-strings. If I had not lived with such a mother I could not have won and seemed to deserve —in part, perhaps, deserved, through transmitted virtues—such a wife . . ."[6]

From earliest childhood, his father took an extraordinarily active role in his education. They were closely bound together, the boy and this handsome, impressive, somewhat frightening minister to whom Wilson later habitually referred as "my incomparable father."

Dr. Joseph Ruggles Wilson was an eloquent preacher, a man of learning, wit and great presence—a personage in the community. His physical appearance, too, was distinguished: he was large and well built, with a gaunt face which conveyed something of the intelligence and moral fiber of its owner.

Dr. Wilson spent much time with his family. There were daily prayers, with all the family kneeling together. Evenings, the Doctor often led in the singing of hymns. Or he would read aloud to the assembled household, his rich bass voice full of expression. The novels of Sir Walter Scott and Charles Dickens were especial favorites. Sundays, Tommy attended church services and listened, awestruck, as his father delivered his carefully composed sermons expounding the austere doctrine of his denomination. Sometimes, when certain sad hymns were played, the boy would cry.

Dr. Wilson was noted for his caustic wit. This he directed not only at his contemporaries but at his young son as well. Tommy never retorted and he never rebelled. Instead, he accepted his father's demands for perfection, tried to emulate him, and interpreted his stinging criticisms as humiliating evidence that, try as he might, he was inadequate. He felt eternally inferior to his father, in appearance as well as in accomplishment. He once remarked: "If I had my father's face and figure, it wouldn't make any difference what I said."[7]

Tommy was not enrolled in school until he was ten. He promptly took his place at the foot of his class. There were family conferences between his father, maternal grandfather and uncle James Woodrow about what to do with a child who performed so poorly. We do not know what corrective measures the family attempted, but perhaps something of the boy's feelings at the time can be inferred from a remark Wilson made many years later that he knew how mortifying it is to a boy to fall behind his class in his studies.[8]

One striking aspect of Tommy's slow development was his ignorance of the written alphabet until he was nine and his inability to read readily until he was eleven. It seems hardly likely that Dr. Wilson, who took such pains with his son's education and who revered masterly use of the English language above all other intellectual skills, would have neglected to teach the boy his letters. One wonders whether Tommy's capacity to learn was not reduced by his father's perfectionist demands. Perhaps the Doctor's scorn of fumbling first errors was so painful (or perhaps the mere expectation of such a reaction was so distressing) that the boy renounced the effort altogether. Perhaps, too, failing—*refusing*—to learn was the one way in which the boy dared to express his resentment against his father. In any case, the significant fact is that coming from a home in which reading was an important daily activity, Tommy's reading proficiency was retarded; in a home saturated in a religious atmosphere, he had difficulty learning the catechism; in a family of scholars, he was a conspicuously poor student.

Once literacy was achieved, great new possibilities for rigorous drilling of the boy suggested themselves to Dr. Wilson. Frequently, after he had spoken to his son about one subject or another, he would ask, "Do you thoroughly understand that?" "Oh, yes," the boy would say. "Very well then, write it out and bring it to me so I can see that you do." Tommy would take great pains to produce a composition that would pass muster. Timorously, he would submit his effort to his father. If the Doctor came upon anything that seemed in the slightest degree ambiguous, he would demand what exactly was meant. Tommy would explain. "Well, you did not say it," Dr. Wilson would snap, "so suppose you try again and see if you can say what you mean this time, and if not we'll have another talk and a third go at it."

Many years later, President Wilson told his wife that time and again he had a fourth and even a fifth "go at it" before his father was satisfied.[9] Another favorite exercise was to examine the classics sentence by sentence and try to rewrite portions of them in better style.

Dr. Wilson had a passion—an obsession—for the most exact use of language. Did the boy, perhaps in the heat of animated conversation, use a word imprecisely? He was interrupted at once and sent to the dictionary to discover his error.

After President Wilson's death, his daughter Margaret summed up her grandfather's pedagogical creed for the benefit of Wilson's official biographer: "His idea was," she said, "that if a lad was of fine tempered steel, the more he was beaten the better he was." [10]

Other relatives, too, had graphic recollections of Dr. Wilson's severity. Helen Bones, Wilson's cousin, reported: ". . . Uncle Joseph was a cruel tease, with a caustic wit and a sharp tongue, and I remember hearing my own family tell indignantly of how Cousin Woodrow suffered under his teasing. He was proud of WW, especially after his son began to show how unusual he was, but only a man as sweet as Cousin Woodrow could have forgotten the severity of the criticism to the value of which he so often paid tribute, in after life." [11]

Another cousin, Jessie Bones Brower, recalled a typical instance of Dr. Wilson's "teasing." The family was assembled at a wedding breakfast. Tommy arrived at the table late. His father apologized on behalf of his son and explained that Tommy had been so greatly excited at the discovery of another hair in his mustache that morning that it had taken him longer to wash and dress. "I remember very distinctly the painful flush that came over the boy's face," Mrs. Brower said.[12]

One can imagine the effect on a boy of such mockery. Indeed, one does not need to resort to imagination. Wilson's own recollections of his youth furnish ample indication of his early fears that he was stupid, ugly, worthless and unlovable. These feelings had rich opportunities for elaboration in his religious convictions concerning the fundamental wickedness of human nature. It is perhaps to this core feeling of inadequacy, of a fundamental worthlessness which must ever be disproved, that the unappeasable quality of his need for affection, power and achievement, and the compulsive quality of his striving for perfection, may be traced.

For one of the ways in which human beings troubled with low estimates of themselves seek to obliterate their inner pain is through high achievement and the acquisition of power. The trouble is that no matter how dazzling, their accomplishments are likely to prove only momentarily satisfying because the deep-seated low estimates persist and in short order begin to clamor anew for assuagement.

Wilson seemed enmeshed in such an unending attempt to prove to his father, to his God—to himself—that he was a capable and worthwhile human being. As a child he determined he would do something magnificent in the world. An old family servant recalls how once Tommy announced solemnly at the dinner table, "Papa, when I get to be a man, I'm going to have a lofty position." [13] Dr. Wilson laughed good-naturedly. But to the boy this was no childish joke. He was in dead earnest. He spent his childhood and youth industriously preparing to be a great man.

It is by now a generally accepted fact among psychologists that in the process of raising their children, parents inevitably arouse a certain amount of resentment against themselves. For to induce a child to conduct himself in a civilized fashion necessarily involves requiring him to abandon many forms of pleasurable behavior. This the child resents and he experiences anger at the parent who thus thwarts him. Specialists in these matters still are not agreed as to what kinds of parental behavior produce what varieties and degrees of resentment. But it is probably not unreasonable to suggest that a boy like Wilson, upon whom very high demands were made, had to contend with an ample load of anger, which was certainly not mitigated by his father's penchant for ridiculing him.

It is also a truism among modern psychologists that the manner in which a child handles his resentment of his parents is of crucial importance in the development of his personality. Some children feel free to express it openly, and in the fortunate event that the parent in question is able to accept the child's hostile feelings and reassure him, a potential source of future difficulty is averted. Some children, on the other hand, are afraid to express such negative feelings openly, commonly out of fear of what reprisals the parent would take if he knew. Sometimes the child is so terrified that he dares not even recognize the existence of such feelings within himself but, rather, seeks constantly to persuade himself of a surpassing devotion to his parent. This seems to have been Wilson's method of handling the anxiety engendered by his hostile feelings.

There is not a shred of evidence that he ever once openly rebelled against his father's authority. Instead, he submitted and became an extravagantly devoted son. It was a devotion which lasted throughout his life. Tommy was always obedient and respectful. He delighted in doing chores for his father. As a young man, he cheerfully helped his father with the dull task of writing the minutes of the General Assembly of the Church. Even in successful maturity, he retained a feeling of incompetence in his father's presence. He once said the most difficult speech he ever had to make was one during which he suddenly espied his father in the audience; he felt exactly like a boy again, as though he would have to answer to his father afterward for what he said.

When the Doctor grew old and ill, Wilson insisted that he live in Princeton with him, although the care of the increasingly helpless old man was burdensome. A fellow professor recalls that when father and son were together the son was a pupil.[14] When Wilson was President of Princeton and involved in an enervating campus imbroglio, he nevertheless found time to try to lift the old Doctor's spirits by singing some of their favorite hymns to him.

Perhaps nothing more vividly illustrates how Wilson venerated his father than some of the letters that passed between them. Here is one, written when Wilson was thirty-two years old, and a rising young scholar. Its tone is typical.

My precious father,

My thoughts are full of you and dear "Dode" * all the time. Tennessee seems so far away for a chap as hungry as I am for a sight of the two men whom I love. As the Christmas recess approaches I realize, as I have so often before, the pain there is in a season of holiday and rejoicing away from you. As you know, one of the chief things about which I feel most warranted in rejoicing is that I am your son. I realize the benefit of being your son more and more as my talents and experience grow; I recognize the strength growing in me as of the nature of your strength; I become more and more conscious of the hereditary wealth I possess, that capital of principle, of literary force and skill, of capacity for firsthand thought; and I feel daily more and more bent toward creating in my own children that combined respect and tender devotion for their father that you gave your children for you. Oh, how happy I should be, if I could make them think of me as I think of you! You have given me a love that grows, that is stronger in me now that I am a man than it was when I was a boy, and which will be stronger in me when I am an old man than it is now—a love, in brief, that is rooted and grounded in reason, and not in filial instinct merely—a love resting upon abiding foundations of service, recognizing you as in a certain real sense the author of all I have to be grateful for! I bless God for my noble, strong, and saintly mother and for my incomparable father. Ask "Dode" if he does not subscribe? and tell him that I love my brother passionately.

. . . Ellie joins me in unbounded love to you both.

Your devoted son,
Woodrow[16]

Dr. Wilson's death in 1903 did not diminish his hold on his son. Joseph Tumulty, President Wilson's private secretary, has told how one day during World War I, the President interrupted a Cabinet

* Wilson's younger brother Joseph.

meeting to receive an old friend of his father. While the old man praised him, the President stood like a bashful schoolboy. Then the visitor said, "Well, well, Woodrow, what shall I say to you? . . . I shall say to you what your dear old father would have said were he here: 'Be a good boy, my son, and may God bless you and take care of you!' "[16] The President wept.

Nothing in the many descriptions Wilson gave of his relationship with his father suggests that he was aware of any feeling other than exceeding devotion to him. If ever he was aware of his hostility toward his father, he seems to have banished it from consciousness and to have lived in fear of the possibility of ever stumbling upon the knowledge. All his life long, he shrank from reflecting about his inner motivations. The very idea of such self-examination made him uneasy. He once wrote in a letter[17] that he had always had an all but unconquerable distaste for discussing the deep things that underlie motives and behavior. He believed the solution to personal difficulties was rigorous self-discipline. Mary Hoyt, a young relative, reported that he tended to be, as she put it, "hard-hearted" toward anyone who seemed to him lacking in self-control. He was critical, for example, of an artist acquaintance who was unable to work because of an attack of melancholia. "Cousin Mary," he said, "it is possible to control your thoughts, you know."[18] He seemed to fear that if he let his thoughts flow freely some nameless danger would overwhelm him. He once remarked that he never dared let himself go because he did not know where he would stop.[19]

Modern psychologists generally agree that unacceptable thoughts and feelings anxiously dispatched from awareness do not obligingly depart once and for all. Rather, they establish themselves elsewhere within the mind and continue to direct behavior, frequently in highly disruptive fashion.

Not only did Wilson grow up with a taste for achievement and power: he must exercise power *alone*. He could brook no interference. *His* will must prevail, if he wished it to. He bristled at the slightest challenge to his authority. Such a characteristic might well have represented a rebellion against the domination of his father, whose authority he had never dared openly to challenge. Throughout his life his relationships with others seemed shaped by an inner command never again to bend his will to another man's. He seems to have experienced men who were determined to make their viewpoints prevail against his own—men like Dean West at Princeton or, later,

Senator Lodge—as an unbearable threat. They seem to have stirred in him ancient memories of his capitulation to his father and he resisted with ferocity. *He* must dominate, out of fear of being dominated. It was a need so strong that nothing—except, on occasion, the lure of achieving higher office—could overcome his determination to bring his opponents to heel. Not the pleas of his friends. Not even the recognition, deep within himself, that sometimes it is necessary to compromise with one's adversaries to achieve desirable goals.

The validity of the foregoing interpretation and of others that follow is necessarily a matter of opinion. No incontrovertible proof can be offered. Nor can any one incident be relied upon to sustain this or any other theory of Wilson's motivation. It is only when the man's career is viewed as a whole that a repetition of certain basically similar behavior is discernible. Let the reader consider whether these patterns of behavior become more consistently comprehensible in terms of the explanations herein offered than in terms of other explanations. That will be the best test of their usefulness.

If Dr. Wilson was a martinet, there were other facets to his personality as well. He could be full of fun. There are tales of games of tag between the dignified minister and his young son, the participants progressing noisily from the study to the garden, to the delighted consternation of the female contingent of the family. The two played chess and billiards together. They took long walks and Dr. Wilson spoke to the boy without condescension of his hopes and problems. He was free in his expression of affection. He often greeted his son with a kiss. "My Precious Son," his letters generally began. His ambition for his son was boundless. Long before it seemed likely that Wilson would enter politics, Dr. Wilson regarded him as presidential timber, but confided to an acquaintance that "the interests" would never countenance such a choice. Once, at a dinner in Princeton, when Wilson was a professor there, the old Doctor, bursting with pride, leaned over and asked a friend in a loudly audible whisper, "Are you listening to Woodrow? Isn't he brilliant?" [20] At a moment when he felt gravely ill in Princeton, he summoned his three granddaughters to his bedside and admonished them to remember always that their father was a very great man.

Dr. Wilson communicated to his son a solid sense of belonging, both to a religious tradition and to his family. He truly nurtured his son, perhaps unwisely in some respects, but with an unflinching acceptance of his responsibilities. It is a fact of fundamental significance that Dr. Wilson's strict training of his son was conducted in the context of genuine concern for the boy and pride in him. If it is necessary in order to understand some of Wilson's later difficulties to postulate a subterranean hostility between Wilson and his father, it is certainly also necessary in order to understand the man as a whole, to underscore the positive influence of the elder Wilson.

# CHAPTER II

# THE APPRENTICE STATESMAN

> The profession I chose was politics; the profession I entered was the law. I entered the one because I thought it would lead to the other.
>
> Woodrow Wilson to Ellen Axson, October 30, 1883.[1]

WHEN TOMMY WAS A YEAR OLD, the family moved from Staunton to Augusta, Georgia, where Dr. Wilson became pastor of the First Presbyterian Church. He performed his duties there with distinction, and was rewarded with one of the much-coveted professorships at the Columbia Theological Seminary in Columbia, South Carolina. The family moved there in 1870. Tommy was fourteen.

In Columbia, he was enrolled in a private school where, again, he was a mediocre student. A classmate remembers him as somehow different from the other boys—aloof and extremely dignified. He was much alone. Not for him the usual boyish sports: he could not even catch a ball properly. He developed a passion for ships and spent hour after hour, day after day, drawing beautifully shaded sketches of various types of vessels. He became the imaginary admiral of an imaginary navy and composed daily reports of its activities. Another favorite exercise was daily handwriting practice, to cultivate a flowing script like that of an admired uncle.

It was a time of preoccupation with religion. In addition to attending church regularly and sitting in on some of his father's lectures at the seminary, he took part in religious meetings conducted by a young theological student. In the summer of 1873, when he was going on seventeen, he applied for, and was granted, membership in the First Presbyterian Church of Columbia.

It was a time, too, of preoccupation with his future. He had by now decided he wanted to be a statesman and set about studying the lives of great men.

Although he seemed "different" to his fellows, he was generally well liked. His distinctiveness was not of the sort that gets a boy labeled "queer" and earns him ridicule. Rather he seemed to be mysteriously marked for eminence and was accorded respect.

A few months before his seventeenth birthday, Wilson entered Davidson College, a Presbyterian institution near Charlotte, North Carolina. His chief interest there was in the debating society. His academic preparation was below average and he was accepted with conditions in several subjects. Whether it was the pressure of study, the strain of being away from home, or some other conflict about which there is no information, the fact is that at the end of the academic year he was in such poor general health that it was decided that he should return home and continue his studies there, with a view to eventually entering Princeton.

He remained at home (first in Columbia and then in Wilmington, North Carolina, where in the fall of 1874 Dr. Wilson became pastor of the First Presbyterian Church) for fifteen months. He read, discussed books and great men with the one good friend he made in Wilmington, wandered dreamily about the docks, paid a few desultory calls on local girls. Those are the essentials of what is known of his activities during this period.

In September, 1875, Wilson entered Princeton. At once, he joined the Whig Society, a debating club, and set about cultivating his oratorical skills. He combed the library for the speeches of great orators through the ages. The woods near Princeton (and, during vacations, his father's empty church) resounded to his rendition of Burke's orations and the speeches of Gladstone, Bright, Patrick Henry, Daniel Webster and Demosthenes. "What is the object of oratory?" he asked in an article published in the *Princetonian* at the end of his sophomore year. "Its object is persuasion and conviction—the control of other minds by a strange personal influence and power." [2] Oratory, he argued, is not an end but a means—a means, indeed, which it behooved any young aspirant to statecraft to master.

He was intrigued by an article he discovered in *Gentleman's Magazine*, entitled "The Orator," which analyzed the role of oratory in political life and evaluated British statesmen in terms of their oratorical abilities. It was a case of an eager mind meeting just the sort of stimulus most capable of stirring its imagination. He began to compare the British and American systems of government, fairly devouring books on political theory, history and politics. To some students, these were dull pursuits. But to Wilson, who read with an eye to giving more specific direction to his own vaulting ambitions, they were excitingly alive. He decided he would like to be a Senator and wrote out a number of cards identifying himself, after his name, as "Senator from Virginia."

There were a number of other young men in Wilson's class earnestly interested in political affairs. With some of them, the would-be Senator formed close friendships. With one of them, Charles Talcott, he made a solemn covenant binding them to school their powers and passions in order to establish the principles in which they believed; to seek knowledge in order to gain power; to drill themselves in all the arts of persuasion. This agreement was no mere effusion of sophomoric idealism. Wilson took it seriously and so did Talcott. Long after their graduation from college they corresponded about ways of implementing it.

Then there was the talk—the endless, earnest talk of college students about everything under the sun. Politics, religion, morality, hopes and ambitions, all were grist for the mill. Many a discussion ended with Wilson saying half jokingly, "When I meet you in the Senate, I'll argue that out with you." [3]

There were lighter moments as well, in the company of good friends. We have glimpses of Wilson speaking about "the ladies," dancing a hornpipe, telling jokes, sometimes in Negro, Scotch or Irish dialect. His humor and gaiety were a delight to his intimates not only at Princeton, but all through his life. He was a master of the cancan. He could make ludicrous faces, which never failed to send any children present into gales of laughter. He could prance about in a feather boa, trailing a velvet curtain, uttering banalities in falsetto voice in imitation of a society lady greeting friends. He had an impersonation of "the drunken man" which became a family favorite along with a delicious rendition of a pompous Englishman. All this impishness somehow did not detract one whit from his dignity and, one suspects, therein lay the special charm of his nonsense. This lighter side of him only his family and close friends knew. To those not close to him, and particularly to his opponents, he seemed austere and humorless. Nor can it be denied that in his relations with them, in fact he generally was.

An inspection of Wilson's grades at Princeton could not lead an impartial observer to the conclusion that he was a brilliant undergraduate. In a real sense, of course, he was. With subjects which did not touch his interest, he had neither patience nor noteworthy success. But when his interest was aroused, he did not need the lure of good grades to motivate him to study, nor was his study in the nature of stolidly committing masses of facts to memory. Through his capacity to relate the contents of books to his own aspirations, all manner of information sprang to exciting life. He could master the rules of order with avidity, for they were to him a highly practical tool. He could absorb histories of political institutions, for he regarded them as the context in which men—men like himself—must function.

The political system which most appealed to him was the British and a major reason for the preference was that in the House of Commons, great leadership was a function of great oratory and debating skill. In the United States, on the other hand, the committee system in Congress tended to reduce the importance of discussion on the floor. He set out to document this hypothesis and the result was an article entitled "Cabinet Government in the United States." It was published in a then prominent journal, *International Review*. (The editor who accepted it, by the way, was a young historian by the name of Henry Cabot Lodge.) Nor were reading and writing about the advantages of the British system enough. He must put his ideas to a practical test. He organized his friends into a "Liberal Debating Club," composed a constitution modeled on the British and was installed forthwith as Prime Minister.

Princeton was a stimulating experience for Wilson. He was able to a large extent to follow his own bent, and made fruitful use of the opportunity. He also gained in self-confidence. He won honors as a debater. He made friends and reveled in the discovery that they accepted him not only as a person but as a leader too. He wrote for the *Princetonian*. His article on "Cabinet Government" was widely praised. Triumphantly he wrote his father of a great discovery: he found that he had a mind!

This happy era ended in 1879 when Wilson was graduated. His great problem was, what next? A young man of twenty-two who wishes to be, simply, a great statesman, is in a poignant dilemma. Society fairly efficiently defines the alternative ways of proceeding toward various occupational goals: a would-be physician must go to medical school; a would-be businessman seeks a job, starts an enterprise himself or, in Wilson's youth, might still strike out west. But what does a young man burning to be a world leader do? Wilson pondered this problem in the months following his graduation and decided to study law. "The profession I chose was politics; the profession I entered was the law. I entered the one because I thought it would lead to the other," he explained in a letter a few years later.[4] In the fall of 1879, he enrolled in the law school of the University of Virginia.

Interested in the broadest problems of government, Wilson found it tedious to memorize endless cases illustrating, to him, abysmally uninteresting points of law. But the conviction that legal training would be useful later on sustained him. He described himself in a letter to his friend Talcott on December 31, 1879, as swallowing vast masses of legal technicalities "with as good a grace and as straight a face as an offended palate will allow." While, of course, he had no idea of abandoning his studies, "one may be permitted an occasional complaint, if for no other purpose than to relieve his feelings. To relieve my feelings, therefore, I wish now to record the confession that I am most terribly bored by the noble study of Law sometimes, though in the main I am thoroughly satisfied with my choice of a profession. . . . This excellent thing, the Law, gets as monotonous as that other immortal article of food, *Hash,* when served with such endless frequency."[5]

Extracurricular activities were more satisfying. He joined one of the two leading debating societies, the Jefferson. He so distinguished himself that some of the debates in which he participated had to be moved to larger halls to accommodate the overflow audience, and some of his remarks were reported in the newspapers. He was elected President of the Jefferson Society. Promptly he revised its constitution, a project he undertook with much contagious enthusiasm and carried to a highly successful conclusion. He contributed articles to the University magazine. He became, in short, a popular and respected student leader.

These successes only intensified his larger ambitions. "Those indistinct plans of which we used to talk grow on me daily," he wrote Charles Talcott on May 20, 1880, "until a sort of calm confidence of great things to be accomplished has come over me which I am puzzled to analyse the nature of. I can't tell whether it is a mere figment of my own inordinate vanity, or a deep-rooted determination which it will be within my power to act up to." [6]

However irksome his formal studies, Wilson was obliged to spend a great deal of time and energy on them. He was also deeply engaged in outside activities, not only debating but daily practice of elocution and composition—and a courtship—as well. This would be a heavy load for almost anyone. It was a crushing one for the tense young Wilson. In December, 1880, he collapsed. The major symptoms, apparently, were gastrointestinal, and so severe that he had to leave the University and return home.

For the next year and a half, he continued his studies alone, doggedly plugging away at his law books and in his spare time training himself for that nebulous great future in which he still had unshakable faith. A casualty of this period was his first name, Thomas. After experimenting with the various ways of signing his name, he decided "Woodrow Wilson" was the most euphonious possibility.

After eighteen months of solitary study, "Woodrow Wilson" resolved to launch his professional career. The thing to do, he decided, was to set up a law office in an expanding community. Atlanta, Georgia, was the city he finally chose.

In June, 1882, the young hopeful arrived in Atlanta, and immediately called on Edward Ireland Renick whom he had known as a fellow student at the University of Virginia. Renick, too, was about to establish a law office. They decided to join forces and the firm of Renick and Wilson was born. Elated, Wilson wrote his parents about the great development. They promptly sent their good wishes, some new shirts and a few pieces of office furniture. In October, Wilson passed his bar examination. In high spirits, Renick and Wilson awaited bids for their services. They waited in vain. Clients did not pour in. They did not even trickle in. Wilson was burning for a chance to demonstrate his forensic brilliance. None materialized. Day after day the partners sat in their office, their time disconcertingly their own.

There was leisure aplenty to become a frequent spectator of sessions of the Georgia Senate, then still crowded with the post-Civil War mediocrities and worse who had risen to local prominence throughout the South. The oratory Wilson heard did not call to mind that of Demosthenes, Gladstone, Calhoun or Webster. The perspiring legislators, with their crude and ignorant ways, repelled him. This was not the statesmanship he dreamed of. And law was not proving to be a steppingstone to even these vulgar local political opportunities. Law, in fact, was not proving to be a way to earn the cost of his room and board, let alone any of the amenities. So far from distinguishing himself in arguing great legal principles, he was unable to hold his own even in the scrabble for the petty claims cases which might at least have been his financial salvation. He seems not to have attracted a single client—except his mother, who entrusted certain business matters to him.

". . . The potentially great firm of Renick and Wilson," he wrote Heath Dabney January 11, 1883, "[is] doing *very* little, but hoping very *much* . . ."[7] The months dragged by. Wilson spent his time reading, mostly history and political science, interspersed with Milton, Shelley and Keats. He practiced composition every afternoon.

The contrast between the intellectual delight his studies afforded and the niggardly opportunities to engage in stimulating work, even if he were successful at obtaining the sort of cases that seemed most readily available, began to weigh on him. The practice of law seemed more and more a blind alley. Less than a year after venturing so exultantly into the world of practical affairs, he decided to return to university life. ". . . I have about made up my mind to study, at Johns Hopkins University . . ." he wrote Heath Dabney, May 11, 1883.

> In doing this I am, beyond all reasonable doubt, following the natural bent of my mind. I can never be happy unless I am enabled to lead an intellectual life. . . . But hereabouts culture is very little esteemed; not, indeed, at all because it is a drug on the market, but because there is so little of it that its good qualities are not appreciated. . . . I suffer very much in such a community for lack of intellectual companionship.
>
> But the greater matter is that the practice of the law, when conducted for purposes of gain, is antagonistic to the best interests of the intellectual life. . . . The philosophical *study* of the law—which must be a pleasure to any thoughtful man—is a very different matter from its scheming and haggling practice . . .
>
> Now, here it is that the whole secret of my new departure lies. You know my passion for original work, you know my love for composition, my keen desire to become a master of philosophical discourse, to become capable and apt in instructing as great a number of persons as possible. My plain necessity, then, is some profession which will afford me a moderate support, favourable conditions for study, and considerable leisure; what better can I be, therefore, than a professor, a lecturer upon subjects whose study most delights me?[8]

The year in Atlanta took its toll of Wilson's political aspirations. Not that those aspirations ceased to exist. They continued unabated.

But exposure to existence without the protection of either home or college atmosphere forced him to the conclusion that he must make an adjustment which would afford him an income and at least some satisfaction, even if not the most deeply desired. As an academician, after all, he could look forward to exerting influence through writing and teaching, even if he could not directly participate in governmental affairs.

The decision to set his sights upon a more attainable occupation than "statesmanship" was facilitated by a momentous event. He fell in love. Before long, he was dreaming of getting married. How could he, though, until he had made some sensible career adjustment?

The young lady was Ellen Louise Axson, who, like Wilson, was a child of the Presbyterian manse. She was, from all accounts, a rare human being. Altogether accepting of her womanly role, she also had literary and artistic interests of her own. Wilson delighted in her capacity to understand his intellectual pursuits and valued her opinions. Above all, she truly understood Wilson's temperament and catered lovingly to his need for a continuous flow of affection and approval. And how he thirsted for her reassurances! "It isn't pleasant or convenient to have strong passions," he once wrote her. ". . . I have the uncomfortable feeling that I am carrying a volcano about with me. My salvation is in being loved. . . . There surely never lived a man with whom love was a more critical matter than it is with me!" [9] This letter was written during their engagement. Many others, written long afterward, testify to the persistence of these feelings.

Wilson and Ellen Axson became engaged in September, 1883, two days before he arrived in Baltimore to enter Johns Hopkins. "My purpose in coming to the university," he wrote on his application form, "is to qualify myself for teaching the studies I wish to pursue, namely, history and political science, as well as to fit myself for those special studies of constitutional history upon which I have already bestowed some attention." [10]

Wilson applied himself to his studies with furious industry. As always, he regarded the formal course work as little more than a necessary evil, and conserved his best energy for the reading and writing projects he prescribed for himself. He undertook the writing of two books. One was a history of American economic thought and was never published. The other was *Congressional Government*, which attempted to evaluate American governmental institutions in terms of the day-to-day operation of our constitutional system.

He labored with a passion for perfection. "I *must* be true to myself," he wrote his fiancée. ". . . No chance of getting my name before the public shall tempt me to do what I should some day regard as beneath my reputation, as weakly done." [11] He berated himself for the deficiencies of his writing style and set himself a standard that few mortals could meet.

In addition to all his other activities, Wilson sought out the debating society and became one of its leading lights. His oratory dazzled its members. Their warm response dazzled Wilson. He enjoyed speaking, he wrote Ellen Axson, because "it sets my mind—all my faculties—aglow." He felt possessed of confidence and self-command when he spoke and was so exhilarated that it was hard to go to sleep afterward. He told her of the "absolute joy in facing and conquering a hostile audience . . . or thawing out a cold one." [12]

Wilson was irresistibly drawn to the debating societies of every university he attended. And he was irresistibly drawn to the task of revising each club's constitution, along the lines of the British parliamentary system. So at Johns Hopkins. At Wilson's instance, its members converted the Hopkins Literary Society into the "Hopkins House of Commons," and adopted a constitution of Wilson's composition. He promptly reported this success and the great pleasure he took in it to his fiancée, and noted: "I have a sense of power in dealing with men collectively which I do not feel always in dealing with them singly. In the former case the pride of reserve does not stand so much in my way as it does in the latter. One feels no sacrifice of pride necessary in courting the favour of an assembly of men such as he would have to make in seeking to please one man." [13] His success stirred his ancient ambitions. He longed, he wrote his fiancée, "to do immortal work." [14]

The course around which the intellectual life of political science graduate students revolved was Dr. Herbert B. Adams' seminar in history. To this group, Wilson read chapters of his *Congressional Government* as he completed them. Dr. Adams and the students were greatly impressed. Wilson toiled away at his manuscript from January to October, 1884. At last it was complete. In some trepidation, he sent it to Houghton, Mifflin and Co. Less than two months later, the young author had stupendous news: Houghton, Mifflin and Co. wanted to publish the book. "They have actually offered me as good terms as if I were already a well-known writer! The success is of such proportions as almost to take my breath away—it has distanced my biggest hopes," Wilson wrote Ellen Axson.[15]

Significantly, the first elation was quickly followed by a siege of depression. He was restless. He could not even for a while rest on his laurels. In a letter to Ellen Axson, he confessed his low spirits and explained that "success does not flush or elate me, except for the moment." The acceptance of the book had pleased him, of course, "but it has sobered me a good deal too. The question is, What next? . . . I must push on: to linger would be fatal." [16]

*Congressional Government* was published in January, 1885. Gamaliel Bradford, reviewing it in the *Nation*, termed it "one of the most important books, dealing with political subjects, which have ever issued from the American press." [17] The book reviews were alive with praise for the brilliant young Hopkins student. Again, Wilson was elated but in the midst of triumph, Ellen Axson sensed an ineffable sadness and gently inquired about it. Wilson wrote her a remarkably revealing reply, dated February 24, 1885:

> Yes . . . there is, and has long been, in my mind a "lurking sense of disappointment and *loss*, as if I had missed from my life something upon which both my gifts and inclinations gave me a claim"; I do feel a very real regret that I have been shut out from my heart's *first*—primary—ambition and purpose, which was, to take an active, if possible a leading, part in public life, and strike out for myself, if I had the ability, a *statesman's* career. That is my heart's,—or, rather, my *mind's*—deepest secret. . . . Had I had independent means of support, even of the most modest proportions, I should doubtless have sought an entrance into politics *anyhow*, and have tried to fight my way to predominant influence even amidst the hurly-burly and helter-skelter of Congress. I have a strong instinct of leadership, an unmistakably oratorical temperament, and the keenest possible delight in affairs; and it has required very constant and stringent schooling to content me with the sober methods of the scholar and the man of letters. I have no patience for the tedious toil of what is known as "research"; I have a passion for interpreting great thoughts to the world; I should be complete if I could inspire a great movement of opinion, if I could read the experiences of the past into the practical life of the men of to-day and so communicate the thought to the minds of the great mass of the people as to impel them to great political achievements. . . . My feeling has been that such literary talents as I have are *secondary* to my equipment for other things: that my power to write was meant to be a handmaiden to my power to speak and to organize action. Of course it is quite possible that I have been all along entirely misled in this view: I am

ready to accept the providential ordering of my life as conclusive on that point. Certainly I have taken the course which will, with God's favour, enable me to realize *most* of what I at first proposed to myself, and I do not in the least repine at the necessity which has shut me out from all other courses of life. It is for this reason that I have never made these confessions so fully before: I did not want even to *seem* to be discontented with my lot in life. I shall write with no less diligence of preparation, both moral and mental, and with no less effort to put all that is best of myself into my books because I have had to give up a cherished ambition to be an actor in the affairs about which only my *pen* can now be busy.[18]

However valiant his disavowal of discontent, every sentence of this letter bespeaks the man's longing for the career of his first choice. His acceptance of his lot and determination to do his best with the opportunities open to him only underline the poignancy of his disappointment. In the quarter century following the publication of *Congressional Government*, Wilson achieved a degree of distinction in the academic world seldom equaled before or since. He earned many honors, some of which truly pleased him. But none of his academic triumphs could obliterate that undercurrent of restless dissatisfaction which was the man's fundamental mood. None could be enjoyed without a nostalgic pang for another kind of triumph which he yearned for to the depths of his soul but which, reason told him, was forever beyond his grasp. In short, for a quarter of a century, Wilson felt, in a crucial area of his existence, painfully unfulfilled.

*Congressional Government* established its author as a promising young scholar. His reputation was by now something more than local. He began to receive offers of teaching posts. The one he accepted was from a college for women which had just been founded—Bryn Mawr. His salary was to be fifteen hundred dollars per year. On such a stipend, a man could support a wife, even if only modestly. On June 24, 1885, Wilson and Ellen Axson were married. "Can you keep a secret?" Ellen had exclaimed to her brother. "He is the greatest man in the world and the best."[19] Her tender admiration lasted until her death twenty-nine years later.

For any period in their marriage, one can dip into their correspondence or the reminiscences of friends and relatives who knew the household well, and emerge with evidence of Wilson's dependence on his wife's love and her unfailingly tender response. Nine years after their wedding, he could write: "It is so *dull* to be away from you. Life is so much more *commonplace* without you. That is one of the depressing and degrading things you have saved me from: a commonplace life. It is so fresh and sweet and interesting where you are." Seventeen years after their wedding, she could write him: "How do you expect me to keep my head, you dear thing, when you send me such letters as you have done recently—when you lavish upon me such delicious praise? Surely there was never such a lover before, and even after all these years it seems almost too good to be true that you are *my* lover. All I can say in return is that I love you as you deserve to be loved,—as much as you can possibly *want* to be loved." [20]

Years after Wilson's death, Mary Hoyt, a young cousin who had lived with the Wilsons for a year and often visited afterward, wrote a memorandum for Ray Stannard Baker: ". . . I cannot express to you the loveliness of life in that home. It was filled with so much kindness and courtesy, with so much devotion between Ellen and Cousin Woodrow, that the air always seemed to have a kind of sparkle." [21]

The Wilsons moved to Bryn Mawr in September, 1885. Wilson dutifully set about preparing his courses, which were in modern history. But he found teaching women uninspiring, and being supervised by a female dean abhorrent. Just six months after he arrived, we find him visiting Washington to investigate the possibility of getting a place in the State Department. Nothing came of this attempt.

His self-esteem suffered another blow. Through the good offices of his friend, Robert Bridges, he was invited to address a Princeton alumni meeting in New York. In his eagerness to perform well he became nervous, solemn and execrably dull. Not this time the joy of "facing and conquering an audience!" To Wilson's mortification, some of his auditors laughed aloud and others walked out. He returned to Bryn Mawr feeling profoundly humiliated and discouraged. Here he was, trapped teaching women which, so he said, relaxed one's mental muscle; he had failed miserably as an orator—for he so magnified the importance of this incident that he tormented himself for years with this idea; his economic situation was critical, for his wife was about to have a baby and even in those days it was no simple matter for three to exist on fifteen hundred dollars a year. There seemed only one thing he could still fasten his hopes to: his writing.

He conceived a plan for a monumental work, tentatively titled *The Philosophy of Politics*, which would trace, in great detail, the origins and development of democratic government. This was to be his magnum opus, a book which would become a classic. He was prepared to devote years to preliminary research before even beginning to write. As a start, he began to collect data on the systems of government of every nation in the world. There was, he found, no adequate single volume on the subject. He undertook to write one, to be called *The State*, for D. C. Heath & Co.

For three years, in his all-too-scarce spare hours, he labored painstakingly on *The State*. His teaching duties increased, but not his pleasure in them. He tried to augment his income by giving outside lectures and writing articles. The time-consuming activities connected solely with earning a bare living took most of his energy. He grew increasingly oppressed by the feeling that on the slim margin of time left over for the pursuit of his own studies, he would never be able to make much headway. "I don't see how a literary life can be built up on foundations of undergraduate instruction," he wrote his wife on October 4, 1887. "That instruction compels you to live with the commonplaces, the A.B.C. of every subject. . . . You get weary of the plodding and yet you get habituated to it, and find all excursions aside difficult—more and more so. What *is* a fellow to do? How is he to earn bread and at the same time find leisure for thoughts detached from the earning of bread?" [22]

The strain began to tell on his health. He confided to an old friend that he feared he would break down if he remained at Bryn Mawr.[23] It was not merely the amount of work but the aridity of it which fatigued him. He began to cast about for some alternative, and was delighted when he was offered a post at Wesleyan University. The salary was higher than at Bryn Mawr. And the students were men!

In September, 1888, Wilson moved his family to Middletown, Connecticut, and began to teach at Wesleyan. The Wilsons occupied a comfortable old house on High Street, which Charles Dickens once described as "the most beautiful avenue in America." The gnawing discomforts, endured throughout their stay at Bryn Mawr, of cramped living quarters and insufficient money, were now eased. Even more important, here Wilson found the students and faculty more stimulating than at Bryn Mawr. They could serve as a foil for his efforts. His spirits soared.

Reminiscences of some of his students testify to the man's genius for communicating his intellectual enthusiasm. He demanded the best of himself; he inspired the best efforts of his students. He quickly gravitated to the University's debating society, and it will not surprise the reader to learn that he decided it needed to be reorganized into a "House of Commons." The idea took hold. "Cabinets" were formed and clung tenaciously to life as equally tenacious young politicians sought to persuade "Commons" to unseat them. The "House of Commons" became an exciting outlet for the students' competitive spirit. The supremacy of football as their favorite sport was threatened!

Wilson even took an interest in football. He was as enthusiastic a rooter as anyone on that football-loving campus. Between games, he would exhort the players to have faith in their ability to defeat even the big-college teams. During games, when the outlook seemed dark, Wilson would rush onto the field and lead cheers. Wesleyan had a hugely successful season. Wilson became one of the most popular professors on campus.

*The State* was published in the fall of 1889, and enhanced Wilson's growing reputation. His outside lectures were beginning to attract favorable attention. He was elected to Phi Beta Kappa and made president of the Johns Hopkins Alumni Association. At last he was, in small measure, at least, finding a way to apply his talents.

"Have I told you," he wrote his wife on March 9, 1889, "that latterly—since I have been here, a distinct *feeling* of maturity—or rather of maturing—has come over me? The *boyish* feeling that I have so long had and cherished is giving place, consciously, to another feeling—the feeling that I am no longer young (though not old quite!) and that I need no longer hesitate (as I have so long and sensitively done) to assert myself and my opinions in the presence of and against the selves and opinions of old men, 'my elders.' "[24]

Despite these various satisfactions, the man felt larger than the opportunity. "Though this is in truth a delightful place to work, it is not a sufficiently *stimulating* place . . . ," he wrote his friend Robert Bridges.[25] From the time he had first thought of teaching, he dreamed of the political science department of Princeton University as his destination. At this time a reorganization and expansion of the department were under way. Bridges was in a position to advance Wilson's candidacy, and Wilson gratefully accepted his help. A meeting with President Patton of Princeton was arranged. Wilson made a good impression. Eventually, an offer was made. Wilson accepted joyfully. His career at Princeton—it lasted twenty years, twelve as professor and eight as president of the university—began in September, 1890.

In a real sense, when Wilson returned to Princeton, he had "arrived." For he did not consider Princeton a mere way station to a better university. Whatever capacity he had for achievement in academic life could be realized at Princeton. Here was an institution fully worthy of his mettle. Now was the time to give vent to every talent. He accepted Princeton as the place where he was destined to do his lifework.

A flood of pent-up energy poured forth. Wilson's performance at Princeton, from the very start, was superlative. His class lectures were celebrated. He applied all his carefully cultivated dramatic skill to the facts of American constitutional law, international law, English common law and administration. Thirty years later, some of his students could still recall his picturesque description of this or that historical event, so that it remained forever meaningful to them. Sometimes, at the end of a particularly brilliant performance—and they were *performances*—the students would impulsively burst into applause.

He took an active interest in faculty affairs. His contributions to the discussions were cogent, frequently witty and enormously stimulating. He had a way of making whatever he spoke about seem important. An aura of dignity and virtue surrounded the man, and he had the gift of communicating a sense of elevating rectitude to those who adopted his viewpoint. Many of his colleagues were attracted to him as a leader, and he quite naturally slipped into the role of their spokesman.

He was writing too, prolifically, and his books and articles spread his fame far beyond Princeton. So did his outside speeches, for which he now had many more invitations than he could accept. He broadened the scope of his talks, spoke about current affairs to men of affairs. He was coming to the attention of the nation's leaders.

Such outstanding accomplishments resulted in literally scores of offers from other institutions. Whenever a university presidency was open, it seemed, Wilson was sought to fill the post. In quick succession, he was asked to become president of the Universities of Illinois, Virginia, Alabama, Nebraska, Minnesota, and Washington and Lee. The more other universities pursued him, the more determined the trustees became to persuade him to remain at Princeton. They approved an unusual arrangement which provided that several friends of Princeton would contribute money to increase Wilson's income substantially in return for his promise not to accept a position at any other university for five years, beginning in 1898.

No scholar could dream of a more secure opportunity to pursue his studies and produce his books than that which Wilson had secured for himself. Yet he was dissatisfied. The trouble was that, try as he would, he could not efface his desire to take an active role in politics. He was keenly aware of the tendency of men of affairs to look with scorn upon ivory-tower academicians. "The genuine practical politician," he wrote in an essay, ". . . reserves his acidest contempt for the literary man who assumes to utter judgments touching public affairs and political institutions. . . . The ordinary literary man, even though he be an eminent historian, is ill enough fitted to be a mentor in affairs of government. . . ." But "the practical politician should discriminate. . . . Let him find a man with an imagination which, though it stands aloof, is yet quick to conceive the very things in the thick of which the politician struggles. To that man he should resort for instruction." [26]

This is one of the recurrent themes of his writings. He tried to establish himself as the sort of practical thinker to whom men in positions of power might turn for guidance. But the role of scholarly guide hardly fitted his deepest aspirations. For he did not want his influence filtered into existence through a medium. He wanted the reins in his own hands. "I am so tired of a merely talking profession!" he once exclaimed to his brother-in-law, Stockton Axson. "I want to *do* something!" [27]

Exactly what it was he wanted to "*do*" he seemed not to have decided. What attracted him, apparently, was the prospect of exercising leadership *per se*. He was then and, indeed, throughout his career, a leader in search of a cause. One feels, almost, that the various causes for which he fought so passionately in later years were in themselves almost incidental to him. A man cannot exercise power in a vacuum, after all. Wilson sometimes seemed hard put to fix on a practical goal to which to wed his ambitions for leadership. His clearly was not the variety of will to leadership which is born of an overwhelming desire to accomplish certain specific programs. Rather, he had a nebulous desire to lead, and adopted specific programs as a means of giving propulsive substance to his ambition.

This fact in no way detracts from the merit of the projects he thus utilized. If the motivation of the heroes of history could only be laid bare, one suspects it might be discovered that they drew for their great works upon energy generated by what are generally considered the baser drives of human nature. But we are getting rather far afield and ahead of our story, for in his days as professor at Princeton, Wilson had not yet latched on to any moral crusade. He was still trapped in a vise constructed on one side of his unquenchable yearning for the direct exercise of power and, on the other, his rational conviction that it was a yearning he would never be in a position to satisfy.

Stockton Axson once asked if he would be interested in becoming a Senator. "Indeed I would, but that is impossible. In this country men do not go from the academic world into politics," Wilson replied.[28]

There seemed no alternative to plodding ahead as a professor and man of letters, trying as best he could to govern his ungovernable ambition. This effort involved him in perpetual tension. At home, his devoted tenderness to his family continued unabated. But members of the household were aware of a subterranean irritability, ever on the verge of erupting into the open. ". . . Cousin Woodrow had attacks of, I suppose, threatened nervous breaks," Mary Hoyt later recalled.[29]

Wilson lashed himself to an increasingly taxing schedule of writing and lecturing, as though through sheer intensity of effort he could wrest fulfillment from his work. Twice, in 1895 and 1899, he broke down. His doctors prescribed rest. Both times, he went to Great Britain and, at a leisurely pace, toured the great universities, the towns where some of his ancestors lived and places hallowed through some association with his intellectual heroes. Leaves of grass from the graves of Adam Smith and Bagehot were dispatched to Mrs. Wilson with instructions for their preservation. In Wordsworth's haunts, he read Wordsworth's poems and reveled in their beauty. His was not the glazed eye of the bored tourist: he had the capacity for taking innocent joy in the great sights.

Both times he returned to Princeton in better health and in better spirits and plunged back to work with the happiest consequences to an already formidable reputation. There was the Princeton Sesquicentennial celebration in the fall of 1896, at which he delivered an address which attracted national attention. His thesis was that universities ought to train students not merely for their individual self-realization but with a view to their serving the nation. There were his outside speeches, which he made to ever more distinguished audiences on ever more important occasions. There were his books and articles, and his popularity with Princeton students and faculty.

All through this difficult period—indeed, all his life long—Wilson sought relief from inner stress through comforting friendships. He had not as a boy felt unconditionally loved. Rather he seems to have felt that he must earn acceptance by molding his attitudes and behavior in accordance with his father's prescription, and to have been perpetually doubtful of his success in this endeavor. Throughout his life, Wilson was greatly concerned with the problem of whether he was lovable and loved, and required an inordinate amount of explicit reassurance on this score. He was aware of his great dependence on the supplies of affection which his friends provided. He wrote literally hundreds of letters thanking this friend or that who had bolstered his spirit.

To an English friend, Fred Yates, after a vacation in England in 1906: "It is always affection that heals me, and the dear friendships I made were my real tonic and restorative." [30]

Or again, in 1914, to Mrs. Edith G. Reid:

> How sweet it is of you to write such notes as that you sent me on the fourth. They cheer me and hearten me and calm me as only the voice of a beloved friend can; and I bless you for them with all my heart. The turmoil and contest and confusing struggle of the life down here drains the sources of joy and confidence in me sadly, and a dear voice like your own, so generous, so full of affectionate reassurance, so sincere and so full of comprehension, is the very tonic I need. It makes the springs run full and fresh again. . . .[31]

To Mary Hulbert, on August 3, 1913, he wrote that he was not made of steel and that, more than any man he ever knew, he was dependent upon his friends' sympathy and belief in him for strength to do his work as President.[32]

Again, to Mrs. Reid, just a few months before his death: "My friends grow more and more indispensable to me. Little as I see them I think more and more about them. . . . I must see my friends or starve." [33]

All of Wilson's close friends—the men, the women, the professors, the politicians, the socialites—shared one characteristic: they were, or at least had to seem to him to be, *uncritical* admirers of the man and of everything he did. Intellectual disagreement or the feeling that a friend disapproved of some project he had in hand aroused intolerable anxieties, the echoes of indelible boyhood impressions. For the boy Wilson had learned that if he did not earn his father's approval by instantly accepting his every opinion and behaving accordingly, he stood in danger of forfeiting his father's love. To the man Wilson, identity of opinion and love were inseparably linked. He never learned that he and a friend could disagree and still retain a mutual affection.

To him, if a friend disagreed with him about a matter of importance, it signified that the friend no longer cared for him. He reacted in the way he once had feared his father would react to him in similar circumstances—he broke the relationship.

Wilson had many female friends. He reveled in their flattery and praise and doubtless, too, in the relative freedom such relationships enjoyed from the danger that disrupting differences of opinion might one day arise. There were the Misses Lucy and Mary Smith, Mrs. Nancy Toy, Mrs. Edith Gittings Reid, Mrs. Mary Allen Hulbert Peck (who, after her divorce, resumed using her first husband's name and became, again, Mary Hulbert).

His relationship with Mrs. Hulbert threatened to become a national scandal in the presidential campaigns of 1912 and 1916. For Wilson had written her, as he had written many others, both male and female, letters expressing his affection and appreciation of her friendship in fervent terms which the ignorant or malicious might misconstrue. Wilson had a way of attributing the noblest human qualities to his friends and their real personalities did not always affect the mental image he formed of them. His idealized view of Mrs. Hulbert through eyes blinded by gratitude seems to have been at some considerable variance with that of more impartial observers who considered her a flighty, sycophantic social climber. Mrs. Wilson knew of all of these friendships. Some she shared. In any case, no one who understands the role friendship played in Wilson's life, who knows his devotion to Mrs. Wilson, his religious scruples and the equally intimate tone of his correspondence with male friends, can give credence to the scandalous imputations made in connection with his letters to Mrs. Hulbert.

Wilson's capacity for idealizing friends was apparent to the more discerning among them. Mrs. Reid, for example, has written:

> His appreciation of an affection given him was out of the ordinary as was his need of personal love. A person, to obtain his intimacy, had to say very definitely, "I like you," or "I love you." After that, if you were sincere, your life became his personal and unfailing concern.
>
> To make one's friends appreciate each other is not an easy matter. His letters of introduction for one of his women friends almost always began, "You will feel her charm at a glance." Of a man he would write, "You will at once realize his fine nature, his powers of right thinking." The recipient of one of these notes often saw none of those charms and was very bored; and the idealized often found it trying to live up to unfamiliar

virtues. It was especially trying when he introduced in glowing phrases two women and each thought the other too awful for words, but dared not say so . . .

With his intense interest in the personality of a friend, and his entire confidence in a quick characterization, which he never failed to make, it is curious how little he did know about any one who was at all subtle. He had a model for men and women, made out of his own traditions, which at first sight he fitted to any one he felt drawn to.[34]

Wilson's closest friend during his Princeton professorship was John Grier Hibben. The Hibbens and the Wilsons saw each other almost daily, for years. When he learned that Hibben was to sail for Europe for an extended stay, Wilson exclaimed in a letter to his wife: "Doesn't that make you feel a little blank? It does me, very. . . . *What shall we do without them?*" [35]

It is not surprising, given Wilson's passion to lead, either that he took a keen interest in Princeton's administrative problems or that he was quick to find fault with the administrators, chiefly President Patton. Aglow with his observations of the pedagogical methods employed at Oxford and Cambridge, Wilson rhapsodized about the possibility of reorganizing campus life so that the students would learn, not facts, primarily, but, more important, how to think. He expounded the virtues of the tutorial system. He had dreams of a great future for Princeton. Many of the faculty—not only those who disliked Patton for one personal reason or another, but those who felt Wilson could provide a dynamic leadership beyond the capacities of the elderly, conservative Patton—began to look to Wilson for direction. When Patton announced his retirement in June, 1902, the trustees unanimously elected Wilson to succeed to the presidency of Princeton. Seldom had the trustees been so single-minded. Never before had the mantle fallen to a layman.

## CHAPTER III

# PRESIDENT OF PRINCETON

The Princeton period was the microcosm of a later macrocosm, and a political observer, had he studied carefully Wilson's career as president of Princeton University, might have forecast accurately the shape of things to come during the period when Wilson was president of the United States. . . . His refusal to compromise in the graduate college controversy was almost Princeton's undoing; his refusal to compromise in the fight in the Senate over the League of Nations was the nation's undoing. Both controversies assume the character and proportions of a Greek tragedy.

Arthur S. Link in *Wilson: The Road to the White House.*[1]

WILSON WAS DELIGHTED at his appointment as President of Princeton. Guiding a university was a species of statesmanship, after all. He exultantly reported to his wife that preparing his inaugural address made him feel "like a new prime minister getting ready to address his constituents." At last he could begin to slake his thirst to be a *doer* instead of a mere *talker*. After so much monumental yearning, he was tasting of fulfillment. Temporarily, at least, the chronic irritation of frustrated ambition disappeared. Wilson felt liberated. "I find, now that I get a certain remove, that my election to the presidency has done a very helpful thing for me," he wrote his wife. "It has settled the future for me and given me a sense of *position* and of definite, tangible tasks which takes the *flutter* and restlessness from my spirits." [2]

One of Wilson's first steps in his new position was to request that the trustees of the University grant him full and independent power of appointment and removal of members of the faculty.[3] The trustees, who customarily had a voice in such matters, had some misgivings. But, expecting great things from the new president, they granted the request.

Wilson at once proposed that Princeton adopt a tutorial system, roughly similar to that practiced in the great English universities. It was an audacious plan, for it required what then seemed huge funds and a thoroughgoing revision of the curriculum. Wilson labored indefatigably. Three years after his inauguration, the new system was installed. Wilson hired fifty tutors, all promising young men. This infusion of new blood invigorated the University's intellectual life. The project was instantly successful and educators heaped praise on Princeton and her enterprising president.

The catalog of Wilson's achievements in the first few years of his tenure is impressive indeed. Not only did he revise the curriculum and install the preceptorial system. He also first enforced existing scholastic standards and then raised them. On the material side, too, the University was burgeoning. Several new laboratories and dormitories stood as monuments to Wilson's energetic leadership.

With characteristic single-mindedness, Wilson was racing toward his goals. No one yet opposed him or challenged his methods, and he made phenomenal progress. He was widely saluted as "Princeton's greatest asset." Nevertheless, at first in isolated instances but in growing crescendo as time passed, criticism developed. Some students and faculty members thought the new discipline too harshly administered. Some of the trustees and faculty viewed Wilson's tendency to grasp at more and more power with mounting alarm. Not only did he demand unlimited authority over the faculty. He insisted, too, that he must have a voice in appointments to the Board of Trustees because, he claimed, the execution of his reforms required a thoroughly sympathetic Board. Disquieting stories of his dictatorial tendencies began to circulate. There was, for example, a conversation he had with Henry B. Thompson.

Thompson, a trustee and member of the grounds and buildings committee, had told Wilson a difference of opinion existed as to the best location of some projected laboratories. "Thompson," Wilson had said, "as long as I am President of Princeton I propose to dictate the architectural policy of the University."[4]

By 1906, several of the trustees, men experienced in financial management, considered that the University's financial resources, real and potential, were strained to the utmost by commitments already made. They thought that no further ambitious reforms ought to be undertaken until the ones already planned were solidly under way.[5]

The most important of the unfinished projects which the trustees felt now had priority was the establishment of a graduate school. A beginning had been made before Wilson's promotion to the presidency of the University. In 1900, the trustees had formally established a graduate school and elected Dean Andrew Fleming West to direct its development. They had given West wide powers to carry out his assignment, which was unanimously recognized to be of cardinal importance in enhancing Princeton's prestige. In his inaugural address, Wilson had specified the building of "a notable graduate college" as one of his goals.

West spent the summer and fall of 1902 in Europe, studying some of the graduate establishments there. On his return, he wrote a report, entitled *Proposed Graduate College of Princeton University*, outlining his ideas. Wilson endorsed West's report in a preface in which he stated: "On the side of University growth, a Graduate College is undoubtedly our first and most obvious need, and the plans for such a college which Professor West has conceived seem to me in every way admirable." [6]

This avowal notwithstanding, Wilson was noticeably loath to push the development of the graduate school, although he expended prodigious energy in other directions. During the first four years of his administration, he and the trustees poured all their efforts into reforms affecting undergraduate life. Dean West supported Wilson unstintingly, but with growing impatience at the repeated diversions of the University's resources away from the graduate school.

In the fall of 1906, West was invited to become President of the Massachusetts Institute of Technology at twice the salary Princeton paid him. But West was an outstanding asset to the faculty, just as Wilson had been in the nineties, and the trustees did not want to lose him. West told the trustees frankly that he would consider staying at Princeton only if he had some assurance that his graduate college plans, in which he had invested ten years of labor, would be brought to fruition. On October 20, 1906, the Board of Trustees adopted a resolution, composed by Wilson himself, earnestly urging West to remain at Princeton. "The Board has particularly counted upon him to put into operation the Graduate College which it has planned," the resolution stated. "It [the Board] begs to assure him that he cannot be spared."[7] Satisfied that he would now receive prompt co-operation in his work, West decided to stay at Princeton.

He was dismayed, therefore, when less than two months later Wilson presented to the Board of Trustees a major reform plan which, if adopted, again would relegate the graduate school to the background. Wilson's proposal was that students be grouped in residential quadrangles patterned roughly on the Oxford and Cambridge models. He argued that it would stimulate the students' intellectual life if freshmen, sophomores, juniors and seniors, as well as graduate students and unmarried preceptors, lived and ate together and thus had ready opportunities for informal discussions.

The Board appointed a committee, with Wilson as chairman, to consider the matter and report its findings at a subsequent meeting. On June 10, 1907, Wilson presented the committee's report. It endorsed his quadrangles proposal and recommended that Wilson be authorized to "take such steps as may seem wisest for maturing this general plan. . . ."[8] The Board accepted the committee's report. West was furious at what he regarded as another attempt by Wilson to divert attention from the graduate school. He was furious too that Wilson should have solicited the Board's approval of so important a project without first having consulted the faculty. A number of the older faculty members, and many of the alumni, shared West's indignation, and their criticisms broke into the open. Wilson declared that he favored full and free discussion of the quad plan. His critics retorted that discussion would have been in order before the plan was presented to the trustees. Now that the Board had accepted the proposal before the faculty had even heard of it, Wilson's offer of full and free discussion was a sham. For he was in reality confronting the faculty with a *fait accompli.*

A great controversy ensued in which the issue of Wilson's highhandedness became inextricably interwoven with wide-ranging arguments for and against the plan. Its opponents claimed that it was far too ambitious a project to undertake before bringing others, such as the graduate school, to completion. Further, many hesitated to stake Princeton's future on what they considered a doubtful experiment. In addition, supporters of the upper classmen's eating clubs, which had been established when fraternities were outlawed at Princeton, protested that the quad plan would destroy the clubs. Wilson's supporters contended this would be all to the good because the clubs embodied the faults of the fraternities and were undemocratic.

The debate raged throughout the summer of 1907. It became obvious that the alumni were preponderantly opposed to the quad plan and would not subsidize it. However, the discussion had focussed attention on some of the faults of the clubs and there was a widespread disposition to effect reforms.

Some of Wilson's most devoted friends on the Board of Trustees urged him to switch his objective to reform of the clubs. That was both a desirable and feasible goal, whereas it would be impossible to realize the quad plan, given the strong opposition to it. But Wilson was adamant. The clubs must go. The quad plan must be adopted. The future of higher education in the United States depended on it. He would not be moved from his original aim.

In the end, Wilson's plan was defeated. On October 17, 1907, the trustees met. Opposition to the quad proposal was so great that the trustees formally requested Wilson to withdraw it. Wilson's reaction to this defeat was momentary despair followed by stubborn determination to fight for his "principle" and win through despite all opposition. He appealed directly to the alumni in a series of speeches in the East and Midwest. This time, however, his masterful oratory availed him nothing: the alumni remained dead set against the quad plan.

In a state of nervous exhaustion, and suffering from neuritis, Wilson sailed to Bermuda for a short rest. The idea met its final defeat on April 8, 1908, when a committee appointed by the trustees defended the clubs and refuted Wilson's criticisms of them.

The final defeat of the quad plan was a bitter blow to Wilson. One of its most painful aspects was that his best friend, John Grier Hibben, had expressed himself in favor of reforming, rather than attempting to abolish the clubs. Wilson was horrified that his inseparable companion, the man to whom for years he had turned for solace in times of personal crisis and for daily companionship, should oppose the quad plan. To Wilson, such a difference of opinion meant they could no longer be friends. So he relinquished Hibben's friendship.

It is difficult to convey a sense of the intense mental anguish that this break occasioned. For Hibben long had been a source of that affectionate reassurance upon which Wilson's sense of well-being was so dependent. Hibben's friendship had been one of the important satisfactions of his life. "Thank you with all my heart for your letter," Wilson once had written him. "It would be hard for me to tell you,—

I fear I never can by word of mouth,—how your thoughtfulness and love touch and delight me. Your letter contained just the things I wanted to hear,—just the items of news, and, above all, just the assurances of being thought of and missed and loved. It gave me the feeling, just the feeling that makes me happiest, that I was *needed*,—needed for pleasure as well as for business." [9]

Mrs. Wilson attributed Wilson's physical collapse in 1908 to the rift with Hibben.[10] In the judgment of his daughter Margaret, it was one of the two major tragedies in his life, the other being his failure to secure United States entry into the League of Nations.[11] When Wilson left Princeton, he tried (unsuccessfully) to block Hibben's elevation to the presidency of the University. In later years, when he returned to Princeton to vote, or for a class reunion, he parried Hibben's friendly overtures with icy formality. It was not until he met Colonel House that Wilson permitted himself so close a friendship again.

The defeat of the quad plan ended the possibility of evading action on the graduate school. Wilson's objective now was to rid Princeton of West. "He had reached the conclusion," his biographer, Ray Stannard Baker, writes, "that Dean West would not submit to any control and would ultimately have to be eliminated altogether if real unity in university affairs was to be achieved." [12]

Wilson's supporters on the Board of Trustees, at his instigation, succeeded in April, 1909, in stripping West of most of his authority over the graduate school and transferring it to a faculty committee appointed by Wilson. West protested against this reorganization and charged that it was inconsistent with the promises made in 1906 to persuade him to reject the offer of the presidency of the Massachusetts Institute of Technology and remain at Princeton. Wilson's reaction was to declare (according to West): "I wish to say to the Dean somewhat grimly that he must be digested in the processes of the University." [13]

The following month, in May, 1909, one of West's close friends enabled him to play a trump card: William Cooper Procter, of the Procter and Gamble soap manufacturing company, offered to donate to Princeton half a million dollars for the construction of a graduate school upon a site "which shall be satisfactory to me." Procter stated that he had inspected the site on the campus which Wilson favored and "in my opinion it is not suitable . . ." [14]

The condition in Procter's offer bore upon a dispute which had been developing between Wilson and West. Wilson was determined that the graduate college be built on the campus. He wanted the graduate students to mingle with the undergraduates and set the intellectual pace of the University. West, on the other hand, preferred a site somewhat removed from the campus in order, he argued, to have room for future expansion. Now West's friend, Procter, was making his offer of financial help in effect contingent upon the adoption of West's point of view.

Here at last was an "issue," something which could be turned into a moral crusade of the sort Wilson required as an acceptable rationalization for the expression of his hostile feelings. A feud had been quietly smoldering between Wilson and West for years. In the days before Wilson's appointment as Patton's successor, West apparently hoped to be selected as the next president of the University. If he was disappointed that Wilson was chosen for the post, he gave no outward indication of the fact. He co-operated loyally with Wilson in the execution of the undergraduate reforms. Nevertheless, Wilson apparently disliked the man and could not bring himself to accept West's attempts to take charge of the graduate school as he had been empowered to do.

Wilson was not a man who could face up to his aggressive impulses. He seems to have feared them, just as he seems to have feared and suppressed them in the all-important relationship with his father. Only in defense of a moral principle was it permissible to give vent to his spleen. That he experienced West as an unbearable threat to his authority he apparently could not confess, even to himself, much less accept as a valid basis for action. This probably accounts for the fact that when West was offered the presidency of the Massachusetts Institute of Technology and was seriously considering accepting, Wilson himself wrote the resolution urging him to stay, despite the fact that he certainly would have been relieved to see West leave Princeton. He had at that point simply been unable to hit upon a sufficiently convincing rationalization, in terms of a moral issue, for his dislike of West. But now he could fight! For now he could argue that West was conniving with a wealthy patron, who presumed that his money could determine educational policy! He could say that the West-Procter conception of a luxurious graduate establishment isolated from the rest of the University was undemocratic!

Wilson insisted that the graduate school must be built on the campus. One of his arguments involved the previously accepted bequest of one Josephine Swann. This generous lady had left $250,000 to Princeton for the construction of a graduate school *on* the campus. Wilson contended it would be illegal to use these funds on any site *off* the campus. (Nine prominent lawyers as well as the executors of Mrs. Swann's will disagreed with Wilson on this point. It was their opinion that it would be entirely legal to use the Swann funds for building on the University golf links, purchased after her death, which Procter approved as a suitable site.)

The entire University community—trustees, faculty, students, alumni—became absorbed in a virulent debate. Wilson demanded that the Procter offer be rejected. Most of the alumni thought it ridiculous to refuse such a large gift on the grounds stated. Wilson contended that by stipulating the location of the building, Procter was attempting to strip the Board of Trustees and the faculty of control of the University. Those sceptical of Wilson's arguments wondered why he had never objected to Mrs. Swann's gift even though she had prescribed not only the site of the graduate college but also, among other things, the prices of rooms, disposition of rents, number of fellowships, and qualifications of fellows as to character, sex and race. Why did Wilson denounce Procter's one condition as an assault on academic freedom and at the same time accept Mrs. Swann's much more sweeping conditions without a murmur?

Wilson's stirring appeals for the protection of the University from the dictates of wealthy patrons failed to persuade a majority of the members of the Board of Trustees. On October 21, 1909, the Board voted to accept Procter's offer.[15]

Having been voted down, Wilson threatened to resign. On Christmas day, 1909, he wrote Trustee Pyne a long letter setting forth his point of view and reasserting that the University's "freedom of choice" had been jeopardized by the acceptance of Procter's gift. For his part, he contended, he had made every reasonable effort to compromise, but had been rebuffed. Just the week previous, he wrote, he had suggested to Procter, by way of compromise, that Mrs. Swann's money be used to build *on* the campus and another graduate establishment be constructed on the golf links with Procter's money. But Procter had rejected the idea. "I am not willing to be drawn further into the toils," Wilson wrote. "I cannot accede to the acceptance of gifts upon terms which take the educational policy of the University out of the hands of the Trustees and Faculty and permit it to be determined by those who give money." [16]

The whole tone of the letter is one of pious self-justification. Wilson represented himself as a man who had tried every compromise and had been rebuffed by unreasonable opponents. He was ready to sacrifice himself on the altar of high principle.

The Board of Trustees met on January 13, 1910. Wilson restated his position: either acceptance of the Procter offer would be withdrawn, or he would resign. Trustee Pyne then electrified all present by announcing that Procter was willing to accept the compromise that Wilson had recently proposed, namely that two graduate buildings be constructed, one on campus with the Swann funds and the other on the golf links with Procter's money. For a moment, it seemed as if a compromise had been worked out at last. But only for a moment. Wilson, taken aback by the sudden concession in his favor on the site issue over which he had created such a furor, blurted out that geography and location were not the fundamental issue after all! What, then, was? Wilson held up a copy of West's report, *Proposed Graduate College of Princeton University*, to which, it will be recalled, he had written a laudatory preface.

"There, gentlemen, in that book is the real reason why the Procter gift must be declined. That book contains Professor West's ideals for the Graduate School. They are his personal ideals; they are not the ideals of Princeton University, and they are radically wrong." As for the site problem, he now dismissed it as a detail: "If the graduate school is based on proper ideals, our faculty can make a success of it anywhere in Mercer County." [17]

One of the trustees asked why Wilson had written a complimentary preface to West's pamphlet. Wilson answered that he had written it without having seen the book, although the incontrovertible fact is that he had corrected the proofs of West's report. Bewildered by the sudden shift in Wilson's argument just at the moment when the long-awaited solution seemed at hand, the trustees deferred action and merely appointed a committee of five to report in the following month on the "whole question involved in Mr. Procter's offer." [18]

Wilson now dedicated himself to demonstrating that his opponents were defenders of special privilege and that he was the uncompromising champion of democracy. West had plans drawn for the graduate college building. Wilson denounced the proposed building as too costly and too elaborate—just another indication, so he claimed, of West's desire to make the graduate school an elegant club for rich boys rather than a suitable setting for hard intellectual endeavor.

Again and again he insisted that the graduate school must be placed at the geographical center of the University to facilitate fruitful interchange between graduate and undergraduate students.

On January 31, 1910, an editor of the New York *Times* solicited Wilson's views and faithfully recorded them in an editorial which appeared in the *Times* on February 3. The editorial denounced those who would "bend and degrade" students into "fostering mutually exclusive social cliques, stolid groups of wealth . . . and the smatterings of culture." Should Princeton allow herself to be invaded by "dilettanti . . . dedicated to the aimless purposes of men who depend for prestige, not upon their own minds and efforts, but upon the brains and the fortunes of their fathers?" the *Times* asked.

The most thorough and objective Wilson scholar of this generation, A. S. Link, after sifting through all the evidence, concluded that "there was no basis in fact for Wilson's charges," and comments: "Who can explain the reasons that led Wilson finally to propound this interpretation of the graduate school controversy? The vagaries of his mind . . . are unfathomable." [19]

Does not Wilson's fanatical battle with Dean West become more fathomable if it is considered in terms of the quest for power and for freedom from domination set in motion in his childhood? It would seem that Wilson construed West's insistence on the validity of his own point of view as a galling challenge to his authority; that at some level West evoked in Wilson the image of his father; that he experienced West's activities as an attempt to dominate him, and resisted with all the violence he had once felt, but never ventured to express, in response to his father's overwhelming domination. He disguised all his volcanic aggressive feelings against West in terms of a great moral crusade in which he championed the "right." The passion with which he invested his various attacks on West derived from this underlying aggressiveness. So it is not surprising that the site issue having been exposed as fraudulent, he immediately seized upon another issue, "democracy" at Princeton, with equal ardor.

On February 6, 1910, Procter withdrew his offer, stating as the cause that Wilson had received it unfavorably. Four days later, the trustees met. The committee of five appointed in January to consider the whole question of the Procter offer reported itself in substantial agreement with Wilson. Since Procter had already withdrawn the offer, discussion seemed superfluous. The trustees voted to accept the report.[20]

Wilson, exhausted, left for Bermuda for a short vacation. In letters to his wife he complained that his difficulties at Princeton were emerging in disturbing dreams, but assured her that he had a clear conscience and could face the future happily.[21]

Procter's withdrawal of his offer and the trustees' endorsement of the report of the committee of five by no means ended the dispute. Most of the alumni were incensed that so generous a gift had been lost. While Wilson was in Bermuda the storm raged. When he returned to Princeton in early March, Wilson decided to explain his position to the alumni personally. He addressed alumni meetings in the East and Midwest, but failed to convince them that his handling of the Procter gift had been in Princeton's best interests. The trouble was that he could persuade few men who knew West and some of his supporters—men who had served Princeton loyally for many years—that they had suddenly begun to pursue the dark objectives that Wilson ascribed to them. The alumni brought pressure on the Board of Trustees and there was considerable sentiment in favor of the election of anti-Wilson trustees as vacancies occurred on the Board.

The Board, its members divided into two bitter factions, but dominated by men who thought Wilson in error, met on April 14, 1910. Wilson, confident of faculty support, requested that the graduate school question be referred to a general faculty meeting. The trustees rejected the request. Wilson was furious.

Two days later, he addressed a meeting of the Pittsburgh alumni. Whatever the cause—whether the defeat he had experienced at the hands of the Board, or the hostility of his audience, or fatigue, or other factors not known—he publicly lost his temper and delivered what he himself later admitted was an ill-advised, intemperate address. He charged that privately endowed colleges pander to the desires of wealthy students and alumni; that "a handful of conspicuous men have thrust cruel hands among the heartstrings of the masses of men upon whose blood and energy they are subsisting." To correct these iniquities, he had dedicated "every power that there is in me to bring the colleges that I have anything to do with to an absolutely democratic regeneration in spirit." "Will America tolerate the seclusion of graduate students?" he demanded. "Will America tolerate the idea of having graduate students set apart? . . . Seclude a man, separate him from the rough and tumble of college life, from all the contacts of every sort and condition of men, and you have done a thing which America will brand with contemptuous disapproval." [22]

The debating continued, but settled nothing. The issue of "democracy" which Wilson was so heatedly raising earned him considerable favorable publicity throughout the country, but many close to the situation could not understand the relevance of his charges to the problem at hand.

On April 25, Trustee McCormick, generally sympathetic to Wilson's point of view, conferred with Procter. Procter said he was willing to renew his offer and assured McCormick that he had no desire to interfere with the administration or the curriculum of the graduate school. In fact, he had heard Wilson's address to an alumni meeting in St. Louis, and afterwards remarked that his ideals and Wilson's seemed to coincide.[23]

The trustees conferred among each other. The pro- and anti-Wilson factions made concessions. Finally a compromise agreement was reached which the trustees fervently hoped would settle the matter once and for all. The agreement stipulated construction of the graduate school on the golf links—this to appease Procter. It also provided for West's retirement as dean of the graduate school and his assumption of the office of provost or resident master instead—this to satisfy Wilson. Hopes that the impasse had been broken, however, were dashed by Wilson's refusal to accept the compromise: the new role assigned West offended him quite as much as the old.

It would not be accurate to assert that this intransigence left Wilson bereft of all support. A few of the trustees and some of the faculty remained loyal to him throughout. However, a large majority of those who had followed the controversy closely were astounded, if not also repelled, by Wilson's stubbornness.

The situation was hopelessly snarled when a stunning act of fate intervened in West's favor. In May, 1910, one Isaac Wyman died. His will provided a bequest of several million dollars for the construction of a graduate college at Princeton. West was named one of the two executors of the will.

Wilson received the news through a telegram from West and his co-trustee. Mrs. Wilson, it is said, heard her husband laughing in his study. She went in and found him poring over the telegram. "We have beaten the living," he said, "but we cannot fight the dead. The game is up." [24] Wilson withdrew his objections to the golf links site and recommended that West remain as dean of the graduate college.

On June 6, 1910, Procter renewed his offer. The Board of Trustees accepted it immediately.

It might be assumed from this sequence of events that Wilson realistically acknowledged he was defeated and was willing to accept the situation. The fact is, however, that he was not a man to yield to pressure, however overwhelming. Later in his career a situation of remarkable structural similarity arose. This was Wilson's struggle with the Senate over the League of Nations in which Senator Lodge took the role Dean West played in the graduate school controversy. In the League fight, too, Wilson refused to compromise despite the most fervent exertions of his friends as well as his opponents, and despite the certainty of defeat if he remained adamant.

In the case of the struggle with the Senate and, particularly, with Lodge, the drama was played out to its inexorable conclusion. Wilson seems to have been locked in the same sort of all-consuming battle with Lodge as with West. He was assuredly driven to his passionate stubbornness by the irresistible, never-articulated need to retaliate against the kind of domination he had once endured at the hands of his father. At the same time, he sensed that true concern for United States participation in the League would naturally lead him to compromise with Lodge. For, as his writings show, Wilson was a discerning student of the political process and social reform. He was fully aware that in order to gain the necessary support for a worthy objective it is sometimes necessary to compromise with one's political foes, especially when they have a legitimate, constitutional basis for participating in the decision to be made. Yet, for compelling inner reasons he could not bring himself to yield an iota to Lodge.

A man of Wilson's high moral standards pays dearly for such intransigence by feeling anxious and guilty. The greater the stubbornness, the greater the internal anguish. Every human being seeks to relieve such inner pain. Wilson's method seems to have been to strive desperately to justify himself to himself by demonstrating his moral superiority over his opponents. He must show how right he was and how wrong they were. He seems to have derived grim satisfaction from the fact that Lodge and his cohorts were "immoral" enough to permit their personal dislike of him to warp their political judgment and to sabotage the peace settlement. Of course, by becoming involved with Lodge on this peculiarly personal level, and refusing to break the deadlock, he brought a monumental defeat upon himself.

It is unlikely, then, that the mere logic of events, the simple fact of Wyman's huge bequest on Dean West's terms, was responsible for deterring Wilson from the battle. Difficulties generally inflamed him to greater effort. So there must have been something besides the Wyman will that turned the scales.

There was. At just this time, other opportunities—*political* opportunities—which had been carefully nurtured for four years were maturing. Let us see what these opportunities were, and who provided them.

Wilson was shepherded into politics by conservatives who hoped he could wrest control of the Democratic Party from the then powerful progressives led by William Jennings Bryan. At the turn of the century, both Democratic and Republican Parties were controlled by determined reformers, whose avowed purpose was to deprive the large corporations of much of their power. It was a day of muckraking and anticapitalist invective. Conservative businessmen and political bosses whose machines were threatened by the reformers were casting about for a leader who could break Bryan's grip on the Democratic Party and once again make it serve their interests. To some of these conservatives, Wilson seemed a possible candidate for the job.

George Harvey, editor of *Harper's Weekly* (at that time financed by J. P. Morgan) and a close associate of both political bosses and industrialists, was one of the first to advocate that Wilson be groomed for high political leadership. At a dinner in Wilson's honor in February, 1906, Harvey publicly speculated about Wilson's becoming President of the United States. Newspapers throughout the country quoted Harvey. Many commented favorably on the idea. From that time forth, Harvey energetically championed Wilson's political career. To Harvey, perhaps more than to any other man, Wilson owed his entrance into politics.

It is easy to imagine, given Wilson's pent-up desire for a political career, how deeply Harvey's efforts in his behalf must have stirred him. Wilson's relationship with Harvey from 1906 to 1910 bespoke his eagerness to enter the political arena. It was an eagerness tempered by caution, lest he be led unwisely into situations which might reduce his ultimate political potentialities. After all, he was over fifty years of age, too old to take frivolous chances. Furthermore, he had to consider his financial security. By skillful management, especially on Mrs. Wilson's part, the Wilsons had been able to live graciously, although modestly. But they were not financially independent. Wilson literally could not afford to venture lightly into a new and uncertain career.

He had to have confidence in his chances for success. And only success of the first order interested him.

Wilson's new friends embarked on a program of bringing him to the attention of the public in a political context. First, they had him appointed to the New Jersey Commission on Uniform State Laws. Next, in the fall of 1906, Harvey, in co-operation with Boss Smith of New Jersey, decided to run him as Democratic candidate for the United States Senate.

In those days, Senators were elected not by the people of the several states, but by the state legislatures. If a legislature were predominantly Republican, Republicans were sent to the Senate. If the Democrats were in control, Democrats were selected. The November 1906 elections placed the Republicans solidly in control of the New Jersey legislature. It was quite clear that the Democratic candidate would have no chance of actual election since the Republicans would surely elect one of their own party. The Democratic candidate, therefore, could hope for nothing more than the honor of endorsement by his own party.

Wilson at first declined to be a candidate. Harvey importuned him to reconsider. Finally, he agreed to permit the Democratic caucus to consider his name. The exciting lure that Harvey held out was his confident prediction that one day Wilson could be elected President of the United States. Getting him the Democratic nomination for the Senate was a maneuver in the effort to build his political prestige.

In December, 1906, Wilson wrote Harvey asking him to name the influential men who, Harvey had assured him, considered him promising presidential timber. He knew, Wilson wrote, that there existed only the mere possibility of his becoming President. Yet one should consider possibilities as carefully as probabilities, and he wished to calculate his course of action on the basis of the hard facts of the situation.[25] Harvey replied, naming some of the most influential bankers, utilities executives and conservative journalists of the country. A powerful group of supporters indeed, but Wilson was shrewd enough to realize the growing importance of the reform movement and the need for finesse in accepting help from this conservative quarter without becoming too identified with their unpopular cause.

Exactly this ticklish problem was posed for Wilson by Harvey's effort to get him the senatorial nomination on the Democratic ticket. For the Democratic Party in New Jersey was bitterly split between the political bosses and reformist elements who were trying to gain control from them. The reformists favored the nomination of E. A. Stevens as Democratic candidate for Senator. Wilson was the candidate of the bosses. Stevens had been Wilson's classmate at Princeton, and they were friends. On December 29, 1906, Stevens wrote Wilson that progressives in the Democratic Party considered his consent to be the bosses' candidate "as a sign of your willingness to allow the use of your name as a club by the very men who every good Democrat feels to have been the bane of the party and whose leadership has made the state hopelessly Republican." [26]

Wilson replied that since only a complimentary vote by the minority party was involved it would be unnecessary to declare that he would not accept the honor of his party's endorsement. Stevens wrote back that there was more at stake than an "empty compliment." The question of party control was involved. Wilson, he warned, was being manipulated by men whose purpose it was to destroy the reform faction of the Democratic Party. He appealed to Wilson to withdraw from the race.[27]

Within a week of Stevens' second appeal, Wilson withdrew his candidacy for the nomination. He evidently considered the certain alienation of the progressive wing of his party too high a price to pay for an empty honor which he was not even certain of obtaining. There remained the delicate problem of placating Colonel Harvey. Wilson wrote him of the decision to withdraw. "My chief regret is that you will be disappointed," he said. "I hope that I may have many opportunities of showing my appreciation and admiration . . ." [28]

Whatever Harvey's chagrin, his plans for Wilson were too important to be affected by so minor an incident. In March, 1907, he helped arrange a private meeting between Wilson and William M. Laffan of the ultra-conservative New York *Sun* and Thomas Fortune Ryan, commonly considered the chief "reactionary" in the Democratic Party. Laffan and Ryan were interested to inspect Wilson as a possible presidential candidate. The meeting was harmonious. Laffan and Ryan were favorably impressed.

A few months later, in August, Wilson wrote a political credo for the perusal of his two new acquaintances. In it he defended the great trusts as the necessary instrumentalities of modern business and declared himself unequivocally opposed to the union movement. Wilson's stock among highly placed conservative Democrats rose immeasurably. No doubt about it: here was a "sound" thinker—just the sort of man people like Laffan and Ryan were interested to have in high political office.

Wilson's views about William Jennings Bryan only further delighted his new friends. Bryan was the leader of the progressive Democrats, and effectively controlled the party. It was to break his power that the conservative Democrats were so eagerly seeking a suitable man.

As far back as 1904, Wilson publicly demanded that Bryan and his followers be "utterly and once for all thrust out of Democratic counsels." In a speech delivered in March, 1908, Wilson referred to Bryan as "the most charming and lovable of men personally, but foolish and dangerous in his theoretical beliefs." Bryan, Wilson once remarked to a friend, had "no mental rudder." [29] So great was his antipathy for the man that he withdrew his acceptance to address the National Democratic Club's Jefferson dinner in 1908 when he learned that Bryan would be present.

The most celebrated anti-Bryan statement Wilson ever made was contained in a letter he wrote on April 29, 1907, to Adrian Joline, President of the Missouri, Kansas and Texas Railway. Joline had sent Wilson a copy of a speech he had made attacking Bryan's proposal for government ownership of railroads. Wilson replied to Joline: "Thank you very much for sending me your address at Parsons, Kan., before the board of directors of the Missouri, Kansas and Texas Railway. I have read it with relish and entire agreement. Would that we could do something at once dignified and effective to knock Mr. Bryan once for all into a cocked hat!" [30] In later years, this particular statement almost wrecked Wilson's political career, but in the first decade of the century, this and similar expressions of a conservative and "safe" outlook made Wilson the white hope of the uneasy tycoons.

Despite impressive evidence of his growing stature as a public figure, Wilson apparently considered his chances for obtaining the Democratic presidential nomination in 1908 too remote to warrant his betraying an interest in it. The Democratic convention was to be held in July, 1908. Colonel Harvey was to attend. As the pre-convention campaign progressed, it became clear that William Jennings Bryan still effectively controlled the party. Wilson himself, in a letter to a supporter on April 10, said that he did not feel he was any longer being seriously considered as a possible nominee.[31]

When the convention met, Wilson was vacationing in Scotland. He wrote his wife that he felt "a bit silly waiting on the possibility of the impossible happening."[32] Reason told him he was not in the running, but he could not suppress all hope of Harvey's being able to work a miracle. Bryan was nominated.

Whereas for many years Wilson had been trying to adjust to being an educator rather than a politician, by 1909 he was ready to reopen the floodgates of his old ambition. "This is what I was meant for, anyhow, this rough and tumble of the political arena," he wrote Mary Hulbert on September 5, 1909. "My instinct all turns that way, and I sometimes feel rather impatiently the restraints of my academic position."[33]

To an admirer who urged him to enter political life, Wilson wrote that he felt with all his heart the country needed a change of leadership, and that if a suitable invitation came from the proper sources "it would be my duty to give very careful consideration to the question where I could be of the most service. . . ."[34]

In January, 1910, Colonel Harvey invited Boss Smith of New Jersey to lunch in Delmonico's in New York City. In November, 1910, a governor of New Jersey was to be elected. Harvey wanted Smith to help make Wilson the Democratic Party's candidate. Smith was sceptical. How would the "Presbyterian priest," as he referred to Wilson, impress "the boys"? Even more important, what assurance did Smith have that Wilson, once elected, wouldn't try to break down Smith's organization? On the other side of the ledger was the prospect of contributing to the political fortunes of a man who could conceivably become President of the United States. What rewards could he not claim if he maneuvered Wilson through the governorship to the presidency? Harvey's suggestion that he get his "boys" at the convention to support the nomination of Wilson was intriguing.

A few months after this meeting, one of Smith's lieutenants, John Harlan, undertook to find out what Wilson's attitude would be toward Boss Smith's organization should he be elected governor. Smith was aware, of course, that in an article entitled "The States and Federal Government," Wilson had pleaded the wisdom of leaving the selection of candidates for public office to those who volunteered to make a business of it. "They are the political bosses and managers whom the people obey and affect to despise. It is unjust to despise them," Wilson had written.[35] But Smith wanted further assurance. On June 11, 1910, Harlan wrote Wilson that while Smith had not the slightest desire for any commitment as to principles, measures or men, he did want to be satisfied that "you, if you were elected Governor, would not set about fighting and breaking down the existing Democratic organization and replacing it with one of your own." [36]

Wilson replied that he would be "perfectly willing to assure Mr. Smith that I would not, if elected Governor, set about 'fighting and breaking down the existing Democratic organization and replacing it with one of my own.' The last thing I should think of would be building up a machine of my own." [37]

This assurance satisfied Smith. He was willing to press Wilson's nomination. In subsequent conferences, Wilson seems to have made no further commitments and, indeed, made his opposition to Smith's views on the politically important liquor problem quite clear. The "Boss," however, seems to have been entirely persuaded by Wilson's statement to Harlan. He set in motion in Wilson's behalf the great, corrupt, New Jersey political machine.

By early June, 1910, faced with defeat at Princeton, Wilson had an opportunity to extricate himself from his unhappy position there by running for Governor of New Jersey. The governorship interested him primarily as a steppingstone to the presidency. He conceived of the governorship as, he wrote a friend, "the mere preliminary of a plan to nominate me in 1912 for the presidency." [38] This bait was irresistible. On July 12, 1910, Wilson told Colonel Harvey and Boss Smith that he was willing to run for governor.

Wilson hoped to wait until after the election to resign his Princeton post. But such was the animosity that he had aroused that in October the trustees sent a delegation suggesting that he resign. One of the trustees was determined to make this private request a public demand should Wilson refuse. The next day, Wilson presented a letter of resignation. The trustees accepted it immediately.[39]

## CHAPTER IV

# GOVERNOR OF NEW JERSEY

My friends tell me that if I will enter the contest and can be nominated and elected Governor of New Jersey, I stand a very good chance of being the next President of the United States.
Woodrow Wilson to Mary Hulbert, winter, 1908.[1]

. . . candidacy must precede election, and the shoals of candidacy can be passed only by a light boat which carries little freight and can be turned readily about to suit the intricacies of the passage.
Woodrow Wilson, *Congressional Government.*[2]

IN EARLY 1910, the men who wanted Wilson as Governor of New Jersey were conservative Democrats. Clearly, if he wanted any sort of political career at all at that time, he would have to encourage their support. Clearly, too, he would have to win the support of the anti-conservative faction of the Democratic Party somehow, if he were to have any real chance of becoming President. His problem was to use the help of his conservative backers to gain the vantage point of the governorship and then to attract the liberal support he needed to proceed to still higher office.

News of Wilson's candidacy for the governorship touched off an avalanche of attacks against him. The Hoboken *Observer* wrote:

There is no denial of the fact that Dr. Wilson was induced to enter the race by a combination of the very elements which the Progressives are fighting, and that these elements have assumed charge of his candidacy . . .

When it is remembered that the leading corporation lawyer in the state, Richard V. Lindabury, who has taken no interest in Democratic politics for fifteen years, and George B. M. Harvey, who is closely affiliated with the Morgan railroad interests, were active with the bosses in the exclusive conference at which Mr. Wilson's candidacy was decided upon: that the Professor has himself alienated all of the union labour men of the state, of which the party is largely composed, by his recent address at Princeton University, and that his position on every other local question is at the time unknown, he will understand the great wave of doubt and opposition which is sweeping through the state.[3]

In his baccalaureate address in 1909, Wilson had criticized labor unions for encouraging the worker "to give as little as he may for his wages" and, indeed, for forbidding workers in some trades to produce more than their least skillful fellows. In mid-August, 1910, the New Jersey Federation of Labor officially denounced Wilson as an enemy of labor. This was a serious blow to his candidacy.[4]

The anti-Wilson protests were loud, numerous and backed by considerable popular feeling. Through it all, with one or two minor exceptions, Wilson remained silent. Journalists peppered him with questions about his views. Did he favor a corrupt practices act? Workmen's compensation legislation? Did he favor a public utility commission with rate-making powers? Direct election of United States Senators? Did he favor legislation against large campaign contributions? Wilson declined to say. Apparently he was unwilling to antagonize Boss Smith or Colonel Harvey before the convention—before they had made the promised efforts in his behalf. The reformers represented Wilson's refusal to commit himself as confirmation of their suspicion that he was the creature of Wall Street and the political bosses.

The Democratic state convention convened in Trenton on September 15. Confronted by the bitter and alarmingly powerful opposition of the reformers, Boss Smith was driven to arrange for the support of an ancient rival, Boss Davis of Hudson County, New Jersey. Even so, the "Big Fellow" had a terrible time corralling the necessary votes for Wilson. All the resources of his machine, including the persuasive solicitations of his race-track cronies, had to be brought to bear on the delegates. The progressives could not marshal sufficient strength to withstand the pressure. At last Smith's will prevailed. Wilson was nominated.

In the latter stages of the battle, the candidate himself was waiting calmly in Colonel Harvey's hotel room. When one of the delegates brought him the news of his nomination, Wilson reacted like a man who had had no doubt of the outcome. "Thanks. I am ready," he replied in a businesslike manner.[5]

He walked onto the stage of the Opera House, where the delegates awaited him. Most of them had never even seen Wilson before. There was a demonstration—Boss Smith was very efficient—but the reformers sat stonily eyeing the man who had triumphed over their own candidate.

Wilson began simply, thanking the delegates for the nomination. He then astonished his audience, still smarting from the whiplash of his machine sponsors, with a declaration of his political independence. "As you know," he said, "I did not seek this nomination. It has come to me absolutely unsolicited, with the consequence that I shall enter upon the duties of the office of Governor, if elected, with absolutely no pledges of any kind to prevent me from serving the people of the State with singleness of purpose. Not only have no pledges of any kind been given, but none have been proposed or desired." He declared himself in favor of the progressive measures which had been included in the platform, and then exhorted the astounded assemblage in front of him to help make the Democratic Party "the instrument of righteousness for the State and for the Nation."[6]

What did all this indicate about his attitude toward Boss Smith? Nobody knew for sure, but there could be no doubt that here was a man of power, an authentic leader. Wilson radiated sincerity and assurance. There was a contagious vitality about him. He spoke as a man confident of overcoming all obstacles to the achievement of his purposes. He was richly endowed with that charismatic quality which can unlock a crowd's emotions and direct the path of flow. On occasion, he could inspire not merely mass submission to his domination but, as well, the wish to participate in an impassioned demonstration of joy and relief at the surrender. His speech to the New Jersey nominating convention was one of those occasions. The delegates rose to their feet and cheered wildly.

Baker has written: "It is the universal testimony of those who were present that the speech, brief and simple as it was, produced an extraordinary effect. . . . He literally brought around his bitterest opponents."[7] One of them, John Crandall of Atlantic County, threw his hat into the air and, waving his cane above his head, shouted, "I am sixty-five years old, and still a damn fool!"[8] Another convert was Joseph Tumulty, who later became Wilson's private secretary.

Wilson's audacious acceptance speech was not an accidental shot in the dark. In quick succession, he made speeches in favor of many liberal measures the reformers of both parties had been advocating for years.

Wilson's new "line" delighted the reformers, including many of the "New Idea" Republicans who deplored the fact that their own party, too, was controlled by a boss-dominated machine. The efforts of the Republican nominee, Vivian M. Lewis, to dissociate himself from the Republican machine seemed pallid compared to Wilson's ringing declarations of independence from the bosses. Time and again, this unusual political phenomenon from Princeton stated bluntly that if the machine leaders thought they could control him they would learn that they had picked the wrong man. The bosses, he was fond of telling his audiences, were like the "young lady of Niger" in one of his favorite limericks. He would then recite:

> "There was a young lady of Niger
> Who smilingly rode on a tiger.
> They returned from the ride
> With the lady inside
> And the smile on the face of the tiger." [9]

However attractive they found Wilson's speeches, the more cautious reformers remained sceptical. Wilson sounded almost too good to be true. If he really meant what he said, how did it happen that the Democratic bosses, usually extremely shrewd in recognizing exactly where their interests lay, continued to support him? And how did it happen that in all the years of his New Jersey residence he had never lent the slightest assistance to the struggling exponents of the reform measures he now so zealously championed?

On October 17, 1910, George Record, one of the most prominent Republican reformers, addressed a series of nineteen questions to Wilson. The answers would reveal once and for all where he stood on the question of boss control in state politics, and on specific reform measures.

Wilson's advisers pleaded with him not to answer Record's questions.[10] But Wilson took his own counsel. In clear and unmistakable language, he repudiated the political bosses and promised unequivocal support of legislation establishing state control of utilities, workmen's compensation, the direct election of United States Senators and corrupt practices control. He candidly admitted that the boss system existed and stated that he hated that system as thoroughly as he understood it. He declared:

You wish to know what my relations would be with the Democrats whose power and influence you fear, should I be elected Governor, particularly in such important matters as appointments and the signing of bills, and I am very glad to tell you. If elected I shall not, either in the matter of appointments to office or assent to legislation, or in shaping any part of the policy of my administration, submit to the dictation of any person or persons, special interest or organization. I will always welcome advice and suggestions from any citizen, whether boss, leader, organization man, or plain citizen, and I shall constantly seek the advice of influential and disinterested men, representative of their communities and disconnected from political "organizations" entirely; but all suggestions and all advice will be considered on their merits, and no additional weight will be given to any man's advice or suggestion because of his exercising, or supposing that he exercises, some sort of political influence or control. I should deem myself forever disgraced should I in even the slightest degree co-operate in any such system or any such transactions as you describe in your characterization of the "boss" system. I regard myself as pledged to the regeneration of the Democratic party . . .[11]

Boss Smith and James Nugent, his chief lieutenant (who was also his nephew), simply could not believe that Wilson really meant what he said. They had come to realize that, as Nugent put it, Wilson was "a terrible man to manage."[12] Nevertheless, they thought (or at least uneasily pretended to) that once elected, Wilson would conveniently forget what they considered the idealistic claptrap of the campaign.

The Wilson-Record correspondence overcame the last doubts of the reformers. They campaigned for him enthusiastically.

On November 8, 1910, Wilson was swept into office with a plurality of almost fifty thousand votes. The Republicans retained a small majority in the upper house of the legislature, but the Democrats won a large majority in the Assembly. It was large enough to outvote the Republicans in any joint session, such as would be held to elect a United States Senator from New Jersey.

Wilson's behavior in the period between 1910 and 1912, from the time he resigned his Princeton post to the time he was elected President, proves beyond doubt that he had the capacity, at least in some circumstances, to be a versatile political strategist. With great skill, by adjusting his views to conform with popular sentiment, by cultivating the favor of men who could advance his interests, by making and breaking commitments as expediency dictated, he maneuvered his way to his goal. He left in his wake a trail of tough-minded and experienced politicians, incredulous that a man they had regarded as a cloistered academician could outwit them at their own game. Outwit them all Wilson did. He proved himself a practical politician without peer, a prodigy in the art of elevating himself to power.

James Kerney, editor of the Trenton *Evening Times,* who had close firsthand knowledge of Wilson during this period, has written that as Governor, Wilson "frequently found it necessary to resort to trading. The kind of things he had condemned uncompromisingly in his writings, and as university professor, were put aside in the rough and tumble of affairs." [13]

Wilson performed two major intellectual somersaults. Both furthered his political fortunes. First, after accepting the help of the political bosses and assuring them that he would not, if elected, fight the existing Democratic organization, he turned on them and the whole boss system and fought tooth and nail to destroy their power in New Jersey.

Even more startling, he transformed himself from a conservative Democrat to a liberal Democrat. Several competent students of these events have emphasized the importance of political expediency in this conversion. A. S. Link, for example, writes:

> Wilson wanted desperately to enter politics, to hold high office, and he must have recognized that the strength of the progressive movement, especially in New Jersey, was growing rapidly, and that a continued adherence to his conservative creed would be almost certainly fatal to his political aspirations. After his nomination for governor, Wilson was forced to make a deliberate choice between conservatism and progressivism, and he knew that the outcome of the election depended upon his decision. The choice was inevitable—he finally capitulated to the progressives.[14]

If Wilson opposed the boss system before his nomination for the governorship, his willingness to allow himself to be sponsored by the bosses indicates the ability to compromise a principle (anti-bossism) in the interest of achieving a desirable goal (the nomination). If, on the other hand, Wilson had no serious objections to the boss system, his denunciation of it after his nomination can only be construed as an attempt to secure votes by pretending to believe what he knew would enhance his popularity. In either case, he was behaving expediently. He was also behaving expediently when he expressed conservative views at a time he needed conservative support and liberal views when he needed liberal support. Wilson had once said: "If you would be a leader of men, you must lead your own generation, not the next. Your playing must be good now, while the play is on the boards and the audience in the seats . . ." The "audience" was in the mood for reform. And Wilson yearned for its applause.[16]

Under a democratic form of government, most politicians in the course of their careers are obliged to accommodate themselves to some extent to public opinion when seeking elective office and, having attained it, to the views of the men with whom they share power. Were they unwilling or unable to do so, their chances of being elected or, once elected, of leading successfully, would be sharply curtailed, if not destroyed entirely. So there is nothing intrinsically remarkable in Wilson's flexibility. What *is* noteworthy is the contrast between his genius for political maneuvering in his pursuit of power and his shattering want of good judgment, having won the Presidency, in his relations with the Senate in connection with the League of Nations. Wilson's adroitness in dealing with the bosses and with the 1911 New Jersey legislature is a measure of the later tragedy of the man—a demonstration of the skill he might have applied to the League fight if only he had been able to cope rationally with his animosity toward Senator Lodge.

Even before Wilson had been sworn into office, Boss Smith provided ammunition which the Governor-elect could use against him. The choice of United States Senators being at that time in the hands of the state legislators, and the state legislators being largely under the thumbs of the political bosses, New Jersey's Senators were usually the bosses themselves or their henchmen.

Boss Smith had served in the United States Senate from 1893 to 1899. He had acquitted himself badly, having been discovered in questionable financial dealings involving misuse of confidential knowledge for personal gain. In the decade following the expiration of his term the Republicans controlled the legislature and were sending Republicans to the Senate. Smith professed to experience this state of affairs as no personal loss at all. He declared repeatedly that he had no desire to return to Washington. Life in the nation's capital bored him, he said, and besides his health was too poor to permit him to perform a Senator's strenuous duties. It was widely believed, however, that in reality Smith was eager for another term of office. A rumor which could not be quelled throughout the gubernatorial campaign of 1910 was that Smith was supporting Wilson in the hope that Wilson would sweep into office with him a Democratic legislature which could be relied upon to restore the "Big Fellow" to Capitol Hill.

In any case, as the campaign of 1910 progressed and the prospects for the election of a Democratic legislature grew, Smith's physical ailments seemed to trouble him less and less. The election results, which assured a Democratic majority in the legislature, dispelled Smith's last doubts as to the attractions of a Senator's life and his fitness to lead it. He set his heart on being chosen for the job.

There was, however, another claimant for the prize: James E. Martine. In 1907, the progressives had succeeded in piloting through the legislature a law which established preferential primaries for the senatorship. The electorate of New Jersey still did not control the selection of their United States Senators, for the results of the preferential primaries were not legally binding upon the legislature. Nevertheless, the 1907 law at least provided a channel for the expression of the popular will. In the election of 1910, the first to occur in accordance with the 1907 regulation as to Senators, less than a third of the Democrats who voted availed themselves of their new privilege. This fraction of the Democratic electorate, however, endorsed Martine by a large majority.

From all accounts, James E. Martine was an affable but vacuous Bryan Democrat who for forty years had been running unsuccessfully for a variety of public offices, high and low. When the time came to select candidates for the senatorial primary, none of the leading Democrats of either faction of the party were willing to come forward. For the general expectation was that the legislature would be Republican-controlled and that the Democratic candidate therefore would stand no chance of actual election. Nonetheless, names were needed for the ballot, and the progressives decided that their perennial candidate, Martine, would simply have to lend his. A committee of two summoned the draftee to inform him of his fate. Martine pleaded to be spared the humiliation of another defeat. To no avail.[16] He was thrust unwillingly into the breach and, in consequence of the Democratic victory, suddenly found himself in possession of a claim to high office. It was no more than a claim, however, since the legislature was not legally bound by the results of the primary. Certainly Martine's candidacy did not deter Smith in the slightest from pressing his own suit.

Smith opened his drive as soon as the election results were in. Whatever his misgivings about Wilson's unnerving campaign speeches, he sent him an enthusiastic telegram of congratulations. He assumed a paternally protective tone, advising the governor-elect to take a vacation before assuming his new office.

A few days later, the "Big Boss" appeared in Princeton to celebrate with the victor in person, and to reap his reward. In high spirits, he declared that his health had greatly improved and that his friends were urging him to make himself available as a senatorial candidate. (As a matter of fact, his friends were doing a good deal more than that. They were seeking out the Democratic legislators and trying to pressure them into supporting his claim.)

Wilson objected immediately. He pointed out that some people thought Smith's support of Wilson's candidacy had been inspired by his senatorial ambitions, and that Smith's interest in any office now would confirm the ugliest suspicions as to his motivation. The "Big Boss" insisted he wanted to be a Senator.

Wilson reminded him that Martine had won the senatorial primary. Smith retorted that the primary was a farce and Martine a fool. Wilson conceded both points, but would not agree to Smith's candidacy. He urged the "Big Boss" to propose a compromise candidate behind whom all Democratic factions could unite. Smith refused.

Wilson now had to decide whether to stand by and allow Smith to exact his tribute, or redeem the spirit of his campaign pledges and lead the battle against the "Big Boss." On this point, he seems not to have hesitated: to capitulate to Smith was unthinkable. Unless he gave up his attempt to bludgeon his way to the Senate, a showdown was inevitable. The ardor with which Wilson held to this morally unassailable position doubtless derived in part from the attractive prospect it held forth of breaking Smith's power and establishing himself as undisputed leader of the Democratic Party in New Jersey.

With the related problem of whether or not to support Martine he seems to have had greater difficulty. As late as November 20, Wilson told James Kerney that he considered Martine unqualified and mentioned another man he thought more worthy of the legislature's consideration. Kerney was struck by the fact that he clearly attached little importance to the primary vote.[17] But the progressives were putting great pressure on Wilson to stand behind the winner of the primary. Reluctantly, he concluded he had no alternative.

On November 15, 1910, Wilson wrote Harvey a letter warning that should Smith become a candidate . . .

I would have to fight him. . . . It would offend every instinct in me,—except the instinct as to what was right and necessary from the point of view of the public service . . .

By the same token,—ridiculous though it undoubtedly is,—I think we shall have to stand by Mr. Martine . . .

Senator Smith can make himself the biggest man in the State by a dignified refusal to let his name be considered. I hope, as I hope for the rejuvenation of our party, that he may see it and may be persuaded to do so.

It is a national as well as a State question. If the independent Republicans who in this State voted for me are not to be attracted to us they will assuredly turn again, in desperation, to Mr. Roosevelt, and the chance of a generation will be lost to the Democracy: the chance to draw all the liberal elements of the country to it, through new leaders, the chance that Mr. Roosevelt missed in his folly, and to constitute the ruling party of the country for the next generation.[18]

Wilson apparently hoped that Harvey would show Smith the letter and persuade him to abandon his senatorial ambitions. But Harvey remained neutral. The others upon whom Wilson prevailed to intervene privately all reported that Smith's determination was unshakable, and that he was bringing all possible pressure upon the newly elected legislators to secure their support. Once again, the "Big Fellow" resorted to making an alliance with Boss Davis, whose word was law with the Hudson County Democratic legislators.

On November 25, the governor-elect went to Jersey City and paid a personal call on Boss Davis. Davis lay abed, in the last stages of the cancer which was to claim his life less than two months later. Wilson pleaded with him to reconsider his position. Davis seemed moved, but said he had given his word to Smith to deliver the votes of the Hudson County legislators, and could not break his promise. Notwithstanding this profession of loyalty to Smith, Davis apparently was not actually so firmly committed to him. For in the days immediately following Wilson's visit, the dying chieftain gave his "boys" to understand that he would not be offended should any of them vote against Smith.[19]

While Wilson was engaged in these behind-the-scenes maneuvers to defeat Smith, the progressives were insistently demanding that he publicly endorse Martine. A great principle—the direct election of Senators—was at issue. If Wilson failed to support Martine, they warned, he would not only betray a principle to which his acceptance of the Democratic platform committed him, but he would stigmatize himself as Smith's lackey. On the other hand, to defeat Smith, to secure Martine's election, would establish him as leader, in fact, of the Democratic Party in his state. It would vindicate the faith of the progressives of both parties who had voted for him, and further his chances for the presidential nomination.[20]

These arguments found their mark. The issues of the election of Martine and the defeat of boss rule had become irrevocably wedded in the minds of the progressives. Wilson had already decided, of course, to oppose Smith. Now, to satisfy public opinion, he must champion the validity of a primary to which he had actually attached little importance, and a candidate to whom he had been opposed. Very well. By the beginning of December, 1910, the election of James E. Martine to the United States Senate had become a holy cause to Wilson.

The legislature was to convene in mid-January. The election of a United States Senator was to be one of the first items of business. All through December, Wilson held conferences with the legislators, individually and in small groups. Tirelessly, he expatiated on the moral obligation which the primary election imposed upon them to support Martine.

On December 6, Wilson made one last attempt to persuade Smith to withdraw from the contest. Smith refused. On December 8, Wilson issued a public statement asserting that "it is clearly the duty of every Democratic legislator, who would keep faith with the law of the State and with the avowed principles of his party, to vote for Mr. Martine." The people of New Jersey did not want to be represented by Smith, Wilson declared. They had expressed a preference in the primary and "for me, that vote is conclusive." [21]

The progressives were elated, and the reaction was nationwide. The redoubtable William Jennings Bryan himself had a word of praise for Wilson's stand.[22]

The contest between Wilson and Smith for the support of the legislators continued. Smith offered the usual bait of patronage, favors —his whole repertoire of the blandishments and threats which had served so well for so long. Wilson offered nothing except the chance to join him in a moral crusade to regenerate the Democratic Party. With seismographic sensitivity to the distribution of power, Smith's old retainers perceived that the "Big Fellow's" star was waning. One by one, they deserted to the vital new leader whose career might reach the very highest pinnacle, the leader who, in any case, seemed likely to exercise the prerogatives that Boss Smith had so boldly preempted for himself.

By the end of December, it was obvious that Wilson had won the battle. A sufficient number of legislators had privately committed themselves to supporting Martine to ensure his election. Wilson had not done with his adversary, however.

On December 23, he issued a public statement outlining the entire controversy. In it Wilson claimed that before he had agreed to accept the gubernatorial nomination, he had received reliable assurances that Smith did not intend to seek to return to the Senate. Smith replied indignantly, denying that he had ever authorized anyone to deliver such assurances to Wilson, challenging the governor-elect to name this so-called "authorized representative," and charging him with ingratitude and unwarranted interference with the legislature. His rebuttal was all but ignored in the deluge of enthusiastic comment on Wilson's performance.

Wilson wound up his campaign for Martine in two spirit-stirring speeches. The smell of victory was in the air. The crowds came to cheer. Wilson, full of verve, gave them the opportunity to shout themselves hoarse.

On January 5, 1911, in Jersey City, Wilson described the Smith-Nugent machine as a wart growing on the body politic and jauntily invited the public to witness its excision. There was a hush as he revealed his magnanimity:

> If I understand my own heart, ladies and gentlemen, I do not entertain personal animosities in this matter. It is not a question of persons and their faults. . . . Mr. James Smith, Jr., represents not a party but a system —a system of political control which does not belong to either party. . . . It is the system that we are fighting, and not the representatives. . . .

Turning theatrically to the somewhat confused star of the whole drama, Wilson declared:

> I appeal to Mr. Martine never under any circumstances to withdraw. We are not in this fight to find the easy way, the complacent way. We are in it to find and pursue the right way, and any man who turns away from the right way will be marked, labeled, and remembered. . . .[23]

The crowd roared its approval.

Wilson chose the routed boss's home city for his final thrust. To the detached reader of his speech some half century after its delivery, it may seem a bit bombastic; but the crowd in Newark's New Auditorium on January 14, 1911, loved it:

Gentlemen, what is it that we are fighting for? Does not your blood jump quicker in your veins when you think that this is part of the age-long struggle for human liberty? What do men feel curtails and destroys their liberty? Matters in which they have no voice. The control of little groups and cliques and bodies of special interests, the things that are managed without regard to the public welfare or general opinion—the things that are contrived without any referendum to the great mass of feelings and opinions and purposes that are abroad among free men in a free country. Whenever things go to cover, then men stand up and know and say that liberty is in jeopardy, and so every time a fight of this sort occurs, we are simply setting up the standard again. One can almost see the field of battle. On the one hand a fort that looks strong but that is made of pasteboard. Behind it stand men apparently armed with deadly weapons, but having only playthings in their hands. And off cowering in the distance for a little while is the great mass of fearful, free men. Presently they take heart; they look up; they begin to move slowly. You can see the dust of the plain gather, and then as they take heart and realize that whether the fort is hard to take or not life is not worth living unless it is taken. And they go on, and, as in the old Bible stories, the first shout of victorious and irresistible free men causes the stronghold to collapse.[24]

Boss Smith found Wilson an entirely flabbergasting opponent. That a man of Wilson's seeming integrity should renege on his pledge not to fight the Democratic machine astounded him. That he should so savagely turn on the man who had helped him to office seemed the act of an unscrupulous ingrate.

The "Big Boss" fought the battle the only way he knew how. But barter, cajolery, threats were puny weapons to pit against the strangely compelling political evangelicalism of his opponent.

On January 24, the legislature started to vote for the next United States Senator from New Jersey. On January 25, the balloting was completed. The final tally was: Martine 47; Smith 3.

"I pitied Smith at the last," Wilson wrote a friend:

It was so plain that he had few real friends,—that he held men by fear and power and the benefits he could bestow, not by love or loyalty or any genuine devotion. The minute it was seen that he was defeated his adherents began to desert him like rats leaving a sinking ship. He left Trenton (where his headquarters had at first been crowded) attended, I am told, only by his sons, and looking old and broken. He wept, they say, as he admitted himself utterly beaten.[25]

Wilson's victory won him national acclamation. His stock as a contender for the Democratic presidential nomination in 1912 soared. It was the kind of plucky success which delighted people all over the country who were disgusted with the old-style political machines and relished seeing one of the most firmly entrenched of them so neatly dispatched.

The press trumpeted the "cloistered professor" who had vanquished the "Big Boss." One joyous writer described how Wilson, "his garments odorous with the vapours of Parnassus, his lips wet with the waters of Helicon—this long-haired bookworm of a professor who had just laid his spectacles on his dictionary, came down to the Trenton State House and 'licked the gang to a frazzle.' "[26]

The temper of the country was overwhelmingly reformist and progressive. Now presidential candidate Wilson must press his advantage further. He must sponsor the sort of legislation which would bring him to the public's attention as an outstanding liberal reformer.

Before his inauguration on January 17, 1911, Wilson had called a bi-partisan conference of progressives to help formulate bills for presentation to the legislature. He was highly receptive to their suggestions and displayed a considerable talent for reversing his long-standing attitudes on a number of issues (including the initiative and referendum, which he had steadfastly condemned until his election).

From this consultation, Wilson emerged with four major pieces of proposed legislation. Each was of great importance. Together, they constituted a sweeping reform program—the materialization of measures the progressives had long been advocating. They were: 1) an election law which would establish direct primaries; 2) a corrupt practices act; 3) a law regulating public utilities; and 4) an employers' liability act.

The enactment of these reforms would require the co-operation of the Republican-controlled Senate. It would also require the elimination of boss control of the Assemblymen's votes. For Smith and Nugent, although down, were by no means out. Staggered by their initial defeat at Wilson's hands, they nevertheless hoped to play their customary role during the legislative session. Their "customary role" had been to instruct the legislators how to vote and to engineer the passage of legislation which would benefit their big corporation allies. They transacted much of their business in the corridors and committee rooms—even on the very floor of the Assembly chamber.

After his departure from Trenton, Smith remained in the fastness of his Newark headquarters. It was Nugent who turned up at the State House in Trenton in February. He promptly began to buttonhole the legislators in an attempt to pledge them to vote against Wilson's legislative program. Wilson summoned him and suggested that he return to Newark. Nugent refused, and continued his activities.

When the election bill was introduced, the battle for the legislators' allegiance became more tense than ever. Breaking all precedent, Wilson attended a caucus of the Democratic Assemblymen. For three hours, he lectured them about the necessity of passing the bill. For the benefit of those who might remain impervious to his arguments, he warned that if necessary he would carry the fight to the people. In that event, of course, he might be forced to criticize certain legislators, whose careers might suffer thereby.

Meanwhile, Nugent was assiduously applying his brand of persuasion to the legislators. Many of them, men of just average ability and limited aspiration, must have felt between Scylla and Charybdis. Their main concern was to align themselves with what would prove to be the winning side in the power struggle. On the one hand, Smith and Nugent had wielded such great power for so long that the aura of authority clung to them even after Smith's defeat in his bid for the senatorship. Perhaps that was just a first skirmish and the "Big Boss" would succeed in re-establishing his sway. On the other hand, Wilson's strength seemed to be increasing, not only locally, but throughout the land. He was obviously a leader of stature, and the question of what his ultimate destiny would be was already the subject of much heady conjecture. Surely it was risky to incur the wrath of such a man.

It soon became apparent that Nugent would be able to control no more than a dozen votes in the Assembly. In desperation, he approached the Republican bosses. If the Republican Assemblymen could be prevailed upon to vote against Wilson, it would still be possible, by combining forces, to defeat the election bill—indeed, to defeat Wilson's entire legislative program.

The possibility of a coalition between the Republican and Democratic bosses alarmed the Wilson camp. Wilson again summoned Nugent. Nugent, surly and defiant, appeared at the Governor's office on March 20, 1911. Baker gives the following account, based on public statements made by both men after the event, of the interview that took place:

"Don't you think, Mr. Nugent," said the Governor, "that you are making a grave mistake in opposing the election bill?"

"No," said Nugent, "and you can't pass it without using the state patronage."

Nugent could have said nothing that would have cut deeper. He was accusing the Governor of bribing the legislators with promises of offices. Wilson met the charge in white heat. He rose from his chair and pointed his hand at the door.

"Good afternoon, Mr. Nugent."

The boss hesitated, trembling with passion.

"You're no gentleman!" he shouted.

"You're no judge!" responded the Governor.

The report of the meeting spread like wildfire. The boss was seen "tearing down the corridor, apoplectic with rage." [27]

Wilson's latest upbraiding of the bosses won him another round of applause from all over the country. There was something infinitely appealing in this supposedly inexperienced scholar's tilting with some of the roughest, toughest men in the country—and doing it successfully!

There could be no mistaking the surge of enthusiasm for the new Governor among the voters of New Jersey. Every day Nugent learned of new defections from his dwindling forces. In the end, he was able to persuade only ten Democrats to vote against the election bill. The Assembly passed it on March 21, 1911, by a vote of 34 to 25.

Now the bill was sent to the upper chamber. The State Senators were far more independent of the political bosses than their colleagues of the lower house. What worried Wilson about the Senate was not the influence of the bosses, but the fact of a Republican majority. Wilson wooed the Senators with a combination of intellectual appeal and personal charm. He conferred with them individually and in groups. He invited them to visit him in his office: he was unfailingly delighted to chat with them.

He even attended some informal social functions with the Senators. In a letter to Mary Hulbert, Wilson described how at one of them he led a Republican Senator whose vote hung in the balance in a cakewalk, several times around the big dining room.

> . . . We pranced together to the perfect content of the whole company. He seemed quite mollified before we got through with him. Such are the processes of high politics! This is what it costs to be a leader! But it remains to be seen whether the sly old fox votes for the bills or not. I would not trust him out of my sight. But this at least seems gained: I am on easy

and delightful terms with all the senators. They know me for something else than "an ambitious dictator." [28]

The "sly old fox" *did* vote for the election bill, as did every single one of the Senators, Republican and Democratic alike. It would be naïve to attribute this result simply to Wilson's social charm. The Senators apparently had accepted the thesis, ably advanced by Wilson's partisans, that the proposed reform program represented the popular will and that anyone who obstructed it would be discredited in the eyes of the voters. It is nevertheless undoubtedly the case that Wilson's affability facilitated their decision to co-operate on his terms.

The battle having been won on the election bill, the corrupt practices act, the public utilities bill and the workmen's compensation law passed both houses of the legislature with relative ease.

The legislative session of 1911 was a triumph for Wilson. Never in the history of the state had there been so fruitful a session. In four months Wilson had succeeded in piloting his entire program through both houses. He had done so by eliminating the two major obstacles on which, in less skillful hands, the whole program might have foundered: boss control of the Assembly, and Republican opposition in the Senate. His masterful performance had increased his availability for the presidential nomination immeasurably. Elated, Wilson wrote Mary Hulbert on April 23, 1911:

Dearest Friend,

The Legislature adjourned yesterday morning at three o'clock, with its work done. I got absolutely everything I strove for,—and more besides. . . .

Everyone, the papers included, are saying that none of it could have been done, if it had not been for my influence and tact and hold upon the people. Be that as it may, the thing was done, and the result was as complete a victory as has ever been won, I venture to say, in the history of the country. I wrote the platform, I had the measures formulated to my mind, I kept the pressure of opinion constantly on the legislature, and the programme was carried out to its last detail. This with the senatorial business seems, in the minds of the people looking on little less than a miracle, in the light of what has been the history of reform hitherto in this State. As a matter of fact, it is just a bit of natural history. I came to the office in the fulness of time, when opinion was ripe on all these matters, when both parties were committed to these reforms, and by merely standing fast, and by never losing sight of the business for an hour, but keeping up all sorts of (legitimate) pressure *all the time,* kept the mighty forces from being diverted or blocked at any point. The strain has been immense, but the reward is great. I feel a great reaction to-day, for I am, of course, exceedingly tired, but I am quietly and deeply happy that I should have been of just the kind of service I wished to be to those who elected and trusted me. I can look them in the face, like a servant who has kept faith and done all that was in him, given every power he possessed, to them and their affairs. There could be no deeper source of satisfaction and contentment!

In view of Wilson's marked inability, when he was President, to utilize the social graces to ease the passage of his programs through Congress, the next portion of this letter is of special interest:

I have no doubt that a good deal of the result was due to the personal relations I established with the men in the Senate, the Republican Senate which, it was feared at the outset, might be the stumbling block. You remember the dinner in New York and the supper at the Trenton country club which I described to you. Those evenings undoubtedly played their part in the outcome. They brought us all close together on terms not unlike friendly intimacy; made them realize just what sort of *person* I was. Since then Republicans have resorted to my office for counsel and advice almost as freely as Democrats (an almost unprecedented circumstance at Trenton) and with several of them I have established relations almost of affection. Otherwise I do not believe that the extraordinary thing that happened could possibly have come about: for all four of the great "administration" measures passed the Senate *without a dissenting voice!* The newspaper men seem dazed. They do not understand how such things *could* happen . . .

What a vigil it has been! I am certainly in training for almost anything that may come to me by way of public tasks. There are serious times ahead. It daunts me to think of the possibility of my playing an influential part in them . . .

All through everything, as the days come and go with their tale of tasks, runs a constant thought of you, a constant solicitude for you, and an abiding consciousness of being (and of being blessed by being),

Your devoted friend,
Woodrow Wilson [29]

However brilliant Wilson's accomplishments in New Jersey had been, and however enthusiastic the public response, he was still far from the presidential nomination. He had, of course, irrevocably alienated the Democratic machine politicians throughout the country. Most of his conservative backers had ruefully concluded that they had misjudged him and, disillusioned, had withdrawn their support. (The original Wilson man, Colonel Harvey, remained faithful for a while longer.) Wilson had cut himself adrift from his initial supporters, without any real assurance that he would be able to attract the backing of the influential progressives of the Democratic Party. It was an audacious strategy he adopted—perhaps the only one offering even the possibility of success—but it required great courage.

For leadership of the progressive Democrats was not to let. Still firmly at the helm, even though past the peak of his power, was William Jennings Bryan. Bryan had won the presidential nomination three times, and three times he had lost the election. Although it was possible that the "Great Commoner" might seek a fourth chance, there was widespread sentiment throughout the country for choosing a new standard bearer. Nevertheless Bryan's great popularity, especially in the South and West, would give him a commanding voice in the choice of the 1912 presidential nominee. Such was Bryan's strength with the people and within the Democratic organization that no liberal presidential aspirant, not even the daring Wilson, could hope to challenge his leadership. Bryan's support would have to be won by the man who would emerge victorious from the 1912 Democratic convention.

Now Wilson's past slurs on Bryan rose to haunt him. He had assailed Bryan's views, had described him as lacking a "mental rudder," had refused to speak on the same platform with him, had prevented him from speaking in Princeton.[30] Could he now hope to win the political blessing of a man he had so disparaged?

Bryan was understandably sceptical when Wilson suddenly proclaimed himself a progressive. He wondered publicly, in the columns of his journal, *The Commoner*, why conservative publications, such as Colonel Harvey's *Harper's Weekly*, were so enthusiastic about the ostensibly liberal Wilson. He called upon Wilson to clarify his position. Wilson's battle for the election of Martine "has tended to reassure me," Bryan wrote him on January 5, 1911. However, he still wondered about Wilson's views on public questions and requested him to comment on the Democratic platform of 1908. Wilson complied in such a way that Bryan declared himself "greatly gratified." The "Great Commoner" undertook to offer Wilson suggestions—for example, that he send a message to the New Jersey legislature urging adoption of the income tax amendment—and found Wilson eager to act upon them.[31]

The two men first met in March, 1911. Bryan had come to Princeton to address the Princeton Theological Seminary. Mrs. Wilson, ever alert to her husband's interests, invited him to dinner. Wilson was in Atlanta, but rushed home to meet the man upon whom his political fortunes hinged.

Next day, Wilson wrote a friend that Bryan "has extraordinary force of personality, and it seems the force of sincerity and conviction. . . . His voice is wholly delightful. . . . A truly captivating man. . . ." [32] Bryan, according to Baker, was "charmed" by Wilson's "gaiety and nimble-mindedness" and "captivated" by Mrs. Wilson.[33] An auspicious beginning!

Three weeks later, Wilson and Bryan both addressed a Democratic meeting in Burlington, New Jersey. Wilson took the occasion to pay Bryan fulsome tribute.

Wilson spent the month of May, 1911, stumping the West. Everywhere, the fame of the recently adjourned New Jersey legislature preceded him. He traveled 8,000 miles and made twenty-five speeches, every one of them a faithful, if somewhat ambiguous, echo of Bryan's point of view on important issues. The Western press, by and large, was cordial. His audiences were enthusiastic.

During the months that his attention was largely focussed on national politics, the New Jersey bosses were planning their revenge. A would-be candidate for the presidency is expected to command the support of his home state's delegates to his party's national convention. Wilson realized the importance of winning the New Jersey presidential primary election on May 28, 1912. Boss Smith's organization, which had worked for his election for governor, now opposed him. And the chairman of the state Democratic committee was still James Nugent. Wilson was faced with the necessity of building an effective organization of his own, one he could pit successfully against the Smith-Nugent machine.

An incident which occurred in the summer of 1911 helped Wilson depose Nugent from his chairmanship of the state Democratic committee. One evening, on July 25, to be exact, Nugent and some friends repaired to a bar for some drinks. In the presence of all and sundry, the by then boisterous boss rose and proposed a toast "to the Governor of New Jersey, the commander-in-chief of the Militia, an ingrate and a liar. I mean Woodrow Wilson. I repeat, he's an ingrate and a liar." [34]

Nugent's toast achieved speedy notoriety. The progressives made a great show of moral indignation, and raised a loud cry for his removal from his position on the state committee. In the end, they were successful. To replace Nugent as chairman, the state committee, on

August 24, 1911, elected Edward R. Grosscup, a loyal Wilson man. Wilson now controlled most of the state party machinery. Many erstwhile Smith-Nugent followers hastened to attach themselves to the Wilson bandwagon. Wilson accepted their support.[35]

The first real test of the relative strength of the bosses and the now largely progressive Democratic organization was to come in the September 26 primaries for the state legislature, which was to be elected on November 7, 1911. The progressives had proposed candidates. So had the bosses.

Wilson toured the state, including Essex County, the Smith-Nugent stronghold, urging support of the progressive candidates. In every county except Essex, the progressives were successful. In Essex County, the Smith-Nugent candidates won handily.

Wilson was caught in a dilemma. On the one hand, he wanted his party to gain control of the legislature. It would be a demonstration of his political strength if the Democrats won leadership of the legislature in a normally Republican state. On the other hand, he shrank from supporting the boss-led Essex County candidates. His progressive following would disapprove his supporting the bosses' candidates even to ensure a party victory. So, too, in all likelihood, would William Jennings Bryan, and Wilson's every important move was calculated with an eye to whether or not it would stand well with Bryan.

Wilson decided to campaign for the Democratic candidates everywhere throughout the state except Essex County. He did so, vigorously. Smith and Nugent, whose desire to avenge themselves against Wilson overrode all other considerations, simply did not campaign for their own candidates. Instead, Smith's two newspapers concentrated on trying to discredit Wilson. Clearly, the "Big Boss" had decided to "throw" the election, thus ensuring Republican majorities in both houses of the legislature and embarrassing Wilson's chances for the presidential nomination. He succeeded.

On election day, November 7, the voters rejected the entire slate of Essex County Democratic candidates. Losses there were of pivotal importance. As a result, the Republicans won large majorities in both houses of the legislature.

Two days after the election, Boss Smith's Newark *Star* editorially quoted the Philadelphia *Evening Telegraph* to the effect that " 'the National Convention will think twice before placing at the head of the ticket a man who was unable to hold his forces together for nine months.'" The *Star* added with ill-concealed relish: "That opinion is taking hold at Trenton, too."[36]

The loss of the legislature was a blow to Wilson's prestige. He must redouble his efforts to make a good showing on May 28, 1912, when New Jersey's delegates to the national Democratic convention would be elected.

In November, 1911, Wilson was a man within range of achieving the dream of a lifetime, the presidency—a statesman's career! He was walking a political tightrope at dizzy heights. There were myriad intricate problems to be coped with as he went along—gaining Bryan's support, battling the resurgent New Jersey bosses, building a nation-wide organization to support his candidacy. The possible pitfalls were many. He must proceed in very gingerly manner to avoid them. Yet he must be bold and imaginative too, and move quickly.

And in reaching the thousand and one perilous decisions which must be made, he was alone. The women of his family and some of his friends adored him, and wished fervently for his success; but they could not help him much with the practical problems at hand. The men he leaned on for aid seemed to him in varying degrees astute and useful and in varying degrees self-seeking. On none of them did he feel able to rely completely. With none of them did he feel free to speak without reserve. Once there had been a person who combined the capacity to enter into his intellectual world with the capacity for satisfying his need for personal friendship—John Grier Hibben. But he had cast Hibben aside bitterly, and there had been no one since to fill the inner void that their broken friendship had left.

This was the man who, on November 24, 1911, went to New York to call on Edward Mandell House. House, he had heard, had been advancing the Wilson cause in Texas, and was in a position to render even greater service. It was a meeting which profoundly affected both men's lives. Before describing it, let us see who House was, what his background had been, and why he was so eager to meet Woodrow Wilson.

## CHAPTER V

# THE APPRENTICE ADVISER

. . . I had no ambition to hold office . . . because I felt . . . that I would fall short of the first place, and nothing less than that would satisfy me. Yet I have been thought without ambition. That, I think, is not quite true. My ambition has been so great that it has never seemed to me worth while to strive to satisfy it. . . .

Edward M. House in an autobiographical essay, "Reminiscences."

EDWARD MANDELL HOUSE was born in Houston, Texas, on July 26, 1858. He was the seventh son of one of the wealthiest men in Texas.

Thomas William House's fortune derived from vast sugar and cotton plantations and banking. Too, during the Civil War, he owned ships which, running the Union blockade both ways, plied between Galveston and nearby West Indian and Central American ports. The cargo from Galveston was usually cotton. The cargo on the return voyage was munitions, clothing and medicine, which Thomas House sold to the Confederate army. Blockade-running was a risky enterprise, but a highly profitable one.

What manner of boy he was and how he developed the political interests which later absorbed him, Colonel House set forth in two long and fascinating memoranda, which are now to be found among his private papers in the Sterling Memorial Library at Yale University. One was written during the summer of 1916, when House was at the zenith of his career. He wrote the other in 1929 when, an ailing old man, he took pleasure in reflecting about his boyhood and youth.

His earliest memories, House recorded, centered about the violence of the Civil War and its aftermath. "My first impressions of life were of human conflict—man battling against man individually and collectively." Toys, as well as the other material amenities which would normally be the portion of a child born into so wealthy a household, were lacking because of the blockade. The all-absorbing game was "war," and the necessary implements were easily enough improvised. At three, House was riding, shooting and participating with other infant stalwarts in mock battles.

The cessation of formal hostilities between North and South ushered in a period of great chaos in Texas. The House family lived on a plantation on the outskirts of Houston, which was then a village of some seven thousand inhabitants, a large proportion of them Negroes. Negroes and carpetbaggers, under the protection of the United States Army, seized the government of the city. The enraged white inhabitants took the law into their own hands in an effort to restore what they considered a feasible way of life. Riots, shootings, murders—these were the typical order of the day. The typical hero was the hothead who risked his life (and frequently lost it!) to pit himself against those newly in power. House wrote:

> Those were lawless and turbulent days. Personal encounters were frequent and nearly always resulted in fatalities. The courage manifested, the accuracy with which the participants shot, were told in detail by every fireside, and the most reckless dare-devil became the greatest hero. But with it all there was something fine and chivalrous. Men took their lives in their hands gladly, and scorned to take advantage of their opponents. Many were actuated by the spirit of the Crusaders. They were bent on the gradual extermination of the parasites who had fastened themselves on a discouraged and defeated people, and were willing to give life for life in the accomplishment of this purpose.

It was not only with their political enemies that the adults in House's world were prone to fight. Outwardly gentle and courteous, they were exceedingly volatile. Unwary strangers often learned—but, alas! the lesson was frequently fatal—that to brag, to bluster, to give the slightest real or fancied offense to these seemingly mild men, was to court disaster. "Unless you knew them and their ways it were better never to come in contact with them," House noted. As a boy, a native of the area, young House did know them and their ways. He admired and emulated them. "I had many warm friends among them—friends upon whom you could count in fair weather and foul."

One of the delights of House's boyhood was hunting. A great variety of game—deer, turkey, quail, prairie chicken, snipe and woodcock—abounded within easy reach. The lad was tutored in the art of hunting by a neighbor whose skill as a woodsman and marksman House still recalled over half a century later.

Young House belonged to a gang. Its leader was his brother James, six years his senior, whom he describes as a boy of courage, tact, ability and imagination. "My admiration for him was boundless, but we fought constantly although I was helpless in his hands."

Like their elders, the children were reckless and violent. They were also armed. Their mock wars, fought with hair-raising realism, sometimes resulted in serious casualties. House's eldest brother had one side of his face shot off and remained disfigured for life. House himself twice narrowly missed killing one of his playmates. Besides hunting and fighting, the gang enjoyed playing pranks. Gullible strangers were the most enticing targets, and many there were who had reason to regret encountering this young crew.

One wonders what impression this rough-and-tumble lad would have made on young Tommy Wilson who, while House was thus engaged in a gregarious outdoor life, was trying solemnly to master the intricacies of English grammar and shrinking from contact with his fellows.

Of House's attitude towards his parents little is known. His mother died when he was fourteen. His autobiographical memoranda make little mention of her. To his father he acknowledges a great debt, for leaving him a fortune and for teaching him "not to place a fictitious value on wealth." He refers to his father as "masterful," and once responded to a letter asking who of all people most influenced the course of his life by saying he supposed his father did.

House was known within the family as "Jimmie number two" because he and his brother James were the most unruly of the children, and gave their parents more trouble than all the others put together. ". . . Many were the dire predictions as to our end." Jimmie and his father clashed, "and many and distressing incidents occurred."

House's early schooling was at the Houston Academy and at a school in Bath, England, where the House family visited for about a year. Of his career at the Houston Academy, he writes:

I did little there except to get into mischief and fight other boys of my age that undertook to challenge my leadership. I was a strong and sturdy little ruffian then, and expert in all the devices essential to win physical supremacy.

At the school in Bath, life for young House and his brother James was equally hectic. The English lads were not used to the ways of their new Texas schoolmates and did not take to them. Jimmie and Ed were in constant "broils" with the other boys.

At last they returned to Texas and their untrammeled sport. Jimmie fell from a trapeze when he was sixteen and died of a brain injury. One day, when House was twelve, he was playing recklessly on a swing, making it go higher and higher. A rope snapped. He fell, striking his head on a carriage wheel. The injury was serious—"it looked as if Jimmie No. 2 was going the way of Jimmie No. 1." His convalescence was prolonged, and its course was interrupted by an attack of malaria. When finally he did recover, he found himself bereft of his robust physical strength. He never regained it. For the rest of his life he bore the unhappy effects of this illness. His health was frail. His energies were limited. Hot weather made him ill.

For a lad who had led the sort of existence House had until this accident, it must have been particularly difficult to adjust to the limitations his physical weakness imposed. No longer could he excel in the rough play of his friends. No longer could he impose his will on them by brute force. He later wrote:

> I will never forget my first essay abroad. I had been walking about the grounds for several days and thought I was strong enough to venture forth in the neighborhood. I had not gone far before I met a little German boy whom I had promised our gang I would whip the next time I met him. Now here he was and I had to make good. My, what a pummeling he gave me! For the first time I realized that Samson had lost his strength but I did not know then that it was gone for good. . . . My fighting, pony-raising, mischief-loving days in Texas were over.

This illness was a serious turning point in House's life. One of its effects was to alter the expression of his urge for mastery: formerly, he had relied heavily on his physical strength; now he would have to resort to more subtle means—intellectual means—to achieve leadership. Of course it is possible that, as boys commonly do, he would have outgrown the earlier stage of physical combativeness in the ordinary course of events, whether this accident had occurred or not. In any case, after this mishap he bested his comrades by his wits rather than through physical prowess, and enjoyed being able to influence and control them by playing upon them psychologically.

"I was a quarrelsome boy," he once told his biographer, A. D. H. Smith. "I used to like to set boys at each other to see what they would do, and then try to bring them around again." [1]

House spent his early adolescence, the years from fourteen to seventeen, at two preparatory schools in Virginia. At both, hazing was the favorite sport. The boys who could not protect themselves were subjected to humiliating and frequently dangerous abuse—hanging, for example, until the victim's face grew purple. House kept his would-be tormentors at bay with a large knife and a six-shooter. For solace, he tramped the mountain woods and hunted, as at home.

At seventeen, House attempted to enter Yale. He took an examination which revealed that, whatever his skill in the highly practical arts of fending off bullies and hunting small game, his scholastic attainments left a great deal to be desired. Dr. Noah Porter, then President of Yale and a friend of House's father, referred the boy to the Hopkins Grammar School in New Haven. There, he was advised, in perhaps two years, he could complete his preparations to enter Yale.

At Hopkins, House became fast friends with Oliver T. Morton, son of the Republican United States Senator from Indiana, Oliver P. Morton. Young Morton was an even more indifferent student than House. His dislike for the intellectual fare offered at Hopkins became a bond between the two boys. But there was another, more positive, attraction: their mutual interest in politics.

Senator Morton was a leading candidate for the Republican presidential nomination in 1876. As young Morton's guest, House went to Washington frequently. He met the Senator and, through him, other Senators and Representatives and even President and Mrs. Grant. As an intimate in the household of an important Republican leader, House was able to observe the behind-the-scenes political maneuvers which play so important a role in lawmaking and in the selection of presidential candidates.

Although a Democrat, House was keenly disappointed when Rutherford B. Hayes, rather than his friend's father, won the Republican nomination. In the ensuing presidential campaign, House sang the praises of Samuel J. Tilden. Morton, with equal fervor, espoused the cause of the Republican nominee. The fact of their political differences did not in the least cool their friendship. In the months before the election, the two boys frequently abandoned Latin and Greek for the joy of visiting campaign headquarters in New York and Morton's home in Washington, where they met the leaders about whom they read so avidly in the newspapers.

It was an exciting life, one that doubtless contributed greatly to their general education, if not to their ability to pass the Yale entrance examinations. The Hopkins faculty, in fact, were gravely concerned. Undaunted, Morton and House decided to try for Cornell. They hired a tutor and crammed for the entrance examinations. Both passed and were admitted.

At Hopkins and at Cornell, House continued to indulge his penchant for pranks. Once, for example, a rather dull-witted lad who had cut classes and was desperate for an excuse to offer the headmaster asked House for advice. House suggested that he say he had gone out sailing early in the morning and had been becalmed. This the boy did. The fact was, as the headmaster and practically everyone else knew, ice had choked the harbor for weeks. The errant "sailor" was properly chastised. House was enchanted.

Shortly after he entered Cornell, House's fraternity asked him to take as a roommate a young man the fraternity was interested in pledging. House agreed. He also determined to find a way to use this turn of events to rid himself of the unpleasant chore of building a fire every day for heat. At last he hit upon a strategy. It was late December and bitter cold. On the day of the young man's arrival, House cleaned the stove very thoroughly, making it look as though it had not been used all winter. The room, of course, became very cold. When his roommate entered, House was cordial and, apparently, entirely comfortable. It was not long before the new arrival anxiously inquired whether House did not find the room chilly. House, in seeming surprise, replied that he did not. The young man asked if House would mind if he made a fire. House said if it would make him more comfortable, he would be happy to have him do so. The young man was moved at what he construed to be House's unselfish subordination of his own preference for an unheated room. Gratefully, he made the fires each day until he chanced to allude to House's kind-heartedness to a mutual friend. After that, they took turns building fires.

House played pranks which provided him with opportunities to feel superior in a very special way. By some small action of his, he set into motion a chain of events which he could then sit back and contemplate with quiet amusement, an amusement tinged with contempt. To "control" people, to be able, while himself seemingly calm and unruffled, to turn their emotions on and off at will, gratified him enormously. It also gave him pleasure in those early days, as it did later, to be in possession of special knowledge or power and then toy with those ostensibly in control of the matter in question. To have his own competence suddenly and dazzlingly revealed without the least show of bravado or self-advertisement afforded him great satisfaction. In his recollections of his youth, House wrote:

> It was always a joy to play such pranks and appear an innocent participant or bystander. I used to ask questions and get minute instructions about how to do this or that thing, or how to play games in which I was already more proficient than those who sought to teach me. In some instances I would gradually show my skill. In others I would do so at once much to the chagrin of my would-be teacher.

From these boyish antics House seems to have derived essentially the same gratification that he did later from influencing governors and presidents, and patronizing great men.

At Cornell, as at the other schools he attended, House was a mediocre student, and managed to get by only by cramming before examinations. His extracurricular life, however, continued to be full of intellectual stimulation. He found numerous companions with whom to exchange ideas and discuss the books about history and politics that he read.

House's pleasant college days were brought to an end in his sophomore year by the illness and death of his father. Why he did not return to Cornell following the funeral is not clear. He did not immediately begin to share with his brothers the task of managing their inheritance. It was a substantial one. House's portion alone produced an income of approximately twenty-five thousand dollars a year.

With one companion and one servant, House went off on a protracted camping trip into the unfrequented, wild tablelands of northwest Texas. The area was almost completely uninhabited. The three wanderers had some narrow escapes from unfriendly Indians, a criminal fugitive and assorted ruffians. Upon his return from this trip, House went East and considered the possibility of entering the Columbia Law School. He finally decided, however, to return to Texas and assume the responsibilities of his estate.

The young heir plunged into the management of his affairs. He inspected his lands. He bought, sold and traded property. There were opportunities to pit his shrewdness against other men's. House took a certain amount of pleasure from his venture into the world of business. With what gusto he recounts in his autobiographical essay the story of his first successful bout with men more experienced in real estate than he! Business was like a game to House. Being a young man of considerable means, he was in a position to be quite unworried about possible losses in one or another transaction. It was perhaps this fortunate circumstance that enabled him to see his interests with the detachment of a chess player trying to assess a situation and plan an intelligent move.

Whatever the joys of moneymaking, however, they did not satisfy House's ambitions. "In the silent watches of the night and in the quieter moments of the day," he later wrote, "I dreamed great dreams, many of which have since come true."

House's interest in politics, according to his own account, began to develop in his early teens. Whatever ambitions to hold office he may have had he abandoned early in life, for he felt "that I would fall short of the first place, and nothing less than that would satisfy me." Once, George Sylvester Viereck asked House whether the presidency would have appealed to him. House replied: "If some one had offered me the presidency on a silver charger, like the head of John the Baptist, probably I would have accepted the gift. But I was too well aware of the realities of politics to indulge in such speculations."[2]

Some of the reasons for House's early abandonment of hope that he might achieve high elective office are immediately obvious. He was a physically frail man. He was plagued by malaria. Hot weather prostrated him. When summer came, he quite literally fled north, or to Europe, as a matter of physical necessity. He simply was constitutionally unable to withstand the grueling routine to which the chief executive of this country is subjected. Furthermore, he lacked the physical attractiveness which figures so importantly in the success of popular political leaders. He was a short man. His chin receded. His voice lacked resonance—it was not the voice of a public speaker.

These must have been hard realities for young House to adjust to. But he *did* adjust to them, realistically, at an early age. Just when and by what process it is not possible to say, but sometime in the 1880's House decided that although he could not hope to attain high elective office himself, he *could* hope, his physical disabilities notwithstanding, to influence men in positions of power, to be a silent, unobtrusive, behind-the-scenes adviser.

In 1886, House and his wife (he had married in 1881) moved to Austin, the state capital. House entertained extensively. His father had left him a name which was known and respected throughout the state. The elder House's mansion had been for years the scene of brilliant social events. He had entertained the state's political and business leaders. Through him young House had developed a wide acquaintanceship, which he now cultivated independently. He began, in his own right, to add to the luster of his name.

He organized his business affairs so that trusted employees relieved him of most of the work of managing his estate. Now he was free to devote himself to the study of politics. He was keenly interested in all aspects of the art of manipulating men. What made people vote for this or that candidate? What made delegates to a nominating convention support this or that man, and by what means could they be swayed in a desired direction? How best can an executive deal with legislators in a variety of situations in order to persuade them to enact this or that legislation? What motivates men to run for office? What sort of man is likely to be amenable to advice, and how can advice be made palatable to a strong-willed man? It was questions like these which fascinated House. He read widely, studied in minute detail the organization of the Democratic Party in Texas, and soaked up the knowledge and wisdom of his numerous guests.

In this period of conscious preparation for a political career, House apparently already had vaulting aspirations. He wanted to be a *national* leader. Local and state politics, according to his diary, interested him only as a means of getting into national affairs—and that as soon as possible. A local career being a prerequisite to acceptance into the larger arena to which he aspired, he resolved to use the state of Texas as a proving ground for his political skills.

In 1892, House, who was then thirty-four years old, saw an opportunity to test his theories of what it takes to win an election in the crucible of a gubernatorial primary. The contestants for the Democratic nomination were the incumbent Governor, James W. Hogg, and Judge George Clark. Hogg's efforts to regulate the activities of the Southern Pacific Railroad had ranged the road, with all its enormous influence in the state, squarely against him and in favor of Clark. It was generally thought that Hogg would be defeated, in view of the money and press support the "interests" were lavishing on Clark.

On the great political question of that era, namely, whether or not big business ought be further controlled by government, House sympathized with the moderate reformers. He went to Governor Hogg and offered to help organize his campaign. Hogg accepted.

One of the facts of political life House had learned in his years of observation and self-instruction in Austin was that painstaking organization is the *sine qua non* in closely contested elections. He concentrated, therefore, upon getting smoothly-working teams of volunteers functioning on the precinct level. House himself remained in the background. The title of Campaign Manager, at his request, fell to another man. But the Governor and those close to the situation relied on House's energetic, if anonymous, generalship.

Governor Hogg won the Democratic nomination and the ensuing election. Gratefully, he bestowed upon House the title of "Colonel." He gave the "Colonel" something much more important, however: the opportunity to advise him concerning legislation, to act as unofficial trouble-shooter in smoothing the way for passage of controversial measures.

For the next ten years, until 1902, House played the role of behind-the-scenes campaign manager and adviser to four Texas governors—James W. Hogg, Charles A. Culberson, Joseph D. Sayers and W. H. D. Lanham.

The appreciative recipients of House's counsel repeatedly sought to reward him with appointment to office. House invariably declined the proffered honors. For he did not covet political office. Rather his goal was to exert influence upon men who held political office. In return for this opportunity, House could put at his patron's disposal a genius for political strategy, a rare ability to detach himself from the heat of political battle, coolly to appraise the essential elements of a situation and then, quietly and without waste motion, to address himself to the tasks which most tellingly advanced his patron's interests. Most important of all, House had the faculty for appearing entirely unselfish and without personal ambition. No crude demands for patronage for having helped in a political campaign, no vulgar scrabble for publicity or credit, ever poisoned the good relations between House and the men to whose careers he attached himself. William Allen White attributed to House what he termed an "almost Oriental modesty, a Chinese self-effacement":

> He seems to be in constant and delightful agreement with his auditor. And this delightful agreement, as one knows him, expresses itself in a thousand ways in an obvious and unmistakable desire to serve. He is never

servile, but always serving; gentle without being soft, exceedingly courteous with the most unbending dignity. He is forever punctuating one's sentences with "that's true, that's true". . .[4]

He shied away from publicity with genuine fervor. He assiduously avoided the official recognition which could have been his at any time during his service in Texas.

With each successful campaign, his stature both in Texas and in the national Democratic Party grew, and so did his desire to move on to the larger stage of national affairs. The difficulty was that during these years and for a decade afterwards as well (with an interruption in 1904), the Democratic Party in the United States was dominated by William Jennings Bryan.

Bryan's ideas about currency seemed to House unsound. He did not think that Bryan could be elected President, that his election would be a desirable thing for the country, or—and this was a crucial consideration—that Bryan would be amenable to his advice. Writing of Bryan, House declared: "I do not believe that any one ever succeeded in changing his mind upon any subject that he had determined upon . . . I believe he feels that his ideas are God-given and are not susceptible to the mutability of those of the ordinary human being."[5]

By 1896, House was eager to participate in a national election, and the national leaders of the Democratic Party were eager to have him do so. However, he remained aloof from the campaign because Bryan was the Democratic presidential nominee. Bryan lost the election to McKinley.

In 1900, Bryan was nominated once again. By this time, House and the "Peerless Leader" were on cordial personal terms, having been next-door neighbors in Austin during the winter of 1898-99. Close personal association with Bryan only confirmed House's assessment of the man and his potentialities. He found him "as wildly impracticable as ever."[6] Once more he declined invitations to participate in the presidential campaign. Bryan lost again, and again to McKinley.

Texas politics began to weary House. He had learned what he wanted to learn and had extracted from his role as ex-officio adviser all the satisfactions that it had to offer him. In the decade of his political activity, he had witnessed the enactment of a series of laws regulating the railroads. He had been a vital contributor to that accomplishment —and it must be remembered that this was an era in which some great railroads succeeded (as in California) in thwarting efforts to curb their activities. He had helped translate into statutes a variety of progressive ideas as to voting procedures and municipal reform. Texas, he felt, had outstripped the other states in enacting liberal legislation. Now there must be a pause for the new laws to be digested, and for the ideas they incorporated to gain nationwide application.[7]

In this frame of mind, the campaigns and the political tempests became burdens to him instead of challenges to his ingenuity. In 1902, House directed the gubernatorial campaign of W. H. D. Lanham. Following its successful conclusion, he disengaged himself from active participation in state politics.

House referred to the years between 1902 and 1911 as the "twilight years" of his life.[8] He longed to function on the national level as he had on the state. During all the years of his work on behalf of Texas governors, he later wrote, "I had never for a moment overlooked the national situation, and it was there that my real interest lay."[9] In order to realize his ambition, however, he needed a very special opportunity. In the first place, a Democrat would have to be elected President. In the second place, this Democratic President would have to be the sort of man with whom House could establish the kind of relationship he desired.

When one ponders the vicissitudes and uncertainties of politics, it seems an astounding piece of optimism on House's part that he hoped—over a period of many years—for the materialization of that unique combination of circumstances which would enable him to achieve his objective.

His chief diversion between the 1900 and 1904 presidential elections was building a ninety-mile railroad to connect the cotton lands near Austin with the main lines. Neither House nor any of his associates in this undertaking (except the engineer) had had any experience as railroaders. They were nevertheless able to raise capital in Boston and to carry the project through. "We had a lot of fun with that little road. . . ." House later recalled. "I'll never forget how we enjoyed all the questions that arose, the fun we had naming the stations and making up time-tables, and so forth. It was new to all of us. But we sold it at a substantial profit. . . . We did it to prove that a railroad could be built, and run, and make money, and still be fair to the people."[10]

In 1904, the Democratic Party was rent by a struggle for control between Bryan-led radicals and Eastern conservatives. The Eastern interests won a temporary victory and nominated Judge Alton B. Parker for President. House was a thoroughgoing (but always practical) progressive, convinced that only a progressive could win the presidency. If he stuck at Bryan's radical ideas about currency, so too was he deterred by Parker's conservatism. Obviously, the 1904 campaign was not the opportunity he had been waiting for, especially as Parker's opponent was the immensely colorful and popular Theodore Roosevelt. House did not participate in Parker's campaign. Roosevelt triumphed with the largest popular and electoral vote in American history to that time. He carried every single state north of the Mason-Dixon line. And not even the "solid South" remained solidly Democratic. If House, the party man, was depressed by the results, at least his faith in the soundness of his judgment must have been fortified. Now he would have to wait another four years for his next chance.

In 1908, the Democrats again nominated Bryan. House was then fifty years old. It is not difficult to imagine his chagrin at the selection of Bryan for yet another presidential race—yet another unsuccessful one. This time, Bryan lost to William Howard Taft.

Taft had been President Theodore Roosevelt's Secretary of War, and Roosevelt's personal choice as his successor to the presidency. A month after Taft took the oath of office, Roosevelt embarked on a hunting trip to Africa and remained abroad until mid-June, 1910. Upon his return, he accused Taft of having yielded to the conservative elements of the Republican Party and jettisoned the progressive programs of his own administration. The breach between Roosevelt and Taft split the Republican Party wide open. The Democrats became understandably optimistic about the party's possibilities in the 1912 presidential election. Governor Wilson in New Jersey and Colonel House in Texas, as yet unknown to each other, studied the political situation with quickening interest, for each saw in it the possibility of realizing his deepest aspiration.

Believing that the next Democratic nominee ought to be an Eastern liberal, House came to New York in the summer of 1910 to look over possible candidates. Bryan had suggested that Mayor William J. Gaynor of New York City was presidential timber. House dined with him, was well impressed, and proceeded to introduce the Mayor to influential Texans whose support would be useful. House also urged Gaynor to run for Governor of New York that year, on the theory that there is an express highway from governors' mansions to the White House but not even a footpath from city halls.

Gaynor rejected the suggestion, arguing that the duties of the Mayor of New York City are infinitely more difficult and important than those of the governor of the state. House was somewhat taken aback at his blank refusal to take prudent account of the political considerations involved. However, Gaynor's qualifications were so outstanding that House resolved to continue trying to assist him.

So that Gaynor could become better known in the South and West, House invited him to visit Texas that winter and speak before the state legislature. Gaynor accepted. House returned to Texas and obtained a formal resolution from the legislature inviting Gaynor. An official invitation was dispatched. When no reply was received for several days, a Texas newspaperman sent Gaynor a telegram asking if he were indeed coming to Texas. Gaynor promptly replied, to House's astonishment, that he had never heard of the project and had no plans for visiting Texas. House decided that Gaynor was not the man he was looking for. "I wiped Gaynor from my political slate," House wrote, "for I saw he was impossible." [11]

In the fall of 1910, House considered the availability of several men —Governor Joseph W. Folk of Missouri, Governor Judson Harmon of Ohio, Representative (later Speaker) Champ Clark, Representative Oscar Underwood of Alabama—who were being prominently mentioned as possible candidates. He even considered the feasibility of promoting the candidacy of ex-Governor, now United States Senator, Culberson of Texas. But Culberson's health was poor and besides House thought an Easterner would have the best chance for success. As for the other men he scrutinized, there was some objection, or some combination of objections, to every one of them. Either, like Harmon and Underwood, they would be embarrassed by conservative affiliations or, like Clark, they were not Easterners, or they were not men of large enough stature, or some other factor, in House's judgment, argued against their availability.

There was another man House began to take note of in that fall of 1910: Woodrow Wilson. Wilson was conducting an arresting campaign for the governorship of New Jersey. A few months before, the progressives in that state had been denouncing him as a conservative and a tool of the bosses. Now they were his enthusiastic supporters. As he toured the state, denouncing boss rule and outlining the legislation he had in mind to work for if elected, Wilson attracted national attention. House began to wonder, as did many other people at about this time, whether perhaps Wilson was a possible candidate. He began to study Wilson's career, his speeches, his writings. As the weeks went by and Wilson, having won the election by an impressive margin, achieved one legislative success after another, House became increasingly convinced that Wilson was the best man then available. In his later reminiscences House wrote: "I decided to do what I could to further Governor Wilson's fortunes. I spoke to all my political friends and following, and lined them up one after another. This was in the winter of 1910-1911." [12]

There is evidence that House was indeed in correspondence with some of his friends about Wilson as early as then, but he was not by any means enthusiastically committed to him. To his friend E. S. Martin, editor of *Life* magazine, House wrote on August 30, 1911:

> The trouble with getting a candidate for President is that the man that is best fitted for the place cannot be nominated and, if nominated, could probably not be elected.
>
> The people seldom take the man best fitted for the job; therefore it is necessary to work for the best man who can be nominated and elected, and just now Wilson seems to be that man.
>
> Then the thing to do is to influence your candidate as far as possible along the lines you consider wise. We may be wrong and he may be right but it is always a satisfaction to have someone carry out our views as nearly as we can influence him to do so.

The Colonel's doubts lingered into the fall of 1911. On October 10, he wrote Senator Culberson:

> Wilson does not altogether satisfy me as a candidate but as between him and Harmon I am for Wilson. It is among the possibilities that you or Underwood or some man not now mentioned may yet get the nomination and that would please me best of all.

Whatever his private hopes, House could hardly have failed to note that Wilson's candidacy had been gaining momentum all through 1911. None of the other men mentioned had captured the public's imagination, on a nationwide scale, the way Wilson had. Underwood and Harmon were both conservatives, and this was not a time the Democrats would be likely to stake the party's fortunes on a conservative. The candidacy of Champ Clark, who actually proved to be Wilson's most dangerous rival, was not yet generally taken as a factor to be seriously reckoned with.

Clark had been an early supporter of Bryan—free silver and all—and Bryan looked upon him with favor. He was a homespun Missouri politician with a record of twenty years of service in the House of Representatives. He had consistently, even if not brilliantly, served the progressive cause. He had many loyal friends in Congress, and was the sort of practical politician that the Democratic machine leaders understood and trusted. William Randolph Hearst admired him. Clark was in no sense an exciting candidate, but his various connections gave his bid for the nomination a great deal more strength than was credited to it in its early stages. It was not until the spring of 1912, however, that Clark's strength became fully apparent. In late 1911, when House was still looking over the field, it seemed that Wilson would enter the Democratic convention with a majority of the delegates pledged to him. House committed himself to Wilson at a time when Wilson seemed by far the strongest contender.

Months before House jumped on the bandwagon, many other prominent Texans were already diligently at work in Wilson's behalf. In August, 1911, they formally launched a Wilson-for-President organization. One of their first projects was to invite him to visit the Dallas Fair in October. House was not in Texas at the time the Wilson organization was formed. Nor was he there when Wilson spoke at the Fair on October 28. He was in New York, where reports of the enthusiastic reaction to Wilson's speech doubtless further convinced him of the Governor's great potentialities.

Had House chosen to be in Texas on October 28, it would have been easy for him to have arranged to meet Wilson. Several of their mutual acquaintances had mentioned House to Wilson as a man of considerable political experience and influence, and had briefed the Governor on House's interest in his candidacy. The groundwork for an introduction was properly laid. But House was not interested in a perfunctory meeting. He wanted to make a vivid impression on Wilson. He had waited patiently for a decade for a suitable opportunity to take part in a presidential campaign; now he had the forbearance to wait for a suitable opportunity for the all-important first meeting with his candidate. In the fall of 1911, Wilson was deeply involved in an election campaign in New Jersey (for the state legislature). His energies were absorbed in speechmaking on behalf of the candidates he favored. "I want to wait until he has quieted down and has some leisure to think and talk," House wrote D. F. Houston on October 27, 1911.

Meanwhile House wrote Wilson. He wrote neither often nor lengthily, but his letters could hardly have failed to whet Wilson's appetite for amplification of the delightful (if exaggerated!) hints they contained. For example:

> I have been with Mr. Bryan a good part of the morning, and I am pleased to tell you that I think you will have his support. The fact that you did not vote for him in '96 was on his mind but I offered an explanation which seemed to be satisfactory. My main effort was in alienating him from Champ Clark and I believe I was successful there. He sent you several messages which he asked me to deliver to you in person which I shall be glad to do sometime when you are in New York provided you return before I go South around December first.[13]

A few days after receiving this letter, Wilson inquired whether he could stop by at the Colonel's New York apartment for a talk. House said he would be delighted.[14]

The stage was set.

# CHAPTER VI

## " . . . THE MAN . . . THE OPPORTUNITY"

Woodrow Wilson should be the Democratic candidate for President. . . . The *World* believes that he would be a progressive constitutional President whom the American people could trust and for whom they would never have cause to apologize . . .

We appeal to Mr. Bryan to throw his great political influence upon the side of Gov. Wilson . . .

New York *World*, editorial,
May 30, 1912.

This is the year of Democratic opportunity but not of Democratic certainty. Let no man delude himself into believing that any Democrat, or so-called progressive Democrat, can be elected . . .

. . . The need of the day is a fearless, able champion of the people to restore the country to a healthy and prosperous state with the statesmanship and dignity that befit the great office of President.

Who is there better able to undertake such vast responsibilities than Woodrow Wilson, Governor of New Jersey?

New York *World*, Letter to the
Editor, June 8, 1912.

At four o'clock on the afternoon of November 24, 1911, Governor Wilson called on Colonel House at the Hotel Gotham in New York City.

The two men liked each other immediately. "We talked and talked. We knew each other for congenial souls at the very beginning," House later recalled. The conversation was wide-ranging and "we agreed about everything. That was a wonderful talk. The hour flew away . . . Each of us started to ask the other when he would be free for another meeting, and laughing over our mutual enthusiasm, we arranged an evening several days later when Governor Wilson should come and have dinner with me."

The second meeting, according to House, was even more delightful. There was time for a more detailed exchange of views. "It was remarkable. We found ourselves in agreement upon practically every one of the issues of the day. I never met a man whose thought ran so identically with mine . . . I cannot tell you how pleased I was with him. He seemed too good to be true." [1]

The Governor called on House several times that winter, and the initial rapport between them was strengthened. House later wrote:

> We found ourselves in such complete sympathy, in so many ways, that we soon learned to know what each was thinking without either having expressed himself.
>
> A few weeks after we met and after we had exchanged confidences which men usually do not exchange except after years of friendship, I asked him if he realized that we had only known one another for so short a time. He replied, "My dear friend, we have known one another always." And I think this is true.[2]

The day after his first meeting with Wilson, House wrote his brother-in-law, Sidney Mezes:

> . . . We had a perfectly bully time. . . . He is not the biggest man I have ever met, but he is one of the pleasantest and I would rather play with him than any prospective candidate I have seen . . .
>
> It is just such a chance as I have always wanted for never before have I found both the man and the opportunity.[3]

*"Never before have I found both the man and the opportunity!"* What high exultation lay behind these words! All during his maturity, House had been seeking to find, to help create, a political situation containing just the combination of elements which existed now. He had sought a Democrat of large stature who could be nominated and elected to the presidency, and who would also be a genial host to his advice. Wilson seemed to be that unique man. Understandably, House was elated. "The more I see of Governor Wilson the better I like him," he wrote Senator Culberson on November 27, 1911, "and I think he is going to be a man one can advise with some degree of satisfaction. This, you know, you could never do with Mr. Bryan." [4]

If House had much to gain from Wilson's friendship so, too, did

Wilson stand to benefit greatly from House's friendship. For House was able to help with the immediate problem of securing the nomination and he was a source of that supply of reassurance which was a crutch Wilson required throughout his life.

At the time of the initial meeting with House, Wilson was desperately anxious to put himself in the good graces of William Jennings Bryan. He was also eager to promote his candidacy in the various states in preparation for the primary elections in the spring of 1912. Colonel House, apparently without any selfish motive and apparently out of sheer admiration of Wilson, offered help on both scores. What more natural than that Wilson should be drawn to such a supporter?

As a personal friend of both Bryan and Mrs. Bryan (whose opinions carried great weight with her husband), House had an excellent opportunity to act as Wilson's advocate while the Commoner pondered the merits of the various candidates vying for his support. Bryan seemed drawn to both Wilson and Clark but doggedly refused to express any preference as between them. House made skillful use of his relationship with the Bryans to advance Wilson's cause.

On the very day after the initial meeting at the Gotham, House wrote Bryan and reported that Wilson's views on various issues were identical with Bryan's. Having thus attempted to win favor for his candidate, House warned that Underwood and Clark were plotting to "make a direct issue with you for control of the next convention . . ."[5] In the months following, House wrote Bryan several letters cleverly reporting conversations with Wilson in which Wilson expressed views which House knew would please Bryan. Subtly he would intimate that Bryan's own worst political enemies—Hearst and the "interests"—were violently opposed to Wilson too, and favorably disposed toward Underwood and Clark. He enlisted Mrs. Bryan's sympathies in Wilson's behalf.

Bryan remained noncommittal in the face of House's propaganda campaign. His replies characteristically contained pointed suggestions for Wilson's offering further proof of his progressivism. On December 28, 1911, for example, he wrote House that he was "glad" Wilson recognized he was opposed by J. P. Morgan and the rest of Wall Street. "If he is nominated it must be by the Progressive Democrats, and the more progressive he is the better. The Washington banquet will give him a good chance to speak out against the trusts and the Aldrich currency scheme."[6]

The "Washington banquet" was the Jackson Day dinner which was to take place on January 8, 1912. Both Bryan and Wilson were to speak. Wilson looked forward to it as a splendid opportunity to further improve his relations with Bryan. Two days before the event, Wilson's enemies exploded a bombshell that shook his whole presidential venture to its roots.

On January 6, the New York *Sun* published the letter Wilson had written less than five years before to Adrian Joline, in which he expressed the wish that "we could do something at once dignified and effective to knock Mr. Bryan once for all into a cocked hat!"

Wilson's supporters were thrown into panic by the appearance of this incontrovertible evidence of Wilson's earlier contempt for Bryan. Wilson himself was uncertain how best to extricate himself. House, ill in Texas, could not help. When Wilson arrived in Washington for the dinner, he and a group of his advisers foregathered glumly in the Willard Hotel. They tried to draft a statement which would smooth the matter over, but the bald facts of the situation could not be obscured by any rhetoric, however skilled. In the end, Wilson decided not to issue any statement after all. He would just have to trust his political fate to Bryan's judgment and generosity.

On the evening of January 8, some seven hundred leading Democrats assembled for the Jackson Day dinner. All the leading Democratic presidential hopefuls were present. The atmosphere was tense as the guests speculated about how (and *if*) Bryan would greet Wilson. Bryan shook Clark's hand warmly. Then he turned and greeted Wilson—with equal cordiality.

In his speech, Wilson praised Bryan in glowing terms as a man who had "based his career . . . upon principle." Bryan later privately termed Wilson's address "the greatest speech in American political history."[7] On the question of who was leading in the contest for his favor, however, the Commoner remained silent.

Apparently Bryan interpreted the disinterment of the Joline letter as an attempt to disunite the liberal wing of the Democratic Party, and he reacted accordingly. "If the big financial interests think that they are going to make a rift in the progressive ranks of the Democratic party by such tactics," he told Dudley Field Malone, "they are mistaken."[8]

It was Wilson's good fortune that the Joline letter episode, if it had to occur at all, burst into prominence at just the time of another equally sensational episode which pleased Bryan greatly. This was the rupture between Wilson and Colonel Harvey, whom Bryan regarded, not without reason, as a spokesman for Wall Street.

Harvey, of course, had been Wilson's first political sponsor. He it was who had convinced some of his conservative friends that Wilson was a man who might capture leadership of the Democratic Party and halt the progressive trend which was so repugnant to them. When Wilson lashed out against the political bosses and "the interests," his original backers—nearly all except Harvey—dropped him in disgust. Dismayed as he was by Wilson's new tack, Harvey continued to support him. Each issue of *Harper's Weekly*, which Harvey edited, carried above the editorial column the slogan: "For President: Woodrow Wilson."

Harvey's continued support of Wilson puzzled Bryan and his followers, who wondered whether it betokened the persistence on Wilson's part of some sympathy for Harvey's political philosophy. As far back as May, 1911, Bryan's journal, *The Commoner*, commented that it would be a good thing for Wilson's candidacy if such conservative publications as *Harper's Weekly* were to repudiate him. Colonel House realized that Harvey was a political liability to Wilson, and suggested to his friend E. S. Martin, an associate editor of *Harper's Weekly*, that it might be politic, from Wilson's standpoint, for Harvey to moderate his support. Intimations to the same effect reached Harvey from other quarters as well.[9] Finally, he decided to broach the subject with Wilson himself.

On December 7, 1911, Harvey, Wilson and Henry Watterson, editor of the Louisville *Courier-Journal*, met at the Manhattan Club in New York to discuss the political situation. Watterson, through his friend Harvey, had been one of Wilson's earliest supporters. At the end of the conference, Harvey turned to Wilson and asked him whether the support of *Harper's* was embarrassing his campaign. Wilson replied candidly that he had been advised that it was, especially in the West. Harvey seemed to accept Wilson's statement in good part and declared he would simply "sing low." [10]

Some days later, *Harper's Weekly* appeared without its theretofore featured slogan, "For President: Woodrow Wilson." Wilson's brother-in-law, Stockton Axson, and his secretary, Joseph Tumulty, suggested Harvey might have been offended. Wilson seemed astonished at the idea, but nevertheless wrote Harvey a graceful letter of explanation. Reflecting on their conversation, he said, he was distressed to find that he had answered the question about *Harper's Weekly* "simply as a matter of fact, and of business," without a word about "my sincere gratitude to you for all your generous support, or of my hope that it might be continued. Forgive me, and forget my manners!" [11]

Harvey assured Wilson in his reply that he had accepted Wilson's response impersonally and had removed his name from *Harper's* "in simple fairness to you no less than in consideration of my own self-respect. . . . Whatever little hurt I may have felt as a consequence of the unexpected peremptoriness of your attitude toward me is, of course, wholly eliminated by your gracious words." [12]

Wilson was not satisfied. He wrote again, reiterating his gratitude and high esteem, and saying he felt "very ashamed" for having unintentionally "hurt" a "true friend."

Harvey declared in reply that "there is no particle of personal rancor or resentment left in me. And I beg of you to believe that I have not said one word to anybody of criticism of you." [13]

In these letters to Wilson, however, Harvey grossly misrepresented his real feelings in the matter. For the fact is that he was furious at Wilson and had resolved to do whatever he could to ruin his political career. He sent a friend down South to urge Watterson to let the world know how Wilson had dealt with his earliest political booster. Watterson, his fine old Southern concepts of gentlemanly behavior outraged, was willing to take up the cudgels in Harvey's behalf. Watterson was the source of many of the rumors which flew about all through the first weeks of January that Wilson had rudely asked Harvey to stop supporting him. However, he delayed issuing the kind of censorious statement which Harvey wanted, and then seemed to have second thoughts on the whole matter. Harvey, apparently, feared Watterson might back down, and seized the initiative himself.

On January 16, 1912, he announced that Wilson's name had been removed from *Harper's* in response to a direct statement by him that the magazine's support was injuring his candidacy. The next day, Watterson publicly denounced Wilson for "discharging" Harvey, without whose help "he would not be in the running at all." [14]

The anti-Wilson press, led by the New York *Sun* and the Hearst chain, pounced on the story of what they termed Wilson's "ingratitude" and headlined it from New York to California. A single story from Watterson's own *Courier-Journal* illustrates the theme Wilson's detractors endlessly elaborated:

> He who would show himself so disloyal to a private friendship cannot be trusted to be loyal to anything. Within a single year Governor Wil-

son's radical change of base, his realignments and readjustments, have been exactly concurrent with his selfish aims. There seems no abasement into which he is unwilling to descend with equal facility and grace. May God preserve Democracy from such a leader and such leadership! [15]

For days the storm raged and it looked as though Wilson's enemies might be able to persuade the public that he was indeed a cold-blooded opportunist. Even some of Wilson's warmest supporters began to vacillate under the impact of the shocking, and unanswered, stories that were appearing about him.

An "angle" hit upon by some of Wilson's imaginative newspaper supporters turned the tide. They contrived a story to the effect that the break with Harvey resulted from Wilson's refusal to accept a campaign contribution from Thomas Fortune Ryan, the financier. Overnight, Wilson was cast once again into the role of the progressive Sir Galahad throwing down the gauntlet to "Wall Street." His relieved supporters rushed to press with editorials praising him for having had the courage to speak the truth to a front man for "the interests." The New York *World* took up the charge of Wilson's "ingratitude" in an editorial which was widely quoted:

> Ingratitude is one of the rarest virtues of public life. "Gratitude" is responsible for many of our worst political abuses. Upon "gratitude" is built every corrupt political machine; upon "gratitude" is founded the power of every ignorant and unscrupulous boss; in "gratitude" is rooted the system of spoils, of log-rolling, of lobbying. . . . The great majority of the voices which are denouncing Wilson's ingratitude are the voices of machine politicians, chief among whose stock in trade is this "gratitude."
>
> No, what we need in public life is a great deal more of discriminating ingratitude . . .[16]

By the end of January it was clear that Harvey's attempt to wreak vengeance on his erstwhile protégé had miscarried. In seeking to harm Wilson he had done him, in fact, a signal service. He had put Wilson in Bryan's good graces! On January 24 newspapers throughout the country carried a statement by Bryan hailing the rupture between Wilson and Harvey. "His former friends are now his bitter enemies and they are proving the sincerity of his present position by the violence of their attacks upon him," Bryan declared. ". . . The venom of his adversaries removes all doubt as to the REALITY of the change." [17]

Although Bryan had been magnanimous about the Joline letter, and had been favorably impressed by Wilson's breach with Harvey, he still gave no indication that he favored Wilson over Clark for the nomination. To win Bryan over remained a major objective. Having recovered from the illness which kept him out of the stormy events of January, Colonel House readdressed himself to the problem.

He managed to let Wilson know tactfully that he was laboring in his behalf with Bryan and, without seeming in the slightest degree vainglorious, to intimate that his intercession was producing good results. The Colonel was wondrously skilled at indirectly conveying the idea that he was almost magically efficient and had mysterious and powerful resources at his command. He would casually relate some incident which, by implication, suggested his prepotency and exalted status. Bryan was to be his guest in Austin, House wrote Wilson on February 2, 1912. "Please let me know if there is anything you would like to have suggested to him, for there can be no better place to do this than by the quiet fireside." [18] A simple statement of fact, to be sure, but so phrased as to conjure up to Wilson a tantalizing picture of House and Bryan engaged in confidential talk, Bryan listening thirstily to House's comments on men and issues.

House also kept Wilson informed of his efforts to influence Bryan through Mrs. Bryan. "Do you recall what I told you concerning the conversation I had with Mrs. B.? I have a letter this morning from her containing this most significant sentence: 'I found Mr. B. well and quite in accord with the talk we had.' " [19]

To William McCombs, Wilson's campaign manager, House wrote on February 10, 1912, that he agreed with McCombs that Bryan's support was "absolutely essential" both to secure Wilson's nomination and, afterward, his election. "I shall make it my particular province to keep in touch with him and endeavor to influence him along the lines desired." Then: "He has evolved considerably in our direction, for when I first talked to him in October he did not have Governor Wilson much in mind." [20]

The letters which Wilson and House exchanged in the months following their first meeting reflect a rapidly developing friendship. Two months after meeting the Colonel, Wilson wrote him declaring that he had come to have a very warm feeling for him and expressing the hope that their friendship would ripen. House replied that he was touched deeply by Wilson's "kindly expressions," for "I have come to have a regard for you that is akin to affection." He added that he hoped, despite recent disagreeable experiences, Wilson could still believe that some people—obviously referring to himself—"are entirely unselfish to you and the cause you represent."[21]

In Texas, House played a leading role in building an efficient organization for the election of Wilson supporters as delegates to the Democratic convention. There can be no gainsaying the value of his contribution. It will be recalled, however, that many months before House had decided to support Wilson, others in the state were working devotedly and effectively in Wilson's behalf. Nevertheless, House blandly fostered the impression that he was at the center of the Wilson movement in Texas. His matter-of-fact, sparely worded statements somehow created an impression of understated accomplishment which a more blatant attempt at self-advertisement could never have achieved.

"I am pleased to tell you that we now have everything in good shape in Texas and that you may confidently rely upon the delegates from this State," he announced to Wilson on March 6, 1912. ". . . In two or three weeks our organization will be perfected, and then I shall leave for the East. . . ."[22]

House's confidence in the selection of a Texas delegation which could be relied upon to support Wilson at the Democratic national convention was demonstrated by subsequent events to have been fully justified. (The Texas delegates, forty strong, backed Wilson unwaveringly through forty-six ballots.) Elsewhere throughout the country, in the spring of 1912, however, Wilson's candidacy was in serious straits.

After the failure of the Joline letter and the Harvey incident to produce the desired effect, the anti-Wilson press, led by William Randolph Hearst, unleashed a campaign of vilification against him which endangered his popular appeal. First, it was charged, as though it were a cardinal crime, that upon his resignation from Princeton, Wilson had applied for a pension from the Carnegie Foundation for the Advancement of Teaching. Wilson pointed out that his application had never been a secret, that having been an educator for over a quarter of a century he was entitled to apply, and that, not having adequate private means, he had felt justified in attempting to provide for the financial security of his family. However convincing this explanation, it never quite overcame the impression that he had stretched his hand out eagerly for money which was, as one Hearst writer put it, "steeped in the human blood of Carnegie's workers . . ."[23]

The anti-Wilsonites systematically combed Wilson's early writings for statements which could be used against him in his new, liberal incarnation. They labeled his new-found progressivism a fraud. Hearst himself publicly described Wilson as "a perfect jackrabbit of politics, perched upon his little hillock of expediency, with ears erect and nostrils distended, keenly alert to every scent or sound and ready to run and double in any direction."[24]

They unearthed passages from Wilson's *History of the American People* which could be construed as unflattering to Polish, Hungarian and Italian immigrants. Wilson soon had to contend with the excoriations of representatives of these politically important ethnic groups, and went to great lengths to try to explain away the uncomplimentary references that rankled with them. He wrote numerous letters to men of Polish, Hungarian and Italian extraction, praising the contributions their respective groups had made and were making to American life. He even acceded to the request of a Polish-American group to rewrite the offending passages for subsequent editions of his *History*. However, neither his protestations of admiration of the groups concerned, nor the fact, hopefully publicized by his supporters, that in 1906 he had joined the National Liberal Immigration League, dispelled the fear among the foreign born that, as President, he might favor restricted immigration.[25]

The primary elections were to take place during the spring of 1912. From January until June, Wilson toured the country, speaking in his own behalf, trying to minimize the effect of the "small missiles" (as he called them) which his enemies hurled at him.

While Wilson was thus engaged in speechmaking, trying to win the people, Champ Clark was quietly lining up the politicians—the men who controlled the machines, who knew how to get the vote out and how to deploy their forces most effectively. Wilson's managers, too, approached the old professionals, but to little avail: had not the New Jersey Governor, in his treatment of Jim Smith, demonstrated his attitude toward the machine politicians for all the world to see?

When all the primaries were over, and the results of battle could be reckoned in the objective fact of how many delegates the various candidates had won, Wilson and his supporters were disheartened. For whereas 436 delegates were pledged to Clark, Wilson could count on only 248. In addition, Clark probably would be able to attract most of the 224 votes controlled by the political bosses. There had been some evidence during the preconvention campaign that Clark, Underwood and Harmon had reached some sort of agreement to combine forces against Wilson. If Clark could now successfully lure into the fold the small blocs of delegates Underwood and Harmon controlled and simultaneously win the machine-controlled votes, he would have the two-thirds total required to win the nomination.

In the face of defeat, Wilson sought comfort in the thought that his motives for seeking the presidency were purely altruistic. On June 9, three weeks before the convention met, he wrote Mary Hulbert: "Just between you and me, I have not the least idea of being nominated . . . I am well and in the best of spirits. I have no deep stakes involved in this game." To his "dear, dear friend," Mrs. Reid, Wilson wrote on May 26 that "I dread the possibility" of nomination, "and yet feel that I must offer myself and not shirk."[26] In a moment of greater self-awareness and frankness, however, Wilson revealed to his friend, Cleveland Dodge, that he did indeed have an emotional stake in his political career, and that the prospect of defeat depressed him. "Bless you for your note of yesterday!" he wrote Dodge on May 16:

> You must have known that I needed it. I do not lose heart . . . but sometimes when I see vast sums of money poured out against me, with fatal success, and it begins to look as if I must merely sit on the side lines and talk, as a mere critic of the game I understand so intimately,—throw all my training away and *do* nothing,—well, I do not repine, but I grow a little sad, and need such a message, of generous love and confidence, as this you have sent me.[27]

Wilson's headquarters in New York City were no longer a place of bustling activity: now only a handful of the faithful manned it. House, too, was pessimistic. He solicited Senator Culberson's reaction to the possibility of having his name advanced in case of a deadlock at the convention. He thought it likely, he wrote Culberson subsequently, that Bryan would be the Democratic nominee. Three days before the convention opened, House wrote Mrs. Bryan pledging his support to her husband in the event of his nomination.[28]

In January, 1912, just when the Joline letter and Harvey incidents were raising a storm in the newspapers, and Wilson was absorbed in a multitude of activities connected with his presidential candidacy, the Republican-dominated New Jersey legislature convened. In a presidential election year, Wilson stood little chance of persuading the Republicans in the legislature, as he had in the extraordinary 1911 session, to accept his leadership. Faced with a situation in which the only possibility for fruitful action lay in patient and unglamorous compromise, Wilson gave up any attempt at leadership, even of the Democratic legislators.

He querulously vetoed about ten per cent of the bills the legislature passed. He even vetoed the major piece of legislation produced in the session, a bill designed to eliminate hazardous railroad crossings. This bill had the reformers' support. Both Republicans and Democrats were committed by their platforms to abolishing these dangerous crossings. Still, Wilson would have none of it, giving as his reason that the measure was too harsh on the railroads! Almost as quickly as Wilson vetoed their bills, the Republican legislators attempted, in several cases successfully, to pass them over his veto.

Wilson was furious. So too were the Republicans of both houses of the legislature. They issued a manifesto censuring the Governor for neglecting state business in his hot pursuit of higher office. Wilson retorted scornfully that the Republican charge was "absolutely false," "uncalled for" and "grossly discourteous."

Writing of the 1912 session to Mrs. Hulbert, Wilson said that nothing much had been attempted except to amend and mar the accomplishments of 1911. "Small men have ignorantly striven to put *me* in a hole by discrediting themselves!" Then, referring to the Senate majority leader, John D. Prince, who also taught at Columbia University, he declared:

> And what shall we say when we find the leader of the petty partisan band a learned and distinguished Professor in a great University . . . with plenty of independent means and plenty of brains, of a kind, but without a single moral principle to his name! I have never despised any other man quite so heartily . . .[29]

How redolent these phrases are of past denunciations of his Princeton opponents, and how prophetic of the future! One suspects that only the lure of achieving higher office enabled him to contain his rage. The situation had that explosive ingredient—what he perceived as a challenge to his authority in his sphere of competence—which never failed to rouse in him an all but ungovernable need to make his will prevail. Had he not been diverted by larger goals, it seems likely that he would have become locked in the same sort of bitter struggle with the New Jersey legislature that engaged him earlier at Princeton, and later with the United States Senate.

April and May of 1912 were dark months in Wilson's career. Having the New Jersey legislature at his heels was a minor problem.

The major one was the deterioration of his candidacy in the face of the loss of state after state to Champ Clark in the primary elections. In view of this poor showing, the New Jersey primary, which was scheduled for May 28, took on added significance. For if Wilson were to prove unable to carry even his own state, his doom at the convention would be all but sealed. New Jersey's Democrats, however, by a large majority, rallied to their Governor's cause—except in Essex County, where Boss Smith's grip could not be broken. Twenty-four of the twenty-eight delegates were instructed to vote for Wilson. When the Democratic convention convened in Baltimore on June 25, 1912, his own state would stand by Wilson.

The story of the 1912 Democratic convention is a thrilling one, and the leading man—always in the center of the stage, and dominating the drama—was William Jennings Bryan.

The first major convention fight revolved about who was to be chairman of the convention. The Democratic National Committee had selected the conservative Alton B. Parker. Bryan, determined to force a reversal of that decision, sought the support of the leading presidential aspirants. Wilson immediately responded to Bryan's appeal with a telegram expressing unqualified support of Bryan's position. Clark, on the other hand, hedged, appealing for party harmony above all else. Parker was named chairman, as it finally happened, but Wilson's forthright position in the matter greatly influenced Bryan in his favor.

In the first ballot, Clark led Wilson 440½ to 324. Votes for all the other candidates combined totaled 321½. To be nominated, a man would need 724 votes. In subsequent ballots, Clark captured a majority of the delegates: he had at one time 556 votes to Wilson's 350½. It seemed certain that Clark would be nominated, for not since 1844 had a candidate received a majority without going on to win the required two-thirds vote. Clark's managers sent Wilson a telegram asking him "in the interests of the party and in vindication of the democratic principle of majority rule" to withdraw his candidacy.[30] Wilson, of course, did nothing of the sort. He clung to the hope that Clark's maximum strength would fall short of the necessary two-thirds, and that when it was realized that Clark could not be nominated, the convention would turn to him.

As fate would have it, the survival of Wilson's candidacy resulted from the fact that House had failed in the fall of 1911 to have the two-thirds rule changed. At that time, it seemed as if Wilson would enter the convention with a majority of the delegates pledged to him. House discreetly set about seeking a change in the convention rules which would provide for nomination by a simple majority. Wilson encouraged him. "I feel very strongly," he wrote House on October 24, 1911, "that the two-thirds rule is a most undemocratic regulation . . . I feel that there would be a certain impropriety in my urging a change because it would be so manifestly in my interest, but certainly any change of the sort would have my entire sympathy and approval. . . ." [31] Luckily for them both, House did not succeed in this project.

A mainstay of Clark's strength was the ninety votes of the New York delegation, which had been delivered over to him by Tammany's Boss Murphy on the tenth ballot. Wilson sent Bryan a message suggesting that all candidates be challenged to disavow the machine-controlled New York vote. For Clark to refuse would be tacitly to admit his obligation to Tammany.

Bryan apparently had been considering some such move himself. He had become increasingly annoyed with what he regarded as Clark's courtship of reactionary support, but he still had not announced his support of Wilson. Nor was it certain that he himself would not seek the nomination. As a member of the Nebraska delegation which had been instructed in Clark's favor he had been voting for Clark. On the fourteenth ballot he broke loose. "As long as New York's ninety votes are recorded for Mr. Clark," he told the noisy and excited delegates, ". . . I cast my vote for Nebraska's second choice, Governor Wilson." [32]

The tide was turned. Clark's strength had touched its highest limit and was now receding. Slowly, Wilson sapped Clark's support. McCombs, working feverishly to swing various delegations behind Wilson, engaged in the usual political "horse-trading" tactics which Wilson, at other crucial moments in his career, disdained. It took thirty ballots before Wilson's vote exceeded Clark's. When Illinois, Virginia and West Virginia switched to Wilson, the battle was over for all practical purposes. The minor candidates withdrew, and Clark released his delegates. After the forty-sixth ballot, Wilson was nominated unanimously.

During the hectic week of the Baltimore convention, Colonel House was resting aboard the S.S. *Laconia*, en route to England. He sailed the day the convention opened, having explained in a letter to Wilson that he felt physically unequal to attending it. He had done everything he could to anticipate every contingency, had informed McCombs which delegates could be most relied upon, and now felt, he wrote, that he could do nothing further than send his best wishes. Wilson replied warmly, expressing sorrow that House would be away and wishing him a good voyage.[33]

House returned to the United States in late August, and immediately wrote Wilson that he planned to devote himself wholly to Wilson's election. Wilson replied that he was delighted to have House back again and was looking forward eagerly to having his help. If House's summer home were not so far away, Wilson declared, he would run up for a visit.[34]

House concerned himself with broad problems of organization, and with preserving harmony within Wilson's headquarters. A bitter feud had developed between the two top men, McCombs and McAdoo. McCombs was exhausted and ill. Unable himself to carry forward the work, he was too jealous to permit McAdoo to assume authority. Wilson was greatly annoyed and distressed at this personal difficulty, which became so envenomed that it threatened to break into the open. House stood aloof from the quarrel. He remained friendly with both men, tried to keep the peace, and thereby earned the even greater gratitude of his harassed chief.

From the start of the presidential campaign of 1912, it was clear that Wilson had an excellent chance to win the election, for the Republican Party was split. The Republican convention had renominated President Taft over Theodore Roosevelt's heated opposition. Roosevelt, in high dudgeon, formed the Progressive Party and, in August, had himself nominated as its candidate for President. The real contest was between Roosevelt and Wilson, Taft being the colorless candidate of conservative business interests.

On the general propositions that the public must be protected from the selfish exploitation of the "interests," and that the government must be responsive to the public interest rather than to the interest of the privileged few, Wilson could be endlessly eloquent, even if disturbingly vague. Until after his nomination, Wilson's attacks on monopolies contained little by way of concrete suggestions for dealing with the problem. On August 28, 1912, however, he met Louis D. Brandeis, then a renowned progressive lawyer and an authority on monopoly control. From Brandeis he received a blueprint of specific measures designed to regulate competition. Thereafter, throughout the campaign, he relied heavily on Brandeis' guidance and drew upon his ideas to find some reason for attacking Roosevelt's proposals for controlling big business. The difference between them, Wilson now said, was that the Democratic Party stood for a restoration of free competition throughout American industry, for the very destruction of monopoly; whereas Roosevelt's party condoned the existence of monopoly and merely proposed to control the evils which sprang from it.

Wilson's whole program—"The New Freedom," he called it—was designed to restore a truly freely competitive economy in which every man would have an equal chance to succeed in business to the degree of his diligence and good judgment. While he specifically declared himself in favor of legislation to better the lot of the working man, he shied away from welfare legislation of the sort that Roosevelt was advocating on a grand scale.

At first, Wilson hoped that he could avoid the usual political stumping, which he considered undignified. Perhaps, he thought, his interests would be as well served if he delivered a few carefully prepared addresses which would carry the burden of his message to the people of the United States. His managers soon disabused him of this notion. Reluctantly, Wilson took to the road and to the rear platforms of trains—and with considerable success.

A number of observers, including several who were Wilson's contemporaries and wrote from personal knowledge as well as the record, have attempted to analyze the sources of Wilson's great appeal as a political leader. William Bayard Hale wrote:

> His learning is precisely of the degree and the kind best calculated to impress the populace. He bears all the outward decorous marks of the scholar, fulfills the popular idea of a philosopher who confers honor upon the sordid concerns of political life by bringing to them the high thoughts and ideals amidst which he lived so long in cloistered contemplation above that which the vulgar are permitted or are fit to enjoy. On the other hand, his philosophy is not too high for human understanding, and is not withheld from the admiring multitude.[35]

Throughout his campaign—throughout his career—Wilson exhorted his audiences to adhere to "reason" in deciding political issues, to "school" their hearts, subordinate emotion to intellect in reaching their decisions. He succeeded in creating an impression of scholarly objectivity, of applying a cool, detached intelligence to public affairs. Actually, however, Wilson's appeal was intensely *emotional,* not primarily intellectual. He had mastered the technique of oratory. He knew the value of repetition, of catch phrases, of pleasing combinations of sound. "Vagueness and reiteration, symbolism and incantation, I take to be the chief secrets of Mr. Wilson's verbal power," Hale remarks, citing a formidable list of examples from Wilson's speeches to illustrate his point.[36]

Charles E. Merriam, distinguished American political scientist, refers to Wilson's "astounding gift of statement," which "enabled him to attract support to a general spirit rather than a specific program, to avoid unpleasant commitments in dubious cases, and to arouse intense enthusiasm for a specific cause." In Merriam's judgment, Wilson "was not primarily profound," but "was extraordinarily gifted with hypnotic power of expression."[37]

There was another secret to Wilson's consummate powers of persuasion: he was a moralist. Whatever course he happened to advocate at the moment, it was not only "right" but intimately bound up with human progress in general. Arrayed on his side were "God," "progress," "the breath of fresh air," "forces of righteousness.' Whereas another man might have been ruined by so many contradictions and reversals of political beliefs, Wilson escaped the usual consequences because he could convince people of his complete sincerity and of the "righteousness" of whatever position he was at the moment taking.

Wilson's impassioned pleas on behalf of great ideals appealed to the noble side of his listeners' nature. He made people feel that by the simple act of following him, they would exalt themselves, enlist themselves on the side of morality and unselfishness. He impressed the public as a forceful leader, a man who knew exactly what was wrong with the country and exactly how to cure its ills. His seemingly impersonal manner attracted many who wished to see knowledgeable competence rather than political bluster applied to the solution of the nation's problems. Furthermore, he seemed positively chivalrous. At the height of the campaign, Wilson referred to Theodore Roosevelt as "gallant," and to President Taft as a man of unquestionable "patriotism" and "integrity." What a relief from the usual campaign mudslinging!

In the latter stages of the campaign, it was widely realized that Wilson would be the winner. The election of November 5, 1912, gave Wilson 435 electoral votes. Roosevelt trailed with 88, and President Taft with 8. A Republican monopoly on the presidency, which had lasted for sixteen years, was broken. Woodrow Wilson had been elected twenty-eighth President of the United States! Moreover, the people had given him a Democratic Congress to work with.

"I was watching his face, and a surprising change came over it—all the gaiety was gone; suddenly he looked serious and grave." So records Wilson's daughter Eleanor, describing her father's reaction to the news that he had been elected President of the United States.[38] To cheering Princeton students who gathered outside his home, Wilson said, "I myself have no feeling of triumph tonight. I have a feeling of solemn responsibility." [39] Baker tells us that despite Wilson's "supreme confidence" in his ability to cope with the responsibilities of the presidency, "his deep inner reaction was one of anxiety." [40]

This was indeed a solemn moment. Since his adolescence, Wilson had felt "marked" for high leadership. Now his destiny had come to claim him. Wilson had great ambitions for the nation. Providence had provided him a matchless opportunity to serve his countrymen. He felt a sacred obligation to lead a crusade for morality, for righteousness in national affairs.[41] Preoccupied with such large thoughts, with the question of organizing his administration, of formulating a legislative program to present to Congress, Wilson wanted, above all else, a chance to think. This is a privilege, however, not freely accorded a President or President-elect of the United States. Each Chief Executive must devise a way to emancipate himself from the impossible demands of would-be advisers, well-wishers and job seekers. Wilson's solution at this time was flight from the turmoil. Intensely irritated by all the assaults upon his time, he decided that on November 16 he would sail with his family to Bermuda, there to rest, think and plan.

Meanwhile, reporters badgered him on the question of Cabinet appointments. Wilson announced he had not yet decided upon any. The reporters persisted. Wilson grew impatient and curt. He grew impatient too with men who wanted to extract commitments from him, who wanted to be certain of impressing their claims upon him. His defense against such importunities was to be frosty and noncommittal. Many a Democrat who had labored mightily for Wilson's election left a reluctantly granted interview feeling rebuffed.

Only House seemed to want nothing for himself, and to understand what Wilson's needs were. So far from making demands upon his time, House quietly set about assembling the information the President-elect needed. During the month Wilson was in Bermuda, House wrote often, and his letters were full of simply presented data about possible Cabinet members, the general political situation and matters of special interest to Wilson. Characteristically, he ended one of them with this sentence: "Please do not bother to answer my letters unless there is something you want me to do." Wilson wrote several notes thanking House for furnishing just the information which was most useful to him. To one of these, House replied that Wilson's words of appreciation "quicken my already keen desire to have your administration succeed beyond that of any other, and my endeavors are leavened by an affection for you deeper than I can well express."[42]

Gratefully, Wilson offered House a Cabinet post—any one the Colonel wanted except that of Secretary of State. House declined, noting in his diary that he much preferred remaining free to advise the President about matters in general. Why limit his activities to one department of government? His poor health was another factor, doubtless. Probably even more important was the realization that, as he indicated to Charles Seymour many years later, if he wanted to retain his personal influence over Wilson he would have to shun official positions. By remaining in the background, House avoided deflecting credit from Wilson for whatever was accomplished, and avoided possible misunderstandings.[43]

After his return from Bermuda, the President-elect visited Colonel House at his New York apartment some half dozen times. Wilson's main purpose in these visits seems to have been to relax, though he and House spent some time discussing the composition of the Cabinet and other public affairs.

Usually, House would meet Wilson at the station and drive with him to the apartment. They would dine alone, go to the theater and return to the apartment. While munching sandwiches, Wilson would speak of his hopes and his apprehensions. The latter House tried to still by telling him that his steadfastness of purpose and the righteousness of his cause ensured success. Sometimes Wilson would talk of the difficulties he had had at Princeton. It seemed to House that whenever, in later years as well, there was no government business to discuss, Wilson would somehow bring the conversation around to his troubles at Princeton—"showing," House once noted in his diary, "how deeply the iron entered his soul."[44]

In the Colonel's soothing company Wilson gave tongue to thoughts which, as he told House many times, he could permit himself to express to no one else. Sometimes he rather shocked House, as, for example, when he said that he did not share the view that war was to be so greatly deprecated (war was economically ruinous, of course, but there was no more glorious way to die than in battle); or when he declared he thought lying was sometimes justified where it involved the honor of a woman or in matters of public policy. "I mildly dissented from this view," wrote House in his diary. ". . . I thought the best thing to do when impertinent questions were put to you, was not to make any reply. He said perhaps I was right and that in the future he thought he would do that. This attitude of mind is interesting to me for the reason that he has so many times grazed the truth in answering questions in regard to his appointments." [45]

One gets from House's diary for this pre-inaugural period a sense of his elation with his role and, above all, a sense of his delighted wonderment at Wilson's desire to be so intimate a personal friend. Congressional leaders waited in vain for Wilson to divulge his plans. All manner of distinguished men unsuccessfully clamored for a few minutes of his time. But Wilson spent hour after hour with House and thanked him warmly for the opportunity. The New York *Herald*, on February 19, 1913, declared:

> Such men as Speaker Clark, Representative Oscar W. Underwood, Senator Hoke Smith, Senator Culberson, and many others of importance in the Democracy have journeyed to Princeton and gone away saying they had no more information now than when they came. One of them said to me: "I know that Governor Wilson was elected President on November 5. I know that he will be inaugurated on March 4. Further than that I know nothing about what has happened or is going to happen." Several of the leaders frankly say, when asked what will happen after March 4: "You will have to ask either the President-elect or Colonel House." [46]

Indeed, House was privy to Wilson's most important plans. The President leaned heavily on the Colonel's recommendations for Cabinet appointments, and assigned him the pleasant task of notifying several of those chosen. The marked attention which the President-elect paid House at a time when he was avoiding almost everyone else made the Colonel the target of literally hundreds of people who thought that, through him, they could reach the President.

Many a man, finding himself in House's extraordinary position, would have been irresistibly tempted to take advantage of every opportunity for publicity, and to boast of his preferred status. Not House. He studiously avoided newspaper interviews. When cornered into speaking of himself, he would profess to be a man of no particular importance. This statement was so manifestly absurd that it only served to inflame the imaginations of his interviewers. House was promptly dubbed a silent man of mystery. Scores of articles speculated about his activities. His avoidance of the press resulted, if anything, in even more publicity than he would have got had he deliberately courted it. The brashest press agent would shrink from ascribing to any client the pervasive powers which the puzzled journalists ascribed to the modest Colonel.

The June, 1913, issue of *Current Opinion* carried an article which, typically, labeled House "a mystery."

> People claim to have seen him just as other people claim to have seen the sea serpent. Photographs are exhibited bearing his name, but the mystéry surrounding him remains and the references made to his methods and the remarkable results he achieves make one's mind revert, for comparison, to characters in fiction, such for instance as the Count of Monte Cristo. . . . What is the secret of this mysterious man's power?

This was a question which intrigued the entire country.

# CHAPTER VII

# FORMULA FOR SUCCESS

What I like about House is that he is the most self-effacing man that ever lived. All he wants to do is serve the common cause and to help me and others.

Woodrow Wilson to Josephus Daniels.[1]

I never argue with the President when we disagree, any more than with any other man, beyond a certain point. When we have talked a matter over and we find that we are opposed upon it, I drop it—unless and until I come across some new piece of evidence to support my views.

Edward M. House to A. D. H. Smith.[2]

[When the President asks for suggestions on drafts of speeches] I nearly always praise at first in order to strengthen the President's confidence in himself which, strangely enough, is often lacking . . .

Diary of Edward M. House, February 8, 1918.

COLONEL HOUSE could and did perform highly useful political services for President Wilson. But there were other, more important, reasons for the close friendship and political collaboration that quickly developed between them. Merely to serve Wilson politically did not suffice to gain his personal friendship and confidence. Bryan served him politically, yet Wilson never really became fond of him nor made him a confidant. William G. McAdoo served him politically too and, in 1914, became his son-in-law. Yet there was in Wilson's attitude toward McAdoo a subtle undercurrent of hostility. Only House seemed in possession of the intricate combination which simultaneously unlocked Wilson's affection and desire to open his mind, to reveal his thoughts and to receive advice on public business.

The attempt to probe the motives of any human being, and most particularly of a great historical figure, is bound to be a complex and controversial undertaking. It is our thesis that underlying Wilson's quest for political power and his manner of exercising it was the compelling need to counter the crushing feelings of inadequacy which had been branded into his spirit as a child.

Had he as a boy felt unimportant? Then anything he or anyone else could do to convince him that he was uniquely qualified to accomplish great things—perhaps even something immortal—would be a balm. Had his father ridiculed his intellectual capacities and made him feel mediocre? Then anything he or anyone else could do to help him feel that he had superior ability and infallible judgment in matters in which he chose to exercise leadership would relieve him—temporarily. Had he grown up in a stern Calvinist atmosphere, subjected to disquisitions on the natural immorality of man in general and his own immorality in particular? Then he must convince himself always of his superior virtue. Had he, as a child, been overwhelmed by feelings of helplessness and weakness in relation to the masterful adults about him? Then, as a man, he must impose his will on others and never permit himself to be subjugated.

His interest in power, in political leadership, was based, we submit, on the need to compensate for damaged self-esteem. The urgent inner need constantly to struggle against these mischievous self-depreciating legacies from his early years crippled his capacity to react objectively to matters at hand.

The suggestion that such early formative experiences influenced Wilson's choice of career and his functioning in public life will appear more credible to some readers than to others. We are hopeful, of course, that the detailed interpretation of his career in these terms will be persuasive. In any case, however, we freely acknowledge that the following account is interpretative in character.

At Princeton, as we have seen, having been challenged in a fashion which most painfully remobilized his early conflicts, Wilson was unable to curb himself in the interest of his educational goals. During the graduate college controversy, he once remarked: "In taking the position I do, I am throwing away any chance of carrying out my educational plans. But what can I do? I must follow what I think is right!"[3]

"I must follow what I think is right!" This is the excuse he invariably offered—and one suspects from his feverish overemphasis that he could not quite convince even himself of its validity—when he became locked in a power struggle with his opponents. He could not compromise at Princeton to save his educational plans. For to compromise meant to yield to interference in that sphere of authority in which he sought compensatory gratifications. He could yield only when a sufficiently attractive inducement in terms of his personal needs—the chance to become Governor of New Jersey, to advance to an even wider field of power—became available to him.

All through his career his most pressing commitment, not by choice but of inner necessity, was to prove to himself that he was, after all, an adequate and virtuous human being. He waged this private battle on fields furnished by his public life. He would become emotionally committed to certain measures the fate of which became in his eyes a test of his personal worth. With his self-esteem at stake, the struggle for the realization of such measures monopolized his energy and seemed to him of transcendent importance.

When Wilson's attention was thus riveted on a particular task of leadership, he frequently neglected other matters of equal or even superior importance. He often referred, aptly, to his "single-track mind." It was a trait which those who worked with him all but unanimously noted, but interpreted variously. Sometimes subordinates dealing with problems which fell outside the limits of his preoccupation were distressed at his unwillingness to provide guidance. Sometimes they misinterpreted his indifference as generous delegation of authority on his part. According to Colonel House, Secretary of Agriculture Houston, for example, regarded Wilson as the finest chief imaginable because Wilson never touched agricultural matters at all.[4] In general, House recalled, Wilson permitted his department chiefs to proceed without criticism or scrutiny. True delegation of authority, however, involves a thoughtful decision on the part of an executive to divest himself of certain tasks while retaining, even if only at the highest level, a supervisory interest. Wilson tended simply to ignore a great many large problems, to let subordinates handle them without any real direction from him at all.

House also noted that Wilson sometimes *did* intervene in departmental affairs very forcefully and that Secretary of State Lansing's experience with the Chief Executive was quite different from Houston's.[5] No detail was too small for Wilson's personal attention if it pertained to an issue on which he had chosen to exercise his leadership and which, therefore, had become emotionally charged for him. Any interference with his plans in a matter which had become thus freighted with personal significance provoked passionate counterattack.

Naturally, there were gradations in the intensity of his commitment to various goals. Some—for example, the preparedness legislation which he sponsored in the winter of 1915-16—were purely instrumental. They engaged him personally far less than certain domestic reforms and the League of Nations, which represented the quintessence of that high and noble achievement to which he aspired with all his being. There were, accordingly, also variations in the amount of anxiety which challenges to different types of goals evoked in him. Where his personal involvement was smallest he could most skillfully respond to the demands of the situation. Where, however, he had harnessed an issue to the task of bolstering his self-esteem he involuntarily responded, in his reactions to what other people did, to his need for protecting his self-esteem. Sometimes, as in his battle with Dean West at Princeton and later with Senator Lodge, he attempted to master his anxiety through unyielding insistence on breaking the opposition. On the other hand, sometimes, as when he was seeking office, he was best able to satisfy his inner requirements by highly expedient behavior.

In an overall appraisal of Wilson's characteristics as a leader, it is necessary to distinguish Wilson the power-seeker from Wilson the power-holder. Once he had rationalized his desire for office in terms of unselfish service to others, Wilson the power-seeker was free to devote every ounce of his intelligence and energy to waging a realistic campaign to attain his goal. For the personal gratifications he sought —to dominate, to do immortal work, to demonstrate his ability and virtue—could be achieved only if he first obtained a specific position of power. If, in order to gain this position, it was necessary temporarily to suppress certain behavior and to engage in practical politicking, Wilson was equal to the self-discipline required. He could confer. He could be socially charming with possible opponents in the New Jersey legislature of 1911. He need not be openly domineering. He could refrain from becoming involved in a fight to the finish with the hostile New Jersey legislature of 1912. However, having attained an opportunity for exercise of power, first as President of Princeton and finally as President of the United States, he was no longer able to suppress his inner impulses toward aggressive leadership.

Wilson recoiled from recognizing that the motive behind his urge for leadership was highly personal; that wielding power in certain ways and seeking great accomplishment were devices for enhancing his self-esteem. His stern Calvinist conscience forbade an unabashed pursuit or use of power for personal gratification. He could express his desire for power only insofar as he convincingly rationalized it in terms of altruistic service, and fused it with laudable social objectives. For the belief that the naked quest for power is wicked whereas a life devoted to unselfish service to the community is supremely virtuous was of central importance in the cultural heritage which was so bindingly transmitted to him. To convince himself of the reality of his selfless motivation, he must painstakingly carve out a sphere of competence, within which he must perform good works. He seemed especially drawn to projects which he could conceive in terms of liberating human beings from their masters—a goal sanctioned culturally and perhaps peculiarly appealing to one who had never himself cast off the yoke of parental domination. The story of his youth. as we have seen, is a saga of conscientious preparation for service. He seems to have experienced the achievement of competence and the adoption of worthy goals as moral sanction to exercise strong, even dogmatic leadership.

Within the sphere of competence he thus carved out for himself, he felt free boldly—almost defiantly—to assert a sense of intellectual superiority. One of his friends, Mrs. Edith G. Reid, in her book about Wilson, cites a letter he wrote at the age of thirty to a former classmate:

"Hiram, I have—as I hope you have not discovered, but as you doubtless have—an intellectual self-confidence, possibly out of all proportion to my intellectual strength, which has made me feel that in matters in which I have qualified myself to speak I could never be any man's follower . . ."

Mrs. Reid comments: "Such confidence in himself might at this time seem merely youth's bravado, but it was part of the essence of his nature—the quality which made people so often exclaim, 'Do you never think yourself wrong?' And the answer would always be the same. 'Not in matters where I have qualified myself to speak.' "[6]

Having legitimized his drive to exercise power by laborious self-preparation and by adopting worthy goals, Wilson felt free to indulge his wish to force others into immediate and complete compliance with his demands. He could even boast about his "fighting blood" and the joy of giving it scope. The extraordinary energy with which he applied himself to the task of making his will prevail was supplied, we suggest, by the pent-up aggressive impulses which could find expression at last through his leadership tactics.

This demand, so uncontrollably pressed, for unqualified submission to his leadership lay at the root of the most serious crises of his career. It also, however, made his initial impact upon the legislative groups with which he successively dealt all but irresistible. It gave him the capacity to stand firm in the face of obstacles that would have confounded a less deeply motivated man. He was tireless in the pursuit of his goals. He was boldly inventive and skillful in devising techniques for creating support, for bringing the wavering to his side, for holding his ranks firm.

In each of the major executive posts he occupied during his life there was an initial period during which the type of leadership he exercised in response to his inner needs coincided with the type of leadership the external situation required for impressive accomplishment. He drove the faculty and trustees at Princeton to accomplish an unprecedented series of reforms. The New Jersey legislature of 1911 was a triumph of productivity in his hands. Later, he was to exact a brilliant performance from the Sixty-Third Congress of the United States.

His political objectives were shrewdly chosen. He was a keen estimator of broad trends of opinion. ". . . No reform may succeed for which the major thought of the nation is not prepared," he once said. "The legislative leader must perceive the direction of the nation's permanent forces and must feel the speed of their operation. There is initiative here, but not novelty . . ."[7] In selecting the projects by means of which to satisfy his ambitions for idealistic achievement, Wilson was a hard-headed realist. They were always practicable possibilities likely to attract widespread public support and capable of realization within a reasonable time. It was the core of the man's genius to be able to choose his issues wisely and to crystallize public opinion in favor of them.

Wilson's difficulties arose when he encountered opposition, often evoked partly in reaction to his own driving demands, and when the chance for further success hinged upon his ability to alter his tactics. The trouble was that, no matter what the external situation, Wilson's inner anxieties remained the same and dictated rigid, even if self-defeating, adherence to his mode of operation. Indeed, he was usually least capable of flexible responses in the situations which most required them. For angry opposition only intensified his anxieties and the more surely dictated a stubborn determination to subjugate his foes.

Wilson's thirst for accomplishment was unquenchable. A project successfully completed might for a moment still his inner doubts—but only for a moment. Baker writes: "Success does not appease him: it only scourges him to harder effort and during the latter part of his course at Hopkins, with triumph on every hand, he is constantly driving himself beyond his strength, he has 'ominous headaches,' he is in a 'low state of health,' he 'worries.'"[8] Did he write a brilliant and highly successful book? Upon its publication, Baker notes, Wilson is "momentarily in a seventh heaven of elation, but this is followed almost immediately by a temperamental reaction which is highly characteristic of the man. Success never long satisfies him. His aspirations are inappeasable. He can rest upon no victory: he must press on to greater things."[9]

Did he achieve a notable legislative victory? Characteristically, he was incapable of pausing even momentarily to savor it but must immediately turn—and insist that his associates also turn—to a new and equally arduous task. Wilson once told House that he always lacked any feeling of elation when a particular object was accomplished. He always thought of the next great work calling for his attention, rather than of the current victory.[10]

He could not moderate his pace. He could not easily moderate his demand for complete compliance with his plans. His method for arriving at decisions regarding what executive proposals to make only compounded his problems with the legislative bodies whose support he needed. For while he was willing to collect pertinent *facts* from others, he was loath to solicit the *opinions* of those who by tradition in this country, if not always by law, had a legitimate claim to a voice in the making of policy.

One of the most disastrous consequences of Wilson's personal insecurity was his inability to consult about matters which had become emotionally charged for him except with those upon whose ultimate approval he could count, or with those who, in the last analysis, were not in a position to exert pressure upon him to adopt their views.

Wilson might indeed confer with key legislative leaders—although his willingness to do even that faded if he anticipated a refusal on their part to do his bidding—but such conferences were more in the nature of collecting information and obtaining commitments of support than an effort to explore other viewpoints and accommodate his own to them.

Wilson once wrote, in one of his scholarly studies of government: ". . . Without a voice in the conclusion there is no consultation. Argument and an unobstructed interchange of views upon a ground of absolute equality are essential parts of the substance of genuine consultation." [11] This is precisely the sense in which he himself did not truly consult. He was loath to give anyone title to a "voice in the conclusion."

Once Wilson had emerged with a decision on an issue, particularly one which mobilized his aspirations for high achievement, his mind snapped shut. In such cases, he felt that his decision was the only possible one morally as well as intellectually. Having conscientiously put himself through a laborious examination of relevant facts, he categorically identified his view with righteousness and would not permit himself or anyone else to question it. His intense religious faith—the conviction that his decisions were guided by God—served to render him impervious to criticism.[12] A dogmatic insistence upon a particular viewpoint frequently followed a protracted period of indecision on the question. Once he had evolved his own position, he was impatient of any delay on the part of others, even those who might still be committed to ideas which he himself only shortly before had held with equal tenacity. He seemed determined to deny the complex interests which lay back of public issues, shadings of viewpoints and the bases of them. For Wilson there were only right and wrong, black and white: and he undertook to judge on which end of the spectrum various positions belonged.

For years, for example, he opposed federal action to establish women's suffrage. When at last, during the war, he was converted to the cause, he began at once to deride the Senators who did not instantly respond to his plea that the Senate concur in a constitutional amendment to enfranchise women. ". . . When my conversion to this idea came," he told a group of suffragettes on October 3, 1918, "it came with an overwhelming command that made it necessary that I should omit nothing and use the position I occupied to enforce it, if I could possibly do so. I pride myself on only one feature of it, that I did understand when circumstances instructed me. There are some men who, I am sorry to say, have recently illustrated the fact that they would not learn. Their minds are provincial. They do not know a great influence when it is abroad . . . I have to restrain myself sometimes from intellectual contempt." [13]

Again, after a period of agonized uncertainty about whether or not to lead the nation into World War I, he convinced himself of the necessity of United States participation and ever afterward vehemently denounced those whose doubts persisted. For, as he wrote Arthur Brisbane on September 4, 1917, the issues had assumed in his mind "a great simplicity." [14]

The instant he took his position on an issue which was emotionally charged for him, he represented it as an expression of what was in the minds and hearts of "the people." When he was battling in behalf of one or another of his programs, Wilson's fine intuitive insight into public sentiment became distorted. For in order to justify his aggressive treatment of his opponents, he needed to regard himself as the best interpreter of the people's true aspirations. His estimate of public opinion became distorted by his need for rationalizing the aggressive tactics through which he sought to impose his will. He tended to oversimplify trends of opinion and to exaggerate public support of his own position. His tragic delusion that the public would rise in wrath against the Republican nominee in the 1920 presidential election, in protest against the defeat of the League of Nations, was only the supreme flowering of this ever-present inclination.

Wilson's leadership tactics, initially successful in the three major executive posts he held during his life, inevitably generated resentment. With a few notable exceptions, such as in the case of the aforementioned preparedness legislation of 1915-16, he did not take effective steps, by consulting them and by otherwise according them deference, to mollify his critics and restore their willingness to accept his leadership. For it was not easy in such situations for him to make those small but important gestures of deference to those whose advice he by-passed or rejected which might have soothed ruffled feelings and conveyed some acknowledgment on his part of the importance of their functions. Rather, in his anxiety, he became defiantly determined to coerce them into submission. His provocative behavior attracted the personal hostilities of his opponents. They, then, attacked him and his programs in a vindictive spirit. Frequently, their allegations came perilously close to exposing various aspects of his inner motivation which it was intolerable for him to recognize, even privately.

It is easy to understand in what poignant need Wilson stood of friends who, at a thousand and one points, could ameliorate his tortured self-doubts, could bolster his confidence. He needed his friends to help him convince himself that he wanted power simply out of a desire to serve others. He needed his friends to confirm his faith—so easily shaken by outer attack because so savagely preyed upon from within—in his great destiny, in his human worth. He needed their tributes to his selfless idealism, particularly when his detractors rudely stripped away his carefully wrought rationalizations and, with cruelly used insight, broadcast the power-seeking, self-centered, arrogant aspects of his behavior.

So acutely did he need the relief which the reassurance of friends afforded that he was willing humbly to lay the treasure of his affection and his confidence at the feet of those who could provide it. He seemed to require only that they have the capacity to help him believe what he wanted to believe—that he was a noble crusader for noble principles; and that this intoxicating incense be offered without in any way intruding into his sphere of power or competing for it.

One of the ways in which Wilson obtained his friends' help was by corresponding with them. It is truly remarkable the vast number of letters Wilson wrote to friends fervently expressing his gratitude for their faith and affection. So far from reducing his energy for this type of letter-writing, the pressure of public business, particularly when he was under attack, seemed to intensify his need to turn for solace to those who restored him with their uncritical approval.

His correspondence with Mrs. Mary Hulbert most dramatically illustrates this point, although one easily also might select the exchange with any one of a number of other men and women to whom he wrote in a similar vein. From 1907 to 1915 (to judge from the number of letters preserved—and there may of course have been others), Wilson wrote her on an average of at least once every two weeks. He could be under pressure of a thousand and one engagements. He could be involved in the most arduous labors with a Board of Trustees, a state legislature or a United States Congress. Scores of crucial problems might be awaiting his attention. Nothing distracted him from the pleasure of composing for Mrs. Hulbert lengthy descriptions of his daily activities, his attitude toward men and events, his political difficulties, his successes, his delight at her letters, his joy at her instinctive understanding of his own motives in public life. He was endlessly solicitous of her health and comfort. He declared her friendship (as he declared numerous of his other friendships) one of the chief joys of his life. He awaited her letters with eager anticipation, and treasured them.

Many of Mrs. Hulbert's letters to Wilson are to be found in his papers. It is evident from them that she used Wilson, in her own phrase, as a handkerchief to weep in. She was an unhappy woman, once widowed, once divorced, responsible for the upbringing of her son and for the care of her sick mother. She herself was constantly suffering from a variety of vague complaints—her letters are full of descriptions of them.

An attractive and clever woman, she was caught up in the whirl of Bermuda society. Her gay social life, however, only highlighted her melancholy. She wrote Wilson of both moods. Her letters are highly self-centered: she pictures herself as a fragile creature bearing her crushing burdens nobly, the star of a great tragedy—her life. And she blesses Wilson for being a friend to whom she can unburden herself.

Of politics she knew little and cared little. She simply had no mind, she protested, so why not throw politics to the dogs and speak of important things like the weather and the beauties of nature and, of course, herself. One thing she did know, though, and conveyed charmingly in every letter: Wilson was a great man with a large destiny. And the attacks against him were so absurd as to be laughable. Her understanding, tender-hearted friend a demagogue? A dictator? An ingrate and a liar? It was so ridiculous that she could even twit him about it, playfully call him a scheming politician, or wonder why his last letter was not brusque in manner as his manner was supposed to be. This drollery was usually followed by a vibrating statement of what a fine man he really was, what a great, good, noble and unselfish man.

It was her capacity always to see what Wilson preferred to believe was his true self that seems to have touched him so deeply. The letters of other friends to whom he felt closely bound—Cleveland Dodge, Thomas D. Jones, Fred Yates, Edith G. Reid, Nancy Toy—all have something of the same flavor. Unreserved paeans to Wilson's noble nature are a thread which runs through them all.

These were some facets of the complex man on whom House pinned his own substantial ambitions for achievement. The role he wished to play was a far more difficult one than that simply of a personal friend to Wilson. For House was not content merely to bask in Wilson's personal attachment. His goal was to exert political influence. He wished, in short, to venture into that most dangerous ground, that most jealously guarded area—Wilson's sphere of power. Truly, this was a daring endeavor. House realized that, as he once remarked to Charles Seymour, if he displeased Wilson at any time, his career would come to an abrupt end. For very good reasons of his own, therefore, he was a keen student of Wilson's character. It was his own estimate that he learned to know his subject well enough to be able to influence him, but "I could never really understand him."[15]

From the first, House kept assuring Wilson that he was one of the greatest men in all history. His letters were punctuated with praise: "My great and good friend"; "I think you never did anything better"; "You are so much more efficient than any public man with whom I have heretofore been in touch, that the others seem mere tyros"; "No man ever deserved better of his country"; "Your letter of acceptance . . . is altogether the best paper of the kind that has been issued within my memory. . . ."[16]

Not only did House himself praise Wilson. He habitually relayed to him the compliments paid him by others. Thus (and this is typical), House wrote Wilson following his war message to Congress on April 2, 1917, that the British diplomat Sir William Wiseman thought that if Shakespeare had written the address it could not have been more perfect. Paderewski had declared that the world had never seen Wilson's equal. As for House himself, it seemed to him the speech had stirred the world even more than he had expected it to. On another occasion, House forwarded a letter from an English correspondent in which it was opined that Wilson was a greater man than Lincoln.[17]

It would be unfair to dismiss House as an insincere flatterer, as some historians have done. It would be more accurate, perhaps, to evaluate him as an exceedingly keen judge of what types of behavior on his part were required to keep him in good standing with Wilson. Very early in the relationship, House became aware of Wilson's extraordinary need for, and responsiveness to, praise, approval and personal devotion. He proceeded to cater to it.

"I do not think you can ever know, my great and good friend," he wrote Wilson on May 20, 1913, "how much I appreciate your kindness to me. All that I have tried to do seems so little when measured by the returns you have made. . . . I shall believe that you will be successful in all your undertakings for, surely, no one is so well equipped as you to do what you have planned. My faith in you is as great as my love for you—more than that I cannot say." "I think of you every day," he assured Wilson in a letter on March 5, 1914.[18]

House avoided making demands on the President's time and energy. He never intruded either his company or his ideas. Wilson had to ask for both. If Wilson failed to write, House neither complained nor showed annoyance. Quite the contrary: he stated explicitly that he was not disturbed. When, on August 3, 1914, for example, Wilson apologized for not having greeted House immediately upon his return from Europe, the Colonel replied reassuringly (on August 5): "I never worry when I do not hear from you. No human agency could make me doubt your friendship and affection. That my life is devoted entirely to your interests, I believe you know and I never cease from trying to serve you."[19]

House quickly learned that in trying to influence Wilson it was expedient to appeal to his vanity. He once stated this frankly to Charles Seymour and added in another conversation that to get Wilson to adopt a particular course of action all that had been necessary was to suggest that it would help ensure a glorious place in history for him.[20] In this House, of course, was oversimplifying and exaggerating to make his point. A great deal more than a simple appeal to vanity was required to move Wilson. House's actions, as well as other statements in his diary, indicate he was aware of that fact.

If Wilson shied away from a recommendation it was House's practice simply to drop it without any indication of displeasure. The Colonel once told his biographer that he never argued with the President beyond a certain point.[21] What argument he did permit himself was presented dispassionately. If the President still remained unmoved, House indicated his dissent simply by falling silent.[22] When events proved House right and Wilson wrong, the Colonel, as he noted in his diary on May 3, 1916, never adopted an I-told-you-so attitude.

When Wilson showed House the draft of a speech or outlined some plan or policy, he was certain of a sympathetic and admiring reception. House was an unfailingly good listener and, to Wilson, unfailingly reverential. "I nearly always praise at first in order to strengthen the President's confidence in himself which, strangely enough, is often lacking," House explained in his diary on February 8, 1918.

Even when privately irritated with the President, House continued to treat him overtly with the soothing balm of flattery, and offered his political advice in seemingly devoted humility. At times when his diary was teeming with criticism of the President, House wrote such messages to Wilson as the following: ". . . I do not put it too strongly when I say you are the one hope left to this torn and distracted world. Without your leadership God alone knows how long we will wander in the darkness." And: "Until you began the direction of the Allied diplomacy it was hopelessly bad." [23] Of course, there is no necessary contradiction between the criticisms and the encomiums, as House may have felt sincerely that Wilson, *guided by him*, was indeed the hope of the world.

Most important of all, House was careful to nurture the impression that he was satisfied to work through Wilson, that he did not covet independent power in an official position. The respective political roles—statesman and adviser—which Wilson and House had cast for themselves complemented each other neatly. House understood the categorical necessity of avoiding creating the suspicion in Wilson's mind that he aspired to any more direct influence upon affairs than his role as adviser afforded.

To this end, he always professed to give Wilson full credit for whatever was accomplished, even if he privately thought *he* deserved it. He protected his position by studiously remaining in the background, avoiding publicity and praise of which Wilson might learn. He habitually rejected requests by journalists for interviews. When it was impossible to avoid reporters, as for example on his missions abroad during the war, House succeeded in telling them nothing and also, strangely enough, in keeping their good will. His avoidance of the press contributed to the impression he strove to create, of modest subservience to Wilson.

As a matter of fact, House's diary indicates a vast susceptibility to praise and flattery, but his insight into Wilson's personality made him uneasy at public commendation. As early as April, 1913, he wrote his brother-in-law, Sidney Mezes, with some concern (if also with some pleasure!) of the publicity he was getting. "I do not know how much of this kind of thing W.W. can stand. The last edition of *Harper's Weekly* spoke of me as 'Assistant President House.' I think it is time for me to go to Europe or take to the woods." [24]

When Mark Sullivan wrote in *Collier's* that many thoughtful folk considered the best thing about Wilson was House and that the team might be equally successful if their positions were reversed, the

Colonel noted in his diary (April 10, 1916): "These are the things I fear most." When, in 1918, Arthur D. Howden Smith showed him the manuscript of a biography he had prepared, House became alarmed. "He writes in the most complimentary way—too complimentary for my safety. . . . I am fearful lest it will lead to trouble." House had Mezes and Walter Lippmann go through the proofs to eliminate the more fulsome tributes.[25] On another occasion during the war when House and Wilson attended church together, the vicar prayed for "the President and his counselor," whereupon House confided to his diary that he wondered how long such things could continue without causing trouble.[26]

House carefully tailored his reports of conversations with various diplomats in order, as he noted in his diary on July 21, 1917, to prevent Wilson from feeling piqued at being by-passed. He also felt it wise not to call the President's attention to the wide scope of his activities. "He does not realize," wrote House on June 8, 1918, "that there is but little of importance that goes to him, either directly or indirectly, that I have not either passed upon beforehand or at least know about. It may be well that this should be so."

House's special status naturally greatly excited the interest of Wilson's other associates, official and personal, though few were in a position to gauge the full range of his functions. House's insight into the requirements of his political role included an acute awareness of the necessity to avoid arousing envy. He had a wondrous facility for self-effacement, and for flattering and making himself useful to those whose good will it was wise for him to retain. Nonetheless, in time, many observers of the relationship perceived that House's approach to the President was highly calculated. Some of them assumed that such behavior *per se* betokened Machiavellian scheming, and disliked him for that reason.

It is true that House consciously tried to manipulate Wilson. The Colonel's conduct was studied, unspontaneous and detached. This is not to say that his motives were dishonorable or that he abused the confidence of his illustrious friend. His manipulative skills notwithstanding, House was not opportunistic in the matter of political ideals. He was what may be described as a conservative reformer, and he aspired to political achievement of the highest order. His political ideals happily coincided with Wilson's. Their collaboration otherwise would have been impossible, for however flexible his tactics, House was devoted to his convictions.

There is every evidence, moreover, that he had a genuine appreciation of the President's qualities of greatness and believed him capable of making his mark as one of the outstanding leaders in the nation's history. In the privacy of his diary, he spoke of Wilson's surpassing intellectual ability, his analytic capacities and genius for clear expression. He confessed the "profoundest admiration for his judgment, his ability and his patriotism." House rejoiced that his mind and Wilson's were closely attuned. [27] His delight at having found such a friend is a major theme of his diary, if also of his correspondence with Wilson.

In judging people, House was a realist. His admiration of Wilson did not blind him to the qualities of the man as a whole. If he coated his recommendations with skillful flattery and assurances of affection, which were at least partially simulated, doubtless he felt justified by the fact that he could not otherwise hope to gain Wilson's acceptance of his advice. If he deliberately exploited his insights into Wilson's personality to augment his own influence, doubtless he felt justified by the hope that he was creating a possibility to serve the President and their shared ideals.

For his part, Wilson seemed to give little effort to analyzing his friend's character and motivation. Rather he reveled in the pleasure of this new friendship—the closest since the break with John Grier Hibben at Princeton. Gratefully, uncritically, he accepted House's practical services and moral support. He attributed to House, as he had done in the past to other friends who had therefore inevitably disappointed him, an ability to sense his opinions, even on complex technical matters, without his having to articulate them. He further assumed that, because House was his good friend, they would naturally always find themselves in essential agreement.

Far from arousing Wilson's suspicions, House's method of bestowing fulsome praise and affection, and carefully yielding on policy issues in order never to permit a difference of opinion to crystallize, seems only to have confirmed Wilson's image of their perfect relationship.

Wilson liked to believe that there was some sort of mystic bond between himself and House. On numerous occasions when he placed House in charge of complex negotiations, he told the Colonel that the need for giving him instructions was obviated by the fact that their thoughts and purposes were as one. On occasion, House encouraged this feeling on the President's part, as is evidenced by a letter he wrote from Europe in the spring of 1915, reporting in mystified pleasure that the President had by a kind of telepathy furnished him a statement which he had thought of requesting but did not for fear of overburdening him.[28]

Wilson's reaction to House was one of uncritical delight. Feeling from the earliest days of their acquaintanceship quite secure with the faithful House, he enjoined the Colonel always to be frank with him and to "scold" him if he seemed to be doing something wrong.[29] House, of course, was wise enough not to construe this invitation literally.

If House's expressions of affection were studied, Wilson's seem to have been quite ingenuous and revealing of a profound gratitude which, considering the services which House performed for him, he doubtless felt from the bottom of his heart.

Again and again, when Wilson thanked him for a service performed, House would declare that such commendation and the opportunity to serve constituted the greatest possible reward. To please Wilson, to serve him and their mutual ideals was all the Colonel wanted. The President, pressured, badgered, criticized and misunderstood by so many people and from so many different directions, was touched, sometimes quite literally to tears, at House's seeming selflessness.

One of the outstanding characteristics of the correspondence between the two men is House's iteration of his desire to serve ("My only concern is that I cannot do more for you," he wrote, typically) and Wilson's repeated expression of heartfelt gratitude. He felt grateful to House all the time, he declared time and again, and everything the Colonel did made him more so.[30]

One of the greatest gratifications Wilson derived from his friendship with House was the feeling that he could relax in the Colonel's presence. In the atmosphere of approval and affection which House created, Wilson felt free to let his thoughts flow without fear of being quoted or misquoted, misunderstood or argued with.

"You are the only one in the world to whom I can open my mind freely," he once told House, "and it does me good to say even foolish things and get them out of my system."[31] To some people he could confide one thing and to others another, Wilson elaborated a few months later, "but you are the only one to whom I can make an entire clearance of mind."[32]

To the ever-sympathetic House, Wilson could denounce this or that Cabinet member, disparage the press and anyone or anything else that aroused his displeasure. He had found in House a safe sounding board, and he rejoiced in this aspect of their intimacy. To House, Wilson could reveal the rudenesses and punishment he would have liked to visit upon those he disliked. Once, House must have appeared somewhat shocked when the President declared his intention never to appoint another Irishman to any office, for Wilson later remarked: "House is always afraid that I am about to do something foolish because I unload my mind on him without reserve, and he is afraid I might do some of the things I tell him I want to do." The Colonel concluded, he wrote in his diary, that the President never meant half of what he said.[33]

It is readily understandable that a man like Wilson who usually felt the necessity for rigid self-control would treasure both opportunities for carefree self-expression and the man who provided them. The President was enormously solicitous of House's health, welfare and comfort. Did House catch a cold? Wilson would write a note of sympathy. A more considerate host when House visited the White House it would be difficult to find. Full of benevolence for the man who so greatly helped him, Wilson was ever eager to give evidence of his esteem. Once, when House was in Washington to spend the Christmas holiday at the home of his daughter and her husband, the President called unannounced as House and his family were gathered around the Christmas tree. Since the President of the United States rarely "drops in" on anybody, it is easy to imagine how much this unusual compliment pleased House.

Most important of all, for a long time Wilson did not recognize that House had personal ambitions—as what human being has not!—which he was striving to gratify through their friendship. "What I like about House is that he is the most self-effacing man that ever lived," Wilson once remarked to his Secretary of the Navy. "All he wants to do is to serve the common cause and to help me and others." [34]

This was a naïve evaluation of House's motivation. He was motivated by a great deal more than a desire to serve the common cause and help Wilson, and it is not to his discredit that he had many personal reasons for his activity in Wilson's behalf. Though persuaded by unalterable circumstances to give up the idea of occupying public office himself, House retained his ambition to direct and control national affairs. His renunciation of presidential aspirations did not stem from any reluctance to accept the awesome responsibility of policy-making on the highest level. As is plainly indicated by his diary, House considered himself adequate to the task of taking the largest decisions concerning national and international problems. Indeed, there is no indication at all through all the years during which he helped decide issues of gigantic import that he was at any time disturbed by uncertainty as to his fitness to play what he considered a leading role in determining mankind's fate.

A clue to the nature and scope of House's ambition is a novel, *Philip Dru: Administrator,* which he wrote anonymously during the winter of 1911-12, shortly after meeting Wilson. Philip Dru, barred by ill health from the military career for which he has been trained, becomes leader of an insurrection against an incompetent administration, and subsequently dictator of the United States. Dispensing with constitutional government, he institutes a series of sweeping reforms by executive decree and then benevolently relinquishes his dictatorial powers in order to re-establish a democratic government under the terms of a new and improved constitution.

The reader will wonder in how far House identified himself with Philip Dru. A letter he wrote in 1915, at a time when he was still trying to conceal his authorship of the book, is revealing: "I am sending you the book of which I spoke," wrote House. ". . . It was written by a man I know. . . . My friend—whose name is not to be mentioned —told me . . . that Philip *was all that he himself would like to be but was not.*"[35] Philip Dru was handsome, dashing—and dictator of the United States.

It seems reasonable to assume that a man with House's goals, ambitions and self-confidence would necessarily have an ambivalent attitude toward the intermediary through whom he had to operate. For no matter how genuinely grateful he was to the man who gave him an opportunity to exercise power vicariously, it was inevitable that at some level in his mind House should have resented the necessity of such an intermediary and the further necessity of deferring to his judgment when differences of opinion arose, lest the favor upon which he was dependent be summarily withdrawn.

Such was the very basis of the relationship that House was obliged to attempt to filter his contribution to public life through the tortuous requirements of Wilson's personality. To an extraordinary degree he succeeded. No account of United States foreign policy between the years of 1914 and 1919 could properly omit extensive reference to his role. House was fully aware of the importance of his work and he approached it zestfully. In the midst of one of his efforts to mediate between the European belligerents, he wrote in his diary: "The life I am leading transcends in interest and excitement any romance."[36] House had forged a position for himself which he valued highly, one which it merited his best efforts to safeguard.

But what when, in matters of great importance, he was unable to persuade Wilson and events confirmed his faith in his own ideas? Beyond a certain point House correctly sensed that he dare not go in pressing his advice. One would expect his latent hostility toward Wilson to come to the fore in situations in which he thought American policy and American interests were suffering in consequence of his restricted authority. Those would be the situations, one might predict, in which House's dissatisfaction with his role would mount to such a pitch that he might succumb to the temptation of acting more directly and forcefully.

House's seeming indifference to the normal rewards of the political arena, then, did not arise out of personal modesty. It stemmed, rather, from his insight into the necessities of his unusual role, and was maintained through the years only by dint of a remarkable capacity for self-discipline.

To a man of Wilson's temperament the mere discovery that much more was involved in House's helpful friendship than an altruistic desire to serve would be disillusioning. House, being an astute psychologist, understood the peculiarly urgent necessity of concealing certain aspects of his motivation from Wilson. That their friendship endured for seven years is a tribute to his skill in this regard.

## CHAPTER VIII

# WILSON AND CONGRESS

> President Cleveland said he had a Congress on his hands, but this Congress has a President on its back, driving it pitilessly. . . . Never were Congressmen driven so, not even in the days of the "big stick."
>
> New York *Times* editorial,
> August 15, 1913.

WOODROW WILSON entered the White House filled with zeal for accomplishment. "The Nation has awakened to a sense of neglected ideals and neglected duties," he had said in accepting the nomination for the presidency. ". . . She has awakened . . . to the conviction that she stands confronted with an occasion for constructive statesmanship such as has not arisen since the great days in which her Government was set up." [1]

He, Wilson thought, must be the constructive statesman for whom the country clamored. The nation, he said, was on the threshold of a new age. To him was given the privilege of being its chief architect. The challenge was prodigious, and so was his sense of responsibility. His blueprints for action, if somewhat sketchily conceived, were on a grand scale. He wished, he told a friend, to create a Renaissance in America—political, artistic and social.[2] Certain economic reforms were a prerequisite to the larger achievements he dreamed of, and must therefore be enacted at once. To begin the great work, he called a special session of Congress to meet on April 7, 1913, a month after his inauguration.

This Congress, the Sixty-Third, is remarkable on at least two counts. At Wilson's insistence, it sat continuously for over a year and a half, from April 7, 1913, to October 24, 1914—the longest congressional session in the nation's history. From it, Wilson extracted an extraordinary amount of excellent legislation.

It was a Congress controlled in both houses by Democrats. About two-thirds (291) of the members of the House of Representatives were Democrats. In the Senate the margin of control was slimmer: there were fifty-one Democrats, forty-four Republicans and one Progressive. Wilson's first impulse was to ignore the reactionary Democrats and to form a working alliance of progressives of both parties. He soon discovered, however, that whereas he had few ways of controlling progressive Republicans, even the most recalcitrant Democrats yielded to patronage and party discipline. He who had seriously considered jettisoning party organization began to wring from Democratic Congressmen the most extraordinary concessions to party loyalty.

The first major issue Wilson wished the special session to consider was revision of the tariff in the direction of reducing protection to American business. Many efforts to lower the tariff had been made. All had been frustrated by the pressure of various business groups.

On April 8, the day after Congress convened, Wilson shattered a century-old precedent by appearing before Congress personally to deliver his message on the tariff. Briefly—the whole address lasted about ten minutes—he outlined his argument for abolition of protective tariffs. Some of the legislators resented what they considered an intrusion of the Executive into their domain, but the reaction was preponderantly favorable: Wilson had injected drama into the usually dull procedure for receiving presidential messages.

The next day, Wilson appeared in the President's Room in the Capitol to confer with the Democratic Senators of the Finance Committee. No President since Lincoln (and he only during the Civil War) had used the President's Room except on ceremonial occasions. After the meeting Wilson told newsmen that he was "sure we will have no difficulty in keeping together on the tariff." [3] He did not mention that the Senators had warned him that they might see fit to amend the tariff bill.

Wilson anticipated some difficulty with the Senate and had already mapped out his strategy should he fail by other means to win sufficient support. If necessary, he told some of his Democratic supporters in Congress, he would make a direct appeal to the people against those Democratic Senators who opposed the tariff measure.[4] This was a strategy designed to meet the worst possible contingency. First, he would try other tactics. As he was dealing with a Democratic Congress, his success would be assured if only he could command the unwavering support of members of his own party. How, though, to gain party unanimity? Wilson solved the problem by making unprecedented use of a traditional party institution: the caucus.

The members of each party in each house of Congress comprised a caucus. Through caucus action a bill could be declared a "party measure." Then members of the party were bound to support that bill no matter what their personal views. Any man who defied party decisions ran the risk of being denied the fruits of party loyalty, such as patronage, party support at re-election time, and desirable committee assignments in Congress. In practice, until Wilson's administration, binding caucus action was rarely resorted to even to secure passage of important legislation. Wilson, however, promptly seized upon the caucus as an instrument for enforcing his leadership.

Under Executive pressure, the Democratic caucus in the House of Representatives duly adopted the Underwood-Simmons tariff bill as a "party measure" and, on May 8, the bill was passed by a vote of 281 to 139.

From the outset it had been clear that the real struggle would come in the Senate. There, the Democrats had only a narrow margin of control. The Republicans stood overwhelmingly against the measure. A number of Democrats claimed that removing the protective tariffs on wool and sugar would wreck the wool and sugar industries in their states, and they too therefore opposed the bill.

Democratic leaders in the Senate Finance Committee urged Wilson to separate the wool and sugar schedules from the rest of the bill, for they feared that the combined strength of the Republicans and protectionist Democrats would defeat the entire measure. Wilson refused and was greatly annoyed at newspaper reports that he was looking for a satisfactory compromise in the matter. In an interview on May 15, he asked the reporters with some asperity to inform the public that "I am not the kind that considers compromises when I once take my position."[5]

The House having a large Democratic majority, lobbyists had refrained from putting forth what they realized would be a useless effort there. It was at the Senate, where Democratic control was precarious, that they directed their campaign against the administration's measure. The lobbyists applied for, but were denied, a hearing before the Senate Finance Committee. Feverishly, they turned their attention to individual Senators. Wilson would have to counter their influence or his attempt at tariff reform, like the attempts of the Cleveland and Taft administrations, would founder on the rock of entrenched special interest. On May 26, Wilson issued a statement condemning the "insidious" influence of men spending money "without limit" in order "to overcome the interests of the public for their private profit."[6]

Wilson's attack on the lobbyists resulted in the creation of a special Senate subcommittee to investigate the role of lobbying on the tariff issue. This prompted Senator Townsend (R., Mich.) to charge that the most flagrant lobbying was that done by the President himself through "withholding of patronage" and "coercion of Senators."[7]

Bitter charges and countercharges were made. The practical result of the tempest was to focus public attention on the tariff controversy and to make it extremely difficult for any Senator to vote against the bill without exposing himself to the charge that he had succumbed to lobby control or was protecting his own economic interests.

Never for a moment did Wilson relax his pressure on the Senate. To supporters he wrote letters of praise. "May I not give myself the pleasure of saying that I am proud to belong to a party consisting of such men as yourself. . . ?" a typical one (to Senator Robinson of Arkansas) read.[8] He pressed his case to groups of Senators at meetings both at the White House and at the Capitol, where he frequently visited. He had a special telephone installed so that he could reach Senators quickly from the White House.

Through the enervating heat of the Washington summer the debate continued. On June 20, 1913, a caucus of Democratic Senators met to consider the tariff bill. The New York *Times* (June 21, 1913) called it "the first caucus of Democratic Senators that any one can remember," and pointed out that previously "less binding conferences . . . have sufficed for discussions of party policy." After an acrimonious debate, in which the propriety of "binding" Senators' votes was a major issue, the Democratic caucus adopted a resolution declaring the tariff bill a "party measure."

Some Democratic opponents of the measure openly chafed at their enforced support of it. Three of the dissidents declared they would vote for the bill but refused to consider themselves "bound" to do so. Senator Hitchcock of Nebraska, whose amendment to the bill had been rejected in caucus, insisted nevertheless upon proposing it on the floor of the Senate. He did so in a speech on August 29, 1913, asserting that caucus rule would mean the end of representative legislation. Once the caucus of the majority party had decided upon its course and bound its members, he argued, debate in the Senate was a farce. (This outburst notwithstanding, Hitchcock voted in favor of the tariff bill.)

On September 19, 1913, by a vote of 44 to 37, the Senate passed the Underwood-Simmons bill. It was a tremendous victory for Wilson. He had overcome an array of interests which two other Presidents had found invincible. Yet, he was incapable of deriving a normal satisfaction from this accomplishment. To Walter Hines Page (an old friend, and his Ambassador to Great Britain), who had sent a message of congratulation, Wilson wrote: "I am so constituted that, for some reason or other, I never have a sense of triumph. . . ."[9]

Wilson signed the Underwood-Simmons bill on October 3, 1913. At the signing ceremony, he expressed pleasure at the occasion but immediately pointed to the next goal: "I hope I will not be thought to be demanding too much of myself or of my colleagues when I say that this, great as it is, is the accomplishment of only half the journey. . . ." he declared. "We are now about to take the second step . . . the currency bill. . . ."[10]

Weary Senators, who had debated the tariff bill through the heavy heat of summer, had hoped to adjourn the special session and postpone consideration of the remainder of Wilson's program until the regular session convened on December 1. But Wilson was determined to force immediate action.

He had, indeed, already lashed the House of Representatives into action. The House, it will be recalled, had passed the tariff bill on May 8, 1913, and the measure was then sent to the Senate. Thereafter, the Representatives were unoccupied. Wilson set them to work on currency reform on June 23, when he appeared before Congress and requested immediate consideration of the administration measure.

The necessity for an elastic currency system based on commercial assets was universally conceded. On three major aspects of the problem of how to attain such a system, however, there were deep cleavages of opinion. They involved a) whether the government or bankers should control the system; b) whether there should be regional banks or one central bank; c) whether the banks should have the right to issue money. Within the Democratic Party, and among Wilson's immediate advisers on the subject—Representative Glass, Senator Owen, Secretary of the Treasury McAdoo, William Jennings Bryan, Colonel House—there were a variety of opinions. The President received a bewildering number of proposals, based on varying combinations of attitudes toward the three factors above enumerated. In this welter of confusion, Wilson turned to Louis Brandeis for advice. Brandeis recommended that the government should control the new system, and that only the government should be empowered to issue currency. Wilson bade Glass, Owen and McAdoo to harmonize their drafts of the bill in accordance with these two principles, and also to provide for regional banks rather than a central bank. The Glass-Owen bill, as Wilson presented it to Congress on June 23, was the product of the President's decision on these basic issues.

His manner in addressing Congress, according to the New York *Times* of June 24, was one of grim determination. " 'We must act now, at whatever sacrifice to ourselves,' said the President in his address," reported the *Times*, "and he emphasized the 'now' with a snap of the jaws." He declared that he had " 'come as the head of the Government and the responsible leader of the party in power to urge action now.' There was something about the second 'now' that suggested defiance." Later, at the White House, continued the *Times*, the President declared that the currency bill "was an Administration measure in exactly the same sense" as the tariff bill. He would tolerate no compromise of its principles, though he was willing to consider alterations of details.

In a tense atmosphere, the fourteen Democrats (who constituted a majority) of the Banking and Currency Committee of the House of Representatives began to consider the bill. A number of them were indignant at the President's injunction that they were to address themselves to "details." It was with the proposed bill's basic provisions that many of them disagreed, and they asserted their right to champion their views by introducing a number of far-reaching amendments. The President promptly intervened, warned the dissidents that their antagonism to the bill as it stood constituted a challenge to his leadership, and requested the committee to report the bill to a caucus of the House Democrats.[11] What the President hoped, clearly, was that a majority of the House caucus would accept the administration bill without substantial amendment and then bind the minority to the caucus decision. Thus assured of unanimous party support, Republican opposition, both in the Banking and Finance Committee and on the floor of the House, would be unavailing.

That is, in fact, what happened. The Democratic critics were voted down in caucus, and on August 28, 1913, the bill essentially as proposed by the President was adopted as a "party measure." The Republicans bitterly attacked the "secret caucus" which had rendered further discussion of the bill futile, but they were powerless in the face of the now solid Democratic phalanx. On September 18, 1913, the currency bill passed the House, 287-85.[12]

On the day after the House passed the currency bill, the Senate passed the tariff bill. The Senators were all but unanimously in favor of adjourning until December. However, Wilson made it plain that he expected the Senate to take up the currency bill without delay.

Senator Hitchcock wrote Wilson that he opposed being "rushed." Even Senator Owen, Chairman of the Senate Banking and Currency Committee, cautioned that there existed a "natural weariness of the flesh."[13] Wilson's response to all the grumbling he heard was to call the Senate's Democratic Steering Committee to the White House and to announce his opposition to any adjournment of more than three days at a time.

Reluctantly, the Senate began to process the bill. The Senate Banking and Currency Committee was composed of twelve members, seven Democrats and five Republicans. The Republicans unanimously opposed the bill, and three of the Democrats (Hitchcock, Reed and O'Gorman) declared themselves opposed to the measure as it then stood. The administration forces on the Committee were thus reduced to a minority of four, against an anti-administration majority of eight.

The immediate danger to the bill was that the Banking and Currency Committee would indefinitely prolong its hearings on the whole subject of currency reform, and thus prevent the measure's consideration on the floor of the Senate. Wilson met this situation with an ultimatum both to the Committee and to the Senate as a whole. Either the Committee would halt the hearings and report the bill within a week and the Senate would vote on it by November 1, 1913, or he would stump the states of his Democratic opponents in an effort to arouse enough favorable public opinion to compel senatorial support.

All through October the newspapers were full of reports of senatorial resentment of Wilson's coercive tactics. A report in the Washington *Post* that he had denounced his Democratic opponents as "rebels and no Democrats" further inflamed the situation.

Nevertheless, on October 6, the Committee on Banking and Currency voted to end hearings on the currency bill by October 25. This would not speed the bill as much as Wilson had demanded, but he let his supporters know that it was concession enough, provided the Committee then reported the bill promptly.

The Democratic dissenters, however, were not yet prepared to knuckle under. By November 6, they and the Republicans on the Committee, a working majority, had passed a series of amendments which altered the basic structure of the currency bill in the direction of making it more acceptable to the nation's bankers.

"The President," Carter Glass later wrote, "was getting mad through and through." As he saw it, the question now was "whether a controlling group of bankers or this administration shall write a currency bill." [14] Obviously, a showdown between Wilson and his Democratic critics was at hand.

The President had some powerful weapons at his disposal. The Democrats had been out of office for seventeen years, and the long-deprived party faithfuls were bringing tremendous pressure on members of Congress to deliver patronage. Wilson was engaged at just this time in making thousands of appointments. It was soon plain that he intended to use the patronage to reward his Congressional supporters and punish his opponents. (In many cases, incidentally, the Senators and Representatives to be rewarded for compliance with his program were machine-affiliated conservatives who, in their own states, especially in the South, were locked in battle with progressives for control of the local party machinery. The progressives had battled the machines, worked valiantly in behalf of Wilson's nomination, and now expected his support in their continuing struggle with the conservatives. Wilson was impervious to their dismayed protests at the wholesale gift of federal appointments to the very elements of the Democratic Party that he had so frequently and so eloquently denounced.) [15]

Wilson's prestige with the voting public was another weapon in his hands. In the off-year elections of November 4, 1913, Wilson candidates in key areas won by large majorities. The elections showed that the voting public heartily approved of the new Chief Executive. The prospect of one day embarking upon a campaign for re-election with Wilson's disapproval to contend with doubtless sobered the Democratic recalcitrants.

On November 8, the President's senatorial supporters called a caucus, to meet four days later. The Republicans, understandably enough, were furious at the decision to make the currency bill a party issue. An equally indignant outcry came from some Democrats—

even a few usually considered pro-administration. In their view, the question of the President's dictatorial attitude transcended in importance the particular issue at hand.

Resentment of the President by members of his own party found open expression on the Senate floor on November 10. Senator Reed denounced the President's attitude toward the Banking and Currency Committee. Even more hostile was Senator Hitchcock, who accused the President of increasing pressure on Democratic members of the Committee following the elections. He termed the move for a party caucus the last and worst phase of Executive pressure on the Committee.

At the November 12 caucus, Senator Owen proposed that the Committee be given a few days more in which to reach agreement. His motion was adopted. The Committee, however, proved to be hopelessly deadlocked. On November 26 the caucus reconvened. Several meetings were held. Precisely what transpired we do not know. By what arguments some of the dubious Senators were swayed we can only guess. From behind the closed doors of the meetings came reports of protest. The fact remains, however, that the caucus adopted the Glass-Owen bill without a single substantial amendment not approved by Wilson.

Following caucus adoption of the bill, overt opposition to it on the Democratic side disappeared. Debate on the Senate floor took place in the first half of December. Republican Senator Cummins expressed the attitude of a number of his Republican colleagues when he declared in the Senate on December 4:

> . . . There is to be no real debate upon the banking and currency bill. That debate has already taken place, the bill has been considered elsewhere; it has been passed elsewhere. . . . My protest is against the caucus system. . . . The real legislation of this body is now taking place in a Democratic caucus. I think a debate upon this measure is a pure farce. . . .[36]

On December 19, 1913, the Senate passed the Glass-Owen bill by a vote of 54-34. Every Democrat present, including Senator Hitchcock, voted in favor of it and, much to Wilson's gratification, a number of Republicans joined in approving it.

The minor differences between the bill as passed by the House and Senate had to be reconciled, as such divergences generally are, in joint conference. Wilson chafed at the short delay. House was with him on December 22 as messages concerning the proceedings at the Capitol were brought to him. That night the Colonel noted in his diary that Wilson had been irritated at what he considered the unnecessarily slow pace of the legislators. They were behaving, he complained, like a bunch of old women.[17]

Wilson signed the bill on December 23, and left for a three-week vacation in Pass Christian, on the Gulf of Mexico. On January 20, 1914, he was addressing Congress again, this time demanding legislation on trusts and monopolies. We have described the passage of the tariff and currency bills through the House and Senate in an attempt to illustrate Wilson's characteristic approach to Congress. There is no need to dwell upon the details of the struggle for trust legislation. Suffice it to say that Wilson's pressure on the legislators was unremitting and that passage of the Clayton Anti-Trust Act and the bill establishing a Federal Trade Commission testify to the President's continuing domination of Congress. The Sixty-Third Congress adjourned on October 24, 1914. Under Wilson's imperative leadership, it had been one of the most productive sessions in the nation's history.

Throughout 1914 the President's energies were increasingly drawn into problems of foreign affairs. There was a protracted crisis in Mexico, in which Wilson involved the United States almost to the point of war. In the summer of 1914 the Great War began in Europe. The task of preserving the United States' neutrality more and more absorbed Wilson's time. There was a hiatus in his drive for domestic reforms.

Wilson did not focus his attention on reform legislation again until spurred to action by the danger of losing the presidential election of 1916. In this campaign there would be no split in the Republican Party to benefit him. Theodore Roosevelt had re-entered the Republican fold and was trying to lead his errant Progressives back with him. Wilson needed to attract substantial numbers of Progressives. Otherwise he would almost certainly be defeated, since the Democratic Party was still traditionally the minority party.

Many reformers had voted for Roosevelt in 1912 because he embraced the social welfare legislation they favored. The Progressives wanted the government to take an active role in defining and protecting the rights of working men. Wilson, too, had declared himself in favor of federal legislation to safeguard labor's interests where labor could not adequately do so; but he had opposed encouraging the government, however benign, to act as the people's "guardian" or "trustee."

Faced with the hard realities of the political situation in 1916, however, Wilson underwent another great intellectual conversion. Link writes that "he became almost a new political creature" and "virtually bludgeoned" Democratic leaders in Congress into helping pass another sweeping reform program. By the fall of 1916, Link points out, a Democratic Congress "had . . . enacted almost every important plank in the Progressive platform of 1912." [18]

By this tactic Wilson succeeded in gaining widespread support among erstwhile Progressives, and they played a crucial role in his victory over the Republican candidate, Charles E. Hughes.

A generation after the Wilson era, surveying the entire history of the United States, the distinguished political scientist E. S. Corwin has written that "the present-day role of the President as policy determiner in the legislative field is largely the creation of the two Roosevelts and Woodrow Wilson . . ." [19]

Wilson came into office following a two-decade eclipse of Democratic power. Democrats in Congress, a chance for leadership and patronage in their hands at last, were disposed to co-operate with the new President. Wilson, as we have seen, quickly exploited this margin of receptivity and pressed the members of his party in Congress into unprecedented subservience to Executive leadership.

Another scholar, W. F. Willoughby, has made the point that the history of Congress is a story of the unceasing conflict between the view that legislators should vote in accordance with their individual convictions and the view that they should subject themselves to party discipline.[20] Only strong leadership can establish centralized control. In the absence of continuing disciplinary pressure there is a natural reversion to individual action.

In England, as in most European nations, legislative leadership is institutionally vested in the Cabinet in power, which participates in the proceedings of the law-making body. The channels of control, the devices for ensuring party discipline are well established, being integral features of the system of government. In the United States, however, the source of legislative leadership is not institutionally prescribed. The Constitution does not specify in detail what the President's role shall be in the legislative process. It has been up to each President to hew out his power relations with Congress. ". . . What the Presidency is at any particular moment depends in important measure upon who is President," observes Corwin.[21] The opportunity for personal impress upon the office is tremendous.

The doctrine of the separation of powers has tended to discourage Executive initiative *vis-à-vis* Congress. Only by a strong act of will can the President establish his sway over Congress. In recent times relatively little exertion has sufficed, for recent Presidents have been able to take advantage of the expectation of Executive leadership created by the most dominating of their predecessors. In Wilson's day, however, the heavy weight of precedent mitigated against the exercise of strong Executive pressure on Congress. In the light of this fact, his immense expansion of the presidential role in law-making seems all the more impressive. He it was who set the stage for what is now generally regarded as one of the most important functions of the President: the formulation of a legislative program, and the exertion of his power to secure its passage.[22]

Wilson's achievement, of course, was not accidental. A lifetime of contemplating the problem of leadership had equipped him with thoroughly considered theories which he was burning to put to the test. The relationship between Wilson's theories of leadership and his own ambitions and life situation merits scrutiny. For throughout his academic career his views seem to have been formulated and changed with an eye to his own potential political role. Wilson wanted to believe, always, that a route existed for a man in his circumstances to rise to the pinnacle of public preferment. He was adept at interpreting governmental institutions to fit this private need. His ideas—many of which were of celebrated cogency—seem to have been molded to an important extent by his desire to solve his perennial problem of finding an outlet for his own talents.

The central question around which his researches revolved, as he stated in his first book, *Congressional Government,* concerned "the real depositaries and the essential machinery of power."[23] His initial conviction was that the principal political power in this nation rested with Congress and that, of the two houses, it was in the Senate that a great orator could become most influential. His youthful ambition was to be an orator and a Senator. Fate seemed to decree otherwise. He was sidetracked into academic life and tried, unsuccessfully, to overcome his ambition to become a statesman. For many years it seemed that the achievement of public office would be denied him. Very well. His early works are shot through with the suggestion that perhaps, after all, it is to men *without* political office that the nation must look for inspired leadership.

In *Congressional Government,* he argued that no government official—not the President, nor the Speaker of the House of Representatives nor any of the chairmen of the standing committees of Congress—was in a position to serve as preeminent party leader. "If there be any one man to whom a whole party or a great national majority looks for guiding counsel, he must lead without office, as Daniel Webster did, or in spite of his office, as Jefferson and Jackson did. There must be something in the times or in the questions which are abroad to thrust great advocates or great masters of purpose into a non-official leadership . . ." [24]

These were the days when he was writing his old friend, Charles Talcott, proposing that they and a few others pool their thought on current issues and "raise a united voice" through their writings, gradually working their way "to a position of prominence and acknowledged authority in the public prints, and so in the public mind . . ." [25]

Wilson's initial assessment of the potentialities of the presidency, as we shall see, was disparaging. As his own chances for occupying the office increased, his view of it became progressively enthusiastic until at last, in *Constitutional Government in the United States* (published in 1908), he asserted that the President can be the pivotal force in government. He also advanced the thesis, which handily disposed of one possible criticism which might be leveled at his own candidacy, that "the office of President . . . really does not demand actual experience in affairs so much as particular qualities of mind and character which we are at least as likely to find outside the ranks of our public men as within them." [26]

Throughout his life, Wilson was a great admirer of the British Cabinet system of government. Representative government, he wrote in *Congressional Government,* "is government by advocacy, by discussion, by persuasion. . . . It is natural that orators should be the leaders of a self-governing people." [27] The British system, he noted approvingly, tends to elevate orators to the highest positions—a circumstance understandably appealing to a young hopeful whose oratorical abilities were one of his chief gifts. Another, and related, advantage of the British system, Wilson argued, is that both executive and legislative authority are vested in the leaders of the dominant party. The Prime Minister and his Cabinet not only participate directly in the legislative process but initiate all important legislative propositions and can properly be held responsible for them. The British system is perfected party government. A Cabinet's tenure of office depends upon the success of its legislative program. Inevitably, the opposition subjects the ministers to the most determined attacks and keenest criticisms. Too, the ministers are daily obliged to establish anew their claim to the confidence of their own party, for opposition to any important measure by a member of the dominant party is tantamount to a demand for the formation of a new government. Debate on the floor of the House of Commons, therefore, "is the very breath of life to such a system." [28] It serves not only to elicit the clearest exposition of contending viewpoints for the benefit of those who must vote on any issue, but also to stimulate an informed public opinion.

The American system, on the other hand, Wilson at first thought, is a hodgepodge of divided authority and responsibility. No single man, no single party, even, is the recognized fount of legislative initiative. Congress conducts its business by means of bipartisan committees, working in private. Bills which emerge from the committees do not represent the policy of either party: rather they embody compromise conclusions which are a composite of the views of committee men of both parties. The debates preceding the compromises have been conducted in the seclusion of the committee rooms. Nobody in particular is responsible for the provisions of the bill. Public debate on the floor of Congress is stultified by the fact that there is no cohesive opposition to a cohesive leadership, no arraignment by a minority party of a party in power, with the prize of leadership at stake on every important issue. The way to correct these inadequacies, Wilson thought, was to adopt some features of Cabinet government.

In his early maturity, when he wrote *Congressional Government*, Wilson considered the power of Congress "irresistible." The Constitution had provided for nicely adjusted balances among the three branches of government. In practice, however, Congress had vanquished the judicial and executive branches.

The Presidency, said Wilson, "has fallen from its first estate of dignity because its power has waned; and its power has waned because the power of Congress has become predominant." The President "is plainly bound in duty to render unquestioning obedience to Congress." His business is "usually not much above routine. Most of the time it is *mere* administration, mere obedience of directions from the masters of policy, the Standing Committees." [29]

By 1908, when he published *Constitutional Government in the*

*United States,* Wilson had revised his ideas on the relationship between President and Congress. Since the publication of *Congressional Government* in 1885, he had discerned a trend toward the expansion of presidential power. Opportunities for constructive statesmanship resulting from the Spanish-American war, he thought, had lifted the Executive into new prominence.[30] Unmentioned, but unquestionably influential on Wilson's thought, was the fact that Theodore Roosevelt had claimed it was within his province as President to guide Congress. Doubtless, too, Wilson's growing personal interest in the office inspired him to explore the possibility of approximating its functions to those of the British Prime Minister, whose governmental role he so highly esteemed. In any case, the new evaluation of the presidency which Wilson made in *Constitutional Government in the United States* stood in striking contrast to the deprecating appraisal of it he had made twenty-three years earlier.

The President, so Wilson now thought, "must stand always at the front of our affairs, and the office will be as big and as influential as the man who occupies it." He is free to be "as big a man as he can." [31] Only his capacity need set the limit. He is the natural leader of his party, the only party nominee for whom the whole nation votes. He alone represents the people as a whole:

> He can dominate his party by being spokesman for the real sentiment and purpose of the country, by giving direction to opinion, by giving the country at once the information and the statements of policy which will enable it to form its judgments alike of parties and of men. . . .
>
> Let him once win the admiration and confidence of the country, and no other single force can withstand him, no combination of forces will easily overpower him. His position takes the imagination of the country. He is the representative of no constituency, but of the whole people. When he speaks in his true character, he speaks for no special interest. If he rightly interpret the national thought and boldly insist upon it, he is irresistible; and the country never feels the zest of action so much as when its President is of such insight and calibre. . . . A President whom it trusts can not only lead it, but form it to his own views.[32]

The Constitution, Wilson noted, authorizes the President to recommend to Congress "such measures as he shall deem necessary and expedient." The President is legally at liberty to press his recommendations to Congress as forcefully as he is able. ". . . Many long-established barriers of precedent, though not of law, hinder him from exercising any direct influence upon its deliberations; and yet he is undoubtedly the only spokesman of the whole people. They have again and again, as often as they were afforded the opportunity, manifested their satisfaction when he has boldly accepted the role of leader, to which the peculiar origin and character of his authority entitle him. The Constitution bids him speak, and times of stress and change must more and more thrust upon him the attitude of originator of policies. His is the vital place of action in the system. . . ." The President's means of compelling Congress, Wilson thought, was an aroused public opinion which would bring the necessary pressure to bear on the legislators.[33]

Wilson had convinced himself, in short, that a President of the United States can function more nearly like a British Prime Minister than he had earlier conceived possible. This was his conception of the presidency when he himself came to the White House in 1913. This was the type of executive-legislative leadership he wanted to provide.

Of central significance in Wilson's new conception of the President's functioning was the role of the Chief Executive as a medium of public opinion. Shortly before his inauguration, Wilson declared:

> . . . I feel first, last, and all the time that I am acting in a representative capacity. I am bidden to interpret as well as I can the purposes of the people of the United States and to act . . . through the instrumentality of persons who also represent that choice. I have no liberty in the matter. . . .[34]

On nearly every public issue there are a multiplicity of attitudes based on differing interests. These varying attitudes usually find spokesmen in Congress. When differences of opinion arose between Wilson and Congress, how did he go about determining what public opinion actually was on the matter in question? He was not a Theodore Roosevelt, with a taste for contact with men of all stations and points of view. Colonel House has recorded that Wilson seldom read the daily newspapers and glanced only cursorily at the weekly press.[35] The man who handled the White House mail throughout Wilson's tenure of office has stated that Wilson "never took much interest in the general run of the mail. . . . The trend of opinion as reflected in letters . . . was of no particular importance to him." [36] To some extent he used House as his eyes and ears, but the Colonel, as has been noted, was careful not to say anything which might offend Wilson's sensibilities. Too, a certain amount of information about public attitudes reached him from people (Cabinet members, for example) he could not avoid seeing, though it was his often-stated wish that he could still further curtail the number and length of his conferences.[37] Moreover, Wilson generally preferred that callers limit their remarks to the specific items of business at hand. He was not interested in their digressions about public opinion or anything else. In sum, he made little use of the usual devices public men employ to keep themselves informed of the public's state of mind.

What he relied on most was his intuition. This intuition, as many of his biographers have noted, was often an uncanny barometer of the public's disposition. But when he had deep personal stakes in an issue, his intuition became the servant of a need to see himself as the people's champion. For somehow he had to justify to himself the aggressive tactics he employed against his opponents. To preserve his own equilibrium, therefore, he *had* to believe that "the people" sanctioned his course. Small wonder, then, that in such cases he was not interested—was, indeed, angered—to receive reports which might disturb this image. In the midst of his battle with Congress over the Shipping Bill, and after his Mexican policy had been roundly attacked, for example, his irritation at critical newspapers burst out. In a Jackson Day address on January 8, 1915, he declared:

> With all due respect to editors of great newspapers, I have to say to them that I seldom take my opinion of the American people from their editorials. So that when some great dailies not very far from where I am temporarily residing thundered with rising scorn at watchful waiting, Woodrow sat back in his chair and chuckled, knowing that he laughs best who laughs last—knowing, in short, what were the temper and principles of the American people. If I did not at least think I knew, I would emigrate, because I would not be satisfied to stay where I am.[38]

There is evidence that Wilson was at least dimly aware that it was not only the demands of the situation itself, but personal requirements which determined his leadership tactics. There is the letter he wrote Mrs. Reid in the fall of 1913, for example, in which he speaks of the loyal and gracious acceptance of his leadership in Congress "even by men of whom I did not expect it." Then: "I hope that this is in part because they perceive that I am pursuing no private and selfish purposes of my own. How could a man do that with such responsibilities resting upon him!"[39] May this not be the overemphatic protest of a man conscious of some obtrusive personal motives about which he feels guilty and from the recognition of which he is trying to shield himself?

Again, there is a revealing entry in House's diary on November 12, 1913, the day of one of the fateful Senate caucuses on the Federal Reserve Act.[40] Wilson told House that a President *ought* to use his power to translate the desires of the people into law. There was no danger in such strong leadership, for unless a President were backed by public sentiment, he continued, Congress would not yield to his pressure. He had been restless the night before, the President said. He had had nightmares and thought he was seeing some of his Princeton enemies. Here once more seems to be uneasy self-justification. This time it is combined with the disclosure that his struggle with Congress evokes the painful memory of the earlier, transparently personal struggle. He sounds like a man frightened of himself, of his own need, no matter what the consequences, to pursue the battle to the end.

Some of his letters to Mrs. Hulbert, too, suggest his inner discomfort. On September 21, 1913, at a time when the newspapers were full of charges that he was dictatorial, he wrote her:

> Do not believe anything you read in the newspapers. . . . Their lying is shameless and colossal! . . . [They] represent me . . . as master of the situation here, bending Congress to my indomitable individual will. That is, of course, silly. Congress is made up of thinking men who want the party to succeed as much as I do, and who wish to serve the country effectively and intelligently. They . . . accept my guidance because they see that I am attempting only to mediate their own thoughts and purposes. . . . They are using me; I am not driving them. . . . And what a pleasure it is, what a deep human pleasure, to work with strong men, who do their own thinking and know how to put things in shape! Why a man should wish to be the whole show and surround himself with weak men, I cannot imagine! How dull it would be! How tiresome to watch a plot which was only the result of your own action and every part of which you could predict before it was put on the boards! That is not power. Power consists in one's capacity to link his will with the purpose of others, to lead by reason and a gift for cooperation.[41]

A week later, Wilson wrote Mrs. Hulbert another letter, this time chronicling quite a different attitude.

> The struggle goes on down here without intermission. Why it should *be* a struggle it is hard (cynicism put on one side) to say. Why *should* public men, senators of the United States, have to be led and stimulated

to what all the country knows to be their duty! Why should they see less clearly, apparently, than anyone else what the straight path of service is! To whom are they listening? Certainly not to the voice of the people, when they quibble and twist and hesitate. They have strangely blunted perceptions, and exaggerate themselves in the most extraordinary degree. Therefore it *is* a struggle and must be accepted as such.[42]

Wilson's shifting evaluation of the character and purposes of Congress and his fluctuating conception of his own role as leader testify to his inner conflict. On the one hand he represents himself as an agent of "thinking men" who "wish to serve the country." He enjoys working with "strong men" and helping realize their common purposes by leading with "reason and a gift for cooperation." On the other hand, in the second letter he denounces the recalcitrant Senators and concedes that his leadership "*is* a struggle."

It might be argued that Wilson's evaluation of Congress in the second letter quoted above contained elements of truth and that his aggressive tactics succeeded and may be regarded as an excellent adjustment to reality. If his tactics were simply an adjustment to the exigencies of this particular situation, why, in the first letter, was he at such pains to deny that he had employed them? The very emphasis with which he rejects the notion that he is "master of the situation" and bending Congress to his will for the passage of two excellent measures betrays his anxiety as to his motivation. His argument that a President can succeed with Congress only if his proposals enjoy wide public support, and that for that reason firm leadership is justified, is indeed convincing—but Wilson apparently never succeeded in convincing himself that that was the explanation of his behavior. His uneasy protestations and his nightmares are evidence of his own distrust of that explanation. He seems to have been plagued by the uncomfortable sensation that somehow his carefully wrought self-justification did not in fact quite cover the case. He seems to have sensed that something else, something within himself, dictated his leadership tactics. That "something else," we suggest, was his need for domination as a means of countering his low self-estimates. This need forced him to contrive rationalizations—such as that he, better than any of his opponents, represented the popular will—which facilitated justification of the aggressive tactics required to dominate. The more uneasy he felt about his aggressiveness, the more desperately he clung to his rationalizations.

"Nothing has to be explained to me in America, least of all the sentiment of the American people. . . ." Wilson once declared. "And the advantage of not having to have anything explained to you is that you recognize a wrong explanation when you hear it." [43]

The President gave members of Congress to understand, not once, but as a characteristic response to disagreement, that their views on various matters were simply "wrong." He habitually stigmatized his opponents as petty and lacking conscience or intellect for their efforts to give representation to their views. This type of behavior, which was only one tributary stream feeding the swelling river of resentment at his tactics, was bound to provoke eventual counterattack.

It came when, in August, 1914, Wilson urged Congress to pass a bill authorizing the government to buy or build ships needed to carry American goods to overseas markets. The outbreak of war in Europe had interrupted the supply of foreign shipping facilities upon which the nation's exporters had become dependent. American trade was disrupted. It seemed unlikely that private investors would be willing to risk the capital required for a great ship-building program. Wilson pressed the administration's shipping bill upon Congress—it was the same Congress which had been sitting in continuous session for over a year—with the same urgency with which he had demanded all his major domestic reforms. Weary, overwhelmed with other business, doubtful of the wisdom of the President's proposal, irritated with his ceaseless pressure, Congress adjourned on October 24, 1914, without acting on the measure.

Congress reconvened on December 7. Next day, Wilson declared that the shipping legislation was "imperatively needed" and "cannot wisely be postponed," and expressed the earnest hope that it would be passed.[44] It soon became clear that Wilson had a full-scale revolt on his hands. The substantive issues which the bill raised need not be discussed here: suffice it to say that it was widely recognized that the use of American ships in foreign trade in wartime would result in numerous problems with the belligerents and might seriously jeopardize our status as a neutral. Baker, however, acknowledges that while "some of the opposition was due to real anxiety over what was regarded as a radical proposal," the fight also involved "a concerted revolt against 'executive domination.'" He adds: "It is not to be doubted that the President's steady, implacable, unrelenting pressure in completing his reform programme and in forcing through various emergency measures . . . was in part responsible for the revolt on the proposal for government ships. . . ." [45]

Two months went by, and favorable action seemed more remote than ever. In the Senate, the Republicans, aided by seven bolting Democrats, were trying to filibuster the bill to death. Finally, in mid-February, Wilson summoned Representative William C. Adamson (D., Ga.) and said:

"I am tired of this obstruction. We need the ships. It is time for Congress to get behind the matter. I want the House, for the moral effect of it, to pass that Shipping bill and send it to the Senate, and I want you to see that it is put through." [46]

Obediently, Adamson arranged a caucus, the Democratic opposition was ordered to vote in favor of the bill, and it was passed by the House on February 16, 1915. Wilson had no such quick success with the Senate. The seven dissident Democrats—men who had been pressured into voting for Wilson's domestic reforms—refused to back down. The Republicans continued to filibuster. Congress adjourned on March 4, 1915. The Senate had not acted on the bill.

Wilson was unable to force action on the shipping bill for more than another year. A new version was introduced in Congress in January, 1916. Administration leaders in both houses this time did their work more efficiently. On May 20, the House passed it. On August 18, following a caucus, the Senate passed it. Not a single Democratic Senator voted against it. Not a single Republican Senator voted for it.

There were other revolts—notably over whether Americans should be prevented from traveling on armed belligerent ships which might be sunk. Congress overwhelmingly favored discouraging such travel, since the loss of American lives on Allied ships attacked by German submarines had precipitated crises which threatened to involve the United States in the war. In February, 1916, Representative Jeff McLemore (D., Tex.) and Senator Thomas P. Gore (D., Okla.) introduced resolutions in Congress warning Americans against traveling on armed belligerent ships. Wilson took the position that Americans were within their rights, according to international law, to travel on such ships, and that the government was in honor bound to uphold the rights of its citizens. ". . . I cannot consent to any abridgment of the rights of American citizens in any respect," he declared. "The honor and self-respect of the nation are involved. We covet peace, and shall preserve it at any cost but the loss of honor. To forbid our people to exercise their rights for fear we might be called upon to vindicate them would be a deep humiliation indeed." [47]

The President remained adamant in the face of all efforts to convince him that standing on the letter of the law might lead to explosive situations which a bit of preventive caution might avert. For a few days it seemed as though Congress might defy the President and pass the resolutions over his objections. That would be a grave step in the midst of an international crisis. The authors of the resolution hesitated. Wilson boldly demanded a showdown, on the grounds that doubt had been created in foreign capitals as to the unity of American foreign policy. Congress—including many Republicans—capitulated. The resolutions were tabled.

As the international crisis deepened, Congressional animosity toward Wilson was held in check by the patriotic obligation Republicans and Democrats alike felt to unite behind the Chief Executive. Mounting anger at the President's high-pressure tactics could be temporarily shunted aside, but it continued to feed upon his increasingly peremptory behavior. The day of reckoning might be postponed, but a day of reckoning there would be.

Colonel House's connection with the domestic reforms passed in Wilson's first administration was peripheral. The measure to which he devoted most energy was the currency bill. There is no evidence that he contributed substantially to the drafting or passage of any of the other important reform legislation. He was, nevertheless, of enormous assistance to the President even before he turned his attention to foreign affairs, the sphere in which they were destined to collaborate most fruitfully.

He encouraged Wilson to press his program forward in Congress. He admired Wilson's bold assumption of the initiative in legislative matters: it accorded with his own theory, expressed in *Philip Dru: Administrator*, that the President should take a more positive role in providing leadership for Congress.[48]

He rendered signal service in the matter of appointments. He helped choose members of the Federal Reserve Board. He was Wilson's closest adviser in selecting men for assignments abroad. Was this man or that mentioned for some important post? Wilson often asked House to check his record and "look him over."

House also lightened the President's burden by seeing people who otherwise would have made demands on his time, by serving as his factotum in countless transactions, and by keeping him informed of various streams of public opinion.

Even before World War I began, House turned his attention to foreign affairs. The outbreak of hostilities intensified his diplomatic activities. From 1914 on, they were his chief interest. He did take time out, however, to contribute his skills to the presidential campaign of 1916.

As early as January, 1915, House was planning the strategy of the 1916 campaign in terms of winning the votes of former Progressives and independents. How to attract sufficient non-Democratic votes to Wilson: that was the problem, and House saw it correctly. As always, he stressed the necessity of effective organization to reach the class of voters who held the balance. He helped select the chairman of the Democratic National Committee—Vance McCormick—and advised him throughout the campaign. He drew up a plan of action which called for a concentration of effort in doubtful states where the most promising opportunity for winning undecided voters for Wilson existed. He devised a system for keeping track of trends of opinion so that campaign resources could be flexibly deployed, according to the needs of the moment. House had a plan for every contingency—including even the President's defeat, in which case he thought Wilson should appoint Hughes Secretary of State and then resign along with the Vice President in order that Hughes could take charge immediately.

All these services he rendered in the context of that close personal friendship which was the oil in the machinery of his "silent partnership" with the President. When, in early 1914, House left for a visit to Texas, Wilson wrote that it was a grief to see him go so far away and that he thanked God daily for the friendship between them.[49]

In August, 1914, an event occurred which shattered Wilson's personal life. His wife, Ellen, died. In his grief, Wilson needed his friends more than ever. His emotional dependence upon House, to judge from House's diary and the letters which the President wrote him, seems to have reached its peak in the period between the death of Ellen Axson Wilson and Wilson's marriage to Mrs. Edith Bolling Galt in December, 1915.

Ellen Axson Wilson, the first Mrs. Wilson, was an extraordinary woman. She was a gifted homemaker, a painter of some talent and, above all, completely devoted to Woodrow Wilson. Wherever the Wilsons lived, whether in a modest house in a university town, the President's house in Princeton, the Governor's mansion or the White House, it is the unanimous recollection of people who knew her well that Ellen Axson Wilson had the capacity for generating an atmosphere of warmth, repose and loving sympathy. Her whole purpose was to provide a setting in which her husband could work and develop. She shielded him from the petty annoyances of day-to-day existence, and carefully kept from him information about his associates which might arouse his anger and waste his energies.

Her letters to him when he was off alone on vacations (she insisted upon his traveling by himself to Europe and Bermuda on several occasions when it was financially impossible for both of them to go) are full of the most tender affirmations of love.[50] From the first, she thought him—and told him that she did—the finest, noblest human being imaginable, a genius no less worthy than the eminent political figures he strove to emulate. Whatever he thought, she thought. His battles became hers. She was his unfailing partisan. But she also knew how to smooth rough edges in Wilson's behavior towards other people in order to advance his career.

Far from attempting to satisfy Wilson's need for affection and approval entirely herself, she encouraged him to find friends—men and women both—who would supply the friendly reassurance he needed. Ellen Axson Wilson and Colonel House were on the friendliest of terms. She created no obstacles to her husband's friendship with House.

On the other hand, the second Mrs. Wilson and House came to dislike each other, a fact which is clear both from House's diary and Mrs. Wilson's published memoirs. At first, however, they professed to find each other delightful, probably because neither cared to risk trying to turn the President against the other. House, of course, could never speak to the President in criticism of his wife. On the other hand, Mrs. Wilson was under no permanent compulsion to maintain the fiction of liking House. She was in a position to try to influence Wilson against him, and she did so. But we are getting ahead of the story.

## CHAPTER IX

# THE GREAT WAR: NEUTRALITY AND INTERVENTION

The President declared if he knew he would not have to stand for reelection two years from now, he would feel a great load lifted from him . . . I could not see what else he could do in life that would be so interesting.

He replied that the thing that frightened him was that it was impossible to make such an effort in the future as he had made in the past, or to accomplish anything like what he had accomplished in a legislative way. He feared the country would expect him to continue as he had up to now, which would be impossible.

I thought the country would neither expect it nor want it. There were other things he could do which would be far more delightful in accomplishment, and would add even more to his fame. *I referred particularly to his foreign policy which, if properly followed, would bring him world-wide recognition.*

The diary of Edward M. House, September 28, 1914.[1]

IN THE FIRST DECADE of the twentieth century Europe was rocked by a series of crises which, thoughtful men on both sides of the Atlantic realized, would one day eventuate in a general European war unless some way were found to correct the underlying causes of the tension. Broadly speaking, the disturbances arose from the challenge of Germany to the hegemony of England and France. Germany wanted colonies and overseas markets. Other nations had already appropriated the most alluring. Germany was determined to build a world empire. The British and French were determined not only to maintain their existing positions but to perpetuate their supremacy by themselves exploiting the most attractive remaining opportunities. Plainly, the situation was explosive.

President Wilson, his vision narrowly focussed by the blinders of his "one-track mind," was largely unconcerned by the turbulence across the seas: he was preoccupied with his domestic program. Colonel House, however, was among those realists who saw that vital interests of the United States, too, were at stake in Germany's bid for power.[2] He realized, as so many of his countrymen at the time did not, that the security which the United States had so long enjoyed in ostensible isolation from Europe stemmed from benevolent British control of the seas; that the interests of the United States were served by the workings of the European balance-of-power system inasmuch as it prevented any nation from gaining control of the European continent and then challenging British power. To prevent a war which might result in a disturbance of the balance of power and, worst possibility of all, in the eclipse of British sea power, would therefore serve the American national interest. Too, House sensed that the era was ending in which the United States could stand aloof from European affairs and passively expect conditions favoring American security to emerge as a by-product of intra-European relations.

Equipped with these insights, the Colonel three times induced Wilson to charge him with peace missions to Europe. The first, undertaken just before the European war started, was designed to explore with the leaders of England and Germany possible alternatives to the dangerous system of alliances to which they were then committed; and, further, to explore the possibility of some accommodation of their clashing aspirations, so that mutual arms reductions would be feasible. This mission, although it seemed to begin auspiciously—the British Foreign Secretary, Sir Edward Grey, and the Kaiser professed interest in House's proposals—was ended by the outbreak of hostilities.

House's interest in promoting a more constructive organization of world power continued unabated. A victorious Germany, he feared, would inevitably threaten the peace and security of the United States. On the other hand, the total defeat of Germany would be equally undesirable for it would create a power vacuum into which Russia would move. House hoped for a third result, a negotiated peace which would preserve the balance of power and convert it to a system for mutual security. In early 1915 and again in the winter of 1915-16 he journeyed to Europe to try to pave the way for American mediation of the war. Both missions failed.

While Wilson approved, even with enthusiasm, House's peace efforts, his general outlook on world affairs was different from that of the Colonel and his fellow realists. Wilson, of course, was familiar with the theory and workings of the European balance of power. However, his antipathy to considerations of balance of power and national self-interest was so extreme that it was difficult for him personally to initiate and justify foreign policy on the basis of such calculations.

Wilson's outlook on international relations had been strongly influenced by the anti-imperialist revulsion against power politics which dominated American opinion at the turn of the century. The war with Spain and the annexations which followed ran counter to deeply rooted national notions of fair play and respect for the weak. In consequence, the idealists and the Utopians succeeded in capturing the nation's conscience and, to a large extent, in discrediting the so-called realists. As President of the United States, Wilson quickly became the leading exponent of the idealist approach to the conduct of foreign affairs, and his eloquence solidified public support of it.

In the idealists' view the struggle for power among nations was due to ignorance, selfishness and an insufficient development of proper institutions. Conflict was not a necessary or inevitable state of affairs, but only a temporary disruption of a natural harmony of interests among individuals and nations. People and nations were capable of putting aside their selfish interests through appeals to better impulses, to reason and to a common desire for peace and justice. Through international agreement, freedom and fair play could be ensured, the causes for conflict removed, and disputes among nations settled. The idealists looked forward to the day when spiritual and moral power would supplant the more brutal instruments of persuasion in international life.

The idealists were not isolationists, even though they were blind to the bearing of disturbances of the European power structure on the security of the United States. Rather they defined the United States' emerging international role in missionary terms. The criteria which should govern the formulation of America's foreign policy, they thought, should be not—as the realists argued—the national self-interest and relevant power considerations, but an altruistic adherence to universal ideals.

The discrediting of the late nineteenth century effort to revive and popularize in the United States a realist philosophy of international relations is of the greatest importance in understanding the response which the nation was to make to the challenge of World War I. It was the internationalism of the idealists, not that of the realists, which was to dominate America's reluctant drift away from neutrality to intervention in the great European war.

The intellectual basis of Wilson's idealism was strongly reinforced by temperamental factors. The idealist approach and, particularly, the moral and altruistic rhetoric in which it was cloaked struck a powerful chord in his personal make-up. It has well been said by Robert E. Osgood, in *Ideals and Self-Interest in America's Foreign Relations*, that "Wilson's national altruism, like [Theodore] Roosevelt's national self-assertiveness, was an integral part of his temperament and his philosophy of life, inseparable from his personality and yet giving universal expression to elemental values of human conduct." [3]

All his life long, Wilson was plagued by bottled-up aggressive impulses which he could not bear to recognize. Most men in public life are capable of perceiving and accepting the fact that an element of self-interest and personal motivation is present in much of their political activity. Woodrow Wilson had what can only be described as a horror of being "selfish" and of the possibility of behaving aggressively for personal reasons.

He tried valiantly to check those tendencies within himself of which he disapproved. The aggressive tinge in his leadership he could justify to himself only if he dedicated this leadership to the highest moral ends. Always he must prove to himself that he, and by extension the nation, acted unselfishly and without hostile intent. What made a nation truly formidable, Wilson held, was its "purified purpose." He maintained that "there is nothing so self-destructive as selfishness. . . . Whereas the nation which denies itself material advantage and seeks those things which are of the spirit works . . . for all generations, and works in the permanent and durable stuffs of humanity." [4]

This compelling personal need to purify the exercise of his power, we suggest, partly explains Wilson's strong distaste for basing his foreign policy actions directly on cold calculations of power and national self-interest. It was all the more fortunate, therefore, that his closest adviser—his alter ego, as he sometimes called him—was thoroughly at ease in the setting of the realist philosophy of international relations. It became Colonel House's task to interpret events from this standpoint and to initiate, and prepare the ground for, some of the most important foreign policy projects which Wilson undertook in response to the European conflict.

Colonel House well understood, as the quotation from his diary at the beginning of this chapter indicates, that Wilson's active interest in world affairs could be roused only by helping him to see that opportunities for great achievement in international relations lay within his grasp.

However, House found it difficult to stir Wilson's idealism and aspirations. Shortly after the outbreak of the European war House told the President that the war offered him an opportunity to bring about a revolution in international morals and urged him to begin to preach the new doctrine. But Wilson was not hopeful of succeeding in such a project, and remained unresponsive.[5]

The reasons for Wilson's reluctance to turn his aspirations for accomplishment to foreign policy were, of course, many and complex. He had entered the presidency expecting to concentrate the efforts of his administration on domestic reform. He had also entered the presidency sharing the general opinion of his countrymen that America should remain aloof from European rivalries. But more subtle personal factors also underlay the reluctance to commit his leadership to projects in the international sphere. Ironically, although Wilson's popular fame is today measured largely in terms of his effort to bring about a new world order, his distinctive gifts of leadership were in reality more suited to the arena of domestic politics than to the sphere of foreign relations.

The type of leadership to which Wilson was temperamentally inclined and for which he had schooled himself rested upon a unique gift for oratorical persuasion. It operated best, as he well knew, in situations in which the machinery for decision was well defined and which, moreover, offered opportunities for an inspirational leader to push through a concrete plan which embodied the "popular will."

However, the field of international relations does not easily lend itself—and particularly did not in Wilson's day—to the persuasive, driving type of leadership in which he excelled. There was then no representative international body for developing world opinion as to what was just and right. Having one's way, obtaining the acceptance of one's program, controlling the outcome of the political struggle presented infinitely more difficult problems on the international scene than on the domestic. In international affairs, after all, Wilson had no patronage to dispense and no caucus to resort to. As his official biographer aptly noted in pointing to the difficulties which Wilson faced when the challenge of international affairs could no longer be avoided, "there was no ready political method of approach, no international congress in which to test the issue and to pass the law." [6]

In domestic politics, as we have already noted, Wilson had been realistic in selecting as his objectives only those political projects which were ripe for realization. For a long time he remained unconvinced of the possibility of achieving in foreign affairs the great works to which he so passionately aspired. However much he wanted to be, as House kept assuring him he could be, the "world figure of your time . . . the prophet of a new day," [7] the President instinctively avoided permitting his personal aspirations to become attached to goals which did not seem quickly attainable through the type of leadership in which he excelled. Being inclined by temperament to demand a quick realization of political objectives once they were formulated, he was reluctant to embrace political goals which required long and patient cultivation to bring them to fruition and the success of which was in any event highly problematical.

In attempting to rouse the President's interest in certain foreign policy projects, House appealed to Wilson's ambition and to his desire to achieve everlasting distinction. He also attempted to turn to account the President's need for affection. Following, for example, is House's description of their farewell to each other on January 25, 1915. House was leaving for Europe to try to pave the way for a negotiated peace which should be formulated under Wilson's aegis:

> The President's eyes were moist when he said his last words of farewell. He said: "Your unselfish and intelligent friendship has meant much to me," and he expressed his gratitude again and again, calling me his "most trusted friend". . . .
>
> I told him how much he had been to me; how I had tried all my life to find some one with whom I could work out the things I had so deeply at heart, and I had begun to despair, believing my life would be more or less a failure, when he came into it, giving me the opportunity for which I had been longing.[8]

The next day, House wrote the President: "My! How I hated to leave you last night. Around you is centered most of the interest I have left in life and my greatest joy is to serve you. Your words of affection at parting touched me so deeply that I could not tell you then, and perhaps never can tell you, just how I feel."[9]

The day before he sailed, House wrote Wilson again: "Goodbye, dear friend, and may God sustain you in all your noble undertakings. . . . You are the bravest, wisest leader, the gentlest and most gallant gentleman and the truest friend in all the world."[10]

It is worth noting that at the time House expressed these sentiments to Wilson, he was filling his diary with criticism of the President's failure to appreciate the importance of the European war. All the more reason then, the Colonel may well have felt, to try to convince Wilson by whatever means necessary to take a more active interest in the conflict. In urging upon Wilson the role of mediator in the European war, then just beginning, House wrote: ". . . The world expects you to play the big part in this tragedy—and so indeed you will, for God has given you the power to see things as they are."[11]

This was a refrain to which the Colonel returned on numerous occasions when, at critical points in the long period of American neutrality, he urged the President to follow a certain line of action: ". . . If we accomplish nothing else, you will be able to do the most important world's work within sight." "He [Rathenau] said it was the noblest mission that was ever given to man and that he would pray that we would not become discouraged." "This is the part I think you are destined to play in this world tragedy, and it is the noblest part that has ever come to a son of man." "A great opportunity is yours, my friend—the greatest, perhaps, that has ever come to any man." "You have before you the biggest opportunity for service that was ever given to man, and I hope you will not risk failure."[12]

These appeals to Wilson's idealism, to his desire for unique achievement, while doubtless consciously manipulative on House's part, were not totally insincere. For House genuinely believed, his diary indicates, that a unique opportunity for American diplomacy had arisen.[13] From House's standpoint, he was merely trying to get the President to grasp the opportunity which history had given him.

Nor were the idealistic principles in which House frequently couched his appeals and advice to Wilson foreign to his tongue. For House's own approach to international affairs, unusual in his day and since, was in many respects a synthesis of both realist and idealist views of world politics. To some extent, therefore, he was able the more effectively to introduce realistic considerations into Wilson's thinking and calculations, and to bring them into consonance with the President's idealistic aspirations.

Nevertheless, House realized that at crucial moments his advice to the President had to accent idealistic considerations. So did the President's other foreign policy advisers—Lansing, Page, Gerard—who also from an early stage were concerned at the threat to American security which a German victory would pose. In time, perhaps only partly consciously, all of them came to rely less and less on hard-boiled arguments of national self-preservation in attempting to move the President towards intervention. For, as Robert E. Osgood suggests in a recent study of the problem,[14] these advisers seem to have sensed that neither Wilson nor public opinion would sanction intervention on realistic grounds but that they *were* open to the arguments of national honor and international morality which the issue of submarine warfare provided.

For a while after the European war broke out Wilson seems privately to have shared the opinion of his advisers that a defeat of the Allies would not be in the American interest.[15] Outwardly, however, he felt it to be his primary task to maintain scrupulously the "strict neutrality" which he quickly proclaimed the official policy of his administration. Despite a natural sympathy for Britain based on personal ties of ancestry, old friendships and memories of happy vacations there, Wilson felt rigidly constrained to prevent his emotional preference for the Allies from influencing his policies. He tried to remain neutral in thought as well as in deed, and enjoined the American people to do the same. He thought that an impartial, unemotional attitude toward the conflict and an open mind as to its causes would enhance his availability as a mediator among the belligerents at some appropriate time.

Such an expedient policy of strict neutrality was fortified by the dictates of Wilson's temperament. Indeed, it seems impossible without taking note of the temperamental factor at play, to account fully for his refusal to be provoked by repeated violations of American rights by the belligerents and his ability to remain impervious to pressure for more forceful action from his advisers and from enraged elements of public opinion. Just because, at bottom, his own interest in power stemmed from hidden aggressive and self-seeking impulses, its exercise had to be kept tightly under control. From an early age he had cultivated and preached self-control, the need to discipline his emotions in order better to exercise reason. He insisted upon the necessity of excluding the influence of emotions, his own and those of the country, upon his judgment and action during the repeated crises which the European war thrust upon him. In answer to public criticism of his refusal to be swayed by the shocking actions of the belligerents he preached his own personal gospel of self-control.

"I am interested in neutrality," Wilson explained in a speech to the Associated Press on April 20, 1915, "because there is something so much greater to do than fight; there is a distinction waiting for this Nation that no nation has ever yet got. That is the distinction of absolute self-control and self-mastery." In another public speech, three days after the sinking of the *Lusitania,* which roused strong passions against Germany, Wilson spoke in a similar vein: "There is such a thing as a man being too proud to fight. There is such a thing as a nation being so right that it does not need to convince others by force that it is right." [16]

Having pointed to House's persistent effort to stimulate Wilson's ambition as a means of inducing him to focus his attention on foreign policy, we do not wish to suggest that when the President did move in this direction it was due primarily to the efficacy of House's appeals.

Despite the Colonel's best efforts, for many months after war began, Wilson would not undertake a military preparedness program. He would not turn his attention wholeheartedly to the possibility of world leadership. It was, rather, events themselves—the increasing difficulty of safeguarding American neutral rights and of staying out of the war—which gradually forced the President to interest himself more actively in the conflict. His approval of House's second mission to Europe early in 1915, for example, appears to have been motivated as much by a desire to find some solution to the controversy with the Allies over neutral rights as by a desire to bring about mediation. And his approval of the bold plan for American intervention which emerged from House's third mission to Europe, as we shall see, seems to have been motivated more by an urgent wish to avoid being dragged into the war over the U-boat controversy than by ambition to play the role of world peacemaker.

As the war ground on, it became painfully apparent even to Wilson that no matter how forbearing he might be, his hand might be forced by German submarine warfare. Still, he drifted with events, and considered each new crisis individually, without any overall plan of action.

House was deeply disturbed at this purely reactive American policy.

If U-boat depredations continued, House (as well as many of Wilson's other advisers) felt there would be no alternative to breaking relations with Germany. Of all the President's advisers, Colonel House was the most dissatisfied by the prospect of entering the war over the relatively narrow issue of neutral right.[17] To do so, he thought, would prejudice the possibility of exerting American power effectively on behalf of a desirable peace and postwar world. House was also concerned lest America's prestige and influence be damaged in the sterile diplomatic struggle over neutral rights. Caught between the belligerents, attempting to protect its neutral rights equally against each, America was irritating both sides and dissipating her moral credit with the world at large.

House came to the conclusion that American foreign policy should recover its flexibility and its freedom of action. It should take the initiative to intervene diplomatically for the purpose of ending the war in a manner consonant with its own long-range interests.

On October 8, 1915, House outlined to the President a bold plan which he had been turning over in his mind.[18] The plan, on behalf of which he went on his last peace mission, was as simple in design as it was to prove difficult of execution: on the basis of a preliminary understanding to be achieved with the Allies, through Great Britain, the United States would demand a peace conference to arrange a reasonable negotiated peace and a new system of postwar security. If Germany refused, the United States would exert diplomatic pressure to compel her. If it should become necessary, the United States would enter the war to force German acquiescence to such a peace.

After sounding out the Allies and receiving encouragement, House obtained Wilson's consent to travel once again to Europe in order to obtain firm backing for the new plan for positive American intervention. After prolonged negotiations, the plan was finally agreed to by the British and approved by Wilson in March, 1916. It came to be known as the House-Grey memorandum.

House's plan was predicated upon an abandonment of strict neutrality in favor of a frank, if not immediately overt, collaboration with the Allies. When these facts became known after the war, many persons in the United States were shocked by what they regarded as a devious scheme to bring America into the war. Various interpretations were offered of Wilson's part in it. Some of his partisans preferred to believe that House had somehow hoodwinked the President into accepting a more far-reaching commitment than he would knowingly subscribe to. The facts appear otherwise. The essence of the plan, its commitments and risks, were known to the President. Despite its radical character, Wilson was more than willing to go along. For he saw in it an opportunity to bring about a negotiated peace before an open rupture with Germany was forced upon him by U-boat warfare. There was in the plan, to be sure, a risk of American involvement in the war. But Wilson seems to have played it down in his own mind, evidently counting it unlikely that once the belligerents were brought to a peace conference any of them would resume the war.[19]

The House-Grey plan for American intervention was highly vulnerable, of course, from the standpoint of American public opinion. In itself, however, this fact did not render the plan worthless. For, as long as the understanding arrived at with the Allies remained secret and as long as the necessity for American military intervention did not arise, considerations of domestic American opinion need not prevent Wilson from using it at least to bring the belligerents together to discuss a negotiated peace. Wilson undoubtedly realized that it would be no easy matter to persuade the American people and Congress to sanction the possible employment of American force against Germany if she refused to agree to a "reasonable" negotiated peace. The President, indeed, made little effort even of an indirect character to prepare the public or Congress for this unpleasant possibility. However, in negotiating the plan with the British, Wilson had appropriately qualified this commitment in recognition of Congress' exclusive prerogative to declare war.

The plan for positive American intervention was noteworthy from another standpoint as well: it marked a historic shift from the traditional American policy of isolation from Europe's affairs. During the negotiation of the agreement with House, the British requested and received from Wilson an assurance that American power would be committed to a league of nations to be set up after the war.[20]

During the summer of 1916, the House-Grey agreement died a slow death. For complex reasons which need not be entered into here, the Allies declined to respond to repeated requests from House and Wilson to invoke the plan. In the face of this, House felt there was little to be done, since it was part of the agreement that the Allies would decide when the plan should be put into effect and the call for a peace conference issued by the President. As it turned out, this was a fatal but perhaps inevitable weakness of the plan. For, as conceived by House, American intervention had to be on terms acceptable to the Allies, especially to the British, whose collaboration he deemed a prerequisite to establishing a desirable postwar security system. House realized, too, that American military unpreparedness in any event ruled out an independent, forceful mediation effort by the United States.[21]

The "big mistake," House wrote Charles Seymour on April 6, 1925, had been the United States' failure to start arming on a large scale as soon as the war in Europe began. If we had, House thought, "both the Allies and Germans would have heeded any threat of intervention, and we might have intervened pretty much on our own terms." [22]

If House's peace efforts failed, they did so perhaps more by reason of circumstances over which he had no control rather than because of any want of skill on his part. Indeed, he had displayed a distinguished talent for exploring passionate questions dispassionately and for bringing divergent views to their closest point of approximation. That there remained a gap which no diplomatic legerdemain could bridge is no reflection upon his ability as a negotiator.

Since we are again to encounter him in the role of diplomat at the Paris Peace Conference, a brief profile of House the negotiator is fitting.[23]

If Wilson was the orator in politics, his closest adviser was a political genius of an entirely different stamp. House appreciated the role of the inspirational orator in politics; he encouraged Wilson to make full use of his talent in this respect. But House also knew that desirable results are to be achieved in political life often only through patient organization and planning. It was as a political tactician and a behind-the-scenes organizer that the Colonel excelled.

In domestic politics, as we have seen, House habitually informed himself thoroughly on all factors relevant to the success of his undertakings. He had a great faculty for recognizing what those factors were. He usually could foresee the difficulties which might arise in various situations. He was wondrously adept at divining the attitudes of those whose actions would have to be co-ordinated to bring about a desired result, and at assessing their motives. He overlooked no pertinent detail, no matter how trivial. He neglected no action, however small in itself, if it would contribute to the eventual realization of his objective. In short, the Colonel had an unusual capacity for working out detailed tactics for implementing an overall strategy.

House's political gifts were readily transferable to the conduct of foreign relations. In many respects they were more suited to meeting the challenges which arise in international negotiation than were Wilson's. House quickly discovered that the planning and implementation of foreign policy were well served by essentially the same type of painstaking groundwork for which he had such a natural facility.

The possibility of effective American mediation in the European conflict, he recognized, required more than idealistically worded appeals and offers of good services. As early as September 5, 1914, we find him outlining in his diary a more deliberate approach in which he had greater confidence: "I am laying plans to make myself *persona grata* to all the nations involved in this European war, so that my services may be utilized to advantage and without objection in the event a proper opportunity arrives. . . . I do not believe in leaving things to chance, and then attribute failure to lack of luck or opportunity. I am trying to think out in advance the problems that the war will entail. . . ." [24]

An unusually broad time perspective entered into House's planning and calculations. He could see the bearing of small, seemingly trivial events and actions upon larger, more distant objectives. He did not believe in the reckless, risky frontal assault. Rather he was willing to settle for the possible as his immediate objective, at the same time keeping larger, more distant objectives in focus.

House realized that the factors on which the outcome of his mediation efforts depended were not all susceptible to his control. However this did not lead him to exaggerate the role of chance. Rather he tried to give what direction he could to events. Systematically he charted his course, controlling whatever was susceptible to a measure of control, and setting into motion developments which, in propitious circumstances, might mature in the fashion he hoped. His patience and long-range view enabled him to accept setbacks without becoming frustrated or losing interest.

House had the capacity to train his thoughts on likely future contingencies. It stood him in good stead not only in his planning, but as an aid to influencing those with whom he negotiated. For example, he was able to argue very effectively with both British and German leaders who seemed bent on pursuing what House thought the foolish objective of total victory. House shrewdly articulated the possible undesirable consequences of the destruction of either British or German power, obliging the European statesmen to consider possibilities they ordinarily preferred to underrate.

On House's peace missions abroad and later at the Paris Peace Conference, he usually tried to discover the current thinking of the European leaders he was approaching before he made any proposals. He also took great pains to inform himself thoroughly on matters of interest to them. He considered this preparation of vital importance to the presentation of his plans in the manner most likely to ensure their acceptance. Unlike Wilson, he neither harangued the men with whom he negotiated nor took them to task for their selfishness. He advanced his ideas as best he could in terms of *their* interests. European statesmen generally considered him an exceptionally well-informed and detached negotiator, a man with whom they could deal comfortably even when agreement was impossible.

His skill at reaching personal understandings with European statesmen notwithstanding, House realized that the possibility of moving leaders and public opinion by verbal arguments is limited. Sometimes only events can change dispositions and policies. All the more reason, House felt, for the United States to wait for the proper moment to launch its mediation efforts. In the meantime, to preserve the possibility of eventual success in such endeavors, House thought it necessary to avoid inflaming public opinion either here or abroad over the controversies concerning neutral rights in which the United States and the belligerents were involved. He also urged European leaders in both belligerent camps to try to moderate the hatreds of their peoples for each other lest they find their freedom to consider sensible national policies circumscribed by public opinion.

House knew it would be well for the leaders and publics of the warring nations to have an image of Wilson which would predispose them to accept his mediation. Both in his conversations and correspondence, he tried to project Wilson favorably and to counter the critical opinions of him which were prevalent abroad.[25]

In the end, as we have seen, House's efforts to secure a negotiated peace were unsuccessful. After the failure of the Colonel's 1915-16 mission, Wilson took the problem of mediating into his own hands. For House's patient, behind-the-scenes diplomatic approach, he substituted one more in keeping with his own temperament and political style.

Wilson's primary motivation in accepting the House-Grey plan for American intervention had been his desire to utilize it to bring about a negotiated peace before the United States should be dragged into the war over the submarine issue. Understandably, therefore, he was much annoyed when the Allies put off implementation of the plan. In the summer of 1916, the President began to move away from the pro-Allied orientation implicit in the House-Grey plan towards stricter impartiality. He was ever afterward suspicious of the Allied leaders. It was only the leaders of the belligerent powers, he came to believe, not their peoples, who were responsible for the continuation of the war.[26]

Still determined to mediate, if possible, Wilson began to turn over in his mind a new approach based upon an appeal for peace to the peoples of warring nations.[27] He hoped that the people would compel their leaders to accept his design for peace. He decided, however, not to act until after the presidential election of November 7, 1916.

In late November, he composed a note which he contemplated sending to all belligerents. He planned, too, to make it public for the peoples of the world to see. The note called upon the belligerents to state the terms on which they would be willing to end the war, and proposed a joint conference of belligerents and neutrals to explore the whole subject of peace.

Before Wilson had released his note, the German government announced (on December 12, 1916) its willingness to discuss peace. Wilson recognized that the German move embarrassed the one he had been planning, but decided to go forward with it anyway. On December 18, he dispatched his note to the belligerents. A few days later, he made it public.

In his eagerness to induce the leaders in the warring camps to co-operate in his peace venture, however, Wilson had failed to reckon with the possibility that this dubious method—appealing openly to the people over the heads of their leaders—could easily backfire and make it the more difficult to elicit a confidential statement of minimum peace terms from each side. Chastened somewhat by the unfavorable European response to his public note, Wilson attempted within a few days once again to use private diplomatic channels for mediation: on December 24 he sent a confidential note to the belligerents, renewing his request that they furnish him with a statement of their terms.[28]

The confidential exchange of views, however, moved slowly and unpromisingly. Oppressed with a sense that time was running out—which indeed it was—Wilson resorted once again to a direct appeal to the peoples of the warring countries. The occasion was a speech before the Senate on January 22, 1917, but his real audience, Wilson later wrote, was "the *people* of the countries now at war." [29] This was Wilson's renowned "peace without victory" address in which he pleaded for a just and moderate peace settlement. To the far-sighted observation that a "victor's terms" would "leave a sting, a resentment, a bitter memory upon which the terms of peace would rest, not permanently, but only as upon quicksand," Wilson added a statement of the general principles of an idealistic peace which, and only which, the American people would help to guarantee. It must be a peace based upon the equality of all nations, the right of self-government, freedom of the seas, reduction of armaments and the formation of an international organization which henceforth should guarantee world peace.[30]

Essentially, this was the peace program which, somewhat elaborated though not greatly clarified, Wilson advocated after the United States entered the war and which he took with him to the Paris Peace Conference. In this speech are illustrated several facets of Wilson the international statesman: his wish, even before America became a belligerent, to transform the war into a great crusade for an ideal peace; his tendency to overrate the efficacy of moral appeals; his inclination to substitute vaguely worded aspirations and general principles for concrete proposals. The "peace without victory" speech, in short, foreshadowed some of those weaknesses in his approach to negotiation which later in Paris cost him so dear.

On January 30, 1917, in the midst of Wilson's efforts to bring about peace discussions, the German government announced a resumption of unrestricted submarine warfare.

Despite his bitter resentment of this move, Wilson resisted all recommendations that he ready the nation's defenses for the war that might be thrust upon it at any moment. Rather, to the very last moment, he refused to accept the inevitability of United States involvement. He explored every remote possibility for preserving United States neutrality, including the unlikely ones of joining together with other neutrals to form a "League of Peace," and of engineering a separate peace between the Allies and Austria.[31] His efforts in both these directions proved fruitless.

Faced by the prospect of unrestricted U-boat warfare, American shipping refused to venture to sea without protection. Tremendous pressure was brought to bear upon Wilson to arm American merchantmen. He refused. His Cabinet, insistent on action, was near open revolt on the issue. At last, after holding out for three weeks, Wilson reluctantly undertook to arm the merchantmen, though he clung to the hope that it would be possible to preserve a state of armed neutrality.

The next weeks, however, deprived the President of his last illusions. The Germans continued to sink ships. There was widespread public demand for immediate action. Among high government officials, according to reports that Colonel House recorded in his diary, there was "something akin to panic" at Wilson's inaction.[32] On March 20, upon his recovery from a ten-day illness, Wilson polled his Cabinet to find its members unanimously agreed that war was inevitable and that a special session of Congress should be called. Heavy of heart, the President issued a call to Congress to convene on April 2 to receive a special message—his war message. To the very moment of its delivery, Wilson was assailed by doubts as to the wisdom of his course, and spent sleepless nights wondering whether indeed he had exhausted all alternatives.

What were Wilson's reasons for wanting so desperately to stay out of war? Why had it been so difficult for him to accept the inevitable even when unrestricted German submarine warfare began to take its toll? We have already spoken of his antipathy to violence. By itself, however, this constitutes a highly oversimplified explanation of Wilson's difficulty in accepting the necessity for committing the United States to battle. For Wilson was not a doctrinaire pacifist. There were circumstances, he had always recognized, in which moral duty might dictate a resort to arms.[33]

He had approved the war with Spain as a noble crusade, though he opposed American efforts to derive material aggrandizement from it. His own administration, though proclaiming the doctrine of nonintervention and the equality of nations, almost immediately had found it necessary to intervene on an unprecedented scale in the affairs of some of the Caribbean republics and Mexico.[34] In doing so, however, Wilson believed that he had the best interests of these nations more at heart than the leaders of these countries themselves. Wilson had even sent American troops deep into Mexican territory and kept them there for several months despite the outraged protests of Mexicans of all political factions. He could countenance such behavior on his part, however, because he believed that it was required to uphold American honor: a band of Mexicans led by Francisco Villa had several times raided United States territory and Wilson sent the troops into Mexico to capture the culprits. Further, Wilson felt justified even in invading Mexican territory because he thought that he was intervening in the complicated Mexican domestic political situation in a way that promoted what was "best" for the Mexican people.

Wilson, therefore, was capable of using force and violence as an instrument of foreign policy if he were convinced of the purity of the cause. He could fight an "unselfish" war.

His difficulty in accepting war with Germany was precisely that he could not convince himself that it was a "holy war" and that America's participation could be justified on high moral grounds. As late as November, 1916, he thought, as he wrote in his first draft of his message to the belligerents asking for their peace terms, that "the reasons for this upheaval of the world remain obscure and . . . it is not known what motives led to the war's sudden outbreak. . . ."[35] As between the German cause and the Allied he found little to choose. He was temperamentally incapable of allowing himself to be swayed by considerations of national self-interest, so was not drawn to the Allies on that account. And in the matter of violating American neutral rights, the British had been almost as provocative as the Germans—indeed, more so in late 1916. From his point of view, therefore, it was extremely difficult to justify leading the nation to war.

The President had always been by nature highly conscientious. He was prone to postpone decisions on matters in which he saw a balance of opposing arguments. At times, as Colonel House observed, Wilson could act quickly and decisively. But sometimes there was so much to be said on both sides of an issue that he delayed decision, waiting unhappily for events to make evident where the "right" lay.[36]

So momentous was the question of entering the war against Germany that Wilson was the more impelled to defer action in the face of opposing arguments. His conscientiousness paralyzed his capacity for action in a situation where it was not possible to do good without risking or accepting evil. He was appalled by the serious consequences that our entry into the war might entail. He could not tally up the arguments for and against, and act on the basis of the sum result. Rather, what he wanted desperately was to see something clearly as "right" and to do that. When a Cabinet member argued that public opinion favored war, Wilson snapped back: "We are not governed by public opinion in our conclusion. I want to do right whether it is popular or not."[37]

Bitter as he was over Germany's declaration of unrestricted U-boat warfare, he resisted breaking relations with her, "obstinately convinced," in the words of his official biographer, "that right was not all on one side" and that the British, too, had disregarded our neutral rights.[38]

Moreover, perhaps recalling the long and bitter imbroglio which his intervention in Mexico had occasioned, Wilson may have experienced doubts as to his personal capacity for being a successful war leader. In any case, House thought that the President suffered from such self-doubts and tried to reassure him on this score.[39]

An argument which Wilson may well have found compelling was that America's entry into the war would rule out the last hope for a military stalemate and the negotiated peace which all along he had believed essential to a reasonable, lasting peace. America's military intervention, he told his friend, Frank Cobb, of the New York *World* on the eve of his war message, would mean "that Germany would be beaten and so badly beaten that there would be a dictated peace, a victorious peace."[40]

To Cobb, too, Wilson confided his fears that the war would brutalize America and dissipate the moderate opinion needed to bring about a reasonable peace, a peace without vengeance. "Once lead the people into war," Cobb recalled Wilson saying, "and they'll forget there ever was such a thing as tolerance."[41]

Wilson resisted war, too, on the grounds that it would have harmful consequences for liberalism and progressivism in the United States. He seems to have feared that a war would provide opportunities for the "reactionary interests" which his administration had attempted to curb to reassert themselves.[42]

As numerous historians have observed, at no time during the critical weeks while he was still resisting intervention was Wilson willing to accept the argument that war against Germany was justified on idealistic grounds or for reasons of protecting American security. Rather, when his power-oriented advisers employed idealistic arguments in order to move him towards intervention they found him surprisingly adept at raising balance-of-power considerations, which he usually found uncongenial, as a reason for staying out! America must remain aloof from the war, Wilson argued back, in order when the destructive war finally ended to safeguard the interests of the "white race" and "white civilization" against the expected challenge of the "yellow race." When Secretary of State Lansing argued that future peace required the destruction of Prussian militarism, he found that Wilson "was not sure of this as it might mean the disintegration of German power and the destruction of the German nation." [43]

Nonetheless, when war was finally forced upon him and he at last made his decision to ask Congress to recognize that a state of war existed with Germany, Wilson placed his action on the highest idealistic grounds. It often has been said that Wilson's habitual practice of idealizing and moralizing his actions was to some extent consciously instrumental, reflecting his appreciation of the deep wellspring of American feeling to which one must appeal in order to mobilize public opinion. This may well be the case. But his propensity toward idealization was certainly instrumental in the first place in a more personal sense. That Wilson struggled with the conscience of the pacifistically inclined nation should not obscure the simultaneous struggle which he waged with his own conscience.

Indeed, so was he constituted that he could overcome the stubborn doubts he had so conscientiously struggled with only by replacing them with an unquestioned faith in the righteousness of America's cause. This pattern of decision-making—replacing extreme uncertainty with extreme certainty—was characteristic of the man.

The protection of America's rights against the flagrant challenge of German U-boat warfare did not present an objective sufficiently elevated to legitimize his war decision. Even when the fatal step was virtually forced upon him, Wilson could commit his leadership and his people to war only by embracing far-reaching idealistic objectives. It must be a war to make the world safe for democracy, a war to end war, a crusade to usher in a new world order. Fighting to accomplish these great ideals was the one way that Wilson could banish his misgivings about leading the nation to war. Now he turned to this tremendous task with a Messianic zeal that far outstripped his personal commitment to any goal he had ever embraced in his entire life.

## CHAPTER X

# UNDERCURRENTS

Unrestricted power to the President to "co-ordinate and consolidate" all the governmental activities as a war emergency is contemplated in a bill offered in the Senate late today by Senator Overman of North Carolina, an Administration supporter.

The measure, which came from the President . . . was criticised tonight as intended to provide assumption of the entire power of Government by the Executive.

Leaders in the Senate, Democrats and Republicans alike, showed anger tonight over the proposal. . . . "We might as well abdicate," said several Senators.

New York *Times*, February 7, 1918.

. . . The President has nearly destroyed all the work I have done in Europe.

Diary of Edward M. House, December 20, 1916.[1]

When the United States entered World War I, President Wilson openly sought that dictatorial power which his critics suspected he had coveted all along. Wilson took the position that he must become the commander-in-chief of a necessarily autocratic organization; that the normal processes of democratic government must be suspended for the duration; that Congress must be willing to equip him with whatever powers he deemed necessary to prosecute the war.[2]

Given the task which confronted the nation, Wilson's demand for authority was not to be denied. With whatever misgivings and distaste —and there was a great deal of both—Congress entrusted Wilson with the job of mobilizing the nation's resources, in Professor Corwin's phrase, "through the simple device of transferring to the President its applicable powers."[3]

Wilson presented Congress with drafts of statutes he wanted passed empowering him in one phase of national activity after another. So comprehensive and numerous were his requests that Congress was hard put simply to keep up-to-date with the business he laid before it.[4] An article in the September 29, 1917, issue of the *New Republic* epitomized the widespread and, in varying degrees, critical realization that basic changes in the relations between the executive and legislative branches of government were taking place:

> The private individual of Congress is dead . . . The traditional separation of powers has broken down. . . . Congress may delay presidential action; but there is evidence enough, even apart from the fact of war, that it is finding it increasingly difficult ultimately to thwart it. . . .
>
> The congressional committees have become less the moulders of legislation than recipients who may alter its details. . . . They interpret the executive will; and we have seen recalcitrant members interviewed on policy by the President himself.
>
> The key to the whole, in fact, has come to lie in the President's hands. The pathway of decision is his own, influenced, above all, by his personal cast of mind and by the few who can obtain direct access to him.

Attempts were made to brake Wilson's power through alterations of the administration's bills. He rebuffed them all. It was his constant purpose to enlarge his authority and to exercise it without restriction. When the suggestion was made that he form a bipartisan Cabinet, he declared himself "utterly opposed to anything of the sort." Republicans "of the finest sort," he told Tumulty, would be willing to work with the Democratic administration, whether or not they were given Cabinet positions.[5]

When the Senate was considering an amendment to the Espionage Bill which would curtail his embargo powers, Wilson summoned Senator T. S. Martin (D., Va.) and requested his help in defeating the restriction. Two days later, the Senate voted in favor of conferring "full and elastic powers of embargo" on the President. During the drafting of the Priorities Bill, some of his critics (Democratic) proposed an amendment to vest authority for fixing priorities in the Interstate Commerce Commission rather than in the Executive. Wilson denounced the idea as a machination of "distinctly hostile" men out to "prevent the very things that are now absolutely necessary." He ordered Tumulty to tell administration leaders in the Senate that "I believe that the granting of the power suggested direct to the Executive is the only wise and feasible thing that can be done in the existing circumstances."[6] The offending amendment was promptly dropped, although several pro-administration Senators had previously agreed to it.

When a clause was inserted into the Food Bill providing for the creation of a committee to supervise war expenditures, Wilson served notice that he would interpret the adoption of such a provision "as arising from a lack of confidence in myself." "The constant supervision of executive action which it contemplates," he wrote Representative A. F. Lever (D., S.C.), "would amount to nothing less than an assumption on the part of the legislative body of the executive work of the administration. . . . I sincerely hope that upon the reconsideration of this matter both Houses of Congress will see that my objections rest upon indisputable grounds. . . ." On the same day he appealed to Senator Ben Tillman (D., S.C.) to help prevent the establishment of "an espionage committee" over him.[7] The clause establishing the supervisory committee was duly stricken from the Bill. Another attempt in the same direction was made a few months later. Wilson notified several Democratic Senators that the creation of an additional authority "would create confusion and make my task twice as complex as it is."[8] The committee was not set up.

In early 1918, criticism of several aspects of the war effort was climaxed by the introduction of two bills by Senator G. E. Chamberlain (D., Ore.) establishing respectively a war Cabinet and a munitions ministry to direct war activities. Wilson announced that he would veto any such measure. Perhaps better co-ordination of the war effort could be achieved, Wilson conceded, but *he* would do the job. What he needed was power enough to reorganize the entire government, to create agencies as he thought them required, to reallocate appropriations as he thought best. A bill reflecting Wilson's desires was introduced by Senator Overman (D., N.C.). The New York *Times* of February 7, 1918, reported that Democrats as well as Republicans were angered by the bill's proposed transfer of so much of the power of government to the Executive. "We might as well abdicate," several Senators were quoted as saying. Editorially, the *Times* suggested that Wilson needed not more power, but better men to help him exercise the vast power he already had.

Congressional leaders of both parties doubted that the President seriously expected the bill to pass. They thought he had had it introduced to divert attention from the Chamberlain bills. In any case, to quote the *Times* again, "the general opinion expressed by Democratic and Republican Senate leaders was that the Overman measure pointed the way toward absolutism, and that Congress could not afford to delegate any such power as is comprehended in the bill. . . . More than one Senator spoke of the bill as aiming at establishing a virtual monarchy." [9] Wilson continued to insist that it was essential to the prosecution of the war that the Overman Bill be passed promptly and without change. Once again, reluctantly, Congress obeyed. The Overman Bill was passed in May, 1918.

The war crisis furnished an excuse for Wilson's subjugation of Congress and his resistance of all attempts to qualify his powers. Republicans and Democrats both were critical of much that he did, not only as to substance but as to manner of execution. Nevertheless, there was a war on and as patriotic Americans they rallied behind him. In something of the spirit of the long-suffering private who dreams of some day settling old scores with his top sergeant, Congress did Wilson's bidding and waited for the war to end. The Republicans, particularly, were looking forward to the mid-term elections of November 5, 1918, as an opportunity to win control of Congress and then force the President to take cognizance of their viewpoints.

In October, 1918, their armies routed all along the western front, the Germans requested Wilson to "take steps for the restoration of peace." [10] To Wilson, it seemed that the end of hostilities would only increase his need for a compliant Congress which would not create difficulties in the task of peacemaking which lay ahead. Already there were ominous signs of the sort of obstruction he most dreaded. It was coming from a faction of the Republican Party headed by Theodore Roosevelt and Senator Henry Cabot Lodge of Massachusetts. Both Roosevelt and Lodge had supported the war while in a sustained state of almost apoplectic rage at Wilson himself. For envenomed denunciation of a man's character and motives, the references to Wilson in the letters which Roosevelt and Lodge exchanged are scarcely to be equaled.

In the Senate, Lodge had opposed most of Wilson's domestic reforms. During the 1916 presidential campaign, Lodge and Wilson had cast doubt upon each other's veracity. The issue was whether or not at one stage during the composition of the protest to Germany over the sinking of the *Lusitania* Wilson had written a postscript designed to intimate to the German government that the note's firm tone need not be taken too seriously, that it was primarily to placate American public opinion. The fact is that there was a substantial basis for

Lodge's charge, although some of its details were inaccurate. Wilson took advantage of this fact.[11] Seeking refuge in technicalities, he denied Lodge's accusation. The two men never forgave each other.

Now, in October, 1918, while he was in the midst of the most delicate negotiations with both the Germans and the Allies in response to the German peace request, Lodge and Roosevelt were publicly blasting his peace program, criticizing his day-to-day course of action, and stressing the importance of the Senate's function in treaty-making. In August, 1918, Lodge had been elected Republican floor leader in the Senate. He was the ranking Republican on the Senate Foreign Relations Committee. Should the Republicans win a majority in the Senate in the November 5 elections, Lodge would be in an even more powerful position.

On October 25, 1918, Wilson issued his fateful appeal to the people to elect a Democratic Congress, "if you have approved of my leadership and wish me to continue to be your unembarrassed spokesman in affairs at home and abroad . . ." He conceded that the Republicans had been pro-war, but "they have been anti-administration." At almost every turn, he declared, they had tried to undermine his control of the war effort. "This is no time either for divided counsels or for divided leadership. Unity of command is as necessary now in civil action as it is upon the field of battle." Wilson continued:

> The return of a Republican majority to either House of the Congress would, moreover, be interpreted on the other side of the water as a repudiation of my leadership. . . . It is well understood there as well as here that the Republican leaders desire not so much to support the President as to control him.

In ordinary times, said the President, he would not feel free to make such a request. "But these are not ordinary times." Wilson declared that he was the people's servant and that he would "accept your judgment without cavil."

A great protest rose from the Republicans. They pointed to their support of Wilson's war policies, and to the fact that many Democrats in Congress had tried to thwart him. All through the war Republicans had put party affiliation aside and worked for victory. Must they now yield representation to Democrats, not because Democrats were more loyal or patriotic, but simply because they were Democrats? The President's statement, one Republican leader after another declared, was a challenge and an insult.

In explicitly staking his prestige upon the outcome of the election, Wilson was taking an enormous gamble. He was not merely gambling on whether or not the public would support him on the issue on which he wanted, in effect, a vote of confidence. He was also gambling on whether, in the first place, the public would vote in terms of that issue. Congressional elections usually revolve about local issues, and voters are traditionally kinder in mid-term elections to the party out of power—in this case, the Republicans. Moreover, he was risking the good will of a large number of Republicans who saw merit in his peace plans. Lodge and Roosevelt, influential as they were, did not represent the entire Republican Party. Such prominent Republicans as ex-President Taft and ex-Secretary of State Elihu Root were disposed to support Wilson's peace program.

It was a daring gamble and, as it turned out, a disastrous one. On November 5, 1918, the nation's voters turned the Democrats out of control of Congress. Both the Senate and the House would have Republican majorities. Both would be organized by the Republicans, with Republican chairmen of the committees—Lodge, Chairman of the Senate Foreign Relations Committee.[12]

Wilson had committed himself to the interpretation that the election of a Republican-controlled Congress would signify the people's repudiation of his leadership. Whether it was a correct interpretation or not, Roosevelt, Lodge and their friends prepared to make the most of it.

The lines of battle between Wilson and the Roosevelt-Lodge bloc were taking shape just as another of Wilson's difficulties, as yet subterranean, was coming to a head. His relations with Colonel House were rapidly moving toward an unhappy climax. Given the complex, subtle basis upon which their political collaboration rested, it is less surprising in retrospect that House and Wilson eventually drifted apart than that their friendship should have lasted as long as it did.

Although his relationship with the President was the source of much heady pleasure for the Colonel, House was not a man to be satisfied by mere *proximity* to the mighty. He had his ideas about public policy and great ambition to see them realized. From House's standpoint, therefore, differences of political judgment with the President, which would not yield to his artful suasion, were the chief frustration he had to endure. Too, it was irritating always to have to minister to the President's quirks as the price of gaining consideration for policy ideas.

House found the President's personal limitations a major and constant obstacle to the achievement of worthwhile policy goals. "As I saw him at the time and as I see him in retrospect," House later wrote of Wilson, "his chief defect was temperamental."[13] The Colonel was sufficiently detached to observe how certain of Wilson's personality traits hobbled his performance as a political leader. To judge from the tone of House's diary, he felt variously sad, chagrined at his own helplessness in the situation, and angry at Wilson. Sometimes he tried to intervene. More often, he stood by silently, aware of the necessity of tact for the preservation of his own position. If he had to hold his tongue, his pen was free. His diary is studded with criticisms of the President. They date back to February, 1913, when House noted that Wilson was too casual in selecting his Cabinet. By April, 1914, House had become aware of Wilson's general reluctance to consult others and recorded on the fifteenth that he almost laughed when the President declared he always sought advice.[14]

On September 29, 1914 (and frequently thereafter), House wrote that Cabinet members were justified in their resentment of the President's failure to consult with them. On the same day he noted that he and Wilson disagreed about the desirability of multiple presidential terms, Wilson's position being that the people should have the privilege of retaining leaders as long as they choose. By November 2, 1914, House and McAdoo, over lunch at the Ritz, agreed that the administration was drifting toward conservatism.[15] On November 14, 1914, House confided to his diary that the President was a peculiar man: he did not want to discuss things with anyone except the Colonel, and this impeded his efficiency as an executive.

On January 4, 1915, House noted that the President did not fully realize the importance of "sociological measures" relating to such problems as unemployment and immigration. On January 12, House was distressed because after dinner at the White House, the President read from A. G. Gardiner's sketches of prominent men instead of discussing important pending business.

When war broke out in Europe, House wrote repeatedly that Wilson was insufficiently aware of the importance of foreign affairs, that he did indeed have a "one-track" mind which could not cope with both domestic and international problems, but must neglect one or the other.[16] In July, 1915, House was vexed that the hot weather prevented his being in Washington for, he noted in his diary, he could stir

Wilson to action only if he were with him in person and himself undertook to implement what they agreed on.[17]

During the summer of 1915, Wilson met a Virginia gentlewoman of forty-three, Mrs. Edith Bolling Galt. The President had been acquainted with Mrs. Galt, a widow, for two months when he asked her to marry him.

House, it is clear from his diary, was distressed at this development. He complained that Wilson's attention was being distracted from his official duties, particularly from the necessity to prepare the country for possible war.[18] As Wilson became increasingly preoccupied with his fiancée he had less time for the Colonel, and became less dependent upon his friendship.

In November, 1915, Wilson visited House in New York twice, but no longer does the diary chronicle beatific talks during which the President unburdens himself. After such a visit the preceding November House had been able to write his brother-in-law that Wilson had seen no one except him and had to be taken unwillingly to lunch with his old friend Cleveland Dodge; on this occasion the Colonel's diary is a testy account of Wilson's attentions to Mrs. Galt, who was also in New York. Not a word is there that indicates any pleasure at the visit. Rather the diary entries have the petulant tone of one who sensed a partial lessening of dependency and a partial withdrawal of affection, and resented it.[19]

During November, 1915, the month preceding Wilson's second marriage, House's private criticisms of the President multiplied, and the note of personal pique in his diary is unmistakable. He disagreed with the President about the Shipping Bill and the tariff. The reports he received from Washington indicated a curious inertia throughout the government largely due, of course, House noted, to the President himself. He was so engrossed with his fiancée that he was neglecting business, the Colonel again complained in his diary on November 22. He would go to Washington, he wrote, but he knew he would not be welcome at this time, especially if he tried to stir the President to action. A shower of criticism of the President's personality followed: he dodged trouble; he had many intense and often unjust prejudices against people, and could not confer with men he disliked.

The third week in November was a particularly trying one for House, for, at a time when he felt so insecure, Wilson aggravated his anxiety by failing to write. Then, on November 26, Wilson telephoned, apologized for his silence and explained that he had been busy preparing an important message. House's diary indicates that he thought this a specious excuse and that the President was more pre-occupied with affairs of the heart than with affairs of state.[20]

All during the time of these difficult personal tensions, House was absorbed in formulating a plan to end the European war. He had suggested, and Wilson had agreed, that it would be useful for him to go again to Europe. On December 7, 1915, House wrote Wilson offering to come to Washington to discuss this mission. In days past, such a suggestion would have prompted a warm invitation from the White House. This time, however, the summons did not come for an entire week, during which the Colonel's irritation found an outlet in the safety of his diary: Wilson ought to have revamped a recently dispatched State Department note to Austria, his failure to do so indicating an overcasual attitude toward important matters; the President did not realize the country was drifting into war or he would certainly undertake a defense program; in the event of a crisis, Wilson might fail to act quickly and might become the target of justified criticism.[21]

One of the difficulties of House's position was that while he was seething with irritation with the President and Mrs. Galt, he was obliged to simulate a liking for her and express his pleasure at the forthcoming marriage. When Wilson first confided to House his desire to remarry, House feigned approval. The Colonel even professed to wish to help the courtship along, going so far as to obtain a number of engagement rings from which the President might select one to present Mrs. Galt. However, in his diary (July 31, 1915) House wrote that he was sorry the President had fallen in love at that time.

House's discomfiture at the advent of Mrs. Galt is readily understandable. The Colonel had perfected a technique for handling Wilson. It included, as we have seen, such devices as avowing personal affection for him, assuring him of his greatness, professing to agree with him on all important issues and approving whatever course of action he took. This behavior was acceptable to Wilson but might easily be perceived by someone else as an indication of insincerity.

The first Mrs. Wilson not only understood her husband's needs but welcomed House's helpfulness without jealousy. Unfortunately for House, the second Mrs. Wilson was more possessive and more protective. In consequence, she was extremely sensitive to anything that might be construed as reprehensible behavior on the part of Wilson's intimates. Doubtless acting out of her conception of loyalty and devotion to the President, she was quick to find fault with one after another of his close associates.

Mrs. Wilson was particularly disturbed and perhaps deeply perplexed by her husband's dependence upon Colonel House. The relationship between them revealed weaknesses in Wilson's make-up which it may have been extremely distasteful to her to contemplate. Perhaps instinctively, she sought to make Wilson independent of House in order to make reality conform with her idealized image of her husband.

House was thus faced with the perhaps unsolvable dilemma posed by the need to continue his indulgent treatment of the President in order to be able to influence him, and the simultaneous need to avoid thereby offending Mrs. Wilson. He tried to cope with the situation by forming an alliance with Mrs. Wilson, apparently hoping that if he encouraged her faultfinding of other members of the President's inner circle he himself could avoid becoming one of its targets.[22]

Despite House's willingness to cater to Mrs. Wilson's dislikes, he did not succeed in gaining her approval. Theirs was an uncomfortable truce, cemented by their desire to please Wilson, and camouflaged by disingenuous expressions of mutual admiration. Even while she was supposedly treating House as a confidant, writing and speaking to him of her displeasure with others around the President, Mrs. Wilson had already begun, according to her own published account, to suspect his sincerity and to question the value of his services as an adviser.[23]

Mrs. Wilson's perception of the Colonel's behavior was not blurred by any desire that the close friendship between him and her husband continue. From her point of view, House may well have seemed an interloper. Shortly after they were introduced House advised her not to succumb to the importunities of friends who might try to use her as a means of influencing the President. This may have struck her as an impertinent attempt to intrude into her personal affairs. When House, as he recorded in his diary on November 30, 1915, advised her to let the President alone to think out his problems in the future as he had in the past, she may have felt that the Colonel was trying to exclude her from what he considered his domain.

Indeed, House doubtless *was* irked at the fact that the new Mrs. Wilson was promptly constituted a third party to previously private conferences with the President. Encouraged by Wilson to do so, she began to take an interest in political problems. It is easy to imagine

House's chagrin—he who for years had studied history and politics and had equipped himself to serve as a presidential adviser—at suddenly being obliged to make obeisance to the political opinions of an undeniably attractive gentlewoman who nevertheless lacked the intellectual training for the role she was now privileged to play. If she sensed that House was vexed, she was, in fact, on solid ground.

The President's new wife soon became suspicious of the Colonel's tendency always to agree with him. In *My Memoir*, Mrs. Wilson tells how, in late 1917, Wilson was preparing a message to Congress in connection with government operation of the railroads. He asked House for comment, and House came to Mrs. Wilson and criticized it sharply. Later, when the President asked his opinion, he said he agreed with every word of it. Mrs. Wilson describes herself as having been "perfectly aghast" at this *volte-face*. "I do not like people to change their minds so quickly," she wrote, "and was never able to forget this little scene." Mrs. Wilson did not keep her misgivings about House to herself. On a subsequent occasion, she said to her husband, according to her own account: "It seems to me that it is impossible for two persons *always* to think alike, and while I like Colonel House immensely, I find him absolutely colourless and a 'yes, yes' man." The President defended House against this charge.[24]

Clearly, Mrs. Wilson had grasped at least fragments of reality regarding House's behavior toward the President. She seems, however, not to have comprehended that House's "yes, yes" characteristics were implicitly demanded by Wilson as the price of maintaining his status as presidential adviser. She seems also to have overlooked the fact (or at least to have attached little importance to it) that House was genuinely sympathetic to the President's political goals and was doing him yeoman's service in the struggle to achieve them. Sharply critical of certain aspects of House's behavior, she seems to have undervalued the mitigating factors in his favor.

The frustrations of House's position were increased by the advent of the second Mrs. Wilson. Whether and to what extent this added tension accounts for it, the fact is that after the marriage the Colonel had much more to say in criticism of the President in his diary.

House noted that Wilson's opportunity for successful leadership was hampered by the fact that he did not like to meet people and isolated himself as much as anyone House had ever known. He thought Wilson a man of unusually strong prejudices, intolerant of advice, except when it came from House himself.[25] Furthermore, Wilson seemed to him lamentably narrow and vindictive in his interpersonal political relations. Almost every time he saw him, House noted in his diary on December 14, 1916, the President had somebody else on his blacklist. House declared he could not understand how Wilson permitted his equanimity to be disturbed by the small matters which so upset him. In a similar vein, the Colonel wrote in his diary on December 30, 1917, that Wilson carried his antipathies so far that they reflected badly on him.

House frequently remarked Wilson's inability to organize his work efficiently:

> No one can see him to explain matters or get his advice. Therefore they come to me and I have to do it at long-range which is difficult and unsatisfactory. The President lacks executive ability and does not get the best results from his Cabinet or those around him.[26]

At times House himself felt inadequately informed as to Wilson's policies Early in their association, he was flattered at Wilson's failure to provide guidance, for he felt he had a latitude in his activities that more explicit direction from the President might have circumscribed.[27] As time went on, however, House seemed to realize that Wilson was not actually delegating policy-making functions to him.

House came to feel seriously hampered by the lack of specific instructions. He once complained to McAdoo:

> . . . The President expects me to keep absolutely abreast of both the domestic and foreign situations and, in addition to that, he expects me to read his mind and know what conclusions he has come to or will come to under certain conditions . . . It is hardly fair to me, and less fair to him.[28]

As an administrator House termed Wilson a failure: ". . . The President does not know what is going on in any of the departments. He does not follow their work and has an idea that every department of the Government is running smoothly and well. . . ." Shortly before, House had complained in a similar vein: "The President is not a man of action and seems incapable of delegating work to others. . . ." Wilson's handling of the press, too, frequently aroused House's critical comment.[29]

In the early months of 1917, as Wilson moved toward the conviction that the United States must enter the war on the Allied side, House's spirits rose: at last, he recorded in his diary several times, he had been able to bring the President to a realization of the role which the United States ought to play in world affairs.

Shortly after the United States entered the war, alarmed by reports of inefficient handling of mobilization problems, House urged Wilson to allow him to organize a "war machine." The President declined. Thereafter, there seems to have been a tacit agreement between them that House would confine himself to questions of foreign policy and the shaping of the peace. The Colonel wrote in his diary on January 17, 1918:

> . . . He [Wilson] knows that I do not believe that he has an effective war organization, and I have been content to let it go at that. The fact that he does not consult me about these matters indicates that he knows we disagree, but he has believed he could work it out along the lines which he has pursued. In foreign affairs, he does nothing without the closest possible collaboration with me, and since I am so much more interested in that than in domestic affairs, I have been willing to accept the situation as he has willed it.[30]

All through the war, in seeking to stimulate Wilson's interest in international affairs, House shrewdly assured him that he could achieve immortality by pioneering a world organization which would insure peace. When the President, his interest finally aroused in the task of creating a new world order, began increasingly to regard the problem of peace as his special preserve upon which no one should encroach, House was repelled. Wilson's reluctance to co-operate with the Allies in developing peace plans drew adverse comment on several occasions in House's diary. For example:

> I wish again to call attention to the selfishness which seems to lurk in the minds of those in authority. The President is anxious to state his peace terms before Lloyd George and Clemenceau have an opportunity to forestall him. It is not team work. While it is impossible to formulate these things together because of the widely divergent opinions, yet nothing should be done by one without some knowledge of the move being known to the others. It is the thing I have complained of so often in this diary, that is, that it is not so much general accomplishment that those in authority seem to desire as accomplishment which may redound to their personal advantage.[31]

House's displeasure with the President at this time was compounded of numerous negative feelings which made it increasingly difficult for him to play his accustomed role with Wilson. For one thing, he considered himself better qualified than the President in matters of foreign policy. On one occasion, for example, when he differed with Wilson and Lansing, House expressed the certainty in his diary that he was better informed than either the President or the Secretary of State; and that his greater firsthand knowledge of the world situation enabled him better than they to arrive at correct judgments.[32] So far from recognizing this superiority and consequently giving him free rein, the President hobbled his efforts, House thought. For example, in early March, 1916, House felt that the delicate negotiations he had been conducting with the British to arrange American intervention in the war had been jeopardized by the ill-timed effort made simultaneously by Wilson and Lansing to disarm Allied merchantmen. Again, in December, 1916, House complained in his diary that Wilson's penchant for gratuitously angering the Allies had nearly destroyed all his work in Europe.[33]

House's diary testifies to his subjective feeling of competence to handle the most complex problems of the presidency. More than once when he attributed some error to Wilson, he outlined what he would have done had *he* been President.[34] It is easy to imagine House's impatience, given this frame of mind, at the necessity to function through and completely at the pleasure of another man, particularly a man like Wilson. Indeed, in "Memories," House acknowledges that "there have been times when I would have liked the office itself instead of being an adviser to him who held it." It was when his advice was disregarded, he noted, that he entertained such feelings.

Although in his letters and talks with Wilson he deliberately minimized his own role in the conduct of foreign affairs, in the intimacy of his diary House casually referred to "my" peace plans.[35] There are suggestions in the diary that House considered himself the author of many ideas which the President accepted and later thought his own. For example, he collaborated with Wilson on the President's message asking Congress to recognize the existence of a state of war between the United States and Germany. The President, according to House's diary (entry, March 28, 1917) "made a memorandum of the subjects he thought proper to incorporate" and "I approved, for most of them were suggestions I have made from time to time. . . ." On the day Wilson delivered the message, House posed the question in his diary whether the President was aware of the contribution which he, House, had made to the speech: Wilson, he noted, had given no indication of realizing House's part in it.[36]

At times, the tone of House's private comments about the President was patronizing. For example, recording his pleasure at the President's reply to the Pope's peace proposals of the summer of 1917, House stated in his diary (on August 23, 1917): "While I should have written somewhat differently myself, I am thoroughly satisfied with the way he has done it, for he has covered all the points I asked him to embrace, and has left out the dangerous points to which I called his attention." Incidentally, it is interesting to note the difference in tone between the foregoing diary entry and House's letters to Wilson about the reply to the Pope. Whereas the diary conveys House's feeling that he was responsible for the contents of the note, the letters do not refer at all to his role and, rather, praise the President extravagantly. "You have again written a declaration of human liberty. . . . You are blazing a new path, and the world must follow, or be lost again in the meshes of unrighteous intrigue," House declared in a letter on August 24, 1917.[37] He wrote Wilson again on September 4: "I believe your reply to the Pope is the most remarkable document ever written. . . ."[38]

House assiduously recorded in his diary scores of compliments, like the following paid him by the British diplomat Sir Horace Plunkett, which have in common that he and Wilson are placed at an equal level: "Thank God," Plunkett told House, "Woodrow Wilson and you are directing matters in this country and are working in harmony."[39] Nor did House seem to think there was any inaccuracy in the remarks of American journalist Lincoln Colcord on August 25, 1917, when Colcord attributed to him direction not only of the foreign policy of the United States but of the Allied governments (including the Russian) as well.

There can be no question that at the zenith of his career, House exercised tremendous influence upon the course of diplomatic negotiations. Making the fullest allowance for his actual (and extraordinary) power, however, one suspects that he had the capacity for exaggerating the importance of his own role in international affairs. A master of flattery himself, he seems to have been naïvely susceptible to the compliments of foreign diplomats, whose expressions of esteem, it seems safe to assume, were not always entirely artless. Ignace Paderewski, for example, once told House:

> Words cannot express what I feel for you. It has been the dream of my life to find a "providential man" for my country. I am now sure that I have not been dreaming vain dreams, because I have had the happiness of meeting you.[40]

On another occasion, Paderewski declared he came to House as he would to his God.[41] Although he recognized the extravagant nature of the praises Paderewski heaped upon him, House set them down in his diary without any indication that he thought them undeserved, insincere, or connected with Paderewski's aspirations for an independent Poland. He recorded in his diary literally hundreds of such expressions of esteem,[42] and it is interesting to note that he had the highest estimate of the abilities of the authors of some of the most glowing ones.

Such intoxicating praise made it easy for House to forget that his power derived exclusively from his association with Wilson. House seems to have come to believe that Allied statesmen sought him out for his own capabilities rather than as a spokesman for another and, in his view, less informed man.

As the war drew to an end, House was in a frame of mind which placed his relationship with Wilson in jeopardy: he was coldly realistic about the President's shortcomings; he was resentful of his own subordinate role in policy-making; he felt he was better qualified than the President to handle United States foreign policy; he deluded himself into thinking that European statesmen sought his advice for its own sake, and not necessarily because he represented the President; and he was prey to grandiose notions of his own importance and capacity to influence the foreign policy of the Allied nations.

His attitude is illustrated by a remark in his diary concerning a difference of opinion with the President concerning whether or not to include a provision creating a world court in the Covenant of the League of Nations. House was in favor of doing so, and included it in his draft. The President deleted the clause. Noting that he and Wilson had been in complete disagreement on the matter, House wrote in his diary on August 15, 1918, that he had consoled himself with the thought that his position would be upheld by the Peace Conference.

On August 15, 1918, President Wilson invited House to accept an appointment as a United States delegate to the peace conference in the offing. A decision of the greatest importance was thus thrust upon the Colonel. On the one hand, he was keenly alive to the danger of accepting an official position in which he might find himself precipitated into a power conflict with Wilson. "Unless I change my mind," House wrote in his diary that night, "I think I should prefer not being one [a delegate—Ed.] unless, indeed, the President should not go himself. . . . There are many reasons why it would be better for me to be on the outside. . . ."

Among the "many reasons," of course, would be House's awareness of the necessity to sidestep situations in which Wilson's jealousy might be aroused. For years he had shunned publicity, remained in the background, subordinated himself to Wilson. Doing so was part of his endeavor to avoid treading on the President's sensibilities, which House knew to be very delicate indeed.

House was hoping, later diary entries indicate, that the President would not attend the conference as a negotiator, but instead would appoint him chief of the United States delegation. Whatever his hopes and expectations, however, House had to decide whether to accept an official appointment before he knew what part in the conference the President would elect to take. House finally decided to accept the official post, and it was understood before he left for Europe to attend the pre-armistice negotiations that he would serve as a United States delegate.

Why did House thus change his mind? It seems likely that he regarded the coming peace conference as the greatest opportunity that would ever come to him to play a role of first-rate importance in world affairs. What ancient ambitions, so long stifled, must have stirred in the Colonel's breast! Further, House was impatient of the President's shortcomings and seemed to feel that he was an obstacle to the achievement of their shared political ideals. To state the matter baldly, House considered that he could better negotiate the peace treaty than Wilson. The stakes were too high and the dangers of failure too great to rely on the limited possibilities which his role as adviser afforded of influencing the President in the right direction. House wanted, for once, to act directly, independently.

For years he had been placating the President, always attaching primary importance to the maintenance of their friendship. Now, for the first time, he was willing to risk the relationship itself. He hoped fervently that Wilson would remain in Washington or, if he came to Paris, that he would participate in the conference only briefly. House would in either of these cases have wide latitude in conducting the negotiations and a good chance of avoiding personal difficulties with Wilson. Wilson, however, decided to remain in Paris as chief United States delegate. By then, House had committed himself to his new role and there was nothing to do but hope he could handle it so tactfully as not to offend the President.

Given Wilson's temperament, House's state of mind of the moment, and the covert hostility between Mrs. Wilson and him, the Colonel was skating on exceedingly thin ice.

# CHAPTER XI

## WORLD LIBERATOR

> Perhaps I am the only person in high authority amongst all the peoples of the world who is at liberty to speak and hold nothing back. I would fain believe that I am speaking for the silent mass of mankind everywhere who have as yet had no place or opportunity to speak their real hearts out. . . .
>
> Wilson's "peace without victory" address,
> January 22, 1917.

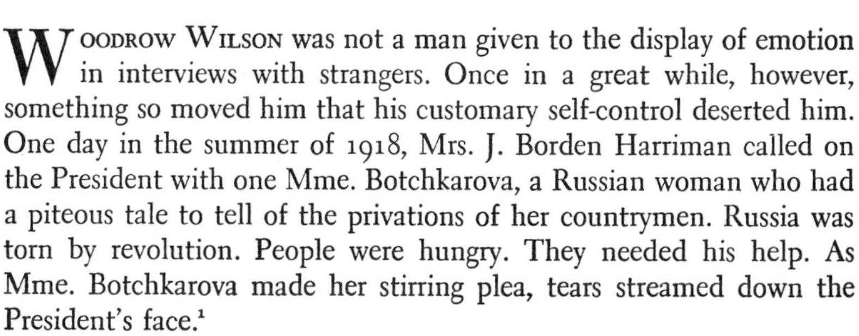

WOODROW WILSON was not a man given to the display of emotion in interviews with strangers. Once in a great while, however, something so moved him that his customary self-control deserted him. One day in the summer of 1918, Mrs. J. Borden Harriman called on the President with one Mme. Botchkarova, a Russian woman who had a piteous tale to tell of the privations of her countrymen. Russia was torn by revolution. People were hungry. They needed his help. As Mme. Botchkarova made her stirring plea, tears streamed down the President's face.[1]

This incident illustrates the depth and quality of Wilson's identification with humanity's suffering. He not only keenly felt the great misery of war-ravaged mankind: he was possessed of the idea that it was his God-given mission to ameliorate it by so reordering the relations of the nations of the world that never again would the plain people of this earth be afflicted with war. In his speeches he had set forth the broad moral principles which he thought must guide any peace settlement if it were to be a lasting one. By the war's end he had fastened upon one item in his program, that prescribing the formation of a league of nations, as the very keystone of the whole, until the wish to shepherd such an organization into existence suffused all his thinking, all his feeling, all his functioning.

Historians who have examined the story of Wilson's struggle to bring about the ideal peace settlement he envisaged have been struck by the series of inexpedient actions which marked the President's effort to achieve his objective. Examined singly and sympathetically, many of his mistakes can be, and have been, attributed to lapses of judgment of the kind to which any human being working under great pressure is liable, or related to various difficulties with which he had to contend: to the strength and cunning of the European forces arrayed against him; to the difficult domestic political situation in which he had to operate; to his illness at two critical junctures in the fight for his peace program; to the immaturity of the American public's outlook on foreign affairs and its reaction, once the war was over, against crusading idealism and internationalism.

When the President's numerous errors in peacemaking are examined in their entirety, however, there remains an important residue, a common thread which links them with one another, which cannot be explained in these terms alone. However sympathetically one views Wilson's noble aspirations and his struggle on their behalf, one is forced to acknowledge, as many historians already have, that temperamental defects contributed to the President's tragic failure. At the root of Wilson's numerous blunders, both in negotiating the Treaty and later in attempting to secure its ratification, was his complicated personal involvement in the objective of an idealistic peace and a new world order.

Wilson undoubtedly faced a difficult and complex situation, both domestically and internationally, when he turned his attention to the task of making peace. To achieve his idealistic peace program in Paris and to secure its ratification at home indeed constituted immense challenges to his skill as a statesman and political leader. Yet, time and again, he was irresistibly impelled to define and structure situations confronting him in ways which excluded the very courses of action that would have best served his political objectives.

The possibility of being the instrument for bringing about an idealistic peace had appealed to the President even before America's entry into the war, and had been among his motivations in attempting to mediate between the belligerents. If Wilson had strong Messianic impulses, the situation in which he found himself, both during the war and after, invited them into the open and fed them richly. In the days of United States neutrality, after all, there was real justification for his belief that he was in a unique position to render service to the cause of peace. The other leading powers of the world were in the grip of war hysteria, which drowned out the voices of reason and moderation. Only America, so Wilson very reasonably thought, had sufficient power and influence to stand a chance of bringing the warring camps to their senses.

As Wilson was unwillingly propelled closer to war, House tried to make the prospect more palatable by suggesting that being a belligerent would entitle America to a commanding voice in the peace settlement.[2] As long as the United States was not yet in the war, however, Wilson was willing to confine his peacemaking activities to those open to him as head of a neutral state: his most compelling wish was to stay out of the war. But once war was thrust upon him, he was free—indeed, then psychologically compelled—to identify himself completely with the mission of becoming chief architect of a new world order.

Wilson had accepted the awesome responsibility of committing American lives and American treasure to Europe's battlefields without being convinced that the Allied cause was righteous or that until the time of America's entry into the war it was being fought over basic moral issues. He had done so without feeling justified—because he was temperamentally incapable of giving primary weight to such considerations—by the fact that the national interest demanded an Allied victory. His only means of justifying to himself his excruciating decision to go to war was to devote every last ounce of his strength to ensuring that out of the holocaust would emerge a moral peace settlement which would ensure that this would be indeed the war to end wars. The realization of such a sublime ideal was the only coin which could purchase peace of mind for him.

To this compelling motivation were wedded others, perhaps even more basic, which sprang from Wilson's urgent inner needs. He had always wanted—*needed*—to do immortal work. Devising a peace settlement which would prevent future wars was a task which appealed to everything within him which strove for self-vindication through accomplishment. For what greater good could a man do than engineer the end to human strife? He had always wanted—*needed*—to dominate. The greatness of this cause provided justification for imposing his moral purpose on the whole world. In the service of such an ideal, he could allow himself to seek control of the peace conference and to impose his will ruthlessly upon those at home who dared question the wisdom of his ideas about the peace settlement. Organizing a league of nations was for Wilson a peculiarly appealing task. He had always been interested in ordering the political relations of men. As a boy, a youth, a young man, he had joined club after club and left in his wake a trail of revised constitutions for them. Now, in sponsoring the League, he saw an opportunity to write nothing less than a constitution for the whole world.

Already, before the war ended, certain Senators had begun to challenge his conception of the peace settlement and to proclaim their intention of exercising their constitutional power in the treaty-making process. They focussed their fire on Wilson's proposed League of Nations. This type of challenge to his authority in a sphere of activity fraught with personal significance to him set into motion that involuntary defense mechanism which doomed Wilson to a course of defiant insistence that his will should prevail. The more his critics found fault with the League of Nations, the more determined Wilson became that the League must lie at the very heart of the treaty.

Any one of the various personal motives which lay behind Wilson's commitment to his peacemaking role in general and to the League of Nations in particular doubtless would have sufficed to spur him to great effort. The confluence of these motives upon the task of peacemaking galvanized Wilson to a performance which came from the depths of his soul and engaged every facet of his being. Conscience as well as ambition and defiance dictated that he apply his entire energies to the accomplishment of his mission. The words of the student attempting to analyze Wilson's behavior do not reflect the passion—for it was nothing less than that—with which he approached his task. It is no exaggeration to say that Wilson was aflame with something akin to a religious zeal to "save mankind." Here, too, reality was the bright sun which brought Wilson's missionary ardor to full bloom. For, in fact, he *was* in possession of an extraordinary opportunity to exert this nation's power for the common good. The United States had no territorial ambitions to satisfy. She was involved in no embarrassing secret treaties, as were all the major Allies. Well might Wilson have felt that only he was in a position to speak for the decent and peaceful aspirations of "the silent mass of mankind" everywhere. America was emerging from the war the creditor of the world, a full-fledged power of the first rank. As this country's leader,

Wilson could legitimately expect a large voice in the peace settlement.

The trouble was, Wilson did not want merely *a* voice in the Conference. He wanted to be *the* voice. And this desire fostered a view of the other negotiators and of his task which reduced his effectiveness as a champion of his own ideals.

Wilson's peace program was embodied in a series of four speeches, the most important of which was the Fourteen Points address to Congress on January 8, 1918. These eloquent statements of America's peace objectives were designed both to reduce the will of the war-weary people of the enemy nations to continue the fight, and to rally the Allied peoples—if not the Allied governments—to a liberal peace program. Among other things, the President called for a peace of moderation, open diplomacy, freedom of the seas, removal of economic barriers in international trade, an impartial adjustment of colonial claims, reduction of armaments, self-determination and, to him most important of all, the formation of a general association of nations—the League of Nations.

In October, 1918, the Germans applied to Wilson for an armistice to be arranged with the understanding that the peace settlement to follow would be based upon the Fourteen Points and his three subsequent pronouncements. Wilson sent Colonel House to Paris to gain Allied approval of the Fourteen Points as the basis of the peace. This was a difficult assignment.

The Fourteen Points were propagandistic in character. Their appeal for "justice" was vague and sloganistic. These qualities had enhanced their appeal to enemy populations and made them a superb weapon of political warfare, but reduced their utility as a practical peace program. The Allies were reluctant to give their unqualified assent to Wilson's highly general pronunciamentos. To assent to such a nebulous set of precepts seemed to the Allied leaders an invitation to later difficulty not only with Wilson but with the Germans, who might one day claim—as, in fact, they did—that the peace terms violated the Fourteen Points.

Colonel House strove to meet these difficulties by having his aides draw up an interpretative commentary to the Fourteen Points. To some extent the commentary clarified Wilson's position on various problems, but it by no means comprised a well-formulated American peace program. Indeed, Wilson cautioned House that the "details of application" of the Fourteen Points must be decided at the Peace Conference itself.[3] It was precisely in these "details" that the Allied negotiators were interested. House's commentary notwithstanding, therefore, the Allies feared that their acceptance of the Fourteen Points might be construed as their agreement in advance to Wilson's as yet undefined concrete terms.

Furthermore, it was perfectly plain to the Allies (as to House and Wilson too) that the division of spoils contemplated by the secret treaties in which the Allies were involved was completely out of keeping with the Fourteen Points, sketchy though they were.

Colonel House listened sympathetically to the torrent of objections which the Allied diplomats raised, but stood firm in his insistence, in the name of his chief, that the United States would be a party to a peace settlement only if it were founded on Wilson's principles. The Allies finally agreed to accept Wilson's Fourteen Points as the basis for the peace settlement except that they reserved consideration of the freedom of the seas question to the Conference and explicitly stated Germany's liability for reparations. Their commitment led to a speedy conclusion of the armistice.

Gaining this Allied commitment to the Fourteen Points was something of a diplomatic triumph for Wilson and House. The acrimonious objections which the Allies had raised and the fact that in the end they had attached two reservations to their approval, however, served to confirm Wilson's distrust of the aims of the Allied leaders. His suspicion of their purposes had a long history: it had been aroused when, to his bitter disappointment, the Allies had failed to seek implementation of the House-Grey plan of 1916, which to Wilson's mind guaranteed them a reasonable peace settlement. His distrust had been unhappily substantiated when, shortly after the United States entered the war, the British Foreign Minister had apprised him of the contents of the various secret treaties between the Allied powers. It had been confirmed once again in December, 1917, when House, in Paris for an interallied conference, had been unable to get the Allies to agree even to a broad statement of war aims consistent with Wilson's ideas.[4] Now the reluctance of Allied leaders at the prearmistice conference to bind themselves to his moral principles lent fresh substance to his conviction that he and only he had an "unselfish" settlement at heart. Doubtless he sensed even then what the Allied leaders were to make so painfully evident to him a few months later at the Peace

Conference: that agreement on principles is not equivalent to agreement on concrete terms; that principles may be variously interpreted and cannot always be easily applied to the complex facts of reality—in short, that principles are no substitute for those concrete proposals which alone can serve as a reliable basis for intelligent discussion and unambiguous agreement.

Unless checked by him, Wilson was convinced, the Allied statesmen would betray the best interests of their peoples. They were actuated by considerations of national security, the balance of power, the quest for new colonies and new markets. To Wilson all this was immorality incarnate.

Clemenceau, left to his own devices, would destroy German power altogether. He would impose just that "victor's peace" which Wilson feared would contain the seeds of a new war. Twice in his lifetime Clemenceau had lived through German invasion of France. Germany had taken advantage of her victory in 1871 to impose upon France a Draconian peace, and since that time she had outstripped France in population, wealth and industrial skill. Now, the moment of French victory, Clemenceau thought, was the time to redress the balance. French obsession with security, the determination that France must never again be threatened by Germany, underlay the entire French approach to the peace settlement.

The British view was more moderate than the French. In a day when the English Channel still constituted a formidable defensive barrier, the British had little fear of direct German aggression. Furthermore, British foreign policy traditionally sought to create a balance of power among the continental nations, a preference which argued against divesting Germany of all power. Wilson's perception of this basic community of interest with the British was blurred by his attentiveness to the divergences which existed between them. He was repelled by the network of secret treaties in which the British were involved, the fulfillment of which would violate the Fourteen Points. He was determined to commit the British to his "freedom of the seas" doctrine whereas the British refused absolutely to agree to curtail their blockade practices, which, they claimed, were their chief defensive weapon. The British were interested in carving out new spheres of influence in the Middle East and Africa. Some of the British dominions wished to annex outright certain German colonies.

As for the Italians and Japanese, they were interested primarily in securing the spoils of war promised them by the Allies in secret treaties negotiated during the war. Wilson was not committed to the secret treaties, and considered them inoperative insofar as they conflicted with the Fourteen Points.

To Wilson the Conference loomed as a gigantic battle between the forces of "good" which he thought he alone represented and the forces of "evil" represented by the Allied statesmen. He did not understand that the problems which required settlement at the Conference were not susceptible of solution simply by the application of universal principles of justice; that the Allied statesmen, in a very real sense, were not free agents, but were bound to their positions by a tortuous history, by old traditions of negotiation and by public opinion. Wilson could not conceive that each of the major statesmen, according to his own lights, was justified in what he was seeking. To him they were a cynical and evil crew.

Before the negotiations began, Wilson had extensively elaborated in his mind the notion that it was his duty to save the people of Europe from their own leaders and that he best of all both knew and represented humanity's interests. World-wide enthusiasm for his Fourteen Points speech and his subsequent pleas for a just peace settlement having a league of nations as its heart, helped confirm him in this conclusion.

We find him on July 5, 1918, saying privately: ". . . Europe is still governed by the same reactionary forces which controlled this country until a few years ago. But I am satisfied that if necessary I can reach the peoples of Europe over the heads of their Rulers." We find him on October 23, 1918, expressing gratitude to and agreement with a correspondent who had written advising him to keep "the throttle of war and peace" in his own hands and not to let the Allied leaders direct the course of the peace negotiations. We find him writing in a letter on the day the armistice was signed: "It is astonishing how utterly out of sympathy with the sentiments of their own people the leaders of some of the foreign governments sometimes seem." [5]

Obviously, a great deal that the Allies proposed to do, Wilson properly opposed. In acknowledging the reasonableness of Wilson's rejection of some of their aims, however, we must not obscure this simple fact: that viewing the Allied negotiators as unenlightened representatives of the wicked old order of diplomacy which must be cast aside in the interests of their own peoples served handily to prepare an excuse for any attempt he might make to impose his will on them during the negotiations.

On November 11, 1918, the day the armistice was signed, Wilson cabled House stating that he planned to participate in the peace negotiations personally and that he assumed he would be selected to preside over the Peace Conference. House was distressed. He had been clinging to the hope that Wilson would stay in Europe only a short while and would place him in charge of the United States delegation before the negotiations got under way. As did many of the President's supporters, House thought Wilson's peace program would have a better chance of realization if he remained in Washington, detached from the day-to-day wranglings of the Conference.

In times past, House had always scrupulously refrained from pressing a point of view which he knew Wilson would find disagreeable. This time, however, he did not deny himself. He cabled Wilson, on November 14: "Americans here whose opinions are of value are practically unanimous in the belief that it would be unwise for you to sit in the Peace Conference. . . ." House indicated further that Clemenceau did not think that Wilson should sit in the Conference on the ground that no other head of state would, and that the British concurred.

Wilson was quick to indicate his displeasure. "Your 107," he cabled back the day he received it, "upsets every plan we have made. . . . It is universally expected and generally desired here that I should attend the conference. . . . The programme proposed for me by Clemenceau, George, Reading and the rest seems to me a way of pocketing me. I hope you will be very shy of their advice and give me your own independent judgment after reconsideration." House "reconsidered" and cabled back: "My judgment is that you should . . . determine upon your arrival what share it is wise for you to take in the proceedings." Then, in response to Wilson's charge that the British and French were trying to "pocket" him, House added: "As far as I can see, all the Powers are trying to work with us rather than with one another. Their disagreements are sharp and constant." [6]

Privately, House expressed his disappointment at Wilson's decision to participate in the negotiations. To his diary on December 3, 1918, the Colonel confided that he wished in his soul that the President had appointed him as chairman of the peace delegation. When later that month Clemenceau called on House to tell him the Allies were willing to agree to Wilson's attending the Conference, the Colonel confessed to his diary that he had found it difficult to simulate a satisfaction he did not feel.[7]

Wilson's cable to House is remarkable for its assertion that "it is universally expected and generally desired here that I should attend the conference. . . ." This was hardly an accurate statement. Secretary of State Lansing, for example, told the President on November 12, 1918, that he thought it would be "unwise" and a "mistake" for him to attend the Conference.[8]

At Lansing's suggestion, Vance McCormick called on the President to urge him not to attend the Conference. "Who can head the Commission if I do not go?" Wilson asked. "Lansing is not big enough. House won't do. Taft and Root are not in sympathy with our plans. I must go."[9] (Taft, it should be noted, was the leading light in the League to Enforce Peace, which advocated creation of a league of nations—the nub of Wilson's program.)

Wilson's political enemies were openly charging that his attending the Conference would be unconstitutional, another indication of his alleged megalomaniacal tendencies and catastrophic because he would be duped by clever and experienced diplomats. Apparently Wilson was so eager to assume leadership of the American delegation that, notwithstanding all these indications of opposition to his venture abroad, he deluded himself (or tried to, at any rate) into thinking that public opinion supported it.

On November 18, 1918, Wilson announced that he would attend the Paris Conference. He did not indicate whether or not he would serve as a delegate, although by this time he had probably decided to do so. Public reaction to this announcement was largely negative, although there was considerable sentiment that it might be useful for him personally to conduct brief preliminary negotiations.

Perhaps most significant, in view of subsequent developments, was the fact that Wilson's decision further irritated the already hostile Senate, and provided additional talking points for those who claimed that he was a colossal egotist, out to cover himself with glory. What right did Wilson have to go to Europe as representative of the American people, demanded the Republicans, when he had just been personally repudiated at the polls?—*personally* repudiated because in his October appeal he had asked for the equivalent of a vote of confidence, and had been defeated. From his deathbed, ex-President Roosevelt stated his attitude:

Our allies and our enemies and Mr. Wilson himself should all understand that Mr. Wilson has no authority whatever to speak for the American people at this time. His leadership has just been emphatically repudiated by them. . . . Mr. Wilson and his Fourteen Points and his four supplementary points and his five complementary points and all his utterances every which way have ceased to have any shadow of right to be accepted as expressive of the will of the American people.[10]

If the public reaction to Wilson's announcement that he would attend the Peace Conference was largely negative, a storm of criticism broke loose when, a few days later, he made public the names of the men he had selected to serve with him as delegates. The other American Peace Commissioners were to be Secretary of State Robert Lansing, Colonel Edward M. House, General Tasker H. Bliss and Mr. Henry White.

Of these, only White was a Republican and he, a career diplomat retired from public life for almost a decade, had never been active in party affairs. Wilson passed over such prominent Republicans as ex-President William Howard Taft, ex-Secretary of State Elihu Root, ex-Supreme Court Justice Charles Evans Hughes (who had been Wilson's opponent in the 1916 presidential election), and Dr. Charles Eliot, President of Harvard. He had also ignored the possibility of naming one or more Senators to the Commission or of inviting them along to the Conference in some other capacity.

The Republicans angrily protested that the President had failed to give adequate representation on the Commission to the party which, according to the latest national election, best represented the will of the people. Furthermore, charged Wilson's critics, the Commission was composed of "yes men," second-raters who would never stand up to Wilson and give him sound, if sometimes unpalatable, advice. *Harvey's Weekly* reflected a widespread view in its comment that the Peace Commission was comprised of Woodrow Wilson, representing himself; Robert Lansing, representing the Executive; Henry White, representing nobody; Edward M. House, representing the Executive; Tasker Bliss, representing the Commander in Chief—in other words that the only point of view given representation was Woodrow Wilson's.[11]

A generation of historians have examined the incident and the general consensus is that the critics had good cause for complaint. Many Americans thought (and still think) that Wilson should have taken House, Bliss and White as advisers and reserved places on the

Commission proper for more important personages, including one or two Senators, whose presence might have eased final ratification of the treaty.

Historians, viewing events a generation or more after their occurrence, detached from the heat of bygone political battles and with the record of subsequent events conveniently at hand, sometimes render overharsh judgments on the errors of great men. One might wonder, therefore, whether Wilson has not been unjustly taken to task on the basis of hindsight for not having taken a few Senators or some prominent Republicans with him to Paris. The fact is, however, that at the time Wilson chose the Commission (and, it may as well be noted here, at the time he committed subsequent blunders in his dealings with the Senate) it was clear to many of his contemporaries that he was erring. Ample warnings were offered, but he rejected them. If Wilson did not recognize the folly of his action it was not because evidence of the probable consequences was lacking at the time. His blindness was a shortcoming peculiar to him. His contemporaries watched in fascinated horror as, by his own actions, Wilson fired salvo after salvo at potential Republican supporters, some of whom (Taft, for example) magnanimously tried repeatedly to provide Wilson opportunities to undo the damage he had wrought.

Wilson made his selections to the American Peace Commission in the teeth of warnings, both public and private, that he must show deference to the Senate generally, in view of its share in the treaty-making power, and to the Republicans in particular. Wilson would do neither. The reasons he gave for not accepting suggestions to appoint one or two prominent Republicans in or out of the Senate demonstrate a remarkable capacity for flimsy rationalization.

He could not appoint Senators, he told Attorney General Gregory, because the Senate is an independent body and it would not be fair or constitutional to ask a Senator to negotiate a treaty which he would later have to judge. However, other Presidents before Wilson, notably McKinley, bound by the same Constitution, had felt free to use Senators as negotiators.

Wilson knew that everything connected with the peace treaty would fall within the Senate's sphere of power by reason of the clause in the Constitution which provides that the President shall have the power to make treaties "by and with the advice and consent of the Senate." The precise lines of authority between President and Senate in this function are not clearly drawn. All through American history, Presidents and Senates have engaged in tugs of war for the prize of dominance in the conduct of the nation's foreign affairs. Always alert to any real or fancied encroachments upon its powers or affronts to its dignity, the Senate has been especially alive to the slightest suggestion of presidential disregard of its constitutional prerogatives in the conduct of foreign affairs.

The difficulties of any President's position are increased by the fact that two-thirds of the Senate must approve a treaty if it is to be ratified. This means that the power of an obstructionist one-third is greatly enhanced. Numerous students of constitutional history have concluded that the present system of treaty ratification is unsatisfactory. Whatever justification there may be for such a conclusion, the fact remains that in 1918 and 1919 Wilson had to function within the existing system. The paramount need was to conciliate the Senate in order to obtain ratification of whatever treaty he presented to it.

Burdened by the usual stresses and strains between President and Senate which are inherent in our institutional arrangements for treaty-making, Wilson's task was additionally complicated by the pent-up hostilities toward him of Senators of both parties. Thus a situation ordinarily beset with difficulties was in this instance particularly delicate. So far from taking steps to solve his difficulties, however, Wilson compounded them at every turn.

Understandably, he did not want on the Commission Republican Senators like Lodge, who were so opposed to him personally that they might have deliberately embarrassed whatever attempt he might make during the negotiations to create a league of nations. This objection did not apply to a number of Republican and Democratic Senators who favored the idea of an association of nations or whose minds were at least open on the subject. It certainly did not apply to men like ex-President Taft, Elihu Root and Charles Eliot, who had publicly championed the creation of an international organization in one form or another before the President had done so.

Even if credence be given Wilson's dubious explanation of why he could not appoint a Senator or two to the Commission, it is hard to escape the conclusion that it was his purpose throughout entirely to eliminate the Senate from the treaty-making procedure. For if, unable to give that body representation on the Commission, he nevertheless wished to co-operate with the Senate so that it could exercise its duty of giving "advice and consent," one would assume that he would take steps to keep it informed of the proceedings. He did not. On the contrary, he deliberately withheld information from the Senate. One would assume that respect for the Senate's functions would have led him to negotiate in such a way that possible Senate amendments to the Treaty would not have calamitous consequences. The fact is, however, that he was careful to negotiate so that, as he publicly proclaimed, the Senate would find it difficult to make alterations.

It mattered little to him that deferring to the Senate might save the substance of his program. The substance of his program, although sustained by a variety of personal needs and intellectual convictions which sincerely committed him to it, was in the last analysis the external vehicle of his need to dominate. His paramount requirement—though he would literally rather die than recognize the fact—was to vanquish the Senate for personal, "selfish" reasons. He must not defer to the Senate. It must defer to him. He must not surrender to Lodge. Lodge—another Dean West, another *father!*—Lodge must surrender to him. His very integrity was at stake!

No matter that a Taft, an Eliot, a Root could render incalculable service in mobilizing support for his League and his Treaty. Wilson could not tolerate the presence with him of men whose prestige might threaten his own pre-eminence at the Conference and whose independence of thought might lead them into infuriating challenges to his authority. It was in the nature of his commitment to the task of creating a new world order, we suggest, that some of the private satisfactions he was seeking would be forthcoming only if he worked alone. From the moment he adopted the league idea as part of his peace program he became extremely possessive of it. Many others, both at home and abroad, had been sponsoring the creation of some such international organization. Wilson steered clear of them all.

The League to Enforce Peace, for example, was an organization dedicated precisely to the proposition that there must be an association of nations to preserve the future peace. All through the war, its members worked to prepare public opinion for American participation in such an international association and to systematize the ideas of thoughtful men on the subject. This organization's leaders were among the most respected men in the United States. By August, 1918, it had enlisted thirty-four state governors to serve as its officers. It had organizations in every state of the union and a roster of fifty thousand volunteer workers.[12] The League to Enforce Peace, in short, was a powerful voice in the nation, a voice raised in behalf of the very thing that Wilson had most at heart. Yet, Wilson frowned upon many of its activities. "Butters-in" and "wool gatherers" he called its leaders.[13] He was contemptuous of their plans for a league—plans drawn by men of the stature of ex-President Taft—although he does not appear to have studied them in any detail. He categorically opposed their composing a draft constitution for the proposed international organization. He opposed their seeking contact with similar groups in Europe.[14] In his eagerness to retain personal control of the league project, Wilson could see all the disadvantages but none of the possible benefits of participation by interested elements of the public in discussion of a league.

One of the chief reasons Wilson gave for discouraging public discussion of a league constitution was that the drafting of such an instrument was a matter for government officials to deal with. The British and French, indeed, had set up official committees for just that purpose. When the British committee had completed a report which the British wanted to make public, Wilson objected on the grounds that to do so would only draw the fire of opponents of the league idea, which would make it all the more difficult to secure a desirable constitution at the Peace Conference.[15]

In the summer of 1917, a Frenchman, Franklin Bouillon, who had been working on a plan for a postwar international parliament, approached the President with an invitation for the United States to attend a meeting on the subject with the French, British and Italians. Wilson rejected the invitation. In his diary on September 3, 1917, House attributed the President's reluctance either to receive or send commissions abroad to his autocratic nature. Wilson believed in one-man authority, the Colonel wrote, adding that despite its advantages, benevolent dictatorship is extremely dangerous and not to be countenanced.

It was not until July, 1918, after House had warned him that unless he took the initiative, public opinion might crystallize around somebody else's league plan, that Wilson turned his attention to drafting a covenant He found the British report unacceptable for the ambiguous reason that it lacked virility and, without any suggestion as to what his own ideas were in the matter, charged House with the task of rewriting it.[16] House's draft was the backbone of Wilson's later versions, which he altered in some degree to accommodate the views he encountered at the Conference.

A fact which stands out above all others, writes Ray Stannard Baker of the documents relating to the origins of the League, is that "practically nothing—not a single idea—in the Covenant of the League was original with the President. His relation to it was mainly that of editor or compiler. . . . He had two great central and basic convictions: that a league of nations was necessary; that it must be brought into immediate existence."[17] To these might be added a third conviction, perhaps the deepest of all: that he, and he alone, must be in charge of ushering the new organization into existence.

As the only Republican on the Commission, and as one who understood the crucial importance of gaining the good will of Republicans both in and out of the Senate, Henry White undertook to solicit the views of various Republican leaders before leaving for Paris. He hoped to be able to function as a tranquilizing intermediary between the President and his critics, particularly Senator Lodge, who had been a personal friend of his for many years. On December 2, 1918, Lodge obliged White with a nine-page memorandum for his guidance at the Conference. In it he warned that the proposed League must "under no circumstances" be made part of the peace treaty. "Any attempt to do this," he declared, "would not only long delay the signature of the treaty of peace, which should not be unduly postponed, but it would make the adoption of the treaty, unamended, by the Senate of the United States and other ratifying bodies, extremely doubtful."[18]

Lodge sent White his memorandum on the very day that Wilson appeared before Congress to deliver his annual message. In his speech, Wilson referred to his forthcoming trip. The peace settlement was of transcendent importance both to us and the rest of the world, he declared, "and I know of no business or interest which should take precedence. . . ." American servicemen had accepted his statement of the ideals for which they were fighting. "It is now my duty to play my full part in making good what they offered their life's blood to obtain."[19]

Congress received the President's words with ominous lack of enthusiasm. The New York *Times* reported that nearly all the Senators, Republican and Democratic alike, sat glumly silent throughout.

Two days later, on December 4, 1918, accompanied by Mrs. Wilson, Secretary of State Lansing, White and a corps of experts who for a year and a half, under the direction of Colonel House, had been collecting data bearing on all problems likely to arise at the Conference, Wilson embarked for Europe aboard the SS *George Washington.*

The President left behind him a clique of bitter personal enemies, likely to carp at whatever treaty he negotiated. He left behind also a group of people who so heartily approved of the plan for a league that they continued to support him in spite of personal antipathy: ex-President Taft, for example, despite his great contempt for the President's choice of Commissioners and for many of the President's actions, continued to campaign for a league. The vast majority of Americans had not yet formulated fixed opinions about the peace. Their minds were—to use one of Wilson's favorite expressions—"to let" on the subject. There existed a great deal of sympathy for the general idea of an association of nations to prevent another war and as yet very little organized opposition. As to the specific nature of such an organization, public opinion had not yet crystallized. Nor were most people greatly concerned with the concrete problems of peacemaking: such difficulties as the high cost of living, the delay in the return of one's "boy" from the army, finding new jobs now that war industries were closing down, seemed of much more immediate importance to most Americans. There was a widespread disposition to let Europeans worry about the complicated problems of Europe, and let the United States reserve all her energies for setting her own house in order.

Ahead lay Europe—the statesmen Wilson felt he must vanquish in order to gain a moral peace settlement and the millions of plain folk on whose behalf he was certain he would be acting. He approached his great undertaking with a mixture of apprehension, born of a deep realization of the magnitude of the task he had set for himself, inspirational zeal and, above all, determination to succeed.

Three days before the *George Washington* reached France, Wilson told the experts that the Americans would be the only disinterested people at the Conference, and that the other delegates did not represent their own people. The job for the United States delegation, he declared, was to achieve a new order, "agreeably if we can, disagreeably if necessary." [20]

On Friday, December 13, 1918, the *George Washington* steamed into Brest. The presidential party disembarked and proceeded at once to Paris.

Men who witnessed the triumphal entry of Woodrow Wilson into

Paris said that never before on this earth had one human being been so revered by his fellows.* Frenchmen whose grandfathers had told them about the triumphant processions of Napoleon down the Champs Elysées, Englishmen who had seen the coronation of George V, Americans, Australians, Greeks, Chinese—men from all over the world—have testified that never was there a welcome to match that accorded the President of the United States when he arrived in Europe to make peace in 1918. In Paris, two million people jammed the Champs Elysées, and paid tribute to "Wilson the Just" with cheers, garlands of flowers, prayers and tears.

Wilson arrived in Paris prepared to get to work immediately. Clemenceau, Lloyd George and Orlando all preferred to postpone the opening of the Conference. Wilson readily agreed to the delay, and spent almost a month making triumphal visits first to England and then to Italy, where millions of people gave him a tempestuous welcome which made all that preceded it seem pallid by comparison. The intoxicating ovations he received undoubtedly reinforced his belief in his mission as deliverer of the common people of the world, and his feeling that he, better than their own leaders, represented the people of Europe.

It cannot be denied that there was some justification for Wilson's feeling that his idealistic pronouncements had won the people of Europe. They looked to him as to a god who could and would right all wrongs. Nonetheless there remained a considerable element of unreality in Wilson's belief that he best represented the will of the Europeans and that, if need be, he could force his adversaries at the Conference to accept his views by winning the support of the people of the several nations they represented.

Differing and complex emotions lay back of the tumultuous demonstrations for Wilson. He had given eloquent tongue to universal human aspirations. To people throughout Europe—even in the enemy nations—his very name had become a rallying point for the expression of the wish for a world of peace and justice. His presence provided a splendid opportunity for people to give vent to their relief that the war was over, their gratitude for American help, their approval of high-minded ideals in general, their joy that the all-powerful President of the United States (and they seemed to invest both the man and

* Among the Americans in Paris when Wilson arrived was Captain Harry S. Truman, on leave from the front: "I don't think I ever saw such an ovation as he received," Truman wrote in a memorandum in 1950.[21]

the country with limitless, almost magical, strength and authority) had dedicated himself to improving their lot.

What Wilson encountered was a diffuse emotional outburst which, at best, signified approval of his most general aims. He was riding the crest of that wave of good feeling which so frequently unites men to high purposes at moments of crisis and deep emotion, and which almost always proves transitory and capricious. Wilson, however, mistook the crowds' adulation for a reliable indication that they would approve his specific attitudes, not yet enunciated, on concrete problems. He had yet to learn that it was one thing to inspire a crowd to cheer itself hoarse for him, for "justice" and for the League of Nations, and quite another to gain its support in opposition to its leaders' specific demands. Clemenceau, Lloyd George and Orlando also spoke of peace and justice. If they and Wilson disagreed as to the best way to the millennium, Wilson had little reason to suppose that on specific issues he, rather than their own leaders, would have the support of the people of Europe.

In late December, 1918, two events occurred which might have given pause to a more realistic statesman than Wilson. First, Lloyd George won an overwhelming victory in the British elections, after a campaign in which he pledged to work for the Draconian peace demanded by a public full of hatred of the Germans. Second, while Wilson was in England sounding the need for a league and a new approach to international affairs, Clemenceau appeared before the Chamber of Deputies and proclaimed his adherence, in his words, to the "old system of alliances called the 'balance of power.'" He declared his unwillingness to entrust French security to the untried schemes proposed with "noble simplicity (*noble candeur*)" by President Wilson[22] The Deputies registered their approval of his position with a resounding vote of confidence.

Colonel House wrote in his diary that Clemenceau's victory constituted "as bad an augury for the success of progressive principles at the Peace Conference as we could have. Coming on the heels of the English elections, and taking into consideration the result of recent elections in the United States, the situation strategically could not be worse."[23]

Wilson's evaluation of public opinion, however, seems not to have been affected one whit by these external events.[24] He entered the council chambers full of the exalted feeling that he represented "humanity" and that, in accordance with God's will, he was going to construct a new world order.

While Wilson was receiving the accolades of worshipful admirers in three nations, French and Italian troops took possession of certain disputed territories and the Allied negotiators had an opportunity—for which they were most eager—to observe Wilson at first hand.

Any proficient diplomat, in formulating his strategy, takes into account the psychological characteristics of his negotiating adversaries the more effectively to advance his own objectives. The British, French and Italian leaders had worked together during the war. They had established among themselves cordial personal relations and, if not agreement on some of the problems which now faced them, at least mutual understanding of their various points of view. Wilson was an unknown quantity. His unprecedented popularity with the people of Europe as well as the conflicting stories they had heard about his personality made him a particularly intriguing mystery.

Lloyd George acknowledges frankly in his account of the Conference that the Allied leaders were curious as to what manner of man Wilson was and what his real aims were. Sir William Wiseman, a young British diplomat who during the war had won the confidence of both Wilson and House, was a rich source of information. For two hours one evening shortly before the Conference began, Lloyd George interrogated him on Wilson's personal characteristics, and eagerly took notes as Wiseman discoursed on Wilson's ambitions and susceptibilities.[25]

To Wilson, of course, the League was, as he termed it, the "central object of our meeting," the "keystone of the arch."[26] Wilson's pre-Conference speeches in France, England and Italy revolved about the necessity for making a league the core of the Treaty. (He represented himself as simply the responsive instrument of American public opinion in thus preoccupying himself with the League—a claim that infuriated his opponents at home.) On the very day Wilson arrived in Paris, he told House that once the League was established, other difficult problems would disappear.[27]

There is considerable documentary evidence to prove that the British and French also favored the establishment of an international organization. However, they attached primary importance to the substance of the specific territorial and economic settlements they were about to make. Such substantive questions Wilson regarded as significant but, after all, transitory problems which did not compare in importance to the establishment of permanent machinery to settle international disputes.

Lloyd George had his first business discussion with Wilson on December 27, 1918. He reported to the Cabinet a few days later that the President had "opened at once with the question of the League of Nations and had given the impression that that was the only thing that he really cared much about." He wanted the League to be the first item on the agenda. "Both Mr. Lloyd George and Mr. Balfour were inclined to agree," state the minutes of the Cabinet meeting, "*on the ground that this would ease other matters, such as the questions of the 'Freedom of the Seas,' the disposal of the German colonies, economic issues, etc.*" [28]

Plainly, the British Prime Minister had gained the impression in his first encounter with Wilson that he could trade his approval for the immediate formation of a league (not a very great concession on his part, since a league was part and parcel of the British program!), for Wilson's agreement to certain British proposals, the adoption of which would conflict with the Fourteen Points. At one point in the Cabinet meeting, the Australian Prime Minister remarked that the League to Wilson was like a toy to a child—he would not be happy until he got it. The British, in their natural effort to explore every means for achieving British aims, had quickly discovered that the President had a deep personal involvement in the League which they could probably exploit.

Whether the French had come to a similar conclusion even before the Conference began—they certainly did later—cannot be established on the basis of available data. It is worth noting, however, that after speaking with Wilson for about an hour at their initial meeting on December 15, 1918, Clemenceau told Wilson that he had been opposed to his remaining at the Conference as a delegate, but now hoped the President would participate in the negotiations as the chief American delegate. To Colonel House, who escorted him downstairs, Clemenceau expressed his "keen delight" with Wilson. "This change of view on M. Clemenceau's part," Lloyd George suggests in his book, "meant that the astute French Premier had found during his conversations with President Wilson that he was more amenable than had been anticipated." [29]

In the period preceding the opening of the Conference, White,

Lansing and Bliss, who had not been taken into the President's confidence regarding the League (or anything else), were at a loss to know precisely how most usefully to occupy themselves: the President had not even indicated how he intended to divide the responsibilities of the Conference among the Commissioners.

Lansing and White had hoped to confer with Wilson aboard the *George Washington*, en route to the Conference. To their disappointment, Wilson had had only a few desultory conversations with them which left them as much in the dark as ever about his plans.

Henry White went to see Clemenceau on the first day he was in Paris. White had once been American Ambassador to France, and they knew each other well. Apparently thinking that Wilson might use White for private exchanges of views, Clemenceau declared himself at White's disposal, day or night. Some years later, in a letter to Mrs. Wilson, White wrote that, to his great regret, he never had occasion to make use of Clemenceau's invitation: the President had given him no opportunity to help in that fashion. White also pointed out that he and his fellow Commissioners were unaware for much of the time of what was going on at the Conference, a fact which made teamwork and the rendering of any real assistance to the President impossible.[30]

Lansing, too, tried to make himself useful in the absence of any assignment from Wilson. He had inferred (he did not *know*, for Wilson had never shown the Secretary of State his plan for the League of Nations Covenant) that Wilson's League Covenant contained a provision committing the United States to punitive military action against aggressors. He foresaw that such a pledge would encounter difficulty in the Senate, and drafted tentative articles of guarantee which, in his opinion, were more likely to be approved than the one he thought Wilson had in mind. Lansing submitted his memoranda to Wilson on December 23. The President never acknowledged them.

Another source of concern to Lansing was the President's apparent lack of a concrete program which would provide the Commissioners with knowledge of the specific positions the President wished them to take in dealing with the multitude of problems they would be called upon to negotiate. As the days passed and Wilson showed no sign of being even aware of the problem, Lansing undertook to bridge the gap by having the legal advisers of the Commission prepare a skeleton treaty covering the subjects likely to be discussed. When, on January 10, 1919, Lansing mentioned this project at one of Wilson's rare meetings with the Commissioners, the President snapped that he did not intend to have lawyers drafting the Treaty. Lansing, being the only lawyer on the Commission (besides Wilson himself), took the remark as a personal insult, and abandoned this work. He also decided not to make any further suggestions about the League Covenant since the President had ignored previous ones.

General Bliss shared Lansing's concern about the President's failure to brief the Commissioners adequately. He wrote his wife (on December 18, 1918) that he was "disquieted to see how hazy and vague our ideas are."[31] On January 11, 1919, he wrote Newton D. Baker that he was disturbed because he did not know the President's exact views on various problems. What would happen, he wondered, were Mr. Balfour, for example, to ask him the view of the American delegation on such and such a matter? American delegates might constantly contradict each other and seem to be in disagreement. Sometimes, wrote Bliss, it seemed to him that it would be better if the United States had only one representative.[32] No more eloquent summary of the President's treatment of him could be composed than the title given by his biographer to the chapter dealing with Bliss at the Conference: "His Wisdom in Shackles."[33]

In varying degrees, all of Wilson's colleagues on the Commission were distressed at their relationship with the President even before the Conference began. Lansing, White and Bliss were vexed by Wilson's obvious unwillingness to permit them to share in the real work of the Conference. Only Colonel House enjoyed the President's confidence. Only to House did the President confide his plans. He sought the Colonel's advice and informed him in detail about conversations with various statesmen. He used House to sound out his European colleagues, and to smooth out difficulties. On January 1, 1919, House wrote in his diary:

> The President and I transact a great deal of business in a very short time. He seldom or never argues with me after I have told him that I have looked into a matter and have reached a conclusion. He signs letters, documents and papers without question.

House's attitude toward Lansing, Bliss and White seems to have been one of faintly contemptuous pity. He wrote in his diary (on January 8, 1919) that although his fellow Commissioners were willing to help, they were in fact a hindrance. The President, he continued, seemed to have no intention of using them effectively.

It is the story of Washington over again. We settle matters between the two of us and he seems to consider that sufficient without even notifying the others. I feel embarrassed every day when I am with them.

Each morning, Commissioner White would present himself at the Colonel's office to receive whatever news House was willing to communicate to him. House thought, as he noted in his diary, that there was something pathetic in White's eager efforts to keep informed.[34] An offhand note in his diary on February 21, 1919, to the effect that he had asked White to attend a meeting in his stead because nothing of importance was to come up, eloquently bespeaks his attitude. When Lansing consulted House about the advisability of drafting a skeleton treaty, the Colonel encouraged him to undertake the project in order to keep him busy, as he noted in his diary (on January 3, 1919).

As we have seen, his preferred status notwithstanding, House, too, was dissatisfied with the President. The core of his disaffection seems to have been his desire himself to head the United States Peace Commission.

By mid-January the Allies were ready to begin work. Wilson, too, was eager to start. Paris was crowded with delegates from all over the world, with representatives of a thousand different causes, each seeking a chance to plead his case, and with a veritable army of newsmen. The stage was set. The principal actors each had a role he wished to play. Together—out of their hopes and fears, reactions to one another and to a myriad of pressures—they were about to create one of the great dramas of human history.

# CHAPTER XII

# THE PARIS PEACE CONFERENCE

> You can imagine, gentlemen, I dare say, the sentiments and the purpose with which representatives of the United States support this great project for a League of Nations. We regard it as the keystone of the whole program which expressed our purposes and ideals in this war and which the associated nations have accepted as the basis of the settlement. If we returned to the United States without having made every effort in our power to realize this program, we should return to meet the merited scorn of our fellow citizens. For they are a body that constitutes a great democracy. . . . We have no choice but to obey their mandate. . . . We would not dare abate a single part of the program which constitutes our instruction.
>
> President Wilson, January 25, 1919, to a plenary session of the Paris Peace Conference.[1]

On January 12, 1919, Clemenceau, Lloyd George, Orlando and Wilson held their first official meeting. Each was accompanied by his foreign minister. It was this group of men, later joined by the two leaders of the Japanese delegation, M. Matsui and Viscount Chinda, which comprised the Council of Ten. The Council met every weekday, except one, for a little over a month, until February 14, when Wilson left the Conference for a brief visit to the United States.

The chiefs of delegation of the five great powers—Great Britain, France, the United States, Italy and Japan—quickly decided that they should maintain strict control over the proceedings and decisions of the Conference. The Council of Ten would decide what subjects the Conference as a whole should consider. Preliminary decisions on the most important issues would be made by the big powers in the Council and then referred to plenary sessions, at which all the victor nations were represented, for formal approval. Meanwhile, the small powers were invited to submit memoranda on any questions of interest to them as well as on several specific subjects.

For reasons which have never been fully explained, the leaders of the big powers failed to adopt any one of several available plans for a systematic procedure of business. Instead, matters were allowed to drift, and the structure of the Conference was erected piecemeal as the Council of Ten perceived specific needs. A great deal of time was consumed in the meetings of the Council itself in hearing detailed factual reports and in long-winded, inconclusive discussions of matters of secondary importance.

Colonel House, confined to his rooms by an attack of influenza, was deeply distressed by the reports he had that the Council was frittering away its time. "Unless something is done to pull the delegates together and to get them down to work," he wrote in his diary on January 21, 1919, ". . . I am afraid the sessions will be interminable." The difficulty, as House saw it, was lack of organization.[2] He thought it essential that committees be appointed to deal with various subjects. Whether or not he suggested this to the President—he *had* taken it up with Sir William Wiseman of the British staff—we do not know. In any case, Wilson, too, was impatient with the Council's lack of accomplishment.

On January 29, after a particularly wearing session, complicated by the fact that the British and Americans had contradictory information before them, President Wilson suggested to two of the American experts that they confer with their British counterparts, and present joint reports. The experts eagerly accepted the suggestion. The other members of the Council, too, approved giving their respective experts the task of co-ordinating their information on various problems and thrashing out as many problems as they could. Within the next few days the Council set up commissions to consider Rumanian, Polish, Czechoslovak, Greek and Albanian affairs. The task of the various special commissions became, in effect, that of drafting what were to become various sections of the proposed treaty. Thus the American experts, to their surprise and pleasure, became negotiators.[3]

The position within their respective national delegations of the American, French and British experts differed in a few crucial respects. Whereas the French and British were informed in detail of the positions they were expected to take in various matters, the Americans were not guided by a detailed plan or draft treaty. The American experts had Wilson's Fourteen Points and a few other general statements as a point of reference, but these policy directives were too vague to indicate a precise position on each of the hundreds of problems at hand. And if the Fourteen Points had relevance to a particular problem, it frequently happened that there were several applicable principles and that a solution which satisfied one principle would violate another. Adequate machinery for arriving at a balanced American position was lacking. Further, whereas their opposite numbers were systematically informed of the proceedings in all the commissions, the American experts worked without knowing how their colleagues were dealing with other, related problems.

Wilson's failure to guide his aides adequately resulted not merely from passive neglect of this aspect of his responsibilities. As we have seen, he actively rejected the Secretary of State's attempt to provide him with a draft treaty. It is not enough to say that Wilson put a stop to Lansing's effort because he lacked confidence in him. Had he wanted a draft treaty, he could have set House or the experts to work on one. This the President did not do. Having chosen not to provide for such a systematic working-through in advance of the problems likely to arise, Wilson conceivably could have used his fellow Commissioners to co-ordinate the work of the experts. As we have seen, however, even before the Conference began, Lansing, White and Bliss had been demoralized by Wilson's obvious wish that they confine their activities gracefully to keeping out of his way. His negative attitude toward them became even more distressingly apparent after the negotiations got under way. Their diaries and letters furnish vivid, sometimes heated, documentation of the fact that Wilson gave them little to do and kept them in abysmal, humiliating ignorance of his own views and plans.

Commissioners Lansing, White, and Bliss, then, were in no position to disembarrass the experts. Wilson deliberately constricted the contribution which subordinates might have made to policy formation. Further, he deliberately stopped up the channels through which guidance usually flows from an executive to his aides. The result was a mutual isolation of the President on the one hand, and his staff on the other. Willy-nilly, the experts (and the Commissioners) found themselves cast into the role of policy makers on the various commissions. To a large extent independently of each other, the President and his staff each engaged in the entire process of policy formation to which each more properly should have contributed a part to form a co-ordinated whole.

From the experts' paradoxical role at the Conference have derived varying and contradictory estimates of whether or not Wilson satisfactorily delegated authority. Some writers, impressed by the fact that the experts enjoyed considerable freedom of action on the commissions, attribute to Wilson a generous willingness to depute authority to others. It must be noted, however, that the experts fell heir to their influence more by virtue of a vacuum created by Wilson's neglect than from any considered delegation of authority on his part.

The degree to which the President wished them to assume a policy-making role being obscure, and his attitude on so many issues unknown, the experts tended to play passive roles in the various commissions. They surrendered the initiative to the British and French representatives, who were more than willing to furnish the plans on which discussion should be based. "One of the extraordinary things about the Peace Conference," writes Ray Stannard Baker (who was himself on the staff of the American delegation), ". . . was the efficiency of the British and French Foreign Offices, or diplomatic machines. They always had a plan ready: always had it minutely worked out. Even in the minor committees, upon one or two of which I sat, no sooner was a question broached than the French or British had an elaborate plan, beautifully typewritten. . . ."[4]

The fact that commission discussions generally revolved about French and British drafts was of great significance in terms of the final text of the Treaty. For, as usually happens, the initial concrete proposals more or less established the context of debate and tended to carry except where there were serious objections. Changes in the proposed drafts could be made only by amendments, which are not only relatively difficult to obtain but, too incessantly demanded, make a negotiator seem obstructionist. In these circumstances, the American negotiators allowed a host of formulations representing the British and French points of view to pass unchallenged into the Treaty.

Wilson's attitude toward his staff reflected his predilection for operating exclusively and for focussing on that which interested him—in this case the League of Nations—to the detriment of other, sometimes equally important, matters. Another unfortunate effect of his tendency to isolate himself from his staff was that it multiplied the chances that in those crucial transactions of which he took personal charge, his shortcomings as a negotiator would find expression. Any statesman who enters into complex negotiations stands to profit greatly from the intellectual ballast which trusted counsel can provide. It can serve to broaden his perception and strain out errors into which personal viewpoints lead him. So many of Wilson's personal goals revolved about the establishment of the League of Nations that, especially in the latter part of the Conference, he was incapable of estimating his negotiating position realistically. He of all men stood to benefit from the sense of proportion that more tranquil negotiators might have infused into United States policy. But he brusquely shunted aside most of the personnel and procedures which might have improved his perspective. He left himself wide open to the exploitation of his skilled antagonists, who were more than a little alert to the possibility of playing upon his personal weaknesses to further their diplomatic objectives.

Not for a moment during the Conference did Wilson's attention waver from what he considered the most important task at hand—the creation of a league of nations. He wanted the Treaty to contain not merely a commitment to form a league at some future time, but the text of its constitution as well.

There was considerable feeling in the various delegations (including the American) that in view of the urgent necessity to restore order in Europe, the composition of the League constitution should be postponed and top priority given to the settlement of those military and political terms acceptance of which would have an immediately stabilizing effect. Wilson would not hear of it. He made speech after speech in the Council of Ten insisting that the composition of the League constitution was the first order of business.

Lloyd George and Clemenceau, somewhat mystified by the President's obsessive concern with the League, were willing to indulge him. On January 22, 1919, the Council of Ten accepted a resolution embodying Wilson's desires, providing for a special League commission to draft a covenant. On January 25, it was unanimously adopted by the Conference in plenary session, after an impassioned speech on its behalf by Wilson.

This obeisance to Wilson's *idée fixe* having been made, the Allies succeeded in turning the Council's attention to a subject which greatly excited their interest—the disposition of the German colonies. On one point, all the great powers were agreed: the German colonies must not be returned to Germany. Beyond that shared conviction, there was a deep cleavage of opinion.

Clemenceau, Baron Makino and Lloyd George, who was under severe pressure from the Dominion representatives, favored a division and outright annexation of Germany's overseas possessions. Wilson regarded these demands as a manifestation of selfish imperialism and argued that the German colonies should be administered in the interest of their native populations by powers appointed by the League of Nations to act as mandatories. As for Italy, Orlando declared himself willing to accept whatever solution the other powers favored, provided Italy were assigned her proper share "in the work of civilization." [5]

Wilson's preference to reserve the problem to the League of Nations startled and angered the Allies, most particularly the British Dominion representatives (including General Smuts, the author of the mandates plan). They wanted immediate satisfaction of their claims, and they did not take kindly to the possibility that their exploitation of these areas might be limited by League regulations. The League was still no more than a dream, they argued, not even yet created, much less in effective operation. Whether it would ever be able to perform the multiplicity of functions which the President envisaged was a moot question. In any case, if Wilson's point of view prevailed, they declared, the Council might as well adjourn until the League came into being. Besides, here in the Council were the major powers who would deal with the issue in the League, so why not at once take the necessary decisions?

The Council meeting of January 28 adjourned with Wilson in seemingly hopeless disagreement with the Allies. On the morning of January 29, General Smuts came to House with a compromise proposal. It provided for acceptance of the principle that the German colonies be administered through mandatories on behalf of the League of Nations—this to satisfy President Wilson. To satisfy the British Dominions, it provided that certain territories, some of which were specifically named, "be administered under the laws of the mandatory state as if they were integral portions thereof." [6] Smuts' formula would place the German colonies under League control, but it would also create one type of mandatory relationship which approximated annexation. House favored it.

It taxed Lloyd George's persuasive powers to commit the Dominion chiefs to this compromise solution. Nothing that he, House or anyone else said or did, however, could draw Wilson that far. He would agree to the Smuts formula, he declared at the January 30 Council meeting, subject to reconsideration when the full scheme of the League was completed. His statement of acceptance pointedly omitted any reference to the various Dominions as mandatories for the particular areas which Smuts had specifically enumerated. The President had given no promise that any state would be handed the mandate to any area. The Dominion representatives fumed at this omission and irately demanded that Wilson rectify it. Wilson declined to do so. For several hours, the air was filled with acrimonious protest. By the end of the day, however, the Dominion chiefs had unwillingly subsided.

Thus the controversy ended with the great powers committed to accepting the application of the mandate principle. Wilson had committed himself only temporarily to the British compromise proposal. All in all, this was a gratifying outcome for Wilson to the first large-scale diplomatic battle of the Conference.

Lloyd George and Clemenceau decided not to sit on the League commission personally, but rather to apply their energies to settling matters of general principles, supervising the work of the various commissions, and being available for consultation when difficulties arose. Wilson, however, decided to sit on the League commission himself. Orlando and the chief Japanese delegates followed suit. Lloyd George was highly critical of the President's decision. Had there been any question of the devotion to the League ideal of the other commission members, he later wrote, Wilson's sacrifice would have been justified. But all were League zealots. The British Prime Minister construed Wilson's action as an indication that "the League of Nations meant, if not the whole Treaty, at least the only part of the Treaty in which he was interested." [7] As second American delegate, Wilson appointed the only other Commissioner for whom he had any regard—Colonel House.

For eleven days, beginning on February 3, President Wilson attended the meetings of both the League commission and the Council of Ten. All of these meetings were long and exacting. A few times the President was in conference until after midnight. In addition, Wilson was daily confronted with piles of important reports, with a long list of callers, with queries and information from Washington. He was deluged with requests for interviews, and for his presence at social affairs.

Wilson had only two stenographers at the Conference. He had made no arrangements for an adequate clerical and secretarial staff and did not make efficient use of the one Colonel House placed at his disposal. "It was a constant grief to me," House wrote in his diary, "to see him working in his lonely, inefficient way when there was so much depending upon the conserving of his strength and keeping his mind clear for sound judgment."[8] Years later, Lloyd George said: "The rest of us found time for golf and we took Sundays off, but Wilson, in his zeal, worked incessantly. Only those who were there and witnessed it can realize the effort he expended."[9]

Wilson dominated the League commission, and drove through his Covenant, with the same tenacity and unalterable determination with which he had dominated (initially, at least) the trustees at Princeton, the New Jersey legislature and the Congress of the United States. Once again, the strength of his motivation and his driving will to overcome all obstacles contributed to his success in an important enterprise. A less strongly motivated man might have contented himself with a general commitment to the League idea. He might have found the difficulties of reaching agreement too formidable to overcome. He might have considered it impossible to work on the League Covenant while simultaneously transacting a full load of business in the Council of Ten. Precisely because his effort was sustained by compelling inner needs, Wilson was able to mobilize what seemed almost superhuman energy for his work and to clear hurdles that would have felled most other men. In speaking so often in the course of this narrative of Wilson's personal involvement in the League as a source of difficulty to him, we do not want to minimize the fact that the root of his successes, too, often lay in his personal involvements.

Wilson wholeheartedly threw himself into the task of drafting the Covenant. Presiding over the commission was a joy to him. Employing his oratorical skills to excellent effect in such a noble purpose was a taste of fulfillment. Many who observed him noted the keen pleasure he took in this endeavor and the exceptional skill he brought to it. House, for example, wrote in his diary on February 7, 1919, after the League commission had met a few times, that the President liked and excelled in this type of work, and did it better than any one he had ever known.[10]

The President had brought from Washington a draft of the Covenant which he had written on the basis of Colonel House's draft of July 16, 1918. Shortly after his arrival in Paris, the President read the proposals for a league drawn up by General Smuts of the South African delegation. He was greatly struck by some of Smuts' formulations, particularly those relating to the functioning of the league council and the administration of backward areas of the world through a system of mandates. Wilson rewrote his own draft, incorporating (with some significant changes) a number of Smuts' proposals. (Incidentally, he contrived to make this new version, completed in the first week of January, 1919, contain thirteen articles—thirteen being his favorite number—by the somewhat awkward expedient of calling six provisions not "articles" but "supplementary agreements.") This draft was circulated for comment to the American Commissioners and to David Hunter Miller, one of the legal advisers to the United States Commission. Utilizing some of their suggestions and additional proposals from European sources, Wilson wrote a third draft of the Covenant, which was printed on January 20.

In addition to Wilson's third draft, there existed an Italian draft, a French draft, and a British draft, written by Lord Robert Cecil, a staunch advocate of the League, who later played a prominent role in it when it began operations.

The American and British drafts were sufficiently similar to warrant an attempt to compose their differences and produce a joint Anglo-American draft. This task House undertook with the assistance of Cecil J. B. Hurst for the British and David Hunter Miller. At first Wilson was pleased with the progress made by the new drafting group and agreed in advance to accept the product of its labors as the basis for discussion in the League commission. When the completed Anglo-American text was shown to him the evening before its scheduled submission to the commission, however, Wilson complained that it had "no warmth or color in it" and said he preferred his own draft.[11] House tried to persuade him to accept the joint Anglo-American text, as he had promised to do. Wilson refused and instructed House and Miller to revise his own text, incorporating a few of the changes suggested in the Anglo-American version, and to have it ready in time for its scheduled presentation. The redoubtable Miller stayed up all night and had the new document ready by breakfast time the following morning.

When the British learned that Wilson had decided, peremptorily, to discard the Anglo-American draft and substitute his own, they were greatly aroused. Only after strong representations from House and a heated last-minute protest by Lord Cecil was the President persuaded to return to the joint Anglo-American draft as the commission's working document.

Thus, though not a single idea in the Covenant originated with Wilson, his constant concern was to reserve to himself final authorship of the document. He had constructed his drafts on the basis of other men's suggestions, but always he had been free to select, reject and rephrase according to his own tastes. For the first time bound by agreement to accept a specific draft Covenant for a specific purpose, he had promptly tried to bolt and re-establish his own unilateral control of the proceedings. At the last moment, however, he had reconsidered and the joint Anglo-American draft was launched for consideration.

The commission's procedure was simple: it took up the Anglo-American draft, article by article, making amendments and other alterations. There were some clashes of opinion, but all were speedily composed. On February 13, by meeting both morning and afternoon, the League commission completed its revision of the Covenant. The document was now ready to be presented to the representatives of all the nations and, accordingly, a plenary session was arranged for the next day, February 14.

The completion of the Covenant before his impending departure for the United States represented the fulfillment of Wilson's most cherished plan. Yet, in his hour of triumph, the President was disturbed by the fact that his draft had been altered as a result of the discussions in the League commission. He confided to House that he still preferred the version they had agreed upon at Magnolia the summer before.[12]

At the February 12 meeting of the Council of Ten, Clemenceau raised the problem of Wilson's impending departure for the United States. Wilson explained that he would be gone from the Conference for about a month, that he did not want consideration of reparations and territorial adjustments held up during his absence, and that he had asked Colonel House to take his place while he was away.[13]

Although Wilson had asked House "to take his place" while he was absent from Paris, he does not appear to have given the Colonel instructions regarding the conduct of the negotiations. On the morning of February 14, the day the President left Paris, he conferred with House. House, according to his diary, took the opportunity to outline the plan of procedure he had in mind: ". . . We could button up everything during the next four weeks. He [Wilson—Ed.] seemed startled and even alarmed at this statement. I therefore explained that the plan was not to actually bring these matters to a final conclusion but to have them ready for him to do so when he returned. . . ." House enumerated the broad problems he thought required immediate attention: German disarmament, Germany's boundaries, reparations and the economic policies to be applied to Germany. "I asked him if he had anything else to suggest in addition to these four articles," House wrote in his diary that night. "He thought they were sufficient." [14]

House's exposition to Wilson of his intended work schedule and Wilson's acquiescence in it are significant in view of the charges made later that House "betrayed" Wilson's program during the President's absence from Paris. It is also significant that House tried to forewarn Wilson of the unpleasant necessity of compromising with the Allies:

> I asked him to bear in mind while he was gone that it was sometimes necessary to compromise in order to get things through; not a compromise of principle but a compromise of detail; he had made many since he had been here. I did not wish him to leave expecting the impossible in all things.[15]

That afternoon at 3:30 P.M., the President read the Covenant to a plenary session of the Conference and made a speech commending it to the assembled delegates. When he sat down, House wrote him a note:

> Dear Governor,
> Your speech was as great as the occasion—
> I am very happy—
> EMH

Wilson replied:

> Bless your heart. Thank you from the bottom of my heart.
> WW [16]

This exchange is worth reproducing because it indicates that outwardly, at least, Wilson and House were still on excellent terms. A few hours later, House (as well as a host of foreign dignitaries) accompanied the President and Mrs. Wilson to a Paris railroad station to see them off. "The President," House recorded in his diary, "bade me a fervent good-bye, clasping my hand and placing his arm around me." [17]

House probably did not realize it at the time, but this was farewell to the intimate friendship which had existed between the President and him for seven years. For after Wilson's return to Paris, he placed a barrier of cool reserve between himself and his old friend which House, for all his eager efforts to maintain the old relationship, could not penetrate.

A host of writers—men who themselves participated in the proceedings, men close to the leading figures in Paris, journalists who did their research while the great events were unfolding—have written of Wilson's impact upon his old world colleagues. Friend or foe of Wilson's ideas, almost to a man they have testified to the blank astonishment with which his colleagues reacted to his singular negotiating manner. In his account of the Conference, Lloyd George wrote:

> It was part of the real joy of these Conferences to observe Clemenceau's attitude toward Wilson during the first five weeks of the Conference. . . . If the President took a flight beyond the azure main, as he was occasionally inclined to do without regard to relevance, Clemenceau would open his great eyes in twinkling wonder, and turn them on me as much as to say: "Here he is off again!"
>
> I really think that at first the idealistic President regarded himself as a missionary whose function it was to rescue the poor European heathen from their age-long worship of false and fiery gods. . . .
>
> . . . His most extraordinary outburst was when he was developing some theme—I rather think it was connected with the League of Nations—which led him to explain the failure of Christianity to achieve its highest ideals. "Why," he said, "has Jesus Christ so far not succeeded in inducing the world to follow His teaching in these matters? It is because He taught the ideal without devising any practical means of attaining it. That is the reason why I am proposing a practical scheme to carry out His aims." Clemenceau slowly opened his dark eyes to their widest dimensions and swept them round the Assembly to see how the Christians gathered around the table enjoyed this exposure of the futility of their Master.[18]

The backbone of Wilson's philosophy of international relations was the idea that nations should be guided in their actions by precepts of the highest moral order. For considerations of self-interest, where these seemed to conflict with this conception, he had nothing but contempt. Toward statesmen whose foremost concern was to secure their own nation's well-being Wilson's attitude was that of a zealous preacher bent upon leading lost souls to the path of salvation.

Human beings and their history being what they are, Wilson's splendid ideal was more likely to be realized not by converting diplomats to the novel theory that the pursuit of self-interest is wicked, but rather by a gradual broadening of their conception of what constitutes self-interest. As it was, Wilson's behavior did not convince Clemenceau and Lloyd George. It amazed them. Such statements as that which the President once made to the Council that "the central idea of the League of Nations was that States must support each other even when their interests were not involved" [19] certainly did not inspire enthusiasm for either the League or its American champion.

As a matter of fact, a very effective case in terms of enlightened self-interest could have been made for many of Wilson's ideas about the peace. The President's tendency, however, was to define the negotiating situation in terms of a simple dichotomy: on the one side, abstract morality; on the other, wicked self-interest. In a self-righteous manner he importuned his fellow negotiators to embrace the former and cast away the latter. The Allied negotiators regarded Wilson as an eccentric—an individual they must humor because of the power which his position conferred upon him, but not one whose views they as "practical" men could take seriously.

If anything were needed to confirm in Lloyd George's and Clemenceau's judgment that Wilson was an impractical visionary, his failure to put forward specific proposals for the application of his principles to the particular problems at hand doubtless served the purpose.

Wilson's approach to negotiation was highly unconventional. He seemed to think that he ought to play a judicial role, simply applying the yardstick of his principles to the proposals which the various foreign statesmen made. Negotiation did not seem to strike him as essentially a bargaining process for the purpose of arriving at a mutually satisfactory accommodation of national interests. "Bargaining" was part and parcel of the evil old diplomacy which it was his purpose to supplant with a higher ethic.

Not for him the tactic, habitually employed by his diplomatic adversaries, of developing demands as bargaining points, deliberately taking exaggerated positions in the expectation of later retreating in exchange for one or another concession. Whenever Wilson retreated, he yielded some of the substance of his position, not nonessentials prepared as an expendable negotiating margin. Others might extract the maximal *quid pro quo* from him, but he would not stoop to such conduct when he assented to the demands of others: issues must be decided upon their merits and if a claim were justifiable it should be unconditionally acceded to.

Nor was the President willing to express himself in a way calculated to cater to the sensibilities of the men with whom he was dealing. He delivered pronunciamentos based on the verities embodied in his principles. For Wilson, truth was truth and justice, justice; and there was no need to modify their expression to suit any man.

House, who shared Wilson's hopes for a reasonable peace, understood the importance of appealing to the various statesmen in terms of their own values. He wrote in his diary on April 14, 1919:

> The reason I get along with Clemenceau better than the President does is that in talking of such matters as this Russian question, the President talks to him as he would to me, while I never think of using the same argument with Clemenceau as I use with the President. One is an idealist, the other a practical old-line statesman. When I told him about Russia and the good it would do France and the rest of us to open it up, he saw at once and was willing. If I had told him it was to save life in Russia and to make things easier there for the sick, for the weak and for the helpless, it would have had no effect.

Once, reminiscing about the Conference, House remarked that Wilson was never able to understand the value of personal appeal in conducting negotiations. He always felt that if logic were on his side, nothing else was necessary. He mesmerized himself with his own speeches, but he did not mesmerize Clemenceau and Lloyd George. They, thought House, probably did not even listen.[20]

Several days before the President's departure for home, Colonel House suggested to him that he invite the members of the Foreign Relations Committees of both houses of Congress to dine with him at the White House for the purpose of discussing the League Covenant. Ominous reports of growing opposition to Wilson had reached the Colonel—indeed, they were being widely circulated in the newspapers—and he wanted to persuade Wilson, if he could, to take the opportunity of his visit home to soothe the ruffled feelings of some members of Congress.

Wilson's first reaction to House's suggestion was to reject it. The most he was willing to do was to make an address to Congress on the subject. To the astute Colonel, who knew the sort of unfavorable impression Wilson in an imperious mood made on his fellows, the alternative which Wilson proposed seemed wholly inadequate. ". . . It would not please Congress," he noted in his diary, "since they would take it that he had called them together as a schoolmaster, as they claim he usually does. There would be no chance for discussion, consultation, or explanation, and they would not regard it as a compliment but rather the contrary." [21]

So keenly aware was he of the disastrous possibilities inherent in the deteriorating relations between Wilson and Congress that House pressed his suggestion despite the President's negative reaction to it. Wilson finally agreed, reluctantly, and arrangements were made for a White House dinner with members of the Foreign Relations Committees of the two houses of Congress.

If Wilson's personal partisans hoped he would take advantage of the opportunity his trip home afforded of placating the Senate, so, too, did adherents of the League idea, such as William Howard Taft, who were not admirers of the President personally.

Throughout the battle in the United States about the League of Nations, ex-President Taft did more, perhaps, than any other individual to mobilize public support for the idea of United States entry into the new international organization. After the Republican victory in the election of November, 1918, Taft warned Lodge and other Republican Senate leaders that "should they develop obstructive tactics while the President is attempting to carry out a policy in the interest of the country and the world the party will be made to suffer for it at the next election." [22] At the same time, he urged Wilson to consult with the Senate Foreign Relations Committee during the peace negotiations, and to appoint a few Senators as negotiators.

Taft considered the establishment of an effective league crucial to the maintenance of world peace. To his mind, the issue transcended party politics and personal feelings. Some of his letters reveal that he disliked Wilson who, as he put it, "by his brutal ignoring of the Senate" and "his determination to hog all the credit of negotiating the treaty" was partly responsible for the growing opposition to the League in the Senate. He summed up his attitude in a letter to J. G. Butler (March 17, 1919):

> I don't like Wilson any better than you do, but I think I can rise above my personal attitude . . . in order to help along the world and the country. I don't care who gets the credit for the League of Nations, if it goes through.[23]

These were not merely idle words. With unflagging energy, Taft devoted himself to the double task of arousing favorable public opinion, and marshaling the support of Republican Senators for the League. In February, 1919, while Wilson was in Paris, Taft toured fifteen states speaking in favor of the League.

While Taft was thus trying to facilitate President Wilson's task, Lodge and his colleagues were perfecting plans to kill the League, and thus inflict a humiliating defeat upon Wilson. Before the League Covenant was published (on February 15, 1919, in American newspapers), the League opponents, having nothing specific to criticize since the Covenant had not yet been presented to them, evolved a formula according to which Wilson could be attacked no matter *what* sort of League proposal he brought home from Paris. *Harvey's Weekly,* edited by George Harvey (once Wilson's most enthusiastic political supporter, and now a mortal foe) had this to say in its issue of February 8, 1919:

> The League of Nations, as we have hitherto pointed out, must be either a strenuous body so transcending nationality as to be impossible of American approval, or a futile thing of pious aspirations and impotent achievement.[24]

In other words, no workable plan was possible: if the League were to have armed forces at its disposal for the enforcement of its decisions, United States sovereignty would be infringed upon and this could never be approved; if the League depended simply on "moral force" to enforce its decisions, it would be nothing more than an impotent debating society. Thus Wilson's enemies hit in advance upon a formulation which made it impossible to satisfy their objections.

It is interesting to note that when the Covenant was first published in the newspapers of February 15, 1919, Wilson's critics had some difficulty deciding whether to take the position that the League would be a futile debating society or unacceptable for the other reason, namely that it would infringe on United States sovereignty. At first, they seemed inclined to discard the latter criticism. Colonel Harvey himself exclaimed, after reading the Covenant:

> Why, there is no force at all created, but the Executive Committee of the League is to "recommend" to the members of the League their proportionate contribution to the armed forces to be used to protect the covenants of the League. Merely "recommend"; and if the recommendation is not favorably received and acted upon, there will be no force at

> all. . . . From the President's own point of view, then, this proposed League would be hopelessly inefficient and futile.[25]

The New York *Sun* committed the blunder of admitting, in its initial reaction to the Covenant, that "it ingeniously and successfully avoids the constitutional objection . . . with regard to the absolute control of Congress over the beginning of war." [26] It was only later, when it became obvious to them that the tactic would be useful, that Wilson's critics were suddenly struck by the dire perils of Article X.

While Wilson was aboard the *George Washington*, the newspapers announced that he would make a speech when his ship docked in Boston—Senator Lodge's home city. This news, and the angry comment of several Senators upon it, came to House's attention in Paris. The Colonel, greatly alarmed, sent a wireless to the President aboard ship urging him to "compliment" the Foreign Relations Committees of Congress by making his first explanation of affairs at the Conference to them.[27]

Wilson did not heed House's advice. The *George Washington* landed on February 24. Governor Coolidge of Massachusetts escorted the President to Mechanics Hall where Wilson, "throwing down the glove of defiance to all Senators and others who oppose the League of Nations" (as the New York *Times* put it the next day), told a cheering audience that the United States must make men free. Otherwise:

> . . . All the fame of America would be gone and all her power would be dissipated. She would then have to keep her power for those narrow, selfish, provincial purposes which seem so dear to some minds that have no sweep beyond the nearest horizon. I should welcome no sweeter challenge than that. I have fighting blood in me and it is sometimes a delight to let it have scope, but if it is challenged on this occasion it will be an indulgence.[28]

It is difficult, a generation after the heat of the League controversy has been dissipated, to convey a sense of the tension which existed at the time between the President and his senatorial opponents. Wilson immediately upon his arrival in the United States had thrown down the gauntlet to his critics. His critics, meanwhile, disregarding the President's request not to debate the Covenant in Congress until after he had had an opportunity to discuss it with them, had been denouncing Wilson and the League from the Senate floor. Most of the Republicans on the Foreign Relations Committees of Congress received the President's invitation to dinner with extreme reserve. Two Senators, Borah and Fall, refused to accept it. By the time the President arrived in Washington, a Republican project was afoot to filibuster and prevent the passage of some essential appropriations bills in the Congressional session then terminating. The strategy was to force Wilson to call a special session of Congress before the beginning of the next fiscal year on July 1. The special session would be organized by the Republicans (in accordance with their victory in the November, 1918, elections) and it would give them an early opportunity to harass the President with criticism from the Senate floor by whatever stratagems they could devise.

In an atmosphere so fraught with personal animosity, it is hardly surprising that Wilson's dinner with the Foreign Relations Committees on February 26 was a dismal failure. The President was courteous and correct in his treatment of his guests. Even Lodge conceded that he was "civil" and "showed no temper." He discussed the League and explained various articles at some length. Then he patiently answered questions. His friends thought Wilson acquitted himself admirably. Lodge and his supporters came away unswayed. Lodge noted in his diary that Wilson "did not seem to know it [the Covenant] very thoroughly and was not able to answer questions. . . . We went away as wise as we came."[29] Senator Brandegee of Connecticut, who, with Senator Knox of Pennsylvania, had been the President's most persistent and hostile interlocutor, expressed himself more picturesquely. "I feel," he was quoted the next day as having remarked, "as if I had been wandering with Alice in Wonderland and had tea with the Mad Hatter."[30]

Two days after the White House dinner, Senator Lodge made a speech in the Senate presenting his views about the Covenant. He urged the postponement of work on the League constitution at least until after a peace treaty with Germany had been concluded. Indeed, Lodge seemed unfavorably disposed to the League at any time—even after the conclusion of a treaty with Germany. He cited Washington's warning against United States involvement in permanent alliances, and warned against abandoning the traditionally honored policy of aloofness without the most careful consideration.

As to the Covenant that Wilson had brought back from Paris, Lodge asserted that it contained hardly a clause about which differences of interpretation did not already exist. As a legal instrument it was imprecise. Imprecisions must be corrected and unacceptable clauses altered before the United States committed itself to such a project. He then outlined his objections to the Covenant: it bound the United States to submit every international dispute to the League, which would therefore be empowered to adjudicate such domestic questions as immigration into the United States: other nations might decide that the United States should admit a flood of Japanese, Chinese and Hindu labor; Article X nullified the Monroe Doctrine, and adherence to it might force this country into war by the decision of other nations; there was no provision for peaceful withdrawal of member nations from the League; it was not specified that a nation might refuse to act as a mandatory.

"Some of these points I think it might be well for those who prepared this draft to consider," Lodge said. "Perhaps I do not regard the drafting committee with the veneration which the Senator from Nebraska [Hitchcock—Ed.] feels toward them; I know some of them, and, without reflecting upon them in any way, I do not think their intellect or position in the world are so overpowering that we can not suggest amendments to this league." [31]

How infuriated Wilson must have been at Lodge's deprecating reference to the intellect of the authors of the Covenant—inadequate intelligence being in both men's eyes one of the most abhorrent of deficiencies—we can only guess. In any event, on the very day of Lodge's speech Wilson received the Democratic National Committee in the White House and gave vent to his rage at his senatorial critics. "If I could really say what I think about them, it would be picturesque," he declared. ". . . The President, if my experience is a standard, is liable some day to burst by merely containing restrained gases. . . . When the lid is off I am going to resume my study of the dictionary to find adequate terms in which to describe the fatuity of these gentlemen with their poor little minds that never get anywhere but run around in a circle and think they are going somewhere. I cannot express my contempt for their intelligence. . . ." He adjured his listeners to "get the true American pattern of warpaint and a real hatchet and go out on the war path and get a collection of scalps that has never been excelled in the history of American warfare." [32]

Wilson also offered the Committeemen a unique explanation for Democratic losses in the Congressional elections of the preceding November. The President did not mention his October appeal, which most observers agreed had boomeranged disastrously against the Democratic Party; nor did he concede that the Republican victory in any way reflected public rejection of his programs. Quite the contrary. Wilson maintained it was because some of the Democratic Congressmen—even if they had been loyal when the time to vote came—had given evidence of a lukewarm attitude toward his programs that the people had voted them out of office. In short, the President advanced the theory that the Republican victory actually signified public wrath against legislators who had been in some degree disloyal to him, their party chief.

Lodge and his friends managed to plant two thorns in the President's side before his return to Europe. On March 4, the day the Congressional session ended, Senator Lodge read to the Senate a declaration, or Round Robin, signed by thirty-nine Republican Senators. The Round Robin made plain its signers' disapproval of the proceedings in Paris and explicitly declared the Covenant in its current form unacceptable. The Round Robin was intended to serve notice on Wilson and on all the negotiators in Paris that more than a third of the Senate were opposed to the Covenant in its current form, and favored the speedy conclusion of a peace treaty with Germany, the problem of a league of nations to be put aside for later consideration. Since ratification of the Treaty would require the support of two-thirds of the Senate, the signers of the Round Robin were numerous enough to kill any treaty which did not meet with their approval. Their unfavorable reaction to the Covenant, therefore, could not be lightly dismissed.

Nor was the Round Robin all. The filibuster which the Republicans had been considering when Wilson arrived in Washington was successfully executed with the result that Congress expired without having passed some indispensable appropriations bills. Wilson would now be forced to call a special session some time before July 1.

Wilson's reaction to events of the preceding forty-eight hours came in a speech delivered in the Metropolitan Opera House in New York on the evening of March 4. Before Wilson spoke, ex-President Taft made a spirited defense of the Covenant. Then Wilson rose and delivered a blistering, defiant speech.

The first thing he would tell the people in Europe, he said, "is that an overwhelming majority of the American people is in favor of the League of Nations. I know that that is true. I have had unmistakable intimations of it from all parts of the country, and the voice rings true in every case." As for the criticisms which had been made of the Covenant: "They do not make any impression on me because I know there is no medium that will transmit them, that the sentiment of the country is proof against such narrowness and such selfishness as that." The President declared himself "amazed—not alarmed but amazed—that there should be in some quarters such a comprehensive ignorance of the state of the world. These gentlemen do not know what the mind of men is just now. Everybody else does. I do not know where they have been closeted, I do not know by what influences they have been blinded, but I do know they have been separated from the general currents of the thought of mankind. . . . I cannot imagine how these gentlemen can live and not live in the atmosphere of the world." He accused his opponents of misinterpreting Washington's utterance about entangling alliances, the meaning of which is clear "if you read what he said, as most of these gentlemen do not." Without mentioning the Round Robin directly, the President revealed his attitude toward its demand that consideration of the League Covenant be postponed until after the peace treaty with Germany had been made. When the Treaty came back, Wilson said, "*Gentlemen on this side will find the Covenant not only in it, but so many threads of the treaty tied to the Covenant that you cannot dissect the Covenant from the treaty without destroying the whole vital structure.*" [33]

An hour after finishing this address, the President and Mrs. Wilson were aboard the *George Washington*, en route back to Paris. On the voyage across, the President seemed to Mrs. Wilson "happy as a boy." [34]

## CHAPTER XIII

# THE "BREAK"

> In a way I realize that in breaking up here it means the end of an epoch in my life, for after the Peace Conference is wound up I feel that I shall do other things than those I have been doing for so many years.
>
> Diary of Edward M. House, June 10, 1919.[1]

The *George Washington*, with the President aboard, arrived in Brest on the evening of March 13. House had come from Paris to greet the President and brief him on events at the Conference during his absence.

What transpired at this first meeting with the President following his return to France is the subject of conflicting accounts. According to Mrs. Wilson, it was a major crisis in the President's life. Immediately after House left, Mrs. Wilson went to her husband:

> Woodrow was standing. The change in his appearance shocked me. He seemed to have aged ten years, and his jaw was set in that way it had when he was making superhuman effort to control himself. Silently he held out his hand, which I grasped, crying: "What is the matter? What has happened?"
>
> He smiled bitterly. "House has given away everything I had won before we left Paris. He has compromised on every side, and so I have to start all over again and this time it will be harder, as he has given the impression that my delegates are not in sympathy with me. His own explanation of his compromises is that, with a hostile press in the United States expressing disapproval of the League of Nations as a part of the Treaty, he thought it best to yield some other points lest the Conference withdraw its approval altogether. So he has yielded until there is nothing left."[2]

In important respects, however, Mrs. Wilson's dramatic account, written some years after the events it describes, does not coincide with the version of the meeting which House committed to his diary at the time. Colonel House's description of the interview in no way suggests displeasure on the President's part with the manner in which the negotiations had been conducted during his absence, though he recorded that Wilson did complain that "your dinner" with the Senators had been a failure. It seems entirely possible that Mrs. Wilson correctly reports the gist of her husband's irritation with House sometime *after* his return to Paris. In retrospect, however, she may have inadvertently attributed to this first meeting at Brest criticisms of House which Wilson made only later.[3]

As a matter of fact, House's critics contradict themselves as to his major misdemeanor during Wilson's absence from the Conference. Mrs. Wilson, as we have seen, reports her husband as accusing House of having compromised on various other issues in order to keep Allied support for the League. On the very next page of her book, however, she makes quite a different charge. Here she writes: "The chief compromise yielded by the Colonel affected the League of Nations, which now was in danger of being dropped from the Treaty and pushed off into the vague future."[4] This second thesis was developed at length by Ray Stannard Baker, who went so far as to accuse House (and Lansing, too) of having acquiesced in the plans of plotters against Wilson and the League during the President's absence from the Conference.[5]

A number of historians, among them Bailey, Birdsall, Miller and Binkley, have examined Baker's sensational charges and rejected them.[6] There are numerous flaws in Baker's argument. For example, he fails to take into account the obviously important fact that House kept Wilson fully informed by cable of the proceedings in Paris to which he (Baker) attaches such sinister import and that Wilson never cabled a word of objection, although he was quick to cable House instructions about other matters.

Baker also implies that House and his fellow "intriguers" were responsible for the fact that during Wilson's absence from the Conference, scepticism grew (and was reflected in the press) as to whether the League Covenant would indeed be included in the Treaty. However, there is no evidence that such scepticism was in any way the result of House's handling of affairs in Wilson's absence. Rather, these widespread rumors may be more reasonably attributed to the growing opposition to the Covenant of certain United States Senators, whose statements were widely publicized in Europe. It would have been extraordinary indeed, in view of the bitter attacks on the President and the Round Robin resolution, had it not been whispered in Paris that perhaps he would be forced to agree to the deletion of the Covenant from the Treaty.

Neither does the charge stand up that House compromised everything in Wilson's absence in order to save the League. For the fact is, as Seymour has stated and as the minutes of the Council of Ten indicate, that House *discussed* but did not *decide* issues of major importance during Wilson's absence. He had attempted to narrow down differences to what seemed an irreducible minimum. His whole effort was to set the stage for the President's decision. The Colonel did not commit the President at all, much less "give away everything" in order to save the League.[7]

As a matter of fact, while Wilson was away, Lloyd George, Clemenceau and Orlando too were absent from the Conference for varying periods of time. A French fanatic shot Clemenceau on February 19, and the aged Premier, incapacitated for several days, missed six meetings of the Council of Ten. Lloyd George and Orlando visited England and Italy respectively. Of the eighteen meetings of the Council of Ten held in President Wilson's absence, Lloyd George attended six and Orlando only two. In these circumstances, the Council postponed basic decisions and concentrated on speeding up the work of the commissions.

Neither of the accusations against House, therefore, appears to be warranted. Both seem to be explanations contrived later for the President's undoubted change of attitude toward House during the second half of the Conference. How, then, is Wilson's perceptible, gradual cooling toward House upon his return to Paris to be explained?

As has been indicated, Wilson's affection for House seems to have been rooted in House's extraordinary capacity for enhancing the President's self-esteem. House's willingness readily to accept Wilson's opinions no matter what his own were, and the fact that he enjoyed status only insofar as Wilson chose to bestow it, figured importantly in the President's ability to accept the Colonel as a close friend and adviser. By the time Wilson left Paris in mid-February, these twin foundations of the relationship were disturbed.

In the first place, House had begun occasionally to give Wilson exceedingly unwelcome advice regarding his relationship to the Senate.

In early January, 1919, House had advised Wilson to announce to the people of the United States that the November elections gave the Republican Party a mandate to legislate, and that therefore he (Wilson) would not make recommendations regarding measures to be enacted, but would leave Congress free to carry out the will of the people.[8] It was House who urged upon Wilson the distasteful dinner with the Foreign Relations Committees of Congress. It was House who cautioned Wilson against speaking about the Covenant in Boston before discussing it with Congressional leaders.

House, in urging Wilson to mollify his senatorial opponents, had begun to add to Wilson's anxiety about his aggressive attitude toward the Senate. Instead of affectionate approval at a time of great inner tension, Wilson received from House painful suggestions in favor of a course of moderation and compromise. Always in the past, the Colonel's reassuring praise of Wilson's forceful leadership, when Wilson was trying to fend off insight into the more personal components of his motivation, had been a soothing balm. Now, however, instead of proclaiming the justice and wisdom of Wilson's defiance of his opponents, House was echoing the strictures which Wilson probably had to endure from his own conscience. So far from serving as a purveyor of psychological tranquillity, then, House now added to Wilson's burdens.

Another disturbance of the original basis of the friendship arose from the fact that at the Peace Conference House occupied an *official* position under the President. To a man of Wilson's temperament, this alteration of the relationship was in itself of major significance. House's right to participate in policy formation and in negotiation was now based on his own official position, rather than on Wilson's largesse. Commissioner House's activities fell within the purview of Wilson's jealous regard for his prerogatives in a way that they never had in the days when House was simply the President's informal adviser. Moreover, there was a subtle but perhaps important difference in the character of the tentative commitments and decisions which House had made earlier, when he was the President's unofficial diplomatic agent or when he had been placed officially in charge of special negotiations with the Allies during the war, and those which he now made as a Peace Commissioner serving directly under Wilson. With the President on hand and determined to play a direct role in the negotiations himself, he was the more likely to feel himself embarrassed by tentative commitments and understandings which House entered into with Allied negotiators.

In later years, House regretted that he had accepted an official appointment to the Peace Commission. He felt that had he continued to serve the President informally, he could have exerted influence without arousing Wilson's "jealousy."[9] Even at the time, House was aware that his new relationship with the President was fraught with peril. Yet, instead of taking even greater precautions, the Colonel knowingly added to the risks by asserting himself much more freely than he had previously permitted himself to do.

House's problem was exceedingly complex. A matchless opportunity to perform great services—services in the interest of Wilson's ideals in which he sincerely believed—was at hand, and it was left largely to him to delimit his own activities. The President's seeming confidence in him, the importunities of the Allied statesmen, the not completely unfounded conviction that his skill as a negotiator exceeded Wilson's and, be it added, that dash of vanity in his make-up so eager for open expression after so long a period of Spartan repression, all tempted him into activities which he knew from his insight into Wilson's character to be rash.

To his diary, even before the Conference officially began, House was already confiding his dissatisfaction with the President's performance, at times implying that *he* would not have made such mistakes. Of one of the President's early discussions with Clemenceau, for example, House complained in his diary that Wilson had been indiscreet, had not properly expounded the plan for a league, and had inadequately presented the United States position on the freedom of the seas.[10]

House's dilemma was complicated by the fact that he felt driven by the crucial importance of the events now being shaped to save the President from making mistakes which might prove irremediable. When, for example, he foresaw that Wilson's defiance of his Senate opposition could have ruinous results in terms of what the President himself most wanted to achieve, could he remain silent? He could not.

Not only did House undertake to play an active role at the Conference and press unwelcome advice on the President: he was also less careful than usual to conceal his role in shaping events and to avoid personal publicity. Some relaxation in this direction was perhaps inevitable in the circumstances. House no doubt justified to himself the risks he was taking on the ground that the importance of the matters at stake left him no alternative. For example, because he thought Wilson was not supplying adequate information to the press, House undertook to meet with journalists daily despite the fact that, as he noted in his diary (on March 20, 1919):

> I am sure the President does not approve of my giving our public as much information as I do, but I shall continue until he protests and then we will have it out together. . . . Publicity . . . is the best thing . . . for the President whose purposes are so commendable.

In addition, indications are not lacking that House was "feeling his oats" and greatly enjoyed his new role as a statesman in his own right. Once he relaxed the self-discipline which had enabled him to preserve his unique position as the President's closest adviser for so many years, the Colonel lapsed into imprudent self-indulgences which would have been unthinkable in the past.

The Allied statesmen had certain very mundane matters on their minds, such as reparations, frontier revisions and the like. Having found Wilson peculiarly difficult to communicate with on these subjects, they took up a great deal of their business with House. Even though the Colonel opposed many of their demands, he was willing to discuss them in language more comprehensible to them than the President's strange preachments. Thus it was that House's quarters at the Hotel Crillon became the focal point of many a top-level negotiation, presided over by House not at the President's instance but because the Allied statesmen presented themselves and their problems to the Colonel in the first place. From the beginning House was aware, as well he might have been, of the explosive possibilities of this situation. "Sooner or later," he wrote in his diary on January 6, 1919, "I suppose I shall get into trouble, but since it is difficult to advise the Governments associated with us to do differently, I shall probably let matters take their course."

During Wilson's absence, it was frequently intimated to House that matters were moving more smoothly now that *he* was in charge of the United States Commission. Lloyd George flatteringly referred to him, the Colonel recorded in his diary, as a Prime Minister, and a number of newspapers suggested that House was accomplishing more than the President had.[11]

One of House's errors, as he himself later realized, was that he placed several relatives and friends on the staff of the Commission.[12] Among them was his son-in-law, Gordon Auchincloss. who appears to have been greatly impressed with his father-in-law's competence, which he apparently construed to be greater than the President's. In an access of injudicious filial zeal, he appears to have furnished newspapermen with a great deal of material highly flattering to the Colonel. Some of the resultant articles are known to have irritated the President and Mrs. Wilson intensely.[13]

In the past the gratifications he had derived from House's friendship had blinded the President to evidences of the Colonel's tendency to manipulate people, and of his ambitions. Wilson had been impervious to attempts to represent House in a bad light. Now that these gratifications were reduced, Wilson was finally capable of viewing House with an altered perspective. More detached than ever before about the Colonel, Wilson could no longer brush aside indications in House's behavior which seemed to validate Mrs. Wilson's longstanding hostile interpretations.

The rift between the two men frequently has been attributed to one or another incident which occurred during the latter half of the Conference, or to Mrs. Wilson's antipathy for House or, again, to the conniving of House's enemies at Paris. While all these factors are important, they do not lie at the core of the breach. For had not the very foundations of Wilson's positive attachment to House been destroyed, it seems likely that the President would have remained unmoved by evidences and stories of House's "misdemeanors" and resisted, as he had in the past, attempts to bring the Colonel into disfavor.

It was an unfortunate combination of circumstances—Wilson's increased sensitivity to House as a possible competitor and House's overpowering desire to "come into his own"—that contributed heavily to the gradual waning of the President's enthusiasm for his closest collaborator. No one incident marks the end of the friendship between Wilson and House. The relationship was never terminated in a clear-cut fashion. Rather, Wilson gradually withdrew his affection and gradually ceased to consult House.

During the first part of the Peace Conference, the new ground on which their friendship rested had not been put to the test. Wilson had been successful in obtaining the League. Despite House's official status and his new habit of pressing unwelcome advice, the two men remained outwardly on the best of terms. The real challenge to the President's peace program, however, had only been deferred. It confronted Wilson immediately upon his return to Paris.

The problems which Wilson now had to face were not new, nor should they have been unexpected. The French had made their views known from the very beginning of the Conference. The Italians had presented a memorandum stating their demands on February 7, a week before the President left Paris. The Japanese stated their case before the Council of Ten in January, in Wilson's presence. As the experts assigned to the various commissions narrowed down the several points of view on each issue, it became clear that on several important ones, agreement would be impossible without broad concessions on all sides.

It was, therefore, an exceedingly sober story which House had to tell Wilson upon his return to France, particularly with regard to stubborn French demands which were incompatible with the Fourteen Points. Still smarting from the show of force which his senatorial critics had made just before he left the United States, Wilson stepped off the *George Washington* at Brest to find that his opponents in Paris were preparing to dismember the Fourteen Points. House not only broke this unpleasant news to Wilson but made it clear that in his judgment amendments to the Covenant should be obtained to satisfy the Senate and that concessions to the Allies were inevitable and should be made quickly.

House considered it of overriding importance to conclude the Treaty speedily. For with each day of delay came desperate reports of unrest and revolution in central and eastern Europe. There was no time to settle disagreements in leisurely fashion. Problems seemingly incapable of solution must be coped with quickly lest prolongation of the current political chaos drive desperate people to desperate action to bring some sort of order—perhaps bolshevist order—to their lives. House understood this. He, as much as Wilson, disapproved of many of the demands which were being bruited about.

"It is now evident," he wrote in his diary on March 3, 1919, "that the peace will not be such a peace as I had hoped, or one which this terrible upheaval should have brought about. . . . I dislike to sit and have forced upon us such a peace as we are facing." [14] But, being realistic, House recognized that concessions would have to be made to the Allies and he thought it would be best for Wilson to face up to the inevitable promptly and complete the Treaty as soon as possible. He wanted to get a necessary job over with before additional problems were caused by fruitless delay. In this frame of mind, House pressed for compromise all along the diplomatic front.[15]

No one can ever know what disturbing thoughts and insights rose to plague Wilson at this juncture. He was trapped in a vise, and whatever he did in an effort to extricate himself would inevitably tighten the screws in another direction. One wonders whether in some way he was not aware of the fact that he himself was partly responsible for the excruciating dilemma in which he now found himself. He had made numerous errors: tactlessly defying the Senate opposition; revealing to the statesmen in Paris his urgent personal involvement in the League; failing at the very beginning of the Peace Conference, when his position was strongest, to face up to the secret treaties and to insist that the Allies were bound by their acceptance of the Fourteen Points in the prearmistice convention.

What human being, in the grip of agonizing conflict and frustration partly of his own making, is not tempted to find a scapegoat upon whom to blame his troubles? And who was more eligible to serve Wilson as a scapegoat than his alter ego, Colonel House, whose friendship in any event no longer yielded the accustomed gratifications? By attributing some of his difficulties to House, the President could avoid having to admit to himself his own partial responsibility for them. By finding fault with House on these grounds, moreover, the President could provide himself with an excellent rationalization for withdrawing both affection and trust from House, whose appeal for him was lessened for other reasons.

It was apparent soon after Wilson's return to Paris that House no longer enjoyed the President's confidence as of old. The two conferred often enough about specific problems, but gone were the days when the President would summon his "dearest friend" for informal discussions about the drift of events in general. Even more mortifying for the Colonel, Wilson no longer kept him informed of what happened at the meetings which took place between him, Clemenceau, Lloyd George and Orlando.

In the second part of the Conference, most of the important business was transacted in great seclusion by the Council of Four, or the "Big Four," as they came to be known. Other members of the Council of Four took subordinates along to these private meetings or made arrangements with each other to obtain minutes of the meetings. To the chagrin of his colleagues on the American delegation, the President not only ventured into these all-important meetings without either a secretary or an assistant, but also issued express instructions that the minutes not be circulated to anyone in the American delegation—not even to House.[16] Wilson now excluded House with the same chilling reserve which House, with patronizing sympathy, had noted earlier in the President's relations with the other American Commissioners.

It is not necessary to dwell upon the personal pique occasioned by the President's deliberate affront to his fellow Commissioners' dignity although, as readily may be surmised, those involved privately bristled with indignation. It is worth noting, however, that the possibilities for effectively relieving the President of some of the tremendous burdens he was carrying now were diminished to the vanishing point. It was difficult enough during the first part of the Conference when the President failed to brief his American colleagues adequately as to his intentions. But then they at least knew what was happening in the Council of Ten, whereas now, as Secretary of State Lansing later revealed, the American Commissioners were reduced to seeking information from the gossip of the staffs of other delegations.[17] If the Commissioners were in the dark so were the American experts, and this lack of information disheartened them. As one of them, James T. Shotwell, noted in his diary on April 8, 1919: "There has been a great wave of despondency over the Conference recently which is due to several things, but among them I believe the main thing is that we do not know what is being done." [18]

House reacted to Wilson's coolness by pretending not to notice it. Never, it seems safe to assume from available evidence, did he question the President about his change in attitude; never did he tactlessly foist himself or his advice upon the President or, in anger, withdraw from the situation. He tried, outwardly at least, to preserve his customary manner with Wilson, to let him set the pace of the relationship and to remain available for whatever assistance he might choose to request.

This unruffled façade, however, covered considerable vexation. The President was imprudent and reckless, wrote House in his diary on April 2, 1919, to venture into the Council of Four meetings without taking along a member of his staff to report the proceedings.[19] During the three weeks following Wilson's return to Paris, House's diary testifies to an unflattering estimate of his chief and also to his feeling of superiority to Wilson. House was extremely disturbed at the impasse in the Big Four's deliberations and at their inability to reach any decisions. He confessed he found it maddening to see valuable time elapse without reaching settlements. As for Wilson, he was becoming stubborn, angry and unreasonable. Since the President never was a good negotiator anyway, complained the Colonel, the situation was disheartening.[20]

The negotiating dilemma which confronted Wilson at this time was basically as follows: he had returned to Paris amidst widely publicized Senate criticism of the League Covenant. Numerous staunch supporters of the League advised him of the absolute necessity of obtaining amendments to the Covenant to meet these criticisms. Otherwise, he was warned, the Senate might reject the League altogether. His first impulse upon returning to Paris was to stand fast against demands to revise the Covenant.

Exactly when the President decided to seek the necessary changes in the Covenant it is not possible to say. On March 18, 1919—four days after his return to Paris—Wilson received a cable from ex-President Taft urging certain amendments and, significantly, pointing out that if these were obtained, "the ground will be completely cut from under the opponents of the League in the Senate. . . ." [21]

The prospect of thus confounding his enemies apparently enabled Wilson to overcome his aversion to seeking the amendments; and shortly after receiving Taft's cable, we find him displaying what House described as a "more reasonable" attitude on the matter.[22]

Within a few days Wilson had typed out four amendments to the Covenant, which drew heavily on Taft's recommendations and also incorporated certain suggestions made by A. Lawrence Lowell and Senator Hitchcock.[23] A number of competent historians are in agreement that the four amendments which the President now sponsored, and ultimately obtained, constituted a serious effort on his part to meet the major objections which had been raised against the Covenant in the United States. These four amendments, which were specifically addressed to Lodge's criticisms, would (a) provide for a recognition of the Monroe Doctrine; (b) exclude domestic, internal questions from League jurisdiction; (c) provide for the possibility of withdrawal from the League; (d) permit a member to refuse a mandate.

Why, then—to anticipate our story somewhat—did the amendments not mollify senatorial opposition? The manner and spirit in which Wilson made his concessions to the viewpoint of his critics provide a partial explanation. What appears at first glance to have been a conciliatory gesture on Wilson's part was not conciliatory at all. Rather it was a device to assure Wilson's triumph in the contest of wills between himself and the Lodge group. The President, though seeking the amendments, did not disguise his judgment that they had not been really necessary. Neither did he give the Senate the satisfaction of a frank avowal that, after all, he did feel obliged to take Senate criticism into account. Underlying senatorial criticism of the League was not only bitter personal hostility toward Wilson but also, as we have seen, resentment at what were considered his affronts to the prestige and powers of the Senate.

The President's visit to the United States had aggravated, rather than reduced, the friction between himself on the one hand and Lodge and his supporters on the other. The precise nature of Lodge's motivation we do not know. It does seem clear, however, that, whatever the reason, Lodge was peculiarly sensitive to Wilson's failure to defer to the Senate, and felt impelled to thwart him. For all the specific objections Lodge made to the Covenant—and some of them were reasonable enough—the core of the trouble lay in Wilson's attitude toward the Senate.

The implication of some of Lodge's statements at this time is that if the President had accorded deference to the Senate, the substantive difficulties involved in the Covenant could have been ironed out. He wrote Henry White on March 5, regarding the Round Robin: "A point had been reached where the Senate made up its mind that it was time the Peace Conference knew that the President was not the only part of the government necessary to the making of a treaty and that there were other views to be considered." [24]

On March 9, White cabled Lodge requesting "exact phraseology of amendments modifying League of Nations Covenant which Senate considers important." But Lodge refused to commit himself, and replied that "the President expressed no willingness to receive any communication from the Senate while that body was in session. If he now wishes to have amendments drafted which the Senate will consent to, the natural and necessary course is to assemble the Senate in the customary way." It seems reasonable to conclude that had Lodge been interested primarily in amending the Covenant, he would have taken the opportunity White afforded him to advance his proposals.[25]

Had Wilson not been shackled in this situation to the rigid reactions which his anxieties made inevitable, he might have confounded Lodge by soliciting the advice of the Senate. He would have lost nothing by so doing since in any case, upon his return to Paris, he did seek to amend the Covenant to meet the most serious objections which had been raised. He could bring himself to yield in substance, but to accompany his concessions with a show of deference to the Senate—that was anathema to him.

The exclusive and haughty manner in which Wilson amended the Covenant and later explained his action did not assuage either the personal hostility of his extreme critics or the more broadly shared feeling within the Senate that he was ignoring its proper role in the treaty-making process. Well might the Senate have concluded from Wilson's behavior that he had decided to obtain the amendments merely as a stratagem the better to assure successfully imposing his will and his treaty upon it. Wilson gave the Senate most of the amendments it wanted, but he deprived it of the deference to its power which it considered its right.

Three of the four amendments which the President sponsored were quickly conceded by his fellow negotiators at the Peace Conference. At the same time, however, they made it clear that they would withhold their approval of the most important amendment of all, that acknowledging the validity of the Monroe Doctrine. Now, there was nothing in the Monroe Doctrine amendment significantly at variance with the interests of either Britain or France. But the perceptive Allied leaders correctly concluded that their power to obstruct Wilson's amendments and, indeed, to withhold support of the League as it was finally constituted, was the most effective bargaining weapon at their disposal. Faced with the formidable task of getting Wilson to agree to their various demands, Clemenceau and Lloyd George let it be known that their approval of the Monroe Doctrine amendment would be contingent upon Wilson's making concessions on the matters uppermost in their minds.

In the name of French security and justice for what the French people had suffered at German hands, the French negotiators wanted to set up a separate Rhenish republic and would settle for no less than an interallied occupation of the German Rhineland; they wanted to annex certain parts of the Saar outright and to impose on the rest of that overwhelmingly German region a non-German government; they wanted not only to operate the Saar's rich coal mines for French profit, but to own them; and they wanted to saddle Germany with an unsparing bill for reparations, to be paid over as many generations as required for its discharge in full. (As merely keeping up with the interest on such a debt would consume Germany's resources, the

French position amounted to a demand to keep Germany in financial bondage in perpetuity.)

Wilson was squarely opposed to the French program for the Rhineland and to the imposition of a non-German government on the Saar on the grounds that the principle of self-determination would thereby be violated. He was sympathetic to the case advanced for French operation of the Saar's coal mines, but did not think the French should own them. As for reparations, he thought Germany should be required to pay a specified sum, based upon her capacity to pay within a single generation.

For two weeks after Wilson's return to Paris, he and Clemenceau engaged in exhaustive and exhausting debates which succeeded only in revealing the magnitude of the gulf between the contending viewpoints. March 28 was a day of crisis. All that could be said, had been, *ad nauseam*. The discussion that morning started down the old familiar path and led, as usual, to a complete impasse. Wilson's patience was exhausted. He played his trump card, the one he had so long rehearsed in his mind as his best means of forcing the Allies to yield:

"Then if France does not get what she wishes, she will refuse to act with us," Wilson declared to Clemenceau. "In that event, do you wish me to return home?"

Clemenceau bristled. "I do not wish you to go home," he retorted, "but I intend to do so myself." His parting shot was that Wilson was pro-German. With that, he stamped out of the room.[26]

If Wilson "returned home," of course, the issue precipitating the disruption of the Conference would be laid before world public opinion. What Clemenceau's gesture communicated to Wilson, in all likelihood, was that he did not fear a public showdown of the kind that Wilson was threatening. The astute French Premier was, in effect, inviting Wilson to do his worst. The lines of battle were drawn. The crisis had come at last.

Clemenceau's outburst was the sort of challenge which ordinarily would spur Wilson to immediate action. This time, however, he must stay his impulse to fly into battle. For he was caught in a terrible dilemma. As he interpreted the situation, he was being forced to choose between two things, both dear to him: either he must compromise his Fourteen Points to secure Allied approval of his amendments to the Covenant, or, by abandoning the effort to do so, place himself at a disadvantage with the Senate. For Wilson, coping with this problem was not merely a difficult intellectual task. It was a painful personal dilemma as well, as is indicated in accounts of his tormented behavior by people who observed him at first hand during this period.

Wilson did not "return home." On March 31, April 1, 2 and 3, he began to yield to Clemenceau, point by point, trying desperately at each juncture to confine the concessions to as narrow bounds as possible. But once the French found a chink in Wilson's armor, they hammered at it, trying to expand the crack into a gaping breach.

What distress such concessions must have caused Wilson can easily be imagined. It was not merely that he was forced from an intellectually defensible position to an intellectually indefensible one, but that he was *forced* at all. When involved in any sort of power struggle, Wilson could not bear to capitulate. His tendency was to resist pressure no matter what the cost. In this instance he was involved in two power struggles, the immediate one with Clemenceau and the impending one with the United States Senate. To improve his position in the struggle with the Senate, he seems reluctantly to have accepted the need to make compromises in Clemenceau's favor which, under other circumstances, would probably have been unthinkable. Even under these circumstances, it was bitterly difficult, almost impossible, to yield.

Clemenceau shared his burden with a few advisers, who helped him plan his assault on Wilson. The President tried to cope with his terrible problem alone. On the evening of April 3, he collapsed and was ordered to bed.

At Wilson's request, House took his place at the Council of Four meetings. House was determined to exploit this unexpected opportunity to serve as chief United States negotiator to bring the Council to grips once and for all with the major problems delaying the peace settlement. He had concluded that American concessions were inevitable, and was disposed to make them without further ado. On April 5, the Council of Four went over the reparations problem again. House afterwards drafted a reparations article embodying Clemenceau's views and, the next day, secured Wilson's agreement to it.

This further capitulation depressed the President profoundly. His will to resist flared up anew. On the afternoon of April 6, he summoned the American Commissioners and told them that unless more satisfactory progress were made within the next few days, he would tell the Prime Ministers if they did not abide by the Fourteen Points he would either go home or insist on taking up the unsettled problems at plenary sessions.

Some time on the evening of April 6, or possibly early in the morning of April 7, Wilson ordered the *George Washington* to Brest, presumably to be ready to carry him home should he decide to leave the Conference. According to Ray Stannard Baker, this "bold gesture" intimidated both Clemenceau and Lloyd George, who now became more conciliatory.[27] However, as Seymour has pointed out, it was Wilson, not Clemenceau nor Lloyd George, who conceded most in the negotiations of the following week.[28]

Mrs. Wilson, in *My Memoir*, describes the President's state of mind:

> The news that came to him was so grave we trembled for the effect on him. . . . Silently I sat beside his bed, knowing that he was formulating his course. At length he said: "I can never sign a Treaty made on these lines. . . . If I have lost my fight, which I would not have done had I been on my feet, I will retire in good order; so we will go home."[29]

Wilson's assertion that he would not have lost his fight had he not fallen ill simply does not stand up under scrutiny. The fact is that he had made a number of crucial concessions *before* he became ill, and that during his absence from the meetings of the Council of Four no commitments were made by Colonel House without his knowledge and approval. And Clemenceau achieved his major victories over the President himself in the days immediately following his return to the Council meetings.

Some historians, notably Charles Seymour, interpret Wilson's reliance on House during his illness as a sign of his continued regard for the Colonel. Another explanation suggests itself when one scrutinizes the facts in terms of just what task it was that the President wished his substitute to accomplish for him. Wilson felt he must capitulate to Clemenceau in order to obtain French approval of the Monroe Doctrine amendment. Since this was personally distasteful, Wilson seems to have turned to House to make the necessary concessions.

That Wilson was unable himself to supervise a strategic diplomatic retreat is highly revealing of his style as a negotiator. The fact is, the process of negotiation which is essentially, after all, the process of intelligent compromise, was itself repugnant to Wilson. He was not a compromiser. It has been truly said of Wilson that he could not bend, he could only break. He must have all that he wanted or he wanted nothing at all. It will be recalled that at Princeton, too, when he could not gain acceptance of the whole substance of his quad plan he was unable to accept the opportunity which his fight had created for reforming Princeton's clubs, and had suffered a nervous collapse.

For him the problem always was to decide what was right and then cleave relentlessly to it. Instead of considering beforehand what would be his maximum and minimum goals, he tended to formulate only one position which was, in effect, both his maximum and minimum stand. He then endowed this position with moral attributes in order better to mobilize his own emotions and energies in the struggle on its behalf.

This approach as a negotiator—and, indeed, as a college president and political leader—had certain advantages in that the stubbornness with which Wilson pressed for his maximum goals and the skill with which he drew a moral dichotomy between his own position and that of his opponents often culminated in brilliant successes. However, it also had some fatal disadvantages. For when his opponents reached the stage where they would no longer capitulate—and often Wilson did not offer them a gracious way out—his inflexibility led to a complete impasse and ruled out compromise solutions which might preserve a good part of his program. Wilson thus habitually abdicated important responsibilities of political leadership, self-righteously but unrealistically relying on public opinion to vindicate him and force his opponents to surrender to him. It was characteristic of the man to structure every major executive position he held into an inexorable moral battle.

It seems likely that Wilson's stubbornness would have led to a complete diplomatic impasse and a breakdown of the Peace Conference had it not been for the fact that the struggle against the Allied negotiators became subordinated in his mind and emotions to the greater struggle with the senatorial opposition. Wilson reluctantly accepted the need to obtain certain amendments to the Covenant and to compromise the Fourteen Points in order to further his strategic plan for forcing the Senate to accept the League.

While the French were playing upon the President's anxiety about the Monroe Doctrine amendment to achieve their aims, the British made a similar effort. Their objective was twofold: to prevail upon Wilson not to raise the issue of the freedom of the seas, which was Point II of the Fourteen Points; and to obtain some sort of assurance that the United States would not compete with Britain in a naval building program. They were successful on both counts.

The President never raised the question of freedom of the seas, despite the fact that before the Conference began he had regarded agreement on this point as one of the essential elements of the peace settlement. During the prearmistice Conference, in fact, he had cabled House instructions to tell the British, who had already begun raising objections to Point II, that "I cannot consent to take part in the negotiation of a peace which does not include freedom of the seas. . . ."[30]

As to their second objective, the British obtained a letter written by House, and approved by Wilson, assuring them that "if the kind of peace is made for which we are working and which will include a League of Nations . . . I am sure you will find the United States ready to 'abandon or modify our new naval programme'. . . ." House wrote this letter in response to a request from Lord Robert Cecil after Lloyd George had baldly told the Colonel on April 7 that he could not support the Monroe Doctrine amendment without first coming to an agreement with the United States about the United States naval program.[31]

At the April 10 meeting of the League of Nations commission, the Monroe Doctrine amendment was adopted as proposed. Both the French and British voted in favor of it.

Most historians, however critical they may be of Wilson's mistakes in peacemaking, offer a sympathetic interpretation of his painful compromises of the Fourteen Points in order to save the League. The necessity to obtain the League amendments demanded by senatorial critics, they concede, left Wilson no alternative to making concessions to the Allied demands.[32] This viewpoint fails to take into account a very significant factor in Wilson's defeat at the hands of the Allied leaders. This is that Clemenceau and Lloyd George succeeded in defining the negotiating situation for Wilson in terms of the bargains they wished to drive. Wilson accepted, apparently without question, their representation of the alternatives open to him: either he must give way on Allied demands or they would block the Monroe Doctrine amendment to the League Covenant, perhaps even the League itself. It does not seem to have occurred to Wilson that he need not accept this definition of the situation, that his negotiating position in seeking the amendments was not necessarily unfavorable, and that the situation could be structured differently and to his own advantage.

Suppose, for example, Wilson had confronted Clemenceau and Lloyd George with the argument that, unless they agreed to the Monroe Doctrine amendment, the Senate of the United States in all likelihood would refuse to ratify the peace treaty and the United States might revert to a policy of isolation. If he had coolly taken this position, the President might have found the fulminations of his senatorial critics of positive assistance in obtaining the necessary amendments instead of the agonizing embarrassment he felt them to be.

One fact which emerges from the annals of the Peace Conference with crystal clarity is that the European statesmen dreaded the possibility that Europe might be left to cope with her postwar problems—particularly the economic problems—without American help. It was to the interest of Clemenceau and Lloyd George to ensure that the League Covenant be made acceptable to the United States Senate. This was widely recognized at the time.[33] Leading Allied negotiators, Lord Robert Cecil, for example, were well aware that in the last analysis the Allies would have to co-operate, in their *own* interest, in securing the amendments to the Covenant demanded by the United States Senate.[34] However, to utilize the demands of his senatorial critics as a negotiating aid would imply his acceptance of the idea that senatorial views were of some legitimate consequence in the making of the Treaty. This was precisely the admission Wilson could not make. He must get the amendments, yes, but not at the cost of paying such open deference to his Senate foes. Their subjugation was his primary, though probably not conscious, goal. To its achievement he was ready to sacrifice everything else, the Fourteen Points and even, as we shall see later, the League itself.

Wilson's embarrassment and trepidation in seeking the amendments were obvious to the discerning Clemenceau and Lloyd George. His anxiety rendered him powerless to ask for them in a cool and detached manner. It left him at the mercy of men who were relentless in the pursuit of their own aims. Although the Monroe Doctrine amendment actually was of little interest to them, they saw that they could use Wilson's need of it as a bargaining lever to pry concessions from him. They did so.

No sooner had the crisis between Wilson and Clemenceau been surmounted than the clash between Wilson and the Italians and Wilson and the Japanese, just as complicated and enervating, took the center of the stage. Both the Italians and Japanese were seeking the rewards promised them in secret treaties which they had made with the Allies before agreeing to enter the war on the Allied side. The United States was not a party to these treaties. The division of spoils these secret pacts contemplated stood in direct violation of Wilson's Fourteen Points. In both cases, Lloyd George and Clemenceau took the position that however unjust to other peoples fulfilling the terms of the secret treaties might be, they were under obligation to redeem the pledges made by their governments during the war. In both cases, therefore, the burden of enforcing the Wilsonian principles of a "new order" in international relations, according to which the peace was supposedly being made, fell squarely upon Wilson himself.

The observant Japanese, having closely analyzed the successes of the French and British negotiators, skillfully applied the same basic strategy in connection with their own claims. Sanction the various secret treaties by which we extend our control in China, they said in effect to Wilson, or we will not join the League. They presented their case with chilling assurance, in a businesslike, unemotional manner which suggested they meant exactly what they said. House took them at their word, and favored making concessions to them. Among the rest of the American delegation the opinion was widespread that the Japanese would not carry out their threat, that they would not jeopardize their nascent status as a world power by dissociating themselves from the new international organization. Wilson, however, was not equal to playing the nerve-wracking game of smoking the Japanese out. Instead, he capitulated in large measure to the Japanese demands.

The Italians were not so shrewd as the Japanese. They did not rely on the strategy of threatening to withhold approval of the League. Interestingly enough, alone of the major powers, they failed to make headway against Wilson.

President Wilson rejected the whole of the Italian claims—both the secret Treaty of London and the additional claims they made. In this position, he was supported by the American experts specifically concerned with Adriatic problems.

During Wilson's absence from Paris, Colonel House, convinced that some concessions to the Italians, just as some concessions to the British, French and Japanese, would have to be made in order to secure agreement on a treaty promptly, started to explore the possibility of working out a compromise solution.

The charge has frequently been made that the Italians were greatly encouraged by House's conciliatory attitude and pressed their claims more zealously than they would have if they had felt the United States delegation solidly opposed them. It is difficult to assess the validity of this charge, but it is a demonstrable fact that Orlando did indeed look hopefully to House to champion the Italian cause.

Orlando's biggest mistake seems to have been a failure in evaluating Wilson's motivations: he sought to use the influence of a man (House) who was no longer influential; and he did not play upon Wilson's anxiety about the League by making Italy's adherence to it contingent upon the satisfaction of her territorial claims.

On April 14, Orlando and Wilson conferred and found themselves at an impasse. Following this unsuccessful meeting, Wilson asked House to seek a solution—apparently, however, without specifying what exactly he had in mind. It was as if the President, not really wanting compromises but fearing they might be necessary, could make only this limited and peculiarly self-defeating concession to the realities of the situation.

During the next four days, from April 15 to April 19, House made an intensive effort to work out a compromise with the Italians. He was unsuccessful. In the first place, Orlando was not disposed to retreat from his position. In the second place, House was no longer working with the President's solid backing: the Adriatic experts on the American staff, indignant at what they considered House's unwarranted injection into the proceedings of the notion that the United States was willing in some degree to accede to the Italian demands, addressed an appeal to Wilson on April 17. In it, they made skillful reference to the President's determination to make a peace of justice, and asserted that the Italians were seeking loot to which they had absolutely no title. Later that day, Wilson conferred with the American Commissioners and repudiated the various compromise suggestions which House had been suggesting.

It is not clear to what extent House cleared his compromise proposals with the President before conferring with Orlando. Certain it is, however, that Wilson had invited House's efforts. Certain it is, too, that he was further alienated from House by the Colonel's attempts to conciliate Orlando.

James Shotwell interprets House's activities at this time as the cause of the rupture in the Colonel's relations with Wilson.[35] Of course, it was not the "cause," but it seems to have furnished Wilson an opportunity to confirm his negative attitude toward House. Here was House, so Wilson may have thought, all too willing to compromise the Fourteen Points, while he, Wilson, was straining to the utmost to uphold them. Indeed it is probably true that House's efforts to negotiate a solution embarrassed the effort of the President and the Adriatic experts to make a firm stand against the Italians. Yet Wilson seems to have permitted House to seek a compromise solution *after* he had decided not to accept any such solution.

What House apparently did not appreciate fully was that Wilson did not feel under the same compulsion to compromise with the Italians as he did with the French, British and Japanese, because the Italians had not applied effective pressure on him, and that attempts to mediate between the contending positions, therefore, stood little chance of gaining the President's approval.

It was at about this time that the final rupture between House and Mrs. Wilson occurred. According to Mrs. Wilson's account, she showed House some articles from the American press which criticized the President while praising House as "the brains of the Commission." Thereupon, visibly embarrassed, House left, taking with him the articles which Wilson had not yet seen. Mrs. Wilson's account adds that shortly thereafter she learned from Dr. Grayson, Wilson's physician, that House and his son-in-law, Gordon Auchincloss, were busily inspiring articles in this vein.[36] According to Colonel House, on the other hand, what happened was that Mrs. Wilson confronted him with an article flattering to him and demanded an explanation, the implication of her query being that he had inspired it. At that point, the conversation was terminated by Wilson's entrance into the room.[37]

Whatever the details of the incident, it is clear from both versions that Mrs. Wilson became openly incensed at House and, furthermore, that she informed Wilson of her suspicions. After this painful conversation, House never again visited Wilson's house in Paris.

Meanwhile, the Italian claims remained unsettled. Orlando, sometimes vehemently, sometimes tearfully, but never with menacing reference to Wilson's League, absolutely refused to moderate his position. Confronted with another stalemate, but this time not deterred by fears for the League, Wilson at last tested his conviction that he better than their leaders represented the true aspirations of the people of Europe.[38] On April 23, he released to the press his views on the question of the Italian claims, the famous appeal to the Italian people.

The President had thought that his statement would rally Italian public opinion to his ideals. The naïveté of this expectation was quickly exposed. From every corner of Italy, from every political element—even from the very liberals on whom Wilson counted—there issued blasts of vituperation against the President such as probably no other head of a friendly state had ever had to endure. What seemed to rankle most was that whereas Wilson had been willing to compromise his principles to achieve a settlement with the British and French, he seemed completely inflexible where Italian interests were at stake. Orlando and Sonnino, whose ministry had been on the verge of falling, overnight became popular heroes for standing up to the man who wished to satisfy his principles at Italy's expense.

Not only had the President grossly miscalculated the popular temper in Italy, but he had not taken an important step which would have minimized some of the risks of an appeal to the Italian people. Although he had discussed his intention of making the appeal with Clemenceau and Lloyd George, who were also opposed to many of the Italian claims, he had failed to commit them to publishing their views simultaneously with his own. Such a co-ordinated Big Three appeal to the Italian people might have been no more successful than Wilson's individual effort, but at least it would have countered the mistaken but widespread impression, even before Wilson's views were made public, that it was only the American President who stood between Italy and the realization of all her claims.[39] As it turned out, when Wilson's public appeal against the Italian leaders boomeranged, Lloyd George and Clemenceau rode out the storm in silence. Belatedly, Wilson urged Lloyd George to publish the British view already set forth in a private memorandum. Lloyd George replied that to do so would only exacerbate the situation.

In reality filled with trepidation at the turn of events, but with a fine show of high indignation for the benefit of the Italian public, Orlando departed from Paris on April 24. Alas for the unhappy Orlando! He hoped that his colleagues on the Council would try to lure him back with concessions, but they knew as well as he did that Italy had far too much to lose by boycotting the Conference to continue on that tack for very long. With an indifference to Orlando's absence that reduced that unfortunate to despair, Wilson, Lloyd George and Clemenceau calmly proceeded with their business. After a week of waiting anxiously in Rome for propitiating gestures which did not come, Orlando quietly returned to the Conference, having gained nothing by his walkout.

Various unsuccessful efforts to solve the Italian crisis were made in May and June. Of these House's were the most ambitious. The President again reluctantly authorized House to explore a compromise possibility which the Colonel had in mind.

Though penalized earlier for having essayed the role of compromiser so distasteful to the President, House was evidently willing to try again. His feeling that a settlement was being blocked by the President's ineptitude and stubbornness was never stronger. "I am delighted to have the matter coming back into my hands," he wrote in his diary on May 14. ". . . There has never been a time when I have felt it could not have been settled if properly and constantly directed."

House's criticism of the President grew more intense as the cleavage between them deepened and the Colonel sensed it was to be permanent. His diary for May 6, 1919, referred to the President as the most prejudiced man he ever knew. As for his latest effort to reach a compromise settlement House felt that once again the President cut the ground from under him just when he had got the Italians and Yugoslavs nearly to an agreement. Subsequent diary entries add detail to House's contention that his effort failed because of the President's intransigence.[40]

Wilson had set out for Paris in possession of one prescient insight: that a vindictive peace was bound to boomerang against its authors, that a settlement of moderation which did not seek the destruction of Germany as a world power would best serve the interests of all. Because of the many concessions Wilson made to the viewpoints of the Allies, particularly that of France, the peace settlement fell appreciably short of this enlightened conception.[41]

It is tempting to speculate whether a significantly more moderate peace treaty could have been obtained had its advocates waged a more skillful diplomatic battle. It is in the area of British-American relations that the most tantalizing possibilities of "what might have been" suggest themselves. Clemenceau was operating in a domestic political context which gave him little freedom of action at the Peace Conference. Either he must gain a substantial portion of the French demands or his government would in all probability fall.

Lloyd George, on the other hand, enjoyed somewhat greater

negotiating leeway. True, a large part of the British public was clamoring for the Kaiser's head and for "making the Germans pay." But there also existed—as evidenced by the cleavage in the British delegation to the Peace Conference—considerable sentiment for a moderate peace which would leave Germany strong enough to preserve the European balance of power, a traditional goal of British diplomacy.

Among the less obvious and less heralded failures at Paris was that of responsible British and American leaders to explore seriously the extent to which the British interest in preserving the balance of power dovetailed with Wilson's conviction that only a reasonable peace could be a lasting one. In March, 1919, when the first effort to curb French demands was made, Wilson and Lloyd George found themselves in substantial agreement on the Rhineland and Saar issues and in partial agreement on the reparations issue. Yet, for reasons not entirely clear, this broad Anglo-American opposition to the major claims raised by the French was never translated into a co-ordinated Anglo-American negotiating strategy. Instead, Wilson and Lloyd George made separate and largely unsuccessful assaults on the French position.[42] As we have seen, in late March and early April Wilson felt himself obliged to make great concessions to Clemenceau in order to get his support for the Monroe Doctrine amendment. Not the least of Wilson's shortcomings as a negotiator was his inability, having decided to compromise, to work out some overall strategy according to which concessions might be held to a minimum and differences between Lloyd George and Clemenceau exploited to his own advantage.

In May, the Treaty was ready for presentation to the Germans. A number of those, particularly within the British delegation, who had worked on and were familiar with only isolated parts of it were appalled at its crushing severity when viewed as a whole. Not only did Lloyd George and some of his colleagues fear that the Germans might not sign; they also felt that the Treaty as it stood reduced German power below the level which would best serve British interests. Thereupon, after the German representatives presented a series of objections to the Treaty, there began a last-minute effort by Lloyd George in early June to secure certain modifications in Germany's favor.

Surprisingly, however, Wilson was not at all eager to take advantage of this opportunity to join forces with the British and undo some of the concessions he had been forced to make earlier. On June 2, Lloyd George proposed that various terms of the Treaty be softened. Clemenceau indignantly refused to consider reopening the issues. Wilson sat by in virtual silence, thus placing the whole burden of battle on his British colleague.

True, on June 3, the President canvassed the situation with members of the American delegation and authorized them to explore the possibility of securing modifications of the Treaty. He conceded that changes should be made if they would bring the Treaty closer in line with his principles. However, he was extremely reluctant to see the issues revived on which he had been forced to compromise earlier. "The time to consider all these questions," he told the American delegation, "was when we were writing the Treaty, and it makes me a little tired for people to come and say now that they are afraid the Germans won't sign, and their fear is based upon things that they insisted upon at the time of the writing of the Treaty; that makes me very sick." [43]

This attitude doubtless stemmed in part from his concern that Allied unity might be disrupted if an attempt were made to ameliorate the terms to be imposed on Germany—the French were incensed at the idea. Further, however, Wilson probably intuitively rejected the idea of any thoroughgoing re-examination of the Treaty at this time because he sensed that any such procedure would reactivate his intolerable crises of conscience of March and April. Indeed, so distressing to Wilson had been his earlier concessions to the French and to others that he seems to have lost track in his own mind of the extent to which he had been forced to compromise his principles. Thus in the critical Big Four meeting of June 2, Wilson endorsed the Saar arrangement as "sound," although he had accepted it in April most unwillingly after a protracted struggle to avoid any suspension of German sovereignty.[44]

Lloyd George was unquestionably, as Wilson put it at the time to Ray Stannard Baker, in "a perfect funk." He was trying every way to enlist Wilson's support. He had Colonel House to lunch to talk the situation over. He tried to persuade Bernard Baruch to solicit the President's co-operation.[45] Wilson remained passive, unquestionably to Clemenceau's great relief. Forced to tilt with Clemenceau unaided, Lloyd George gained some of the changes he had proposed, but the basic structure of the Treaty remained unaltered.[46]

The question of what it might have been possible for Wilson to accomplish at Paris by more skillful negotiation is obviously enormously complicated. The question of how wise it would have been, even had he been able to apply more effective pressure on the Allied negotiators, to force his views upon them, is equally difficult. It is clear, however, that had he been free of his painful personal involvement in the proceedings he might have been better able than he was to perceive the possible alternatives at hand, and to consider them flexibly in terms of the ultimate fate of his idealistic goals.

After House's unsuccessful and unwelcome intervention in the Italian problem in May, the Colonel found himself cast progressively further toward the periphery of affairs.

By May 30, his association with the President had so ebbed that House wrote in his diary: "I seldom or never have a chance to talk with him seriously and, for the moment, he is practically out from under my influence. When we meet it is to settle some passing problem and not to take inventory of things in general or plan for the future. This is what we used to do."

The Colonel's diary entry for the next day was a dismal reflection of the deteriorating relationship. House deplored the President's secrecy and exclusiveness. He noted that he was continuing to furnish journalists with necessary information about the Conference, in spite of Wilson's disapproval. He explained that he absented himself from plenary sessions because he thoroughly disapproved of the way the small countries were kept uninformed of matters of vital concern to them until the moment they were made public at the plenary sessions. He was in despair that Wilson had failed to communicate the text of the Treaty to the Senate, even though it had already been presented to the Germans and was publicly available on the newsstands.[47]

As the Peace Conference drew to a close, the Colonel realized that his close relationship with Wilson was not to be revived and that their intimate friendship had run its course. "In a way," he wrote in his diary on June 10, "I realize that in breaking up here it means the end of an epoch in my life, for after the Peace Conference is wound up I feel that I shall do other things than those I have been doing for so many years."[48]

This was indeed a prophetic utterance. On June 28, 1919, the Treaty of Versailles was signed. The President, eager to plunge into the task of getting it ratified by the Senate, decided to leave for home that very evening. House, sensing that difficult times lay ahead, had a last conversation with him and urged him to meet the Senate in a conciliatory spirit.

"House," replied Wilson, "I have found one can never get anything in this life that is worth while without fighting for it." House persisted, reminding the President that Anglo-Saxon civilization was built on compromise.[49] On this discordant note, the discussion ended.

Later that evening, House went to the station to see the President off. This was their final farewell. They never saw each other again.

## CHAPTER XIV

# BATTLE WITH THE SENATE

If the President adheres to his position that we must ratify it [the Treaty] without crossing a "t" or dotting an "i," my best judgment is that he will fail.

Senator Lodge to Henry White, July 2, 1919.[1]

ALL THE TIME President Wilson was in Paris spending himself to the utmost first to secure the League Covenant and then to amend it, his enemies at home, led by Senator Lodge, plotted his defeat. When Lodge read the revised Covenant in the newspapers on April 28, 1919, he immediately concluded that Wilson's Herculean effort to amend the Covenant satisfactorily had been in vain. ". . . It is obvious," he stated to the press the next day, "that it will require further amendments . . ." Thereafter, he took the position that, so far from being an improvement over the original, the revised Covenant was "much worse than it was before." The Senate, he indicated, would have to save the country from the perils into which the President's feckless leadership, unless checked, would lead it.[2]

Lodge, indeed, did not even have to examine the Covenant to be certain that it was a dangerous proposition. He had long since decided that while it would be "a mistake" to reject the *idea* of a league of nations—everyone, after all, favored the preservation of world peace—it would be possible to confound any practical plan, no matter what its terms. More than two months before the Covenant first emerged from the Peace Conference, Lodge wrote ex-Senator Beveridge of Indiana, an outspoken critic of the whole notion of American participation in any league:

Now the strength of our position is to show up the impossibility of any of the methods proposed and invite them, when they desire our support, to produce their terms. They cannot do it. My own judgment is that the whole thing will break up in conference. There may be some vague declarations of the beauties of peace, but any practical League that involves control of our legislation, of our armies and navies, or the Monroe Doctrine, or an international police, and that sort of thing, then our issue is made up, and we shall win.[3]

Throughout the battle over Senate ratification of the Treaty of Versailles, Lodge piously maintained that his position was dictated by an overriding concern for safeguarding the interests of the United States, and that he favored American entry into the League of Nations if only the Covenant could be so changed that basic American interests would be protected. It was widely suspected at the time, and frequently has been suggested since, that Lodge was out first and foremost to humiliate President Wilson, and that he had no use whatever for Wilson's League in any form. Since a policy of outright rejection would surely fail because of widespread public endorsement of the League, Lodge shrewdly feigned a more moderate position. He did so, according to this theory, the better ultimately to kill Wilson's creation or, at the very least, to change it and force the proud President to bow to the Republican-controlled Senate, thus yielding prestige, both personal and political.

In the light of Lodge's maneuvers throughout the Treaty fight, this interpretation is persuasive. It gains all but irresistible plausibility from the fact that when at last the Senate rejected the Treaty, League and all, Lodge felt, as he declared in a letter, that he and his colleagues had done very well. To one of his Senate colleagues, he referred to the outcome of the controversy as a "victory."[4] Further, at the Republican Convention of 1920, Lodge refused to urge ratification of the Treaty with the reservations he had so vociferously advocated but preferred, instead, to leave the way open for a complete repudiation of the League. And when, indeed, the Republicans won the election of 1920, Lodge exultantly declared that so far as the United States was concerned, the League of Nations was dead.[5]

Lodge personally detested Wilson, a fact to which his letters and papers eloquently testify. Quite apart from this highly personal consideration, however, as a Republican political leader Lodge had his eye upon the next presidential election, an event which has seldom failed to magnify the partisan component of issues before Congress for long months before its occurrence.

Whatever complex combination of personal, partisan and patriotic motives animated Lodge, certain it is that as soon as the Germans sued for peace in October, 1918, he turned all the resources of a cunning mind to the task of publicly embarrassing Wilson at every turn. He who had once proclaimed that where questions of foreign policy were concerned his politics always stopped at the water's edge,[6] attempted, via Henry White, to furnish Allied diplomats at the Peace Conference a memorandum suggesting that the President's ideas misrepresented the real sentiments of the people and Senate of the United States. His purpose, he stated frankly, was to strengthen the hands of these foreign diplomats in their dealings with Wilson.[7] Lodge organized the Round Robin, which struck Wilson's prestige a mighty blow at just the moment the President needed all his authority to induce the Allies to moderate some of their demands. At the height of the Italian crisis, while Wilson was standing foursquare against the Italian claim to Fiume, Lodge issued a statement to the Italians of Boston upholding the Italian position. The Shantung settlement, the justice of which was indeed debatable, provided Lodge and his cohorts with a splendid excuse to heap further abuse upon their favorite villain.[8]

As the *George Washington* bearing the President home from the Peace Conference coursed toward American shores, Senator Lodge was deep in plans to bring to his knees the man he hated more, he once confessed, than he had ever expected to hate anyone in politics, the man whom, James Buchanan perhaps excepted, he judged to be the worst President in the nation's history.[9] The great alarum which he and his friends were spreading the length and breadth of the land was that Wilson's League was fraught with dire danger for the United States and that the Senate must now change the Covenant to make it safe.

Almost any man who was confronted with opponents as intelligent and resourceful as Lodge and his cohorts would be distressed and angered. A more detached leader than Wilson, however, might have been capable of dispassionately countering Lodge's tactical maneuvers and of taking practical steps to mobilize all possible Senate support for the Treaty. Wilson's particular anxieties rendered him incapable of meeting Lodge's challenge with such equanimity. Because he was so peculiarly vulnerable to them, Lodge's barbs affected him as the proverbial red flag affects the proverbial bull.

Wilson had deep-seated doubts, which originated in his early years, of his intellectual competence, his moral worth and his strength. He had tried to overcome these self-doubts by rigorous training and ceaseless self-vindicating demonstrations through accomplishment that he was indeed of superior intelligence, of good and "unselfish" character, and of sufficient strength to escape the degradation of capitulating to anybody. With an unerring sense of where his adversary's weak points lay and with an air of patronizing superiority, Lodge peppered him with just those personal attacks which intensified Wilson's inner anxieties.

Did Wilson, after suffering much mortification for his "slowness" as a child, joyfully discover in his adolescence that he "had a mind" and thereafter take especial pride in his intellectual attainments? Lodge was not at pains to conceal his contempt for Wilson's "mind." In a Senate speech on February 28, 1919, it will be recalled, Lodge had derided Wilson as one whose intellect and position in the world he found something less than overpowering. As for being the "scholar in politics"—until Wilson's star eclipsed his own, Lodge had enjoyed that popular appellation—why, Wilson was no scholar at all, Lodge maintained. (As evidence of this, in a book he subsequently wrote, the learned Senator cited the fact that in making a classical allusion, Wilson had once confused Hercules with Antaeus, a blunder which Lodge considered "incredible.") [10]

Did Wilson, trained by a father obsessed with the importance of proper use of the English language, take great pains with his style and inordinately value mellifluous phrases and graceful expression? "As an English production," Lodge once remarked of the Covenant, "it does not rank high. It might get by at Princeton but certainly not at Harvard." [11]

Did Wilson secretly fear his "selfish" motives in exercising leadership and continually proclaim his own disinterestedness and, by extension, the disinterestedness of the nation in dealing with other nations? Lodge thought Wilson self-seeking, unprincipled, egotistical, timid, narrow-minded, a demagogue interested exclusively in his own aggrandizement—and he made no secret of his opinion.

Did Wilson, desperately eager to undercut Lodge's position, make the most painful compromises during the latter half of the Peace Conference in order to obtain amendments to the Covenant which would meet the major objections which had been raised against it? Lodge, so far from being nonplussed by Wilson's coup, summarily dismissed the revisions as worthless and served notice that the Senate would have to make further changes. Unless the President accepted these changes, he warned repeatedly, the Treaty would be defeated.[12]

Not only was the substance of Lodge's thrusts unbearable to Wilson: the Senator's manner stung him to the quick. Even one of Lodge's lifelong friends, William Lawrence, in summing up Lodge's career regretfully noted that "Cabot" had "a certain quality of voice in making his brightest and most penetrating remarks" which could mortally offend. "His thrusts of sarcasm, his occasional sharp wit, with his manner and voice, sometimes more than counteracted the matter and sentiment of an otherwise fine and lofty speech." [13]

As a Harvard undergraduate, Lodge had participated with such deadly effect in a traditional parody of the foibles of various members of his class that a number of his classmates were alienated for life and the tradition was abandoned. Over half a century later, recalling Lodge's manner as he lampooned his fellows, a witness of the performance declared: "I can still hear today the exultant voice of the orator. The savageness . . . repelled me utterly." [14]

Lodge trained all this capacity for sneering sarcasm against Wilson. There was something contemptuous in the very calmness of the man: it was as though he felt the objects of his scorn unworthy even of his enmity.

Once before, long ago, Wilson had had to endure barbed criticism. Once before, long ago, he had been sent in humiliation to revise and re-revise some carefully wrought composition. And long ago, overwhelmed by his masterful father, he had submitted to sarcastically made demands and to aspersions on his moral and intellectual worth. He had submitted in seeming docility. Perhaps the rage that he had suppressed then emerged in full force against those he encountered in later years who reawakened the disagreeable sensations of half a century and more before.

Wilson's emotional commitment to the League was, as we have seen, of surpassing intensity. Even in connection with projects of far less personal significance to him, he habitually experienced any interference in his exercise of power as an intolerable threat. Small wonder, given the very real menace Lodge presented both to the League and to Wilson's inner equilibrium, that the mere mention of the Senator's name caused Wilson to clench his teeth in rage.

President Wilson arrived home from Europe on July 8, 1919. Two days later he appeared before the Senate to lay the Treaty before it for ratification. Shortly before leaving the White House to address the Senate, Wilson held a press conference. One of the reporters inquired whether the Treaty would pass if the Senate attached reservations to it. "I do not think hypothetical questions are concerned," Wilson flashed back. "*The Senate is going to ratify the treaty.*" [15]

If his address to the Senate had a somewhat less peremptory tone, its plain implication was the same: the Senate *must* ratify the Treaty—it was God's will. It was not a perfect instrument, the President conceded. Many "minor compromises" had been made but, he declared euphemistically, the settlement "squares, as a whole, with the principles agreed upon as the basis of the peace. . . ." The Treaty's most important accomplishment was the creation of the League of Nations. "Dare we reject it and break the heart of the world?" Rejection was unthinkable. America, as had been universally recognized, "entered the war to promote no private or peculiar interest of her own but only as the champion of rights which she was glad to share with free men and lovers of justice everywhere." Now the world looked to America for moral leadership, and it was our duty to accept the responsibility of providing it. "The stage is set, the destiny disclosed," the President concluded. "It has come about by no plan of our conceiving, but by the hand of God who led us into this way. We cannot turn back. We can only go forward, with lifted eyes and freshened spirit, to follow the vision. It was of this that we dreamed at our birth. America shall in truth show the way. The light streams upon the path ahead, and nowhere else." [16]

Unfortunately, as their immediate comments disclosed, many of the Senators saw "the light" streaming upon a number of alternative paths that the zealous President did not espy; and they regarded the destiny for America which Wilson envisaged more as a product of the plans of Woodrow Wilson than as a manifestation of the "hand of God." What about reservations, a number of them demanded. The President had not even mentioned the subject, which was uppermost in the minds of the Senators. Instead he had treated them to, as Senator Brandegee (R., Conn.) put it, "soap bubbles of oratory and soufflé of phrases." [17]

The Treaty having been formally placed before the Senate, it was immediately referred to the Senate Foreign Relations Committee. The chairman of this Committee, of course, was Henry Cabot Lodge.

Though chairman of the Foreign Relations Committee and leader of the majority party in the Senate—there were 49 Republicans and 47 Democrats in the Senate newly organized in accordance with the results of the 1918 elections—Lodge was in an extremely difficult position. The nub of his dilemma was that public opinion overwhelmingly favored *a* league and, after Wilson succeeded in amending the Covenant in Paris to eliminate most of the dangers its opponents professed to see in it, the public plainly favored *the* League. Several polls testified to that fact. So did the tidal wave of favorable comment in the press and in lecture halls and pulpits throughout the land, of resolutions of endorsement by farm and labor organizations and by state legislatures.[18]

Senator Lodge was greatly concerned over this state of affairs. He was shrewd enough to realize that, given the temper of the country and even of a goodly number of his Republican colleagues in the Senate, any immediate showdown between the supporters of the League and its opponents would result in a rout of the latter. To A. J. Beveridge he wrote in February, 1919:

> The situation . . . practically must be treated with great care. I have no doubt that a large majority of the people of the country are very naturally fascinated by the idea of eternal preservation of the world's peace. . . . Now I do not think it would be wise for us at this stage to make it a party issue, nor to confront it with a blank negative. I think what is necessary for us to do is to begin to discuss it and try to get what it involves and what it means before the American people. . . . I think the second thought is going to be with us, but the first thought is probably against us. Therefore, we must proceed with caution . . .[19]

Lodge accordingly felt that it was necessary to gain time to influence opinion against the Treaty as it stood. The thing to do, Lodge thought, was to proclaim the supposed dangers inherent in Wilson's League from the Atlantic to the Pacific, from Canada to Mexico. Money aplenty was available for this enterprise. Speeches by Lodge and other critics of the League were printed and distributed by the hundreds of thousands. Meetings were held at which speakers warned that Wilson's League impaired American sovereignty, surrendered the

Monroe Doctrine, entangled us in European and Asiatic intrigues, thus flouting George Washington's time-honored advice, and subjected American boys to the authority of a foreign agency which might at any time order them into battle for remote causes in remote parts of the world. Worse still, our boys might be ordered to fight in causes which would be plainly repugnant to any freedom-loving American, such as the quelling of Irish revolutionists for the benefit of their English oppressors.

Several minority groups were highly susceptible to these arguments. First, there were the Irish-Americans, bitterly resentful of Wilson because he had not fought for Irish self-determination at the Peace Conference. Then there were the German-Americans, some seven million strong, and in varying degrees incensed at Wilson for his role in the ignominious defeat of the Fatherland. Too, there were the Italian-Americans, up in arms against Wilson for his implacable opposition to awarding Fiume to Italy.

Other groups, based on mutually shared viewpoints rather than national origins, opposed the Treaty. There were, for example, the liberals, who were deeply disillusioned at what they considered Wilson's betrayal of his own principles at the Peace Conference. One of the leading liberal weeklies, *The Nation*, referred to the League of Nations as, to quote the title of one of its articles on the subject, "A Colossal Humbug," and analyzed one of the President's attempts to depict the disadvantages of rejecting the Treaty under the heading, "Mr. Wilson Rants." [20]

More numerous and an even greater stumbling block to the League were the isolationists—those who still thought America could be a land unto herself and exist without sullying her hands in the endless broils of the rest of the world. To them, the League represented a dangerous departure from the principle, which had served so well in the past, of avoiding foreign entanglements. Once enter the League, they cried, and the United States would find that she had surrendered her sovereignty to a mongrel superstate. The isolationists drew strength from the fact that theirs was the hallowed national tradition. Their predictions of the dire consequences of venturing into new international relationships gave their more forward-looking compatriots many sober second thoughts.

All of these groups were natural targets for anti-League propaganda. Lodge and his political friends tirelessly fanned the flames of their various fears and resentments. The resultant cacophony of anti-League and anti-Wilson invective made many a citizen, not associated with any special group, wonder whether there must not be a kernel of truth in all the criticisms of the League; whether, after all, it would not be wise to "Americanize" the Treaty as so many people so loudly and so urgently recommended. By the time Wilson returned from Paris, there was still a widespread disposition to accept the Treaty and enter the League, but it was qualified by the growing feeling that perhaps the Treaty ought to be changed to further protect American interests.

If opinion throughout the country was growing more confused by the day as the result of the anti-League campaign, opinions in the Senate were in confusion twice compounded. For not only were the Senators prey to all the intellectual cross-currents abroad in the land: in addition, they were swayed by two other factors. First, it was in the nature of the case that the Senators, as politicians, should have politics on their minds—and the 1920 presidential election was little over a year away. Second, many a Senator, on both sides of the aisle, welcomed the opportunity to settle old personal scores with Wilson, now that the war was over and they no longer felt obliged to suppress their antagonism. They would give Wilson an object lesson in respect for the legislative branch of government, using his beloved Treaty as the text.

Historian Thomas A. Bailey, after noting that "one competent writer has estimated that four-fifths of the opposition to the League was nothing more than unreasoning hatred of Wilson," comments: "This is probably an exaggeration, but there can be no doubt that the Republican leaders, and many of the Republican rank and file, hated the President with a consuming bitterness, and were prepared to stop at nothing to bring about his downfall and at the same time (so they claimed) save the Republic." [21]

From a strictly partisan point of view, it would never do to allow Wilson, singlehanded, the great accomplishment of which he dreamed. On the heels of such a success, the Republicans feared, he might seek a third term—and might even win it. From the Republican point of view, Wilson's League must either be defeated or, at the very least, so "Republicanized" that the GOP could claim credit for some of its good features. That the Treaty would be ratified and the United States would enter the League, however, seemed a foregone conclusion. A large proportion of Republican Senators were willing to content themselves with making only minor changes in the Treaty. They, together with the Democrats, constituted a majority of the Senate and could probably attract sufficient additional votes to make up the necessary two-thirds for ratification.

It was into this complex situation that Lodge entered as majority leader of the Senate. It was a situation which filled the enemies of the Treaty with despair, for it seemed inevitable that, with some minor alterations, the Treaty would pass. One evening, Senator James E. Watson of Indiana dined with Lodge to discuss means for meeting the challenge posed by the Treaty. "Senator," Watson declared, "I don't see how we are ever going to defeat this proposition. It appears to me that eighty per cent of the people are for it."

Lodge replied, "Ah, my dear James, I do not propose to try to beat it by direct frontal attack, but by the indirect method of reservations."

Watson was puzzled and asked Lodge to elaborate. Lodge did so, for two hours, until Watson, as he later wrote, "became thoroughly satisfied that the Treaty could be beaten in that way." [22] For sheer brilliance of conception Lodge's strategy stands without parallel in American history. For the finesse with which he applied it, Lodge stands without peer as a master tactician and psychologist.

Lodge's whole plan of action was based upon his estimate that Wilson would never consent to accepting Senate reservations to the Treaty. To Lodge, as he later wrote, Wilson "was simply an element to be calmly and coolly considered in a great problem of international politics." It was the Senator's "calm" and "cool" judgment that Wilson would do all he could to "prevent the acceptance of the treaty with reservations. . . ."

I based this opinion on the knowledge which I had acquired as to Mr. Wilson's temperament, intentions and purposes. I had learned from a careful study of the President's acts and utterances during those trying days—and it was as important for me to understand him as it was for his closest friends—that the key to all he did was that he thought of everything in terms of Wilson. In other words, Mr. Wilson in dealing with every great question thought first of himself. He may have thought of the country next, but there was a long interval, and in the competition the Democratic Party, I will do him the justice to say, was a poor third. Mr. Wilson was devoured by the desire for power. . . .

This conviction held by me as to the governing quality in Mr. Wilson's mind and character was reached very slowly and only finally arrived at when I found myself confronted with a situation, the gravity of which in its public importance could not be exaggerated, and when a correct analysis of Mr. Wilson's probable attitude was an element of vital moment to me in trying to solve the intricate problem which I and those with whom I acted were compelled to face.[23]

Given this conviction and the intrepidity to stake his whole strategy on it, Lodge was able to map out a plan of action at once beautifully simple and subtle. All he had to do was tack reservations onto the Treaty, and most particularly onto the League Covenant, which Wilson held so dear. Then, if his theory was correct, Wilson could be counted on himself to destroy what he had invested his lifeblood to create. Lodge's first problem, therefore, was to make certain that a majority vote could be commanded for his reservations.

Of the forty-nine Republican Senators, fifteen, who came to be known as "irreconcilables" and "bitter-enders," were opposed to the Treaty in any way, shape or form. Led by William Borah of Idaho, a man of incorruptible conviction so fiercely determined to keep this nation out of the League that it was commonly believed he would bolt the Party in 1920 if dissatisfied with Republican leadership on the Treaty issue, the "irreconcilables" had unequivocally announced their intention of voting against the Treaty, amended or unamended, with reservations or without.

On April 29, 1919, three weeks before the new Congress was to convene, Lodge conferred with Borah for the purpose of enlisting his support for amendments and reservations. Lodge told Borah that in his judgment "the great mass of the people, the man in the street, to use a common expression" favored Wilson's League, and that "the vocal classes of the community"—clergymen, educators, newspaper editors, and opinion leaders generally—were also advocating the League as it stood. "With these conditions existing, I said to Senator Borah, it seemed perfectly obvious to me that any attempt to defeat the treaty of Versailles with the League by a straight vote in the Senate, if taken immediately, would be hopeless, even if it were desirable." There was only one thing to do, Lodge argued, and that was to attach amendments and reservations to the Treaty. If the Treaty then failed of ratification, Borah and his colleagues would be satisfied. If it passed, it would at least bear Republican improvements. Borah agreed with Lodge's analysis of the situation and pledged himself to vote for amendments and reservations, with the understanding, of course, that on the final vote he would vote against ratification of the Treaty. Lodge was greatly pleased with this outcome—it "confirmed me in the opinions which I had formed as to the proper way of dealing with the treaty when it came before us." [24]

Next, Lodge turned his attention to the organization of the Committee on Foreign Relations, the composition of which would be, as he later wrote, of unusual consequence. Lodge loaded the Committee with "irreconcilables," deliberately rejecting such middle-grounders as Senator Kellogg, because Kellogg declined to commit himself blindly to Lodge's leadership. Of the ten Republicans on the Committee, six were "irreconcilables" and three were strong reservationists. The Republican "mild reservationists" were appalled. It could be seen immediately, Lodge later blandly recorded, that it was a "strong" committee of the kind the situation required.[25]

The dozen or so "mild reservationists" in the Senate, as their name implies, favored reservations, though of a generally minor character. Lodge could count on them to support *some* program of reservations. He would have to feel his way along to see how broad a one they would swallow. He could also count for support on three or four Democrats, who stood ready to defy Wilson and work for the interment of the Treaty.

By the time Wilson returned to Washington in July, 1919, Lodge could be certain that the one condition upon which his hopes rested —that Wilson would be confronted with the necessity of accepting reservations on pain of seeing the whole Treaty go down in defeat— would be fulfilled.

The arithmetic of the problem was inescapable. No matter what he did, Wilson was caught by it. There was only one exit from the trap: compromise on reservations. The possibility that the President would bow to the realities of the situation and accept reservations, either those of the "mild reservationists" or, if need be, Lodge's own, was the great vulnerability of the anti-Treaty strategy, the waking nightmare of those interested in defeating the Treaty during the nine months that it was before the Senate. Lodge remained imperturbable.

On one occasion, Senator Watson said to him, "Senator, suppose that the President accepts the Treaty with your reservations. Then we are in the League, and once in, our reservations become purely fiction."

Lodge smiled. "But, my dear James, you do not take into consideration the hatred that Woodrow Wilson has for me personally. Never under any set of circumstances in this world could he be induced to accept a treaty with Lodge reservations appended to it."

"But that seems to me to be rather a slender thread on which to hang so great a cause," Watson replied.

"A slender thread!" exclaimed Lodge. "Why, it is as strong as any cable with its strands wired and twisted together."[26]

In later years, Lodge was able to write with some satisfaction that he had made no mistake in his estimate of what President Wilson would do under certain conditions.[27]

Once in the hands of the Foreign Relations Committee, the Treaty was at the mercy of Lodge and the "strong" colleagues he had so carefully selected to assist in the contemplated operation upon Wilson's brain child. First, however, the patient had to be very, very carefully examined—and no one could hurry Dr. Lodge, for he and his fellow Republicans controlled the Committee.

Lodge began by reading the entire Treaty aloud—all two hundred sixty-eight pages of it. It took him two weeks. Much of his performance was witnessed only by the Committee clerk. On one occasion, even this captive audience departed. Undaunted, Lodge soliloquized. The reading finally completed, the Committee began hearings. Representatives of numerous groups which had failed to satisfy their aspirations at Paris gave vent to their spleen before the sympathetic Senators. Their complaints furnished excellent publicity for the alleged iniquities of the Treaty. The hearings also served to give the Treaty's opponents, both in and out of the Senate, further time in which to educate public opinion to the dangers which they claimed would envelop the United States were the League Covenant to be allowed to stand unchanged.

Critics of the Covenant heaped abuse on it from its first word to its last, but major fire was concentrated on four points. First it was alleged that the Covenant as it stood gave the League the right to meddle in the domestic affairs of its members. Did we want to authorize a foreign superstate to interfere with our immigration policies, to tell us, for example, that we must admit Orientals into this country on an unrestricted basis? Or, to take another example, to authorize the League to dictate our tariff policy? Wilson's supporters pointed out that it was to meet this very criticism that the President, when he had returned to Paris in March, had secured an amendment to the Covenant providing that if a dispute between contending parties "is claimed by one of them, and is found by the Council, to arise out of a matter which by international law is solely within the domestic jurisdiction of that party, the Council shall so report, and shall make no recommendation as to its settlement."[28] This formulation, Wilson's critics retorted, left it to the Council of the League to decide whether or not a dispute fell within the domestic jurisdiction of one of the parties. The United States should have this decision in its own hands where any question involving this country arose.

Second, it was alleged that the Covenant endangered the Monroe Doctrine. Wilson's supporters drew attention to a second amendment to the Covenant he had obtained while still in Paris stipulating that "nothing in this Covenant shall be deemed to affect the validity of international engagements, such as treaties of arbitration or regional understandings like the Monroe Doctrine, for securing the maintenance of peace."[29] To this Wilson's critics replied that the Monroe Doctrine was *not* an "international engagement" or a "regional understanding." It was a unilateral policy of the United States, and must be expressly exempted from interpretation by foreign powers.[30]

Third, it was alleged that the provision for withdrawal from the League was unsatisfactory. A third amendment to the Covenant which Wilson had secured in Paris in response to criticism at home provided that "any Member of the League may, after two years' notice of its intention so to do, withdraw from the League, provided that all its international obligations and all its obligations under this Covenant shall have been fulfilled at the time of its withdrawal."[31] But who would decide whether a withdrawing nation had fulfilled all its obligations, it was demanded. Obviously, declared Wilson's supporters, the withdrawing nation would, since the League was nowhere empowered to decide such a question. This answer failed to satisfy Wilson's detractors. To them, the provision was, at best, ambiguous, and there must be no ambiguity in such a matter: the world must know that the United States alone would decide whether or not her obligations had been fulfilled and would expect the unconditional right to withdraw.

Fourth, having been uncertain for a time whether to regard Wilson's League as a powerless debating society or a dangerous superstate, Lodge and his friends took the latter position and fell upon Article X of the Covenant. Article X read:

The Members of the League undertake to respect and preserve as against external aggression the territorial integrity and existing political independence of all Members of the League. In case of any such aggression or in case of any threat or danger of such aggression the Council shall advise upon the means by which this obligation shall be fulfilled.[32]

This provision plainly overrode the United States Constitution, Wilson's critics charged. Under it, the League could order American boys into battle, or order the United States to impose economic boycotts on other nations. The Constitution, however, provides that only Congress can declare war, and all bills to raise revenue or affecting revenue must be passed by Congress and signed by the President. Wilson's defenders pointed out that since the Council's decisions required unanimity, it could not act without the assent of its United States delegate. This would prevent the Council from taking actions obnoxious to the United States. Further, the Council's action in any case was only *advisory*. It had no power to issue a legally binding order. Its advice created a moral, rather than a legal obligation, the point being that a moral obligation left room for the exercise of discretion and judgment. It would be up to Congress to decide whether to accept the Council's advice, and to determine what action to take in any particular case.[33] If there were only a moral obligation, the anti-Wilsonites retorted, then what avail Article X? Every nation could construe the Council's advice as it pleased and the Council would then amount to nothing more than a toothless forum, after all. Wilson and his supporters replied that in such matters, there is a national good conscience. Nations generally attempt to fulfill solemn obligations, moral as well as legal. The mere acceptance of a moral obligation by nations toward each other was an excellent step forward in international relations.

There had been a time, not so many years before, when Lodge had cordially endorsed this very idea. Speaking at Union College in New York in June, 1915, he had declared:

. . . Turn it back and forth as we may there is no escape from the proposition that the peace of the world can be maintained only . . . by the force which united nations are willing to put behind the peace and order of the world. Nations must unite as men unite in order to preserve peace and order. The great nations must be so united as to be able to say to any single country, you must not go to war, and they can only say that effectively when the country desiring war knows that the force which the united nations place behind peace is irresistible.[34]

In May, 1916, speaking at a meeting of the League to Enforce Peace, Lodge had reiterated the view that the only hope for future world peace lay in the creation of an international league with force at its disposal. "I know the obstacles," Lodge then had said:

> I know how quickly we shall be met with the statement that this is a dangerous question which you are putting into your agreement, that no nation can submit to the judgment of other nations, and we must be careful at the beginning not to attempt too much. I know the difficulties that arise when we speak of anything which seems to involve an alliance. But I do not believe that when Washington warned us against permanent alliances he meant for one moment that we should not join with the other civilized nations of the world if a method could be found to diminish war and encourage peace.[35]

A man can change his opinions, however, and when his earlier views materialized in Wilson's Covenant, Lodge invoked the Founding Fathers to vindicate his opposition to Wilson's League in general and Article X in particular.

Wilson's adherents complained that the League's critics spoke as though the Covenant's provisions applied exclusively to the United States; as though the League were nothing but a gigantic conspiracy against the sovereignty of the United States. Britain, France, Italy and other nations were as concerned as we were to preserve their freedom of action and to keep control of their domestic problems in their own hands. All members would be bound by the same rules, these Wilsonians asserted. That being the case, and the other nations being as jealous of their prerogatives as the United States, in practice no great sacrifice of sovereignty would be required.[36] Therefore, the safeguards which so many people were demanding in the form of changes in the Covenant were unnecessary because they were already clearly implicit and tacitly accepted by the other powers.

It will be obvious to the reader, even from this abbreviated account of some of the points of contention, that many arguments could be mustered to support a variety of views concerning each of them. Many were. The newspapers carried column after column of intricate legal discussions, with opinions and counteropinions, with accounts of complicated parliamentary maneuvers in the Senate and of a dizzying variety of views on a dizzying number of the Treaty's provisions. The public was rapidly becoming thoroughly confused, though through it all it remained clear that most people and most Senators wanted the League and the Treaty in some form. Why not, then, attach reservations, even if only to still groundless fears, and get the whole bothersome business out of the way once and for all? This feeling grew, both in and out of the Senate, as the dispute wore on.

Faced with this tangled situation, President Wilson struck an attitude which is as simple to describe as it is difficult to analyze. He would not consent to the embodiment of reservations or amendments to the Treaty in the resolution of ratification. He would consider, however, the possibility of issuing a separate statement of "reasonable interpretation(s)" simultaneously with the resolution of ratification. He took this position on the day he presented the Treaty to the Senate.[37] He reaffirmed it when he met with the Senate Foreign Relations Committee on August 19.[38] From start to finish, he did not deviate one jot from this position. It was on this issue of the *form* of the reservations, as well as of the content of the final version of the reservation to Article X, that the whole Treaty foundered.

Wilson based his refusal to have amendments or reservations embodied in the resolution of ratification on the grounds that such changes then would have to be approved by every nation—including Germany—which had signed the Treaty. Other nations, too, might follow our lead and start changing the Treaty. The floodgates would be thrown open, and the whole Treaty might have to be renegotiated.[39] On the other hand, a separate statement of interpretations issued along with the resolution of ratification, the President held, would not require positive action on the part of the other signers of the contract.

This point involved a technical question of international law about which differences of opinion existed. Wilson and the Republicans were in agreement that any textual amendments to the Treaty would indeed have to be submitted for the approval of all the other signatories, Germany included. They differed, however, on the automatic necessity of so submitting reservations for approval. The Republicans thought it was generally accepted that the mere silence of other parties to the Treaty with reference to reservations would constitute acceptance of such reservations.[40] And they were not content to settle for acquiescence by silence. That, they feared, might create doubt and later confusion as to whether our reservations bound the other signatories. By midsummer, 1919, all the reservationists, both mild and strong—a clear majority of the Senate—were agreed that reservations must be riveted to the resolution of ratification and, further, that they must be unequivocally accepted by the major Allied signatories.[41]

Wilson had taken the narrow view before and during the Peace Conference that the negotiations were his exclusive prerogative, that the Senate's "advice and consent" were required only after the completion of the Treaty. Now that the Treaty was completed he argued that the slightest alteration of its language would endanger the whole noble project. In what way, then, and when, did he believe the Senate could legitimately exercise its prerogatives? His opponents cried that Woodrow Wilson wanted to transform the Senate of the United States into a rubber stamp. Lodge and his friends harped on this theme and skillfully exploited the personal hostility many Senators felt toward the President. For his part, Wilson proceeded with glacial disdain for the interpersonal aspects of his problem. In so doing, he furnished his opponents much grist for their mill.

There was, for example, the matter of his secretiveness about the terms of the Treaty. The Treaty had been presented to the Germans in May. Within a few days, its text had been leaked to the press, and published in newspapers all over the world, including the United States. One of the American financial experts had sent an unofficial copy of it to some of his Wall Street associates and they, in turn, had passed it along to Lodge. There was a great furor in the Senate over the fact that though the newspapers and Wall Street had copies of the Treaty the President had not deigned to inform the Senate, even unofficially, of its contents. True, Wilson and his fellow negotiators had pledged themselves to keep the terms secret until the Germans had accepted them. Events had outmoded this pledge, however. Nevertheless, Wilson elected to observe it to the letter. His stiff-necked rectitude cost him dear in that most valuable of coins, senatorial goodwill.

Then there was the matter of the French Security Treaty. One of the concessions that Wilson had made to Clemenceau was a treaty committing the United States to come to France's aid in the event of unprovoked aggression by Germany. This Treaty specifically stipulated that the President present it to the Senate at the same time that he presented the Treaty of Versailles. Wilson did not so present it. He preferred, he explained to newspapermen, to take it up separately—it was complicated, and he had not yet got around to writing his message on it.[42] This plain, if intrinsically minor, violation of the terms of the Security Treaty gave his opponents still another excuse to flay him. Finally, nineteen days late, Wilson laid the French Security Treaty before the Senate. (Of its fate, Lodge later wrote that it was duly referred to his Committee but was never even taken up.[43] It died quietly—except in France, where Wilson was castigated as the blackguard of the century. But that is another story.)

Lodge badgered Wilson with requests for records of the Paris negotiations, claiming they were necessary to the work of his Committee. He also demanded the texts of treaties which were still being negotiated with some of the smaller nations. Wilson refused many of these requests. Whether the President was justified in doing so or not, Lodge capitalized on every instance of his reticence as further proof of his disrespect for the Senate. On August 1, Lodge presented to the Senate the Treaty with Poland, to which the United States was a party, noting that it had been placed before the British Parliament two weeks before and that it was for sale in London.[44]

This running battle over information was a diversion probably calculated by the Senator, at least in part, to sustain bad feeling toward the President on the part of the "mild reservationists" who, despite all, were attracted to the Covenant and genuinely interested in seeing it and the Treaty ratified. On July 17, Wilson began a series of conferences with individual "mild reservationists" and strong reservationists whose minds he thought might still be open. His purpose, be it noted, was not to explore their viewpoints and the possibility of compromise. Rather, he wanted to persuade them to ratify the Treaty as it stood, adding interpretations, if they must, in a separate resolution. Almost to a man, these Senators warned Wilson that unless he accepted binding reservations, the Treaty would not be ratified. To a man, they assured reporters who avidly questioned them as they left the White House that the President had not caused them to change their views. Bailey has aptly commented on the poor strategy of these conferences: the individual Senators "were forced into an awkward position. The news that they were going to the White House was heralded in advance on the front page of the newspapers. The question on the public lip was, 'Will they bend the knee?' . . . The whole business savored of the naughty boy being called into the principal's office for a scolding. The natural disposition of the proud senators was to show their mettle by making up their minds in advance that they would not yield anything, and none of them apparently did." [45]

Nevertheless the "mild reservationists" were working in good faith for the passage of the Treaty and took the initiative in trying to arrange a compromise with Wilson. On August 1, seven of them issued a set of four mild reservations which satisfied them, and which they hoped would rally the Democrats and a sufficient number of other reservationist Republicans to make up the necessary two-thirds vote for ratification.[46] These first mild reservations, by common consent both at the time and in the judgment of historians, were entirely innocuous. They simply made explicit what Wilson felt was implicit in the wording of the Covenant regarding the right to withdraw, the exclusion of domestic questions from League jurisdiction, the validity of the Monroe Doctrine and the exclusive right of Congress to order the use of American military or economic resources. Their authors, however, had stipulated that these reservations were to be made part of the resolution of ratification, and to be formally approved by the other powers. If Wilson had made common cause with the "mild reservationists" at this time, the likelihood is that he would have had his Treaty with only these few minor alterations.

It is futile to pursue the interesting "if's" of the situation. The fact is that Wilson did not grasp the opportunity afforded by the proposal of the "mild reservationists." Instead, the White House was entirely silent on the subject for two weeks, during which, however, Wilson's Senate spokesman, Gilbert M. Hitchcock, termed the proposal a fresh indication of the "muddle" in the "opposition" camp. In the end, Hitchcock confidently predicted, "the fight of the League opponents will come to nothing at all, with the Treaty being ratified exactly as submitted to the Senate."[47] On August 15, Hitchcock conferred with Wilson, and the two dealt the "mild reservationists" another blow. A headline on Page 1 of the New York *Times* the next day read: HITCHCOCK SAYS THE PRESIDENT WON'T CONCEDE EVEN "THE CROSSING OF A 'T'." Even mild reservations would prove tremendously embarrassing, Hitchcock quoted Wilson as saying, and in any case this was no time for friends of the Treaty to be talking or even thinking of compromises.[48] Wilson was clinging fast to his opposition to any changes in the Treaty, however slight, which would be included in the resolution of ratification and thus require the approval of the other powers. Again on August 26, after another White House conference, Hitchcock reported that he and the President were in agreement that "the Treaty will be ratified and there will be no changes in it."[49]

All through the summer, Wilson and his spokesman issued bold assertions that the Treaty would pass exactly as it stood.[50] The "mild reservationists," knowing full well that it was impossible for the Treaty to pass "exactly as it stood," were depressed and angered at the rebuffs their helpful efforts invariably encountered. But they could not believe that Wilson would wreck the entire Treaty over the question of whether the reservations should be included in the resolution of ratification. They could not believe he would remain blind to the fact that they were offering him an alternative to the far more stringent reservations which the Lodge group were preparing, and against which they were willing to hold out as long as there was hope of reaching agreement with the Democrats. So all through the summer of 1919, they polished their reservations and tried every way short of agreeing to omit them from the resolution of ratification, to make them palatable to Wilson.

By the end of July, ex-President Taft, who regarded the Treaty as acceptable as it stood, sadly concluded that whatever the merits of the case, the situation in the Senate was such that without reservations, the Treaty could not be ratified. No man had done Wilson greater service in the cause of the League. No man was more eager to see the Treaty ratified. On July 21, Taft wrote Hitchcock that in his judgment the administration would have to satisfy the Republican Senators by accepting interpretations which would be "within the Covenant itself. . . ." He earnestly advised Hitchcock to work with the "mild reservationists." [51] Hitchcock publicly termed Taft's letter an attempt to save the Republican Party from defeat in its opposition to the League and declared it affected neither the situation nor his opinion that the Covenant would be adopted as it stood.[52] Taft made a public statement on July 23 reiterating that the Treaty was satisfactory as it stood, but that he now favored mild reservations. It was necessary, he declared, "to recognize the exigencies, personal, partisan and political." When he heard the news, Lodge chortled, "Brother Taft has dropped off his perch." [53]

Wilson was now face to face with his inner demons. He had tried, and failed, to convince the most reasonable of the Republicans that they must support the Treaty as it stood. He made another attempt at courteous explanation of his position on August 19, when he met with the Senate Foreign Relations Committee and, for over three hours, submitted to sharp questioning. His words fell on deaf ears. The "irreconcilables" emerged from the meeting as antagonistic toward the Treaty as ever; the strong reservationists emerged proclaiming their determination to rivet their reservations to the Treaty.[54] The lines were drawn taut. The only way to save the Treaty was for Wilson to compromise—at this stage, not with Lodge, but with the "mild reservationists" who so eagerly awaited any such overture from him.

Whatever the exigencies of the situation, however, Wilson could not help feeling as he had some months before when Senator Martin, then Wilson's spokesman in the Senate, had warned him that the Treaty as it stood probably could not be ratified.

"Martin!" Wilson had blazed. "Anyone who opposes me in that, I'll crush!"[55]

# CHAPTER XV

## DEFEAT

> In the final analysis the treaty was slain in the house of its friends rather than in the house of its enemies. In the final analysis it was not the two-thirds rule, or the "irreconcilables," or Lodge, or the "strong" and "mild reservationists," but Wilson and his docile following who delivered the fatal stab. . . . With his own sickly hands Wilson slew his own brain child. . . .
>
> Thomas A. Bailey, *Woodrow Wilson and the Great Betrayal.* [1]

WILSON WAS A MORALIST. What is "right"? That is a question which had preoccupied him, in one form or another, all his life long. Now he was at a fateful crossroad. What was the "right" thing to do? Wilson knew. He was an historian and, as his writings show, was well aware that the "right" thing for a statesman to do is to accomplish what he can in a practical manner. He had expressed himself often on this very problem: leaders "must not be impossible. They must not insist upon getting at once what they know they cannot get!" [2]

What is a President to do when he finds himself at an impasse with Congress? This question, too, Wilson had pondered deeply, and he had published his views in *Constitutional Government in the United States*. If the President be blocked by the House of Representatives, he can appeal to the nation. Public opinion may then make the House thoughtful of the next congressional elections. However, "The President has not the same recourse when blocked by the Senate. . . . The Senate is not so immediately sensitive to opinion and is apt to grow, if anything, more stiff if pressure of that kind is brought to bear upon it."

But there is a course the President may take to prevent an impasse from arising in the first place: "He may himself be less stiff and offish, *may himself act in the true spirit of the Constitution and establish intimate relations of confidence with the Senate on his own initiative, not carrying his plans to completion and then laying them in final form before the Senate to be accepted or rejected,* but keeping himself in confidential communication with the leaders of the Senate while his plans are in course . . . in order that there may be veritable counsel and a real accommodation of views instead of a final challenge and contest." This course was not only the President's privilege but his "plain duty," Wilson had written.[8]

By the summer of 1919, Wilson had flouted much of his own good counsel. He had excluded the Senate from the peacemaking process and, having carried his own plans to completion, had indeed laid them before that body in final form, for acceptance or rejection. There still was the opportunity, however, to retrieve his errors, to be "less stiff and offish" with the "mild reservationists" and by yielding on the matter of permitting reservations which would require the approval of the Allies, gain support which would help his Treaty pass. But Wilson could not yield. It is probably not accurate to say that he would not yield. He *could* not. His decision to spurn the "mild reservationists" and appeal to the people—to turn his back on "plain duty" and take a course which he must have known held little hope of success—was not the result of rational calculation. It was the result of emotional necessity.

Men require ways of expressing their aggressions and of protecting their self-esteem. Wilson's ways of doing both, unhappily, involved demanding his way to the letter and hurling himself against his opponents no matter what the odds, no matter what the cost. Reason told him he must stay in Washington and compromise to save his League. Feeling forbade his doing so. Feeling obliged him to jeopardize his beloved League—feeling he could neither understand nor bear to examine nor resist. Jeopardizing the League—the whole Treaty—for personal reasons, for those "selfish" motives he so deplored, was an unpardonable sin. Yet the knowledge that he was doing so, that he was not able to efface himself and think first of the Treaty, lay deep within his soul and drove him to frantic efforts to allay the guilt and anxiety he felt in consequence. He *must* fight to have his way. But in doing so he must prove his devotion to the Treaty. He must demonstrate that he had no personal motive for taking the position he took, that matters of great principle were involved. He must demonstrate his moral superiority and his opponents' "selfishness." He must be ready to die for his cause.

In late August, Wilson decided that as a last resort he would tour the country, pleading his case before the people. He was by this time almost exhausted, physically and emotionally. He had begun to suffer from daily headaches. The summer heat had sapped his energy. Mrs. Wilson watched with an anxious heart as the effects of the strain the President was under became daily more obvious. Tumulty, fearing that his chief was on the verge of a nervous breakdown, pleaded with him not to undertake this venture, which would have taxed the constitution of an athlete. Wilson replied that he had to try to save the Treaty: ". . . I am willing to make whatever personal sacrifice is required, for if the Treaty should be defeated, God only knows what would happen to the world as a result of it. . . . Even though, in my condition, it might mean the giving up of my life, I will gladly make the sacrifice to save the Treaty." [4] Dr. Grayson solemnly warned his patient that to take such a trip would be to court disaster. Wilson, greatly moved, said he could not consider his personal fortunes when the Treaty was at stake.[5]

So, reluctantly, Wilson's aides began to prepare itineraries for the swing out West. Wilson rejected plan after plan as being not extensive enough. He struck out provisions for days of rest. "This is a business trip, pure and simple, and the itinerary must not include rest of any kind," he told Tumulty.[6]

Before leaving Washington, Wilson gave Hitchcock a draft of four "interpretations" which he would be willing to communicate to the Allies at the time of depositing "the formal instrument of ratification." [7] In short, they were interpretations which were not to be a part of the resolution of ratification. In substance, Wilson's four interpretations and the four reservations then being sponsored by the "mild reservationists" were all but identical.[8] Wilson authorized Hitchcock to use his interpretations in any way he saw fit. Surely Hitchcock and the "mild reservationists" could have bridged the gulf that separated their respective positions on the four questions at issue. But Hitchcock could not make the one concession that was necessary. He could not say that Wilson would permit the interpretations or reservations to be included in the resolution of ratification. He could not say that Wilson was willing to make them binding upon the other signatories of the Treaty. There was the rub.[9]

At eleven o'clock on the night of September 3, 1919, the President boarded the special train which was to carry him to "the people." With him were Mrs. Wilson, Dr. Grayson and Tumulty. The pressure of other business and his headaches had robbed him of the chance to prepare any of the scores of speeches he was scheduled to make. Tumulty later recorded that he had never seen the President look so weary.[10]

In the next twenty-two days, Wilson delivered some forty addresses, traveled eight thousand miles, took part in a dozen parades, shook thousands of hands. He attended luncheons, dinners, receptions. He gave interviews and sacrificed his privacy even aboard his train to allow local politicians to travel with him from one stop to the next.[11]

The faithful trio with him watched in helpless dismay as Wilson grew more and more drawn and tired. The intermittent headaches began to merge until he was in almost constant pain. Through it all he insisted on adhering to his crushing schedule, pouring his soul into the task of enlisting popular support in the life and death battle in which he was engaged. Some of his audiences were enthusiastic. Some were not enthusiastic. Some were not even polite. At the Indiana State Fair, for example, the crowd moved about noisily, and the meeting was temporarily disrupted.

Wilson's speeches were long—they averaged about an hour each.[12] In them, he took up the major objections which had been raised against the Treaty and answered them, point by point. He and his supporters had stated their position time and again, and there was nothing significantly new in what the President said. On the all-important question of what his attitude was toward changes in the Treaty, he reaffirmed the position he had taken upon his return from abroad in July: the text of the Treaty must be approved as is; a separate statement of interpretations to accompany the resolution of ratification was permissible. The Treaty was not susceptible of misunderstanding, "but if the Congress of the United States wants to state the meaning over again in other words and say to the other nations of the world, 'We understand the Treaty to mean what it says,' I think that is a work of supererogation, but I do not see any moral objection to it." However, any *condition* to our ratification—reservations or amendments which would require the assent of the other signatories of the Treaty—would not constitute adoption of the Treaty. "Our decision, therefore, my fellow citizens, rests upon this: If we want a League of Nations, we must take this League of Nations, because there is no conceivable way in which any other League of Nations is obtainable. We must leave it or take it."

They were passionate speeches. The fate of mankind, Wilson felt, hung upon the outcome of the decision America was to make. If America did not assume her responsibilities in the world community, the world was doomed to terrible new wars. "Ah, my fellow citizens, do not forget the aching hearts that are behind discussions like this. Do not forget the forlorn homes from which those boys went and to which they never came back. I have it in my heart that if we do not do this great thing now, every woman ought to weep because of the child in her arms. If she has a boy at her breast, she may be sure that when he comes to manhood this terrible task will have to be done once more." Everywhere his train stopped, it was surrounded by children. "I look at them almost with tears in my eyes, because I feel my mission is to save them. These glad youngsters with flags in their hands—I pray God that they may never have to carry that flag upon the battlefield!"

The Treaty was "a liberation of the peoples and of the humane forces of the world," "a great human enterprise." The world looked to America for leadership. To exercise it, we must accept the Treaty. "It is inconceivable that we should reject it. It is inconceivable that men should put any conditions upon accepting it. . . ." If the "inconceivable" should happen, he would feel like calling every American boy who had fought overseas to some great field, and he would want to stand up and say, "Boys, I told you before you went across the seas that this was a war against wars, and I did my best to fulfill the promise, but I am obliged to come to you in mortification and shame and say I have not been able to fulfill the promise. You are betrayed. You fought for something that you did not get."

For the men who stood in the way of immediate and unqualified ratification Wilson did not hesitate to express his scorn. Opposition to the Treaty sprang either from "downright ignorance" or some malicious "private purpose." The malicious would be "gibbeted" in the annals of mankind, and "they will regret that the gibbet is so high." As for the merely "ignorant," those who "do not understand English," the President suggested that they equip themselves with French dictionaries and resort to the French text of the Treaty—

perhaps they would find that more to their taste. Ignoring the various plans to accept the Treaty with reservations, the President declared from East to West that those who opposed the Treaty offered no substitute and that they ought to "put up or shut up." Every lover of justice "must support the unqualified adoption of this treaty," Wilson asserted. The only organized opposition to it came from "certain bodies of foreign sympathies," "the elements that tended toward disloyalty" during the war. Germany was the beneficiary of America's vacillation. Germany would be the beneficiary of America's rejection or qualification of the Treaty.

He began his trip confident that he rather than the Senators represented the people's will. He ended it convinced that "the overwhelming majority of them demand the ratification of this treaty." He was certain that the "ultimate outcome will be the triumphant acceptance of the treaty and the League." Any man with open eyes could see "the facts coming, coming in serried ranks, coming in overwhelming power, not to be resisted by the United States or any other nation. The facts are marching and God is marching with them. You cannot resist them. You must either welcome them or subsequently, with humiliation, surrender to them. It is welcome or surrender. It is acceptance of great world conditions and great world duties or scuttle now and come back afterwards."

In Washington, the President's contemptuous references to his opponents raised practically everyone's hackles. Even Senators who agreed with much of what Wilson said—that the League *was* the hope of the world and that the United States should ratify the Treaty—were incensed at his insistence that no valid basis for differences of opinion existed; that his opponents must be either knaves or fools. The "mild reservationists" had been fending off Senator Lodge and his more stringent reservations. Theirs were entirely inoffensive and, in spite of repeated disappointments, they were convinced that Wilson would agree to them. But once again, and most provocatively, Wilson was cutting the ground beneath them by proclaiming he would accept no binding reservations at all. It would be either *his* Treaty, exactly as it stood, or no Treaty at all.

On September 9, one of the "mild reservationists," Spencer (Mo.), declared that he would reject the Treaty rather than accept it without change. "I say with all the conviction in my power that the treaty of peace as it is now written will never be ratified by the Senate of the United States." Reservations, he warned, "must be inseparably interwoven with the ratification itself." Next day, another "mild reservationist," Senator Kenyon (Iowa), angrily referring to Wilson's talk of "gibbeting" his opponents, said: "The Senate is not going to be bulldozed. It has its duty to do, and it proposes to do it." On both days, the New York *Times* reported that the "mild reservationists" were rapidly moving toward the Lodge camp. Wilson had done more than any other man to drive them there.[13]

Lodge, meanwhile, was proceeding with the delicate skill of a picador whose graceful thrusts have begun to have the desired effect. On September 10, he presented to the Senate his Committee's majority report on the Treaty. It recommended ratification, but with some fifty amendments and four reservations. Amendments would have required resubmission of the Treaty to Germany as well as to the Allies. Lodge's reservations covered the same subjects as those of the "mild reservationists" and as the "interpretations" Wilson had left with Hitchcock. But they were more restrictive, particularly in rejecting any obligation under Article X, legal *or* moral, except by action of Congress. The report, as Lodge's biographer has judiciously described it, "was marred by a spirit of contentiousness and by an unseemly use of irony and sarcasm."[14] A document ostensibly addressed to great issues, it nevertheless had a curiously intimate tone, as though it were part of a poisonous and very personal dialogue with Wilson.

"This covenant of the league of nations," the report stated peremptorily, "is an alliance and not a league. . . . The Committee believe that the league as it stands will breed wars instead of securing peace." Great Britain "very naturally" had ratified the Treaty at once (Lodge did not elaborate the implication that the British had succeeded in "putting one over" in the Treaty and therefore hastened to put it into effect) but the Committee would not be hurried by the artificial clamor, which the Administration had inspired, for speed in its deliberations. The impossibility of securing necessary information "from those who had conducted the negotiations" had compelled the Committee "to get such imperfect information as they secured from press reports. . . ." "We have heard it frequently said that the United States 'must' do this and do that in regard to this league of nations and the terms of the German peace. There is no 'must' about it. 'Must' is not a word to be used by foreign nations or domestic officials to the American people or their representatives."[15]

On September 12, Lodge's Committee shot another bolt at the

hated foe who, toiling through Idaho and Washington, was rapidly coming to the end of his physical resources. Up to the hearing room they brought William C. Bullitt, who had resigned from the American staff at the Peace Conference in protest against the Treaty. Before he left Paris, Bullitt testified, Secretary of State Lansing had confided to him that he considered many parts of the Treaty "thoroughly bad," especially those pertaining to Shantung and the League of Nations. If the Senate and the people understood the implications of the League, Lansing had said, the Treaty would never pass. Bullitt's testimony created a national sensation. "BULLITT ASSERTS LANSING EXPECTED TREATY TO FAIL," the New York *Times* headlined. In August, Lansing himself had testified before the Committee and had not been able to conceal his disapproval of the Shantung settlement or the fact that he had played only a minor role at the Conference. His own testimony had been embarrassing enough to Wilson, but Bullitt's revelations, coming in the midst of the President's tour, struck a terrible blow against Wilson's effort to win public support for the Treaty.[16] As if that were not enough, Wilson's enemies dispatched a troupe of "irreconcilables" to follow him about the country, preaching their own gospel about the Treaty.

In the face of this concerted assault, the President grew thinner and paler and more tired each day. He never publicly referred to the Bullitt testimony. As for Lodge's report, he made it plain in every speech subsequent to its issuance that in his judgment the acceptance of the proposed reservation to Article X, alone, would constitute rejection of the Treaty. It nullified even the moral obligation upon Congress to act.

And yet, perhaps the terrible burdens imposed upon him from without were less wearing than the knowledge which, we suggest, weighed upon him from within, that he was obstructing his own cause. "If I felt that I personally in any way stood in the way of this settlement," he protested in Omaha, "I would be glad to die that it might be consummated. . . ." [17] Desperately, from city to city, he tried to dispel the terrifying notion that his own personal motivations were involved in the Treaty dispute. Over and over again, he claimed that he had not expounded his own ideas in Paris but, in creating the League, had served merely as an instrument of the people's will. "I had gone over there with, so to say, explicit instructions," he declared, instructions which he would not "dare come home without fulfilling."

In Salt Lake City on September 23, Wilson addressed a crowd of fifteen thousand jammed into the Mormon Tabernacle. The air was so fetid that Mrs. Wilson almost fainted. Wilson's speech that night was one of the longest of the entire trip. When it was over, his clothing was soaked through with perspiration. At his hotel, he continued to perspire profusely, and it was plain that he was utterly exhausted. Mrs. Wilson pleaded with him to take a few days of rest. He refused, saying he had caught the people's imagination and would be failing in his duty if he interrupted his schedule.[18]

On the morning of September 25, he lashed his spent body to the effort of a speech in Denver. "I thank God that on this occasion the whole issue has nothing to do with me," he proclaimed, continuing at greater length than usual to insist that he was simply the instrument of the people's will. That afternoon, he was whisked to the fairgrounds in Pueblo, Colorado, for yet another speech. He had a splitting headache. The end was near. "The chief pleasure of my trip," he declared, "has been that it has nothing to do with my personal fortunes, that it has nothing to do with my personal reputation, that it has nothing to do with anything except great principles. . . ." He then made one of the most moving appeals for unqualified acceptance of the Treaty that he had ever made. Some in the audience wept. Even the hard-bitten reporters were moved. The speech at Pueblo was the last public address Wilson ever made.

On his train that night, the pain in his head grew unbearable, and he became very restless. Nothing that either Grayson or Mrs. Wilson did relieved his distress. In the middle of the night, feeling that he must move about, the President dressed. At 4 A.M. Grayson called Tumulty, who found his chief sitting pitifully in his chair, one side of his face fallen. "Looking at me, with great tears running down his face," Tumulty later wrote, "he said, 'My dear boy, this has never happened to me before. I felt it coming on yesterday. I do not know what to do.' He then pleaded with us not to cut short the trip." Lodge and his friends, Wilson said, would call him a "quitter" and say the western trip was a failure, and the Treaty would be lost.[19] At about 5 A.M., Wilson fell asleep. Two hours later he awoke, shaved and changed his clothes. The train was nearing Wichita, Kansas, and there was a speech to be given! Tumulty, Grayson and Mrs. Wilson urged him to give up the rest of the trip and rest. Grayson told him that to go on might cost his life. "No, no, no," he insisted. "I must keep on." Only after Mrs. Wilson implored him, for the sake of his cause, to pause to recover his strength, did he give in.[20]

Tumulty announced that the rest of the trip was canceled. Grayson issued a statement explaining that the President was in a state of "nervous exhaustion" and would require rest and quiet "for a considerable time."[21] The tracks before it were cleared, and the President's train, shades drawn, sped back to Washington, arriving on the morning of September 28.

Four days later, Fate struck: Wilson suffered a stroke. His left side was paralyzed. Without revealing the nature of the difficulty, or even that there had been a sudden, new crisis, Dr. Grayson announced that the President was "a very sick man" and that "absolute rest is essential for some time."[22]

That their quarry lay stricken gave no pause to the anti-Wilson cabal. Commenting on the President's breakdown, George Harvey wrote in *Harvey's Weekly*:

> In his unapproachable egotism he is quite capable of believing anything that he wishes to believe; even that his tour has been a triumphal march. . . . He has gained the immense gratification of holding the center of the stage for a time, in full glare of the limelight. . . . He has received a considerable share of the adulation which is ever so dear to his heart. . . . Undoubtedly he had the time of his life "slangwhanging" the United States Senate and insulting every American citizen who ventured to disagree with him. . . . He has had his say. He has shot his bolt. He has done his worst. He is no more to be considered. Now let the Senate act.[23]

The majority report of the Committee on Foreign Relations—Lodge's report—was only one of three the Committee issued on the Treaty. There were two minority reports: one, by the Committee's Democrats, urging unqualified acceptance of the Treaty with neither amendments nor reservations; the other, by Senator McCumber, the mildest of all the "mild reservationists," who urged ratification with a series of "mild reservations" which should be made "part of and condition of such ratification." For all their annoyance with Wilson, the "mild reservationists," in short, were still keeping the door open to compromise.

All through October and the first week of November, the "mild reservationists" united with the Democrats to vote down Lodge's proposed textual amendments to the Treaty. But again and again they served notice that they would stand firm on their reservations. In the absence of any new instruction from the President, Hitchcock continued to insist on ratification without reservations which would recommit the Treaty to the other signatories.[24] He did not even introduce the "interpretations" which Wilson had entrusted to him before setting out on his western trip until November 13. By that time the "mild reservationists" had abandoned hope of compromising with the Democrats and had succumbed to Lodge, who was busily reintroducing in the form of reservations the substance of what had been voted down in the form of amendments.

Hitchcock was in an extraordinarily difficult position. In the first place, he was only acting minority leader. The official minority leader was Senator Martin of Virginia. A protracted illness (which ended in his death shortly before the Treaty came up for vote in November) deprived Martin of his role in the drama. Hitchcock, an uneasy and not conspicuously able stand-in, was thrust to the fore. Even more handicapping was the fact that he did not enjoy Wilson's esteem. Early in 1918, when Hitchcock was chairman of the Foreign Relations Committee, Wilson had tried to depose him and had told Senator Martin, among others, that he did not trust Hitchcock and would not consult him whether he was chairman or not.[25] At various times during the Treaty fight, it was rumored that Hitchcock had been displaced as Wilson's spokesman. The fact that the President conferred only infrequently with the Nebraskan lent plausibility to such talk.[26] Hitchcock, insecure as to his standing at the White House, seemed desirous first and foremost of being efficient in carrying out Wilson's wishes to the letter. He took little initiative in trying to arrange a compromise with the "mild reservationists." He exercised little independent judgment as to the requirements of the situation.

Not once during the whole month of October did Hitchcock confer with the President.[27] Wilson lay paralyzed in the White House, guarded from visitors by Mrs. Wilson, Grayson and Tumulty. What government business was transacted with the President had to be filtered through Mrs. Wilson. She, concerned first of all with saving her husband's life, tried to shield him from disturbing problems. The doctors had warned her that any strain or emotional upset might cost his life. So, with an eye to preserving his equanimity, she passed judgment on what people and what papers the President should see, and when.[28]

In the first part of November, Lodge's reservations, which now numbered fourteen, were adopted by the Senate. Having been unable to make headway with Wilson or Hitchcock, the "mild reservationists," in disgust, finally threw in their lot with Lodge, and it was their votes which wedded his reservations to the Treaty. From that time forth the question was, would Wilson accept the Treaty with the Lodge reservations or would he, by persuading the Democratic Senators to vote against it, engineer its defeat?

It may be argued that Lodge's reservations were offensively worded. It may be argued that his motives in presenting them were questionable. *But the reservations did not nullify the Treaty. They did not even seriously embarrass full participation of the United States in the League of Nations. In practice, they would have been of little significance.* That is the consensus of a generation of scholars who have subjected the Lodge program to minute scrutiny.[29]

As the day for the final vote on the Treaty approached, Wilson's friends and the friends of the Treaty were in anguish. It seemed incredible that a man would destroy his life work—a work affecting the welfare of the entire human race—over a few paltry phrases. And yet, it was perfectly plain that that would happen unless Wilson permitted his followers in the Senate to vote for the Treaty with the Lodge reservations. For without Democratic support, the two-thirds vote necessary for ratification could not be secured. Mrs. Wilson kept from the stricken man nearly all the visitors who wanted to plead with him to relent. She discreetly filed, returned or herself answered most of the written entreaties. Nevertheless, some representations to Wilson were made. Bernard Baruch begged the President to compromise. So did William Gibbs McAdoo. To no avail. Senator Hitchcock was admitted to the invalid's room and reported that not even a simple majority, much less a two-thirds majority, could be mustered for the Treaty without reservations. "Is it possible, is it possible," groaned Wilson.

"We might compromise, Mr. President," Hitchcock ventured.

"Let Lodge compromise, Senator," came the reply.

"Well, we might hold out the olive branch," Hitchcock rejoined.

"No, let Lodge hold out the olive branch." [30]

Mrs. Wilson was besieged by letters and visits from men she knew to be devoted to the President and his ideals, and they implored her to intervene on behalf of the Treaty. At last, she went to her husband. "For my sake," she said, "won't you accept these reservations and get this awful thing settled?" Sadly, he took her hand. "Little girl, don't you desert me; that I cannot stand. Can't you see that I have no moral right to accept any change in a paper I have signed without giving to every other signatory, even the Germans, the right to do the same thing? It is not *I* that will not accept; it is the Nation's honour that is at stake." [31]

On November 18, Wilson dictated his final verdict to Hitchcock, for the instruction of the Democratic Senators. In his opinion, the President wrote, the Lodge resolution of ratification containing Lodge's reservations "does not provide for ratification, but rather for nullification of the treaty. I sincerely hope that the friends and supporters of the treaty will vote against the Lodge resolution of ratification. I understand that the door will then probably be open for a genuine resolution of ratification." Wilson was hoping that after the Treaty with Lodge's reservations failed, the "mild reservationists" would hastily come to the support of the Treaty exactly as it stood, or with Hitchcock's interpretative reservations.[32]

As the day for final action drew near, and the anxiously awaited word that Wilson would break the deadlock failed to come, friends of the Treaty turned desperately to Hitchcock. It was common knowledge that many Democrats wanted to vote for the Treaty, even with the Lodge reservations. If Hitchcock would give his consent, enough Democrats would support the Lodge resolution of ratification to ensure its passage. Taft wrote Hitchcock a moving appeal to vote for the Treaty with the reservations: "Oh I beg of you, Senator, to consider the consequences if you defeat the Treaty," he declared. ". . . The Treaty even with the reservations represents enormous progress toward better conditions as to peace and war in the world. The barking dogs of opposition will cease their noise and the real conscience of the U.S. will assert itself in its actual participation in the doings of the League. We are in sight of the promised land. Don't, don't prevent our reaching there." [33]

But Hitchcock proved impervious to the suggestion that he disregard the instructions of his chief. Undoubtedly one factor that entered into his decision was Wilson's resolve, revealed to Hitchcock in their last interview before the vote, to pocket the Treaty if it came to him with the Lodge reservations.[34] Given Wilson's attitude, to defy him would be a useless gesture and, with elections less than a year off, a highly embarrassing one to all concerned. So Hitchcock remained faithful to Wilson to the end, and did his best to induce the other Democrats to vote down the Lodge resolution of ratification.

At last the momentous day arrived. The Senate convened on November 19, 1919, to take a final vote on the Treaty. There were last-minute speeches. Hitchcock appealed to those "on both sides" who wanted the Treaty "to get together and see if they can compromise their differences." He charged that the Lodge reservations had been dictated by men who did not believe in the Treaty at all—the "irreconcilables" —and had been put to the Democrats highhandedly, on a "take it or leave it" basis.

This statement exasperated the "mild reservationists." Hitchcock's "passionate appeal," retorted Senator Kellogg, came "a little late and with bad grace." Time after time Hitchcock had announced that the Treaty would be ratified without any reservations whatever, an attitude tantamount to demanding that the Senate abdicate its rights. Time after time the "mild reservationists" had sought compromise and Hitchcock had "stood there like a wall to prevent any compromise." Senator McCumber seconded Kellogg's remarks. Every one of the Lodge reservations, he declared, represented a compromise of views. The reservations as they now stood "are just as mild and inoffensive as could possibly be obtained and yet command enough votes on this side of the Chamber as, added to all you could muster on that side, would make the necessary two-thirds vote for ratification." He besought the Democrats not to "scuttle" their ship because they had suffered some "minor reverses."[35]

The time for speechmaking was at an end. Voting then began. First, Lodge's resolution of ratification was passed upon. The Republican reservationists and four Democrats—39 Senators in all—voted in favor of it; the rest of the Democrats and the "irreconcilables"—55—voted against it.

Hitchcock then attempted to secure a vote on the Treaty with the reservations he had introduced four days earlier. Lodge succeeded in blocking such a vote. The reservationists, "mild" and strong alike, with the support of a few dissident Democrats, defeated Hitchcock's motion.

Unconditional ratification of the Treaty was then voted upon. The vote was 38 in favor to 53 against. This time, the Democrats and Senator McCumber had voted "yea"; the reservationists and "irreconcilables" had joined forces and voted "nay."

The Treaty had been unable to command a simple majority vote—much less the required two-thirds—either with the Lodge reservations or without. Democratic Senator Swanson (Va.), shaken, came over to Lodge and asked, "For God's sake, can't something be done to save the treaty?"

"Senator," came the calm reply, "the door is closed. You have done it yourselves." [36]

The door was not "closed," however. Public opinion would not permit it to be. Less than a score of the Senators had declared themselves unalterably opposed to the Treaty. The rest, about eighty, ostensibly favored ratification, and all eighty had sanctioned one set of reservations or another. To the public—even to the legal experts—the differences between the various sets of reservations seemed so minor as to make it absurd to wreck the whole Treaty over them. Surely a way could be found to reach agreement. Newspapers, civic groups, prominent leaders clamored for a reconsideration of the Treaty and a compromise. The demand was irresistible. Wilson was to have that rarest of privileges in a politician's career—a second chance. The big question was, would he take advantage of it?

Few men pondered that question as deeply, as discerningly, and with such a fervent desire to help, as Colonel House. All through the summer of 1919, and into the fall, the Colonel had remained in Europe, dutifully but discontentedly, at Wilson's express request. He wanted to come home. He felt there was little work of importance he could do abroad, and a great deal he could accomplish at home. His personal situation in Paris was awkward—leading members of the American staff were jealous and resentful of him. In the circumstances, House longed to leave the scene. Wilson, apparently not wanting the Colonel to be in the United States during the Treaty fight, insisted that he stay abroad.[37] House confided to his diary that he was greatly upset at the President's attitude and feared it might lead to a serious controversy between them.[38]

From his enforced exile, House followed the news of Wilson's battle with the Senate with a sinking heart. For a year and more he had realized that Wilson's manner with the Senate stood to bear bitter fruit. He had been much disturbed by Wilson's October, 1918, appeal for a Democratic Congress. He felt that Wilson had steadily built a fire underneath himself and was now getting scorched by it. Avidly, he followed the news of Wilson's western tour. It was all such a gamble, House exclaimed in his diary. Wilson owed it to his great cause to ensure the Treaty's success. Instead he was needlessly endangering ratification. Everything that Wilson and he had worked for was now at stake, House realized. He was convinced that he could help the cause by testifying before the Senate Foreign Relations Committee. More important, he thought that if only he could talk with Wilson he stood a chance of persuading him to save the Treaty through compromise.[39]

Finally, late in September, House took matters into his own hands. He decided to return to the United States, and so informed the President. By then, Wilson lay cloistered in the White House. Unluckily, House himself fell ill at just about this time, and had to be carried off the ship on a stretcher upon his arrival in New York. From the White House, all was silence. Then a note, dated October 17, arrived from Mrs. Wilson. She had not told Wilson of House's illness or even of his departure from Paris in accordance with her policy of keeping unimportant or distressing news from him. She knew how anxious the President had been for the Colonel to remain in Paris.

House, taken aback, replied that in several cables and letters to the President he had indicated his intention of sailing, and took Wilson's silence as approval. He invited Mrs. Wilson to call upon him for whatever service he might do either the President or herself. Mrs. Wilson promptly wrote back that she did not know whether or not the Colonel's various letters had reached Wilson: he had been so busy while traveling out West, and so ill since his return that a mountain of documents lay unexamined. She acknowledged with thanks House's offer to be of service, but said she could think of nothing to ask at the moment.[40]

His offer to help thus declined, House watched helplessly from the sidelines as the Treaty went down to defeat in November.[41] Even then, all was not lost. Wilson could still save the Treaty, if only he would. House could not restrain his desire to try to sway Wilson from the catastrophic course he was following. He embodied his advice in a letter to Wilson, dated November 24. He entrusted Attorney-General Gregory to hand it personally to Mrs. Wilson, along with a note to her.

To Mrs. Wilson, the Colonel wrote that he was reluctant to write while the President was ill, but that the issue was a vital one—Wilson's place in history hung on the outcome. Objectionable reservations could be corrected later: the essential thing was to make the President's great work live. House's letter to Wilson suggested that Wilson return the Treaty to the Senate, and advise Hitchcock to ask the Democratic Senators to vote for ratification with reservations. It would then be up to the Allies to decide whether or not to accept our ratification on that basis. Wilson could feel that he had discharged his duty to them by having tried his best to secure ratification without reservations. If the Allies rejected the Treaty with the Lodge reservations, Wilson's previous opposition to reservations would be vindicated. If they accepted the reservations, we would be in the League and time would vitiate their effect.

Gregory duly delivered the letters to Mrs. Wilson, and reported to House that she had regarded the Colonel's suggestions the counsel of surrender. Wishing to leave no room for misinterpretation, House wrote the President again, on November 27, emphasizing that he was advising, not surrender, but action which would ensure passage of the Treaty, probably with only mild reservations.

Neither of these letters was acknowledged in any way. Whether the President ever saw them is not known. House concluded that his advice was not welcome. He never offered any to Wilson again.[42] As the Treaty fight neared the climax of a second vote, House disconsolately noted in his diary that he once had thought Lodge the worst enemy of the Treaty, but now had to admit that first place went to Wilson.[43]

During December, 1919, and January, 1920, various attempts were made to work out some way to get the Treaty passed. The whole vast debate began again. The drama of the "mild reservationists'" futile attempts to unite with the Democrats was relived. Lodge again performed his breathtakingly skillful balancing act between the "irreconcilables" who wanted to yield nothing, on the one hand, and the "mild reservationists" who threatened to bolt his leadership unless he made an effort to come to terms with the Democrats, on the other. None of the bustling activity and stirring oratory, however, could change one all-important fact—that Wilson's position remained precisely the same after the November defeat as before. If there was to be any compromising, the others would have to do it: he was not willing to budge an iota.

Lest anyone suspect that his determination was flagging, Wilson proclaimed his attitude in a White House statement, issued December 14, declaring that he had "no compromise or concession of any kind in mind." [44] A few weeks later, he did so again in a message to the Jackson Day dinner, and this time he had in addition a serious proposal for his party's leaders. He had known from the first, the message said, "that the overwhelming majority of the people of this country desire the ratification of the treaty." His impression to that effect had been confirmed during his speaking tour. However, "if there is any doubt as to what the people of the country think on this vital matter, the clear and single way out is to submit it for determination at the next election to the voters of the Nation, to give the next election the form of a great and solemn referendum. . . ."[45]

It was as true on Jackson Day, 1920, as it had been in October, 1918, when Wilson had issued his disastrous appeal for the election of a Democratic Congress, that voters make their decision on the basis of many issues, some of them purely local. There is no way in a national election in the United States to get a reliable expression of public sentiment on a single issue. Besides, what exactly was the issue? Ratification without any reservations at all? Even Wilson had concluded that "interpretations" were necessary. Ratification with Wilson's "interpretations" as against the Lodge reservations? Not one citizen in a hundred could be expected to grasp the nice distinctions between them, especially when some of the most learned men in the land confessed that they could not see that in practice there would be any significant difference between them. Outright rejection of the Treaty?

Many prominent Democrats themselves were weary of the whole confusing wrangle and wanted nothing better than to vote for reservations—Lodge's if need be—and settle the problem promptly. They were not attracted to the idea of following Wilson into a crusade without any real cause. Wilson's insistence on dragging the Treaty fight into the impending national campaign might split the Democratic Party wide open, they feared.[46] Further, as any clear-headed realist could see, even if every Democrat up for re-election to the Senate won in 1920 and every Republican whose Senate seat was at stake lost, the Democrats would not have the two-thirds majority necessary for ratification.[47] Would Wilson then decide the issue would have to be settled in 1922, or 1924, while the rest of the world patiently waited?

Wilson's appeal for a "solemn referendum" in 1920 was only the best known of his schemes to put it up to the people to vindicate his stand. He hatched another, which can only be described as preposterous. Wilson's idea, which he committed to paper in late January, was to challenge over fifty Senators who had opposed him in the Treaty fight (i.e., nearly all the Republicans and a few Democrats) to resign. They could then seek immediate re-election, on the issue of their position with regard to the Treaty. If a majority of them were re-elected, Wilson promised, *he* would resign. One need only imagine the reception such a proposition undoubtedly would have received, particularly from those Senators whose terms had a long time to run, to be grateful that more sober counsel prevailed, and that it was never made public.[48]

Wilson's implacability notwithstanding, efforts to break the deadlock continued. In view of the President's attitude, however, Senator Hitchcock was unable to conduct meaningful negotiations with the "mild reservationists," the strong reservationists or anyone else. The fact was, he had no negotiating leeway whatever. On December 19, Mrs. Wilson had written him saying the President felt it would be a serious error for the Democrats to *propose* anything, or even intimate the possibility of any concession or compromise. Let the overtures be made by the other side! In early January, Hitchcock had plaintively explained to Mrs. Wilson that hope of ratification rested upon reaching an understanding with moderate Republicans; and that to reach such an understanding, the Democrats would have to make concessions, which thus far the President had been unwilling to consider.[49] Wilson's "unwillingness" never abated. Hitchcock had to try to "compromise" with the Republicans, without having anything he could yield.

In mid-January, goaded not only by public opinion but, more immediately, by the "mild reservationists," Lodge agreed to participate in a bipartisan conference which should seek to break the deadlock. Lodge's attitude toward the proceedings, according to a New York *Times* reporter, seemed one of "tolerance and amusement."[50] Well it might have been, for Lodge had every reason to be confident that Hitchcock would not be able to meet even the "mild reservationists'" minimum demands—Wilson's recent public utterances gave evidence of that fact. He could afford, therefore, to meet with others who were desperately eager to find a solution and even to give some ground, in the comfortable knowledge that in the end, the effort would be wrecked on the rock of Wilson's intransigence. He, meanwhile, would seem the most reasonable of men! So Lodge and eight other Senators met for two weeks, from January 15 to January 30, and went over the reservations, one by one. Some minor alterations of the reservations and of the provision stipulating the form of Allied acceptance of them were agreed upon. But Lodge was not prepared, as he assured the alarmed "irreconcilables," to concede anything that was essential or that was anything more than a change in wording.[51]

Wilson, too, was immovable. On January 26, he wrote Hitchcock rejecting a compromise proposal, then under consideration, to Article

X. He explained that while he adhered to the substance of the reservation, its "form" was unfortunate, and would "chill" our relationship with the other nations. He could, however, accept the Hitchcock reservations of November 13, 1919.[52]

There had been a time when the "mild reservationists" probably would have leaped at the chance to reach agreement on the basis of the Hitchcock reservations, but that had been many months before. In the interim, they had gravitated toward Lodge's formulations. Besides, Wilson *still* evinced no willingness to allow even Hitchcock's reservations to be embodied in the resolution of ratification. This despite the fact that Lodge was now willing to settle for acceptance by silence on the part of the other powers, rather than formal written acquiescence.[53]

The conference bogged down completely over Article X. It being clear that neither Lodge nor Wilson was willing to concede anything, the meetings were disbanded on January 30. Ten days later, the Senate began to reconsider the Treaty with the Lodge reservations, slightly altered. Again the issue was drawn. Again the Treaty would be voted upon. Again the question was, would Wilson yield?

One of the main arguments upon which Wilson relied to justify his refusal to accept binding reservations was that such reservations would be obnoxious to the Allies. On the day after the bipartisan conference collapsed and it became clear once again that it would be ratification with the Lodge reservations or no ratification at all, Wilson's position was shattered by the publication of a letter in the London *Times*. Its writer was one of the most distinguished British statesmen of his day, Viscount Grey.

During the war, growing old and growing blind, Grey had retired. He was a staunch advocate of the League of Nations, and had followed the development of the Covenant with keen interest and approval. When, in the summer of 1919, the gravity of the crisis between Wilson and the Senate became obvious, Grey was prevailed upon by the British government and partly, also, by Colonel House, to undertake a special mission to the United States to help the beleaguered President realize that Europe would prefer the United States to ratify the Treaty with reservations rather than altogether forfeit her participation in it.[54] Grey had come to America in late September, just after Wilson's collapse, and he waited for almost four months for an invitation to visit the President. The invitation never came, although by December and January Wilson was receiving other callers. Finally, his mission unaccomplished, Grey went home, but what he had wanted to say to Wilson was far too important to be left unsaid in view of the impending final Senate vote on the Treaty.

So, presumably with the approval of the British government, he took to the columns of the leading English newspaper with what was ostensibly an appeal to British opinion to be tolerant of the Lodge reservations. Some of the Lodge reservations, Grey conceded, were "material qualifications of the League of Nations as drawn up at Paris." Yet probably in practice neither the "difficulties and dangers which the Americans foresee" nor "the weakening and injury to the League" which Europeans apprehended from the reservations would materialize. Better for the United States to enter the League "as a willing partner with limited obligations" than "as a reluctant partner who felt that her hand had been forced." [55]

The sentiments expressed in Grey's letter were echoed in the French press, which for some time had taken the position, in probable reflection of the official French view, that it would be far better to have the United States accept the Treaty with reservations than to have the Senate reject the Treaty altogether. (Some years later Clemenceau wrote that the Senate had rejected the Treaty because Wilson had refused to consent to "a few harmless compromises." [56])

The Grey letter, reproduced in leading newspapers throughout the United States, gave the Lodge position a tremendous boost. If the British government and the French, too, were willing to accept the reservations, and if Wilson had acknowledged that he did not disagree with the substance of the reservations, but only their form, what was all the fuss about? The great fear that the Allies would balk at them now had been exploded. Therefore, let the Senate ratify the Treaty with the Lodge reservations!

One might expect on first thought that the removal of the specter of Allied disapproval of the reservations would have greatly relieved the worried President. However, no one who remembers how thoroughly upset Wilson was at a comparable moment in his battle with Dean West at Princeton will be surprised to learn that Wilson was angered by Lord Grey's statement, and composed a stinging rebuke, fortunately never issued, castigating him for his action.[57] It will be recalled that at a crucial moment in the battle with West, the opposition suddenly relented on the question of the site of the proposed graduate college, about which the whole controversy supposedly revolved. Far from being relieved, Wilson had been taken aback, and after a few confused moments had declared that the issue was not after all the site, but "democracy" at Princeton. He had not *wanted* a compromise solution to the problem: he had wanted to defeat Dean West. So now, he did not *want* to reach a compromise agreement with the Senate. He wanted to defeat the Senate, and especially Lodge. If he could not overcome his enemies, it would be less painful to him to sacrifice the Treaty than to make concessions. He could relieve his sense of guilt for having provoked his own defeat by picturing himself martyred in a great cause and by seeking vindication from "the people"—a vindication for which he strove to his dying day.

On one occasion earlier in the League fight, Jules Jusserand, French Ambassador to the United States, came to Wilson with a draft of reservations which he had been responsibly informed would be acceptable to some key Republican Senators. If only Wilson would accept them, the Ambassador declared, the Treaty would be ratified, and he could assure the President that the British and French governments would accept the reservations.

"Mr. Ambassador," declared Wilson, "I shall consent to nothing. The Senate must take its medicine."[58]

Most men's personal tragedies are played out in relative privacy. But Wilson was President of the United States; and he was acting out his personal conflicts in a public matter of the highest importance. The world was his stage. His "lines" were printed in every newspaper in the land, and eagerly scanned in every capital on earth. No tragedian could have composed them more artistically. The white-hot light of publicity beat upon him as day after day, confronted with the same rending conflict—whether or not to accept the Treaty with the Lodge reservations—he made the same inevitable choice, to the disbelief, the indignation, the despair of sympathetic onlookers.

In late February, Senator Glass—he who had served Wilson so well in framing the Federal Reserve Act, and who had given the President his unstinting and worshipful support ever since—was deputed to visit Wilson and find out whether he would pocket the Treaty if it were passed with the Lodge reservations. Wilson replied that he would.[59] This was disheartening news to Democratic Senators who thought they might help get the Treaty passed by voting for the Lodge reservations even without that explicit consent which it was evidently so difficult for Wilson to give. But what point if Wilson would not accept the Treaty even then?

In the Senate the debate ground on, and the Lodge reservations were hammered into final shape. As the day of final decision approached, Wilson's friends again importuned him not to cast the whole Treaty away because of the minor imperfections the Senate's action would create. Wilson himself had remarked during his speaking tour that the Senate had addressed itself to "little picayune details here and there" and had lost sight of the "majesty of the plan." [60] Precisely, his friends pleaded. It would be a tragic mistake to abandon everything just because some "picayune details" of the Treaty had been changed. But Wilson could not be turned from his self-destructive course.

On March 8, 1920, he wrote Hitchcock for the explicit purpose of giving "guidance" to the Senate Democrats. He had concluded, Wilson stated, that the reservations, particularly that to Article X, in effect nullified the terms of the Treaty. He had heard of "reservationists" and "mild reservationists" but could not understand the difference between a "nullifier and a mild nullifier." Once again he had taken his stand: the Treaty with the Lodge reservations must be rejected.

Until the very end, friends of the Treaty hoped that the President would change his mind; it would be enough if he merely freed his supporters to vote in accordance with their own judgment. On March 11, Senator Ashurst (D., Ariz.) declared: "As a friend of the President, as one who has loyally followed him, I solemnly declare to him this morning: If you want to kill your own child because the Senate straightens out its crooked limbs, you must take the responsibility and accept the verdict of history." Even the New York *World*, which had followed Wilson through thick and thin, announced in favor of passing the Treaty with the Lodge reservations.[61]

Wilson did not change his mind. The Democratic Senators were left to wrestle with their own consciences on the question of whether to disregard their party chieftain's wishes and vote for the Treaty in the only form in which it could pass. March 19, 1920, was the day of decision. The resolution of ratification with the Lodge reservations was called to a vote. The Democrats were under agonizing pressure. Clearly, if enough of them voted in favor of it, the Treaty would pass. Hitchcock insisted that their duty was to vote "nay." Twenty-one Democrats defied him and voted in favor of the Treaty, along with the Republican reservationists. Twenty-three Democrats bent their will to Wilson's and, along with the "irreconcilables," voted "nay." The count was 49 in favor to 35 against. A majority had voted in favor of the Treaty, but not the necessary two-thirds majority. *If seven more Democrats had bolted, the Treaty with Lodge's reservations would have passed the Senate.* Some years later, Hitchcock admitted that he had had "all I could do" to hold enough Democrats in line to beat the Treaty.[62]

The last name was called, and the final tally announced. Senator Brandegee, an "irreconcilable," turned to Lodge. "We can always depend on Mr. Wilson," he said. "He never has failed us." [63]

The Treaty was dead.

*There is considerable evidence that despite his shattered health, despite the ruinous defeat into which he had led his party, and despite the then unbroken tradition against third terms, Wilson wanted to be the Democratic standard bearer in 1920. He waited hopefully at the White House for the call to candidacy from the Democratic Convention in San Francisco, but his name was not even proposed. One of his warmest supporters wired him that he did not command sufficient support to win the nomination and that putting his name forward in the circumstances would embarrass the party. The nomination went to Governor James M. Cox of Ohio, with an up-and-coming young politician, Franklin D. Roosevelt, as his running mate.*

*The Republicans chose Senator Warren G. Harding, who had been one of the strong reservationists. It is impossible from Harding's campaign speeches to discern just what his stand was concerning the League. This confusion was probably intentional, since he wished to alienate neither the Taft pro-Leaguers nor the "irreconcilables" among Republican ranks, and any consistent position inevitably would have offended one group or the other. Although Cox declared himself squarely in favor of the League, his position, too, was ambiguous as to precisely the reservations or "interpretations" he favored. Neither candidate, therefore, took an unequivocal stand on the League. Besides, the public was weary of the whole complicated debate. Such issues as Prohibition and the high cost of living were uppermost in the minds of many voters. Obviously, the election was not the "solemn referendum" for which Wilson had called.*

*In any case, it took place on November 2, 1920. Harding won a smashing victory, rolling up popular majorities unprecedented in American history. Two days later, speaking ("bloviating," as he liked to say) from the porch of his Ohio home, Harding declared Wilson's League "now deceased."*

*Wilson moved from the White House to a comfortable house on "S" Street in Washington. There, for the remaining three years of his life, he devoted himself to trying to undo the decision of the Senate on the Treaty of Versailles. With the help of a group of loyal friends, he drafted a statement of principles, revolving about the theme that America must resume her international obligations and leadership, to be used in the 1924 presidential campaign. He seems to have cherished the pathetic hope that he might be summoned out of retirement to run for President in 1924.*

*Wilson lived to see the Senate ratify a separate peace with Germany in 1921. He lived to see the utter collapse of his plan to adjust the iniquities of the Treaty of Versailles through corrective action by a virile League and through the moderating influence of United States representatives on the various bodies (especially the Reparations Commission) charged with carrying the Treaty's provisions into effect. The failure of the United States to become a member struck the League a crippling blow from which it never recovered; her failure to help implement the Treaty, particularly its reparations clauses, left the Germans at the mercy of the French—a dénouement from which German pride and the German economy could not recover. Wilson lived to have heaped upon him the abuse of the Allies, who felt betrayed because they had entered into the arrangements made at Paris on the assumption that the United States would discharge her proper share of the responsibility for making them work. He lived to see the United States enter a period of heedless "normalcy," of trying to shut out the concerns of the rest of the world, in hot pursuit of false prosperity, a false sense of security and frenetic gaiety.*

*In the twilight of his life, he grew more dour and querulous. But he never lost faith. On Armistice Day, 1923, a throng of well-wishers gathered in front of his "S" Street house. Wilson appeared on the balcony and, overcome by emotion, made a brief speech. "I am not one of those that have the least anxiety about the triumph of the principles I have stood for," he concluded. "I have seen fools resist Providence before and I have seen their destruction, as will come upon these again—utter destruction and contempt. That we shall prevail is as sure as that God reigns." (The main headline in the New York* Times *the day Wilson's remarks appeared read, across three columns:* HITLER FORCES RALLYING NEAR MUNICH.)

*In early 1924, Wilson began to fail seriously. By February he was abed, his strength slowly ebbing away. It was clear to his physicians that he would not live. Grayson told him the end was near. Wilson accepted the news bravely. "I am a broken piece of machinery. When the machinery is broken—" The faint voice trailed off. "I am ready," he murmured.*

*On February 3, 1924, Woodrow Wilson died.*

*Writing in mid-century, one cannot end the Wilson story on the note of death and failure. In many respects his vision was true. Today in New York City the headquarters of the United Nations stands in testimony of that change of policy he so confidently predicted. And there the United States is represented by—Henry Cabot Lodge, Jr.*

*Wilson sought vindication. For advocating his great ideal in the face of isolationist opposition, history has vindicated him. For keeping the United States out of the League of Nations for a whole generation because of the Lodge reservations, he has not been vindicated. Very probably, he never can be.*

# RESEARCH NOTE

It was inevitable that, sooner or later, specialists in psychology should turn their attention to the intriguing puzzle of Wilson's personality and career. Freud himself collaborated in a study of Wilson which is as yet unpublished. The extraordinary role of "conscience" and "stubbornness" in Wilson's political behavior, noted by numerous of his contemporaries and biographers, will certainly kindle the interest of students of personality and raise the question as to how far their specialized theories about such matters are applicable to Wilson. The interest of the psychologically-oriented biographer is also likely to be aroused by the discerning observation of a gifted man of letters, Edmund Wilson, who said of Woodrow Wilson's career:

> As President of the United States, he repeated after the War his whole tragedy as president of Princeton—with Lodge in the role of West, the League of Nations in the place of the quad system, and the Senate in the place of the Princeton trustees. It is possible to observe in certain lives, where conspicuously superior abilities are united with serious deficiencies, not the progress in a career or vocation that carries the talented man to a solid position or a definite goal, but a curve plotted over and over again and always dropping from some flight of achievement to a steep descent into failure. ("Woodrow Wilson at Princeton," *Shores of Light*, N. Y.: Farrar, Straus and Young, Inc., 1952, 322.)

Our own research on Wilson dates back to 1941 when the senior author prepared a paper on Wilson's personality for a graduate course on "Personality and Politics," given at the University of Chicago by Dr. Nathan Leites. Receiving encouragement from Leites, Dr. Harold D. Lasswell and others, he prepared a second version of the study, which was presented before the Society for Social Research at the University of Chicago in 1949. More recently, in September, 1956, at the annual meeting of the American Political Science Association, we gave a paper on problems of data collection and interpretation encountered in the study. These papers, especially the first two, were technical in character and terminology. In this book, however, we present our findings in relatively nontechnical language, hoping thereby to achieve better communication with general readers as well as with the many diversely oriented specialists who share an interest in political leadership.

There have been important modifications of the study since its inception. The initial characterization of Wilson as sharing traits associated with the compulsive character type, while helpful in many ways, had important limitations. As with most diagnoses confined merely to identification of deeper layers of motivation, it was static, and did not identify the specific types of situations in which his behavior was narrowly circumscribed in range and flexibility.

Our initial impression of Wilson's "compulsive" personality underwent considerable revision when we began to examine his entire career in detail. We were confronted by evidence of an unusual flexibility of behavior in many situations; a knack of selecting as his political goals only those projects which were ripe for realization; and, finally, a skill in political maneuver and in the tactics of leadership which was at times both shrewd and inventive.

Though burdened with serious, at times crippling, temperamental defects, Wilson was capable in many types of situations of behaving expediently in the pursuit of his political objectives and of acting creatively and constructively in political life. The impressive successes which Wilson was able to achieve as President of Princeton, Governor of New Jersey and President of the United States, it emerged, were due in no small measure to the fact that he was able to harness and adapt the driving ambition and energy engendered by personal maladjustment into an effective pattern of leadership. Though forced to operate within a governmental system of divided powers and checks and balances, Wilson's driving, essentially autocratic leadership was for a number of years politically acceptable and successful. This achievement was due in large measure of course, to the character of the situation at the time, which favored political reforms and strong leadership. But it owed something also to his ability to adapt his desire to function as a prime minister to conditions as he found them and to rationalize the type of leadership he offered the country in terms of democratic theory and the national interest.

We have tried, therefore, to identify the many facets of Wilson's personality and to study them in the context of his life history. This approach reflects a growing trend in the investigation of personality and character within the psychological sciences. The complexity of personality organization, the important role of ego functioning, and the variety of ways in which given personality factors may express themselves in a political leader's behavior—all these emerge only when the career as a whole, not merely a few isolated episodes from it, is examined in detail.

The developmental analysis of political leaders—our case study of Wilson is an attempt in that direction—draws upon both genetic and dynamic propositions about personality. In recent years numerous students of personality development have felt the need to revise and broaden Freud's theory concerning the relationship of character formation to early sexual experience. As a result, the investigator who now attempts to use genetic psychology for purposes of political biography is confronted with an impressive array of propositions and hypotheses which have not as yet been fully integrated. Most helpful for our purpose, therefore, has been Dr. Harold D. Lasswell's synthesis and restatement of the state of knowledge about personality development from the standpoint of its implications for the study of political leadership.*

The present consensus among specialists in personality development appears to be that a variety of early childhood experiences may exercise an important formative influence on basic personality structure, but that, in any case, it is an oversimplification to explain adult behavior exclusively in these terms. In the developmental biography, accordingly, the investigator must be concerned with the development of the subject's total personality throughout his formative years and, indeed, sometimes well into adult life. He attempts to trace the subject's efforts from early childhood on to cope with his anxieties. He attempts to identify

* See his *Power and Personality*, New York, W. W. Norton, 1948; especially Chapter III, "The Political Personality"; see also his "The Selective Effect of Personality on Political Participation" in Richard Christie and Marie Jahoda, eds., *Studies In the Scope and Method of "The Authoritarian Personality,"* Glencoe, Illinois, The Free Press, 1954.

not only the development of defenses against these anxieties but also the adjustive and constructive strategies devised by the individual in an effort to harness his anxieties and to avoid situations in which they might have severely disruptive effects. In tracing the individual's elaboration and structuring of a personality system and his development of an outlook on life, the investigator pays particular attention to his familial, cultural and social milieu. For it is in interaction with his milieu that the individual "finds himself" and learns ways of expressing himself in a satisfying manner. It is from this standpoint that the biographer examines the development of the subject's interest in politics and in leadership, and attempts to account for the subject's selection of a particular political role for himself. It is from this standpoint, too, that he studies the subject's efforts to develop the skills appropriate to the political role which he has chosen. (See Chapters I and II.)

In a developmental biography the interaction between personality and situational factors throughout the subject's career is studied chronologically and cross-sectionally. Important episodes and actions in the life history are selected for intensive analysis; in these cross-sectional analyses of behavior, the individual's previous life history is regarded as a set of learning experiences which have structured predispositions operative in the present situation.

The general purpose of situational analysis of personality functioning is to identify the dynamics of the subject's political behavior and to characterize his ego functioning. It may be relatively easy to identify a personal value (power, approval, affection, deference, security, rectitude, etc.) for which the subject seeks some satisfaction in political life. But few political leaders who are at all successful in a democratic environment, even those who, as Wilson, are noticeably power-oriented from an early age, pursue a single value in political life to the exclusion of others.

In the case of someone like Wilson, certainly a multi-valued political personality, the task of establishing underlying motivational forces is difficult and complex. For it becomes necessary to assess the *relative strength* of individual value demands, the ways in which competing or conflicting value demands are *reconciled* in choosing one's goals, and the *conditions* under which one or another value or value pattern has primacy in motivation. Not only is the strength of the demand for some values perhaps greater than that for others, but their relative importance and operative role in specific situations may vary with the subject's shifting *expectations* as to the possibility of satisfying them.*

As a result of a detailed analysis of Wilson's career we have formulated what we hope is a consistent set of interrelated observations about the dynamics of his personality and political behavior. In the book itself this is stated most fully in the first part of Chapter VII. There we also seek to explain some of the contradictory aspects of Wilson's behavior, when his career is viewed as a whole, by distinguishing between Wilson the power seeker and Wilson the power holder, by distinguishing between political objectives which enlisted his aspirations for

* Thus, for example, Wilson also sought satisfaction in the political arena for his pronounced need for affection and approval. But the operative role of these value demands was muted for several reasons. He seems to have realized that the masses are a highly unreliable source of approval and affection; and, perhaps, he was concerned at times lest to seek popular approval and affection interfere with his overriding need to be "right" and to dominate. While he was delighted at evidences of the public's affection and approval, he continued to rely throughout his life upon family and friends as a more reliable source of the continuous supply of affection and approval which he needed.

great achievement and those which did not, and by differentiating some of the conditions under which he did and did not consult.

We recapitulate here in somewhat more general terms the analysis of Wilson's political functioning in order to illustrate problems encountered in a developmental analysis. The basic hypothesis concerning the dynamics of Wilson's political behavior is that power was for him a compensatory value, a means of restoring the self-esteem damaged in childhood. (This general hypothesis—evidently of wide application in the study of political leaders—is stated and elaborated by Lasswell, *Power and Personality*, pp. 39 *ff*. Evidence that the hypothesis applies to Wilson is presented in Chapter I.)

But power was not the only operative value in Wilson's political behavior. He did not—evidently could not—seek naked domination over others. He could indulge his hidden desire to dominate only by "purifying" his leadership, by committing it to political projects which articulated the highest moral and idealistic aspirations of the people. His desire for power was mitigated by a simultaneous need for approval, respect and, especially, for feeling virtuous.

To succeed in dominating others and in achieving great works in his chosen field of politics was necessary for Wilson if he was to gain external bolstering of his self-esteem. This requirement of success was no doubt reinforced by the emphasis in his religion upon "good works" and "service." The faith in which he was reared perhaps also served to spur him to bring his desire for domination into consonance with his need for approval, deference, and a feeling of righteousness. In any case, Wilson hit upon the highly constructive strategy—constructive both from his standpoint and that of the nation—of committing his desire for domination and his ambition for great accomplishments only to reform projects which already enjoyed considerable support and were within reasonable possibility of achievement. By doing so, the vast energies unleashed by his personal involvement in politics were committed to political objectives both desirable and feasible.

This strategy was a constructive one insofar as it reduced the likelihood that, if fastened to political projects which did not command widespread support, Wilson's underlying need for domination would encounter political opposition which, in turn, would rouse his anxieties and lead him into stubborn, self-defeating behavior.

Wilson entered each of his executive positions at a time when reform was the order of the day, and with a substantial fund of good will to draw upon. The Princeton Board of Trustees, the New Jersey State Legislature, and the United States Congress under Democratic control were in each case willing to give him a chance and to follow his leadership. In each position, Wilson was initially highly successful in driving through a series of reform measures, only to encounter equally impressive political deadlocks or setbacks later on.

In the last analysis, therefore, the constructive strategy proved unavailing. Why was this so? The explanation seems to lie in three factors. First, there was Wilson's demand for *immediate* compliance with his desires. This characteristic was of a piece with Wilson's unmistakably oratorical temperament, a need for quick domination once he had committed himself to a major reform project.

Second, there was Wilson's insatiable ambition. He was unable to derive normal gratification and pleasure from his achievements. (". . . I am so constituted that, for some reason or other, I never have a sense of triumph.") Success never long satisfied him. No sooner did Wilson put through one reform plan than he would discover another great work calling for his attention. He was soon pressing it upon legislators as something urgently and immediately to be accepted. His ambition, in other words, was compulsive. As a result, he found it difficult to pace his political demands prudently in order to assure a continued, though slower, series of achievements. The demand for immediate and complete domination on each single issue together with his compulsive drive for reform upon reform, achievement upon achievement, generated in time the opposition of others who shared in the power of decision. The cycle tended to repeat itself in each of his three executive posts.

There is some evidence that Wilson sensed the dangers implicit in his compulsive ambition. To House, Wilson spoke of nightmares in which he relived his struggles at Princeton, and of his fear that the pattern of success-defeat might repeat itself in the Presidency. He spoke anxiously, too, of the difficulty of maintaining during the last two years of his (first) term the level and pace of achievement he had accomplished in 1913-14.*

There is also some evidence that Wilson was casting about for ways of avoiding a repetition of his highly distressing experience as a reformer at Princeton. Thus, for a while, he cultivated the notion that with the passage of his major legislative program of 1913-14 the task of reforming American economic life along progressive principles had been completed. Such a thesis, which Wilson publicly stated in November, 1914, was unrealistic from a political standpoint; not surprisingly, it puzzled and dismayed leaders of progressive opinion.** Its political naïveté makes Wilson's thesis all the more interesting from the standpoint of ego functioning. The implication that he had already made his major political contribution suggests a rudimentary effort to find a means of protecting himself—through resignation or, more likely, refusal of a second term—against the compulsive ambition which was causing anxiety.

Third, Wilson was unable to develop within the American system of government a means for resolving his power conflicts with the legislature before disruptive anxieties, which opposition to his will generated, came into full play. In other respects, Wilson did much to transform the Presidency into an instrument of party leadership and a vehicle for legislative leadership, to bring it closer to the British system of Cabinet government which he had admired from an early age.

At the very beginning of his first term Wilson had recognized that, in undertaking this creative transformation of the Presidency, some means would have to be found for breaking deadlocks between the President and the legislature and for holding the President responsible in a manner comparable to that in which a prime minister is answerable to the legislative branch. "Sooner or later," he wrote, "it would seem he [the President] must be made answerable to opinion in a somewhat more informal and intimate fashion, answerable, it may be, to the Houses whom he seeks to lead, either personally or through a Cabinet, as well as to the people for whom they speak." But, he concluded, "that is a matter to be worked out—as it will be inevitably—in some natural American way which we cannot yet even predict." ***

But the problem, which Wilson correctly identified, proved more difficult of solution than he had imagined. His own efforts in this direction failed; yet they are of particular interest because they go to the kernel of the personal problem of his leadership. Because he generally fastened his aspirations for leadership to projects which articulated the moral and political aspirations of the people, he was able to assert with some plausibility that he directly represented the will of the people. Thereby, he justified to himself and to others his efforts to force Congress to do his will.

* House diary entries, 11/12/13, 12/22/13, 9/28/14, in Seymour, I, 119-20, 295-6; the last of these is quoted at the beginning of Chapter IX.

** Link, *WW&PE*, 79-80.

*** WW to Representative A. Palmer Mitchell, 2/13/13, quoted in H. J. Ford, *Woodrow Wilson, the Man and His Work*. New York: D. Appleton & Co., 1916, 323-4.

His need for achieving a feeling of rectitude, however, could not be so easily satisfied. He was ever sensitive to charges that he harbored autocratic tendencies and seems subconsciously to have feared this was the case. On several occasions he revealed his own concern in the matter by arguing in his self-defense that the pressure he was exerting on Congress on behalf of his legislative proposals could not be considered evidence of autocratic behavior because, after all, Congress would not yield to him unless public opinion favored the measure. It was not pressure from him—so he wanted to believe—but the pressure of the nation back of him which really caused Congress to pass what he wanted. (See pp. 149-51.)

What Wilson needed for peace of mind, when political deadlocks with his opponents developed, was a practical device which would enable him to "test" his contention that he better represented the will of the people than did Congress (or, in other situations, the Princeton Board of Trustees, the New Jersey Legislature, the Allied negotiators at Paris), a device which, therefore, would serve as a psychological and political safety valve against any autocratic tendencies within him. The device which he most often used for this purpose was the "appeal to the people."

That "public opinion" could be made the immediate arbiter in his power conflicts with his opponents was indeed a comforting thesis. It served to relieve Wilson of the responsibility to compromise when deadlock was reached. He could seek to impose his will in such situations, without meeting the need for compromise inherent in our system of divided and shared power, by self-righteously relying upon public opinion to uphold him—or, by defeating him, to save him from being guilty of autocratic behavior. The eagerness with which he turned to the device of an appeal to the people, and the poor judgment and unrealism he often displayed in so doing, testify to the highly personal function of the device in his hands.

In practice, as we have noted, the "appeal to the people" was for Wilson a poor substitute for the "vote of confidence" lacking in our system of government. Another alternative open to a prime minister in a Cabinet system of government—his resignation when defeated by parliament on an important vote—Wilson seems never to have seriously considered, though it is said that he spoke of the possibility on several occasions.* For the President to resign in such circumstances was obviously useless in a system in which Congress would not at the same time be dissolved in order to give the nation an opportunity to pass on the issue.

In his effort, through personal leadership rather than constitutional amendment, to transform the role of President into that of a prime minister, therefore, Wilson failed precisely at the point at which he most needed institutional safeguards against the disruptive tendencies of his personality and leadership.

* Baker, IV, 415; Lawrence, 310-11.

# NOTES AND BIBLIOGRAPHY

Since this book is largely a synthesis and reinterpretation of well-known facts of Wilson's career, documentation of the basic events which enter into the story has been held to a minimum. The bibliographical statements at the beginning of the notes to each chapter are restricted to the main sources utilized. Footnotes are generally reserved for new data utilized from the House and Baker Papers, for quotations and materials perhaps not otherwise easily located, and for adding supplementary observations to the text. Titles for the most frequently cited sources are abbreviated. (See key to abbreviations, below.) For all other sources, the full citation is given the first time only.

Manuscript collections consulted in preparation of this volume were the Wilson, Baker, Hitchcock and Lansing Papers, all at the Library of Congress, and the House Papers at the Yale University Library. The study was almost complete when permission to examine the Wilson Papers was granted. Therefore, we have been able to use that collection only sparingly, mainly for the purpose of checking our interpretations on certain points.

*Key To Abbreviations*

| | |
|---|---|
| WW | Woodrow Wilson |
| EMH | Edward Mandell House |
| Bailey | Bailey, Thomas Andrew, *Woodrow Wilson and the Lost Peace*. New York: The Macmillan Co., 1944. |
| Bailey, *WW&GB* | Bailey, Thomas Andrew, *Woodrow Wilson and the Great Betrayal*. New York: The Macmillan Co., 1945. |
| Baker | Baker, Ray Stannard, *Woodrow Wilson: Life and Letters*. Garden City, New York: Doubleday, Page & Co., 1927, 1931, 1935, 1937, 1939, 8 vols. |
| Baker Papers | The Ray Stannard Baker Papers, Library of Congress. (This collection has been reorganized since we consulted it. Accordingly, we cite only the "series," but not the "box" number, in which the item in question was located.) |
| Baker, *WW&WS* | Baker, Ray Stannard, *Woodrow Wilson and World Settlement*. Garden City, New York: Doubleday, Page & Co., 1922, 3 vols. |
| Buehrig | Buehrig, Edward Henry, *Woodrow Wilson and the Balance of Power*. Bloomington: Indiana University Press, 1955. |
| Corwin | Corwin, Edward S., *The President: Office and Powers 1787-1948*. New York: New York University Press, 1948. |

Fleming — Fleming, Denna Frank, *The United States and the League of Nations*. New York and London: G. P. Putnam's Sons, 1932.

*Foreign Relations, U. S.* — *Papers Relating to the Foreign Relations of the United States, Paris Peace Conference, 1919*. Washington, D. C.: U. S. Government Printing Office, 1942-47, 11 vols.

Garraty — Garraty, John A., *Henry Cabot Lodge: A Biography*. New York: Knopf, 1953.

House Papers — The diary and letters of Colonel Edward M. House, Sterling Memorial Library, Yale University. (Unless otherwise indicated, the diary entries and letters referred to are from the original manuscripts in this collection.)

Kerney — Kerney, James, *The Political Education of Woodrow Wilson*. New York and London: The Century Co., 1926.

Lawrence — Lawrence, David, *The True Story of Woodrow Wilson*. New York: George H. Doran Co., 1924.

Link — Link, Arthur Stanley, *Wilson: The Road to the White House*. Princeton: Princeton University Press, 1947.

Link, *WW&PE* — Link, Arthur Stanley, *Woodrow Wilson and the Progressive Era, 1910-1917*. New York: Harper & Brothers, 1954.

Lloyd George — Lloyd George, David, *Memoirs of the Peace Conference*. New Haven: Yale University Press, 1939, 2 vols.

Lodge — Lodge, Henry Cabot, *The Senate and the League of Nations* New York and London: Charles Scribner's Sons, 1925.

Miller — Miller, David Hunter, *The Drafting of the Covenant*. New York and London: G. P. Putnam's Sons, 1928, 2 vols.

Nevins — Nevins, Allan, *Henry White: Thirty Years of American Diplomacy* New York and London: Harper & Brothers, 1930.

*Public Papers* — Baker, Ray Stannard, and William Edward Dodd, eds., *The Public Papers of Woodrow Wilson*. New York and London: Harper & Brothers, 1925-1927, 6 vols.

Reid — Reid, Edith Gittings, *Woodrow Wilson: The Caricature, the Myth and the Man*. London, New York, and Toronto: Oxford University Press, 1934.

Seymour — Seymour, Charles, *The Intimate Papers of Colonel House*. Boston and New York: Houghton Mifflin Co., 1926, 1928, 4 vols.

Smith — Smith, Arthur D. Howden, *Mr. House of Texas*. New York and London: Funk & Wagnalls Co., 1940.

Tumulty — Tumulty, Joseph P., *Woodrow Wilson As I Know Him*. Garden City, New York: Doubleday, Page & Co., 1921.

Wilson, E. B. — Wilson, Edith Bolling, *My Memoir*. Indianapolis and New York: The Bobbs-Merrill Co., 1938, 1939.

## INTRODUCTION

The characterization of House is from a New York *Times* editorial of March 29, 1938. The statements by Harris E. Kirk (9/30/25), Thomas F. Woodlock (3/10/25) and Lindley M. Garrison (11/18/28) are in the Baker Papers, Series IB. The statement by William Allen White is from his *Woodrow Wilson: The Man, His Times, and His Task* (Boston and New York: Houghton Mifflin Co., 1924), 152. Wilson's letters to his wife (12/7/84 and 8/29/02) are quoted by Baker, *Woodrow Wilson: Life and Letters*, I, 242, and III, 160. Wilson's statement to Tumulty is from the latter's *Woodrow Wilson As I Know Him*, 457. Wilson's observations on reform and leadership are from his *Leaders of Men*, 41, 43-5.

## Chapter I: WILSON'S BOYHOOD

In preparing his official biography of Wilson, Ray Stannard Baker assembled an important collection of material on Wilson's early life and schooling. Much of it was thoughtfully and sensitively presented in Volume I, *Youth, 1856-1900*, of his eight-volume study. This and the Baker Papers, especially Series IB, are the main sources for the factual material presented in this chapter. Additional material on Wilson's early years was collected by William Allen White for his *Woodrow Wilson: The Man, His Times, and His Task*.

1. Baker, I, 49-50.
2. *Ibid.*, 57.
3. *Ibid.*, 68.
4. This story has been widely quoted. See, for example, George A. Riddell, *Lord Riddell's Intimate Diary of the Peace Conference and After* (London, Victor Gollancz, Ltd., 1933), 90.
5. Baker, I, 25.
6. WW to Ellen Axson Wilson, 4/19/88, Baker, I, 35.
7. Baker, I, 31.
8. WW to Cyrus McCormick, 12/21/08, Baker Papers, Series I.
9. Wilson, E. B., 57-8. For other details of Wilson's schooling under his father, see Baker, I, 37-9, and Baker Papers, Series IB, Memorandum of Talk with Miss Margaret Wilson, 3/12/25.
10. Memorandum of Talk with Miss Margaret Wilson, 3/12/25, Baker Papers, Series IB.
11. Helen Bones to Baker, 7/2/25, Baker Papers, Series IB.
12. Jessie Bones Brower to Baker, 5/9/26, Baker Papers, Series IB.
13. Henry B. Kennedy to Lena Rivers Smith, Nov., 1925, Baker Papers, Series IB.
14. Myers, William Starr, *Woodrow Wilson, Some Princeton Memories* (Princeton: Princeton University Press, 1946), 2.
15. WW to Joseph Ruggles Wilson, 12/16/88, Baker Papers, Series I (also published in New York *Times*, 5/17/31).

16. Tumulty, 464-5.
17. Written some time in 1911, from State of New Jersey Executive Department, Baker Papers, Series III.
18. Mary Hoyt Memorandum, p. 17, Baker Papers, Series IB.
19. Memorandum of Talk with Helen Bones, Baker Papers, Series IB.
20. Memoranda of Interviews with Cary Grayson, 2/18/26 and 2/19/26, Baker Papers, Series IB.

## Chapter II: THE APPRENTICE STATESMAN

The major source of data on the development of Wilson's interest in a political career and on his assiduous cultivation of the knowledge and skills appropriate to such a career is, once again, the official biography by Baker, Volumes I and II.

1. Baker, I, 109.
2. *Ibid.*, 92-3.
3. *Ibid.*, 104.
4. *Ibid.*, 109.
5. *Ibid.*, 116.
6. *Ibid.*, 118.
7. *Ibid.*, 152.
8. *Ibid.*, 154-6.
9. WW to Ellen Axson, 12/7/84, Baker, I, 242.
10. Baker, I, 172.
11. WW to Ellen Axson, 6/5/84, Baker, I, 182-3.
12. WW to Ellen Axson, 11/25/84 and 3/18/84, Baker, I, 187.
13. WW to Ellen Axson, 12/18/84, Baker, I, 109.
14. WW to Ellen Axson, 11/9/84, Baker, I, 242-3.
15. WW to Ellen Axson, 11/28/84, Baker, I, 219.
16. WW to Ellen Axson, 12/2/84, Baker, I, 220.
17. Baker. I, 223.
18. *Ibid.*, 228-30.
19. *Ibid.*, 239.
20. WW to Ellen Axson Wilson, 8/2/94, and Ellen Axson Wilson to WW, 8/27/02, Baker, II, 66 and 67 respectively.
21. Baker, I, 289. On the personal atmosphere in the Wilson home, see also Margaret Axson Elliott, *My Aunt Louisa and Woodrow Wilson* (Chapel Hill: University of North Carolina Press, 1944).
22. *Ibid.*, 292-3.
23. *Ibid.*, 293.
24. *Ibid.*, 315.
25. WW to Robert Bridges, 1/27/90, Baker, II, 6.
26. Baker, II, 26-7.
27. *Ibid.*, 23.
28. *Loc. cit.*
29. Mary Hoyt Memorandum, p. 14, Baker Papers, Series IB.
30. WW to Fred Yates, 11/6/06, Baker, III, 301. On friendships necessary to Wilson, see Baker, III, 156-69.
31. WW to Edith Gittings Reid, 3/15/14, Baker, III, 166.
32. Baker Papers, Series IC.
33. WW to Edith Gittings Reid, Reid, 235.
34. Reid, 64-5.
35. WW to Ellen Axson Wilson, 3/11/1900, Baker, II, 53-4.

## Chapter III: PRESIDENT OF PRINCETON

For this period of Wilson's career the official biography by Baker (Volume II) contains essential materials and some perceptive insights. Another authoritative and more objective account of the Princeton period is to be found in Arthur S. Link's *Wilson: The Road to the White House,* which is based upon a thorough sifting of primary sources.

In an early essay, the literary critic Edmund Wilson saw important aspects of Wilson's personality revealed in his struggles at Princeton. He interpreted Wilson's strengths and weaknesses in terms of Puritan culture and a Presbyterian environment ("Woodrow Wilson at Princeton," reprinted in his *Shores of Light.*) William Starr Myers (ed.), *Woodrow Wilson: Some Princeton Memories,* contains interesting impressions of Wilson by a number of faculty members.

1. Link, 90-1.
2. WW to Ellen Axson Wilson, 7/19/02 and 8/10/02, Baker, II, 134 and 138 respectively.
3. Annin, Robert E., *Woodrow Wilson: A Character Study* (New York: Dodd, Mead & Co., 1924), 11.
4. Baker, II, 175.
5. Annin, *op cit.*, 18, 27-8; Link, 63.
6. Link, 60.
7. *Ibid.*, 63; Baker, II, 210.
8. Baker, II, 231; Link, 48.
9. WW to J. G. Hibben, 1/26/07, Baker, II, 252.
10. Baker, II, 266.
11. Reid, 108.
12. Baker, II, 290.
13. *Ibid.*, 289-90; Link, 64-5.
14. Baker, II, 294.
15. *Ibid.*, 310.
16. *Ibid.*, 315-9.
17. Link, 70.
18. Quoted in Baker, II, 324.
19. Link, 76.
20. *Ibid.*, 72-3.
21. WW to Ellen Axson Wilson, 2/17/10, 2/25/10, 2/21/10, Baker, II, 330-1.
22. Link, 83-4. Link notes that the page proofs of this address, which Link quotes from the *Princeton Alumni Weekly,* X (April 20, 1910), 470-1, were corrected by Wilson before it was published in the weekly.
23. Link, 79.
24. Baker, II, 346.
25. Link, 101-2; Baker, III, 21-2.
26. Baker, III, 24-5; Link, 104.
27. Baker, III, 25-6; Link, 105.
28. WW to George Harvey, 1/6/07. Baker, III, 26.
29. Link, 96; for Wilson's 1908 remark see Kerney, 32-3.
30. Link, 353. This letter was published in the New York *Sun,* 1/8/12.
31. WW to H. J. Forman, 4/10/08, Link, 119-20.
32. WW to Ellen Axson Wilson, 7/6/08, Baker, II, 277.
33. Baker, III, 47.
34. WW to Adolphus Ragan, 7/3/09, Baker, III, 39-40.

35. Kerney, 26.
36. Baker, III, 53.
37. WW to John Harlan, 6/23/10, Baker, III, 53.
38. WW to David B. Jones, 6/27/10, Baker, III, 56.
39. Link, 90.

## Chapter IV: GOVERNOR OF NEW JERSEY

The major sources used in preparing this chapter were Baker, III; Link, *Wilson: The Road to the White House*; Kerney, *The Political Education of Woodrow Wilson;* Tumulty, *Woodrow Wilson As I Know Him;* John M. Blum, *Joe Tumulty and the Wilson Era* (Boston: Houghton Mifflin Co., 1951).

1. Hulbert, Mary Allen, *The Story of Mrs. Peck* (New York: Minton, Balch & Co., 1933), 170.
2. Wilson, Woodrow, *Congressional Government* (Boston and New York: Houghton Mifflin Co., 15th ed., 1913), 43.
3. Baker, III, 68.
4. *Ibid.*, 70.
5. Link, 167.
6. Quoted in Baker, III, 78-80.
7. Baker, III, 79-80.
8. Tumulty, 22.
9. Kerney, 71-2.
10. Baker, III, 97 *ff*. See also Link, 189-97.
11. Baker, III, 100-1.
12. *Ibid.*, 94.
13. Kerney, xi.
14. Link, 123. See also 180.
15. Wilson, Woodrow, *Leaders of Men*, edited, with introduction and notes by T. H. Vail Motter (Princeton, N. J.: Princeton University Press, 1952), 29.
16. Kerney, 78.
17. *Ibid.*, 81.
18. Link, 213.
19. *Ibid.*, 216.
20. *Ibid.*, 210, 221.
21. *Ibid.*, 219.
22. *Ibid.*, 222.
23. Baker, III, 124; Link, 230.
24. Link, 232-3.
25. WW to Mary Hulbert, 1/29/11, Baker, III, 126-7.
26. Quoted in Baker, III, 127.
27. Baker, III, 143.
28. WW to Mary Hulbert, 4/2/11, Baker, III, 146.
29. Baker, III, 169-72.
30. Link, 120.
31. *Ibid.*, 316-7.
32. WW to Mary Hulbert, 3/13/11, Baker, III, 210.
33. Baker, III, 210.
34. Link, 280-2.
35. *Ibid.*, 282 *ff*.
36. Newark *Star*, 11/9/11.

## Chapter V: THE APPRENTICE ADVISER

There is no adequate biography of House. A. D. H. Smith's *The Real Colonel House* (New York: George H. Doran Co., 1918) and his *Mr. House of Texas* do contain useful material, but they are uncritical and unreliable. Charles Seymour's *The Intimate Papers of Colonel House* was not intended to be, and is not, a personal biography. It is indispensable as a reference to House's activities and thought, but is not adequate as an interpretation of the man and his motivation. (See also reference to George Sylvester Viereck's *The Strangest Friendship in History* [New York: Liveright, Inc., 1932] in notes to Chapter VII, below.)

The major sources of the present chapter are the two long autobiographical memoranda written by House, "Reminiscences" in 1916 and "Memories" in 1929, which are to be found among his private papers in the Sterling Memorial Library at Yale University. They were used by Seymour in Volume I of *The Intimate Papers*. We have drawn liberally upon the unpublished portions of these memoranda. (Unless otherwise indicated, our account of House's early years and his political apprenticeship in Texas is based upon these two memoranda.) It is interesting to speculate in how far House's recollections of his childhood exploits are objectively true and in how far they represent wishful thinking as to his prowess. He was a small man, and therefore most likely a small child. His elder brother was leader of the gang, and perhaps House had to struggle to keep up with the others. Perhaps, in fact, it was feelings of inadequacy as youngest son in a large family and as the small boy among bigger playmates, as well as the fall from the swing when he was twelve, that made him so eager a manipulator of others.

There is very little in "Memories" and "Reminiscences," or in his diary and papers, of House's affective life. The contrast with Wilson in this respect is striking.

1. Smith, 11.
2. Viereck, *The Strangest Friendship in History*, 22.
3. House diary, 9/26/14.
4. White, *Woodrow Wilson*, 233-4.
5. Seymour, I, 39.
6. Quoted in Seymour, I, 39.
7. Smith, 30.
8. *Loc. cit.*
9. Seymour, I, 38.
10. Smith, 36. See also Seymour, I, 18-9, and St. Clair Griffin Reed, *A History of the Texas Railroads* (Houston, Texas: St. Clair Publishing Co., 1941), 402.
11. Seymour, I, 42. See also Smith, 33-5.
12. Seymour, I, 43.
13. EMH to WW, 11/18/11, Kerney, 166.
14. Smith, 41.

## Chapter VI: ". . . THE MAN . . . THE OPPORTUNITY"

For personal materials we have relied, as before, on Baker (Volume III), the Baker Papers, and the House diary and Papers. (Many of the relevant House letters are quoted in Seymour, I.) The House-Seymour conversations of 2/17/22 and 12/16/21 strengthen the impression gained from House's diary and other materials as to the reasons for House's unwillingness to take an official position under Wilson. Wilson's speeches in the campaign of 1912 were published under the title *The New Freedom* (New York: Doubleday, Page & Co., 1913).

There are numerous accounts by participants in the events leading to Wilson's nomination and election in 1912. Most of them are useful but must be weighed carefully. Of scholarly researches, Link's *Wilson: The Road to the White House* is outstanding and has been most useful for our purposes. The actual importance of House's contribution to Wilson's nomination and election has been variously assessed, being often exaggerated or underplayed. Link rightly dissipates the legend that House was the "president-maker" in 1911-1912 and also moderates the appraisal of House's role in swinging Texas to Wilson and in cementing relations between Bryan and Wilson. He concludes, too, that House did not play a decisive or even important role in deciding the strategy of the campaign (Link, 334-5). Link also corrects Baker's minimization of McCombs, Wilson's campaign manager, but appears to underrate Bryan's importance to Wilson at the Baltimore convention.

We have not discussed in detail the differences in political philosophy and program between Theodore Roosevelt and Wilson in 1912. For thoughtful analyses of the nature of liberalism and progressivism in America, see Richard Hofstadter, *The Age of Reform* (New York: Knopf, 1955); Louis Hartz, *The Liberal Tradition in America* (New York: Harcourt, Brace & Co., 1955); and Eric Goldman, *Rendezvous with Destiny* (New York: Knopf, 1952). See also William Diamond, *The Economic Thought of Woodrow Wilson* (Baltimore: The Johns Hopkins Press, 1943).

Wilson faced the various dangers to his candidacy for the Democratic nomination in 1912 with remarkable equanimity. His faith in Providence sustained him at this and other critical junctures in his career. After the publication of the Joline letter by his enemies (see p. 95) Wilson wrote to a friend that such attacks affected his spirits for a short while but that "for the most part I go serenely on my way. I believe very profoundly in an overruling Providence, and do not fear that any real plans can be thrown off the track. It may not be intended that I shall be President. . . ." (to Mary Hulbert, Baker, III, 257-8).

The most balanced accounts of the Harvey affair are those by Link, 359-78, and William O. Inglis, "Helping to Make a President," *Collier's Weekly*, LVIII (October 7, 14, and 21, 1916). W. F. Johnson's *George Harvey: A Passionate Patriot* (Boston and New York: Houghton Mifflin Co., The Riverside Press, Cambridge, 1929), 174-200, presents important documentary data, but his interpretations are biased in favor of his subject. See also Baker, III, 246-55; Kerney, 161-77; Tumulty, 82-93; Isaac F. Marcosson, *Marse Henry, A Biography of Henry Watterson* (New York: Dodd, Mead & Co., 1951), 192-200.

1. Smith, 42-3.
2. Seymour, I, 45.
3. EMH to Sidney Mezes, 11/25/11, House Papers (quoted in part in Seymour, I, 46).
4. Seymour, I, 46.
5. *Ibid.*, 50.
6. *Ibid.*, 52.
7. Baker, III, 265-6.
8. *Ibid.*, 261-2.
9. See Baker, III, 249, footnote 1, and Link, 362. For House's part in the incident, see also Seymour, I, 53-4, and Viereck, *The Strangest Friendship in History*, 32-3.

10. For an account of the incident, see Baker, III, 246-55; Link, 359-78; and Johnson, *George Harvey*, Chapter 20.
11. WW to George Harvey, 12/21/11, Link, 363. These Harvey-Wilson letters were also published in the New York *Evening Post* (and throughout the U. S.), 1/30/12.
12. George Harvey to WW, 1/4/12, Link, 363-4.
13. WW to George Harvey, 1/11/12, and George Harvey to WW, 1/16/12, Link, 364-5.
14. Baker, III, 252.
15. Bell, Herbert C. F., *Woodrow Wilson and the People* (Garden City, N. Y.: Doubleday, Doran & Co., 1945), 72.
16. Link, 372.
17. *Ibid.*, 373.
18. Seymour, I, 56.
19. EMH to WW, 6/7/12, Seymour, I, 62.
20. Seymour, I, 56.
21. WW to EMH, 1/27/12, Baker Papers, Series I; EMH to WW, 2/2/12, House Papers.
22. Seymour, I, 58.
23. Link, 350.
24. *Ibid.*, 382-3.
25. *Ibid.*, 384-7.
26. Baker, III, 321, 316.
27. *Ibid.*, 315-6.
28. EMH to Culberson, 5/1/12, Seymour, I, 60; EMH to Mrs. Bryan, 6/22/12, Link, 422-3.
29. WW to Mary Hulbert, 4/1/12, Baker, III, 292.
30. Quoted in Baker, III, 357.
31. Baker, III, 299.
32. *Ibid.*, 355-6.
33. EMH to WW, 6/20/12, Seymour, I, 64-5; WW to EMH, 6/24/12, Baker Papers, Series I.
34. EMH to WW, 8/21/12, House Papers; WW to EMH, 8/22/12, Baker Papers, Series I.
35. Hale, William Bayard, *The Story of a Style* (New York: B. W. Huebsch, Inc., 1920), 246.
36. *Ibid.*, 247.
37. Merriam, Charles E., *Four American Party Leaders* (New York: The Macmillan Co., 1926), 60, 86.
38. McAdoo, Eleanor Wilson, *The Woodrow Wilsons* (New York: The Macmillan Co., 1937), 181.
39. Link, 524.
40. Baker, IV, 3.
41. Baker, IV, 180.
42. EMH to WW, 11/22/12, Seymour, I, 92; WW to EMH, 11/30/12, EMH to WW, 12/6/12, House Papers.
43. House diary, 1/8/13, Seymour, I, 100; House-Seymour Conversation, 2/17/22, House Papers. See also House-Seymour Conversation, 12/16/21, House Papers, and House conversations with Viereck in Viereck, *The Strangest Friendship in History*, 43-4.

    House's reluctance to accept appointive office appears to have had a highly personal motivation as well: a certain pride of independence, which bordered upon necessity. This comes out most strongly and clearly in a note which

House provided George Sylvester Viereck, a sympathetic biographer. "If Wilson had really wanted to break with me," wrote House of the difficulties arising in their relationship during the Paris Peace Conference, "all he had to do was to refuse to sanction my actions. That would have discredited me at once. He understood my temper well enough to know that had he done this even once, I would have made some excuse to quit and go home. *I had never been in a position in my life when I had to take orders and that is one of several reasons why I refused to accept an office under him or any other executive. Our friendship and collaboration in public affairs had to be on something like equal terms.* Wilson sensed this at the outset and was willing for it to continue. . . ." (Viereck, "Behind the House-Wilson Break," Chapter 12 of *The Inside Story*, by Members of the Overseas Press Club of America, New York: Prentice-Hall, Inc., 1940, pp. 153-4; italics supplied).

44. House diary, 1/22/14. See also diary entries for 1/24/13 and 4/28/14.
45. House diary, 2/14/13.
46. Seymour, I, 101.

## Chapter VII: FORMULA FOR SUCCESS

The first part of the chapter provides the fullest statement in the book of our interpretation of the motivations underlying Wilson's interest in political power and of the dynamics of his political leadership.

The discussion of the complex bases on which the successful relationship between Wilson and House rested, in the second part of the chapter, derives largely from materials in the House diary and House Papers. House's conversations with Charles Seymour, in which he reflected on various aspects of his collaboration with Wilson, generally corroborate and strengthen the interpretation derived from his diary and other materials, and show more clearly the extent of House's insight into the relationship.

Various interpretations of the Wilson-House relationship have been offered and many of them contain useful insights. The fullest and perhaps most satisfactory account is that in Seymour, Volume I. George Sylvester Viereck's *The Strangest Friendship in History* offers some interesting first-hand data and a number of discerning observations; but the book as a whole is marred by the author's tendency to make sweeping assertions without presenting supporting evidence.

Some of Wilson's admirers have been perplexed and distressed by Wilson's dependence upon House. Accordingly, they tend to turn an unsympathetic eye on House's behavior as if criticizing the Colonel could obliterate weaknesses in Wilson that the relationship reveals.

1. Josephus Daniels to Katharine Brand, p. 13, Baker Papers, Series IB.
2. Smith, *The Real Colonel House*, 277.
3. Baker, II, 341-2.
4. House-Seymour Conversation, 2/17/22, House Papers.
5. *Ibid.*
6. Reid, 48-9.
7. Wilson, *Leaders of Men*, 41, 43-4.
8. Baker, I, 189.
9. *Ibid.*, 219-20.
10. House diary, 10/16/13, Seymour, I, 119.
11. Wilson, *Congressional Government*, 233 (15th ed.).
12. See Baker Papers, Memorandum of Talk with Mrs. E. B. Wilson, 1/27/25, and Talk with Margaret Wilson, 3/12/25.

13. *Public Papers, War & Peace*, I, 272.
14. Baker, VII, 258.
15. House-Seymour Conversation, 4/28/22, House Papers.
16. The quotations from the first four House letters to Wilson are from Baker, III, 302-3; the last quotation is from EMH to WW, 8/21/12, House Papers.
17. EMH to WW, 4/4/17 and 8/4/17, House Papers.
18. House Papers.
19. *Ibid.* (quoted in part in Seymour, I, 117).
20. House-Seymour Conversations, 2/17/22, 3/31/22 and 4/28/22, House Papers.
21. Smith, *The Real Colonel House*, 277.
22. Seymour, II, 463, and I, 265.
23. EMH to WW, 10/27/17, House Papers; EMH to WW, 2/3/18, Baker, VII, 521.
24. EMH to Sidney Mezes, 4/24/13, Seymour, I, 150.
25. House diary, 2/14/18 and 5/14/18.
26. House diary, 2/24/18.
27. House diary, 3/4/15, 4/17/14, 7/10/15, Seymour, I, 387, 123-4, 124-5 respectively.
28. EMH to WW, 4/17/15, House Papers.
29. House diary, 4/14/13.
30. EMH to WW, 6/5/17, and WW to EMH, 1/24/17 and 6/1/17, House Papers.
31. House diary, 1/13/15. See also entry for 1/25/15, Seymour, I, 358.
32. Seymour, I, 116 (date given as some time in summer of 1915).
33. House diary, 8/16/18.
34. Josephus Daniels to Katharine Brand, p. 13, Baker Papers, Series IB.
35. EMH to Mrs. F. L. Higginson, September, 1915, House Papers (italics supplied).
36. House diary, 3/10/16.

## Chapter VIII: WILSON AND CONGRESS

Our treatment of Wilson's impressive achievement in the field of domestic legislation is necessarily highly selective and is focussed upon the methods of leadership he used in order to drive his reforms through Congress. We have relied largely upon the New York *Times* and primary materials reproduced in Baker, IV and V, and in Wilson's *Public Papers*.

Wilson's creative transformation of the Presidency into a vehicle for legislative leadership has been the subject of many scholarly analyses. Particularly useful are Corwin, *The President: Office and Powers*; W. F. Willoughby, *Principles of Legislative Organization and Administration* (Washington, D. C.: The Brookings Institution, 1934); James Hart, "Classical Statesmanship," *Sewanee Review*, October, 1925; and Wilfred E. Binkley, *The Powers of the President* (Garden City, N. Y.: Doubleday, Doran & Co., 1937). See also Louis Brownlow, *The President and the Presidency* (Chicago: Public Administration Service, 1949); George B. Galloway, *The Legislative Process in Congress* (New York: Thomas Y. Crowell Company, 1953); Clinton Rossiter, *Constitutional Dictatorship* (Princeton: Princeton University Press, 1948); Lawrence H. Chamberlain, *The President, Congress and Legislation* (Thesis, Columbia University, 1946); Stephen K. Bailey, *Congress Makes A Law* (New York: Columbia University Press, 1950); Bertram M. Gross, *The Legislative Struggle* (New York: McGraw-Hill Book Company, 1953); William Diamond, *The Economic Thought of Woodrow Wilson* (Baltimore: The Johns Hopkins Press, 1943).

Willoughby (Chapter 34) notes that as a result of the unprecedented use of the caucus in Wilson's first term, feeling against it in Congress was so strong that shortly thereafter both parties decided to restrict use of the caucus for purposes of coercing the vote of members.

For a fuller discussion of the substance of the progressive legislation passed under Wilson's leadership in 1913-1914, see Arthur S. Link's *Woodrow Wilson and the Progressive Era, 1910-1917.*

House's contribution to Wilson's legislative achievement of 1913-14, particularly with regard to the Federal Reserve Act, has been the subject of speculation and controversy. House himself felt that he had steered this legislation into existence (see diary entry for 1/29/18). Charles Seymour's assertion (I, 160) that House was "the unseen guardian angel" of the Federal Reserve Act, so enraged Carter Glass, who as Chairman of the Banking and Currency Committee in the House of Representatives himself had played an important role in its passage, that he wrote a book to disprove what he termed Seymour's "profanation of history" (*An Adventure in Constructive Finance*, Garden City, N. Y.: Doubleday, Page & Co., 1927). The book is intemperate in tone, but is nonetheless convincing in its thesis that House's role was a peripheral one. Doubtless House performed a useful service in acting as informational middleman between the President and important segments of public opinion, particularly the banking community. There is no evidence, however, that House contributed in a direct and substantial way to the drafting of the bill or to its passage. See also Samuel Untermeyer, *Who Is Entitled to the Credit for the Federal Reserve Act?* (40-page pamphlet, date and publisher not given); William Gibbs McAdoo, *Crowded Years* (Boston and New York: Houghton Mifflin Co., 1931); Robert L. Owen, *The Federal Reserve Act* (New York: The Century Co., 1919); Mary B. Bryan (ed.), *The Memoirs of William Jennings Bryan* (Philadelphia and Chicago: John C. Winston, 1925); and a folder of comments on Carter Glass' book in Baker Papers, Series I.

1. WW speech accepting Democratic nomination, 8/17/12, *Public Papers, College & State*, II, 453.
2. Percy MacKaye to R. S. Baker, Baker, IV, 180.
3. New York *Times*, 4/10/13.
4. *Ibid.*, 4/7/13.
5. *Ibid.*, 5/16/13.
6. *Ibid.*, 5/27/13.
7. *Ibid.*, 6/7/13.
8. 5/20/13, Baker, IV, 122.
9. WW to Walter Hines Page, 9/26/13, Baker, IV, 129. See also House diary, 10/16/13, Seymour, I, 119.
10. *Public Papers, The New Democracy*, II, 52.
11. New York *Times*, 7/26/13. See also Glass, *op. cit.*, 130-1.
12. Baker, IV, 181. Also Glass, *op. cit.*, 154. The tabulation of the vote is from the *Congressional Record*, Vol. 50, Part V, 5129.
13. Baker, IV, 182.
14. Glass, *op. cit.*, 193-4.
15. Link, Arthur S., "Woodrow Wilson and the Democratic Party," *Review of Politics*, Vol. 18, No. 2, April, 1956. In employing the patronage weapon and other devices of control Wilson was resorting to the very tactics which, as a student of government, he had so roundly condemned as illegitimate means of influencing the action of Congress (see his *Constitutional Government in the United States*, New York: Columbia University Press, 1908, pp. 70-1).

16. *Congressional Record*, 12/4/13, Vol. 51, Part 1, 160, 63rd Congress, 2nd session.
17. House diary, 12/22/13.
18. Link, *WW&PE*, 224, 226, 229.
19. Corwin, 267 (2nd ed.).
20. Willoughby, *op. cit.*, 521 *ff*.
21. Corwin, 29 (2nd ed.).
22. Willoughby, *op. cit.*, 71; Corwin, 314-5 (2nd ed.).
23. Wilson, *Congressional Government*, 10-1 (15th ed.). The full quotation is: "The leading inquiry in the examination of any system of government must, of course, concern primarily the real depositaries and the essential machinery of power. There is always a centre of power: where in this system is that centre? In whose hands is self-sufficient authority lodged, and through what agencies does that authority speak and act?"
24. *Ibid.*, 204.
25. WW to Charles Talcott, 11/14/86, Baker, I, 280-1. An indirect expression of his urgent claim to political leadership, at a time when the prospect of holding public office was still remote, appears also in Wilson's *Leaders of Men*, which he delivered as an address several times during the 1890's. In this essay, Wilson argued that men who are leaders in thought are as much entitled to be considered "leaders of men" as those who lead in action.
26. Wilson, *Constitutional Government in the United States*, 65.
27. Wilson, *Congressional Government*, 208-9 (15th ed.).
28. *Ibid.*, 119.
29. *Ibid.*, 43, 273-4, 254.
30. *Ibid.*, xi, xii. See also Wilson, *Constitutional Government in the United States*, 59.
31. Wilson, *Constitutional Government in the United States*, 70, 79.
32. *Ibid.*, 68.
33. *Ibid.*, 73, 71.
34. WW speech in Trenton, New Jersey, 1/13/13, Baker, III, 434.
35. House diary, 11/14/14. See also Baker, V, 57 (footnote).
36. Smith, Ira R. T., *"Dear Mr. President . . .": The Story of Fifty Years in the White House Mail Room* (New York: Julian Messner Inc., 1949), 98.
37. See, for example, House diary, 11/14/14, and Lawrence, 215, 222-3. On Wilson's view that the Cabinet was an executive, not a political body, and as such was to be used primarily for advice in the conduct of government rather than in the formulation of political policy, see his *Constitutional Government in the United States*, 76-7. Norman J. Small, *Some Presidential Interpretations of the Presidency* (Baltimore: The Johns Hopkins Press, 1932), 53-4, finds that Wilson's use of his Cabinet generally conformed with his theoretical view of its role.
38. Baker, V, 124-5.
39. McAdoo, *The Woodrow Wilsons*, 259.
40. Seymour, I, 119.
41. Baker, IV, 183.
42. WW to Mary Hulbert, 9/28/13, Baker, IV, 184.
43. Statement in New York, 3/4/19, *Public Papers, War & Peace*, I, 453.
44. Wilson's Second Annual Address to Congress, 12/8/14, *Public Papers, The New Democracy*, I, 220.
45. Baker, V, 122, 119.
46. *Ibid.*, 132.

47. WW to Senator William J. Stone, Baker, VI, 168 (also published in the New York *Times*, 2/25/16).
48. Seymour, I, 151-2, 156. It should be noted, at the same time, that House was aware of the need for Wilson to moderate the tempo of his demands upon Congress for legislation. Thus, in September, 1914, on the ground that relations between the President and Congress were at the breaking point, he advised Wilson against attempting to push the ship purchase bill through during the current legislative session (see House diary, 9/29/14).
49. WW to EMH, 1/28/14, House Papers.
50. These letters (Ellen Axson Wilson to WW) are to be found in Baker Papers, Series IB.

## Chapter IX: THE GREAT WAR: NEUTRALITY AND INTERVENTION

The complex problems of neutrality and intervention are dealt with in highly selective fashion since the objective of the chapter is to characterize the collaboration between Wilson and House in matters of foreign policy, their outlooks on international affairs, and personal aspects of Wilson's decision-making. In depicting House's role we have relied upon the detailed account of his activities presented in Seymour, I and II. For material on Wilson's foreign-policy thoughts and actions during this period the main sources have been Baker, V and VI, and Harley Notter, *The Origins of the Foreign Policy of Woodrow Wilson* (Baltimore: The Johns Hopkins Press, 1937).

The vast literature on American neutrality and "reasons" for American intervention in World War I has been ably referenced and interpreted in the bibliographical essay by Richard W. Leopold, "The Problem of American Intervention, 1917: An Historical Retrospect," *World Politics*, II, April, 1950, 405-25. Particularly useful is the author's indication of the shifting perspective from which American intervention has been historically viewed.

Of the numerous interpretive accounts of the period, we have drawn upon several recent publications: Edward H. Buehrig, *Woodrow Wilson and the Balance of Power;* Robert E. Osgood, *Ideals and Self-Interest in America's Foreign Relations* (Chicago: University of Chicago Press, 1953); Arthur S. Link, *Woodrow Wilson and the Progressive Era*, Chapters 6 and 8.

It is difficult to arrive at a balanced account of House's contributions to American foreign policy during this period and of his influence upon Wilson in this respect. His confidential relationship to Wilson at the time and the later publication of parts of his diary in *The Intimate Papers of Colonel House* encouraged somewhat exaggerated images of a powerful, pervasive, behind-the-scenes influence. On the other hand, apologists for Wilson and pro-Wilson scholars have belittled and criticized House's activities as an informal diplomatic trouble-shooter. Baker in his official biography and, to a lesser extent, Harley Notter contend that on his peace missions abroad House exceeded his instructions and did not keep Wilson properly informed of his activities. On the other hand, Arthur Link has found only one instance in which House failed to render a faithful account to Wilson of what he did and said on his behalf while abroad (*WW&PE*, 203). House's concern with power factors and his methods of diplomacy, which repelled scholars and idealists of an earlier generation, are likely to be viewed more sympathetically by the post-World War II generation, with its more mature image of world politics (see, for example, the favorable estimate of House in Buehrig's book).

House undoubtedly exercised an important influence upon the conduct of American foreign policy. In this chapter we attempt to indicate the broader contribution which House made in this respect rather than day-to-day assistance which he rendered on specific matters. We also indicate some of the important limits to House's influence and relate them to Wilson's attitudes and personality. Despite his achievements and the enjoyment of his role, House was far from satisfied with the degree of success he achieved in influencing Wilson's foreign policies and actions. (On this point, see Chapter X, "Undercurrents.")

Thomas A. Bailey, *Woodrow Wilson and the Lost Peace*, 16-7, 330-1, offers extremely suggestive observations regarding Wilson's growing tendency, after his war decision, to confuse the causes and objectives of American intervention.

1. Seymour, I, 295-6. Italics supplied.
2. The discussion of House's attitude toward the European balance of power and toward the European war as it affected United States security is based on Seymour, I, 191-2, 209-10, 233, 235-40, 251, 255-6, 260-1, 281-2, 285, 297-302, 318, 326-9, 337-8, 358 *ff*.; II, 84-5; Buehrig, 187-200; Osgood, *op. cit.*, 160-3.
3. Osgood, *op. cit.*, 175. On Wilson's idealistic approach to international affairs, see also Baker, V, 24-7.
4. *Public Papers, College & State*, II, 81.
5. House diary, 8/30/14, Seymour, I, 294-5. On Wilson's slowness in turning his interest to problems of foreign policy, see also Baker, V, 20-1, 29-30, 40.
6. Baker, VI, 119.
7. EMH to WW, 7/1/14, House Papers.
8. House diary, 1/25/15, Seymour, I, 357-8.
9. EMH to WW, 1/26/15, House Papers.
10. EMH to WW, 1/29/15, House Papers.
11. EMH to WW, 9/18/14, Seymour, I, 324-5.
12. EMH to WW, 2/23/15, 3/21/15, 11/10/15, 2/9/16, and 11/30/16, Seymour, I, 382, 402-3; II, 92, 165, and 395 respectively.
13. House diary, 9/28/14, Seymour, I, 295-6. See also entry for 5/24/16, Seymour, II, 295.
14. Osgood, *op. cit.*, Chapters 8 and 9.
15. House diary, 8/30/14, Seymour, I, 293; Osgood, *op. cit.*, 174; Notter, *op. cit.*, 373, 403, 422. See also Spring-Rice to Grey, 9/3/14, in George M. Trevelyan, *Grey of Fallodon, The Life and Letters of Sir Edward Grey* (Boston: Houghton Mifflin Co., 1937), 355-6.
16. *Public Papers, The New Democracy*, I, 305, 321. On the temperamental basis for Wilson's ability to resist provocations and pressure for action, see also Robert Lansing, *War Memoirs* (Indianapolis: The Bobbs-Merrill Co., 1935), 349-50. On Wilson's desire for neutrality in thought as well as in deed, see Baker, V, 17-20.
17. Seymour, II, Chapter 4; Buehrig, 172-87, 200-4.
18. For our account of the House-Grey plan for positive American intervention we have relied upon Seymour, II, Chapters 4-7; Buehrig, 205-28; Link, *WW&PE*, Chapter 8, "Devious Diplomacy." Baker, VI, Chapter 5, and Notter, *op. cit.*, contain useful materials but questionable interpretations.
19. Link, *WW&PE*, 205; Baker, VI, 128; Buehrig, 228.
20. Seymour, II, 89-92, 116-7, 293-8; Baker, VI, 125-6, 130-1, 141-2; Buehrig, Chapter 6.
21. House diary, 7/10/15, Seymour, II, 18-9.
22. Seymour, II, 83-4, 289-90, 129, 17-21.
23. The profile of House as a negotiator is based upon an analysis of materials presented in Seymour, I and II, describing House's activities in foreign-policy matters.

24. Seymour, I, 322.
25. See, for example, Seymour, II, 160-3.
26. Link, *WW&PE*, 218-20; Buehrig, 229-46; Seymour, II, 284-5, 304 *ff.*, 316.
27. Baker, VI, 226-7; Buehrig, 245-6, 250-3.
28. Colonel House strongly and repeatedly advised Wilson not to issue the note of December 12, 1916, but Wilson, determined to act for peace before being dragged into war by a resumption of unrestricted U-boat warfare, ignored this advice. In the end, Wilson sent the note without showing the final draft to House (Seymour, II, 390-404). For the U.S. note of December 24, 1916, see *Papers Relating to the Foreign Relations of the United States*, 1916, Supplement, p. 112, quoted in Baker, VI, 406-7.
29. WW to J. P. Gavit, 1/29/17, Baker, VI, 414.
30. Baker, VI, 426-9.
31. *Ibid.*, 453-4, 464-9.
32. House diary, 3/22/17, Seymour, II, 461.
33. See, for example, Wilson's address of May 7, 1911, *Public Papers, College & State*, II, 294. See also Notter, *op. cit.*, 293, 298, 461. On Wilson's attitude toward the war with Spain and the annexations which followed, see Notter, *op. cit.*, 270-2, and Osgood, *op. cit.*, 175-7.
34. Link, *WW&PE*, Chapter 4, "Missionary Diplomacy," and Chapter 5 on Wilson's intervention in Mexico provide concise summaries and perceptive interpretations. See also Notter, *op. cit.*, Chapter 5.
35. The first draft of Wilson's note of December 18, 1916, is published in full in Baker, VI, 380-6.
36. Comment by Colonel House, 10/29/25, Seymour, II, 18. See also Seymour, II, 51. On Wilson's conscientiousness in decision-making, see also Lansing, *War Memoirs*, 349-50.
37. This is the well-known exchange between Burleson and Wilson, quoted in Baker, VI, 503.
38. Baker, VI, 449-50.
39. House diary, 3/27/17, Seymour, II, 464-5.
40. Heaton, John L., *Cobb of "The World"* (New York: E. P. Dutton & Co., 1924), 269.
41. *Ibid.*, 270.
42. Baker, VI, 461-2.
43. Lansing, *War Memoirs*, 212-4; Houston, David F., *Eight Years with Wilson's Cabinet*, 1913-1920 (Garden City, New York: Doubleday, Page & Co., 1926), I, 229.

## Chapter X: UNDERCURRENTS

The major source of data on House's increasing dissatisfaction with his role as Wilson's adviser is, as the text and footnotes indicate, the House diary, particularly hitherto unpublished portions of it.

On Wilson's wartime powers and relations with Congress, our major sources have been Baker, VII, the Baker Papers, and the New York *Times*. Of the commentaries on this subject we have relied upon Corwin; Small, *Some Presidential Interpretations of the Presidency*; Clarence A. Berdahl, *War Powers of the Executive in the United States* (Urbana, Illinois: University of Illinois, 1921); Clinton Rossiter, *Constitutional Dictatorship* (Princeton: Princeton University Press, 1948).

When the Senate successfully filibustered his proposal to arm American merchantmen in the spring of 1917, Wilson issued a strong denunciation of the action and demanded a change in the rules of that body. Early in the next session of Congress, the Senate adopted for the first time in its history a cloture rule (Baker, VI, 480-2; Corwin, 2nd edition, 273).

1. House diary, 12/20/16. For context of this quotation see rest of this diary entry, Seymour, II, 405.
2. Small, *Some Presidential Interpretations*, 11; Baker, VI, 309; Interview with Harry A. Garfield, 3/18/25, and Interview with A. S. Burleson, p. 48, Baker Papers, Series IB.
3. Corwin, 190 (2nd ed., revised).
4. *Ibid.*, 273-4.
5. Tumulty, 265.
6. WW to Tumulty, 6/14/17, Baker, VII, 112-3.
7. Quoted in Baker, VII, 185-6.
8. Quoted in Baker, VII, 251.
9. New York *Times*, 2/8/18.
10. Quoted in Baker, VIII, 454.
11. Lodge, 32-63; Garraty, 329-32; Blum, *Joe Tumulty and the Wilson Era*, 97; Lawrence, 144-7.
12. Wilson's appeal for a Democratic Congress is reprinted in *Public Papers, War & Peace*, I, 286-8. His reaction to the election results, as stated in various letters written shortly thereafter, was to evince a greater stubbornness and determination, and to avow once again his faith that divine Providence would find a way to bring about the realization of the great things for which he was striving. (See Baker, VIII, 562, 574, 591; see also the curious explanation for the Democratic defeat Wilson gave several months later in a speech to the Democratic National Committee, cited in our text, pp. 237-8.)
13. Seymour, I, viii. For House's observations on Wilson's shortcomings see also *ibid.*, 124-8.
14. House diary, 2/24/13 and 4/15/14, Seymour, I, 111 and 126 respectively.
15. House diary, 9/29/14 and 11/2/14. For Cabinet resentment see also entry for 6/30/17 and 4/1/17. For Wilson's position on multiple terms see also entry for 2/14/13.
16. See House diary, 9/28/14, 7/10/15, 7/24/15, 3/29/16, 6/23/16, and 5/19/17. See also Chapter IX.
17. House diary, 7/10/15 (quoted in part in Seymour, II, 18-9).
18. House diary, 7/31/15.
19. EMH to Sidney Mezes, 11/19/14, and House diary, 11/4/15 and 11/5/15. In later years House commented on several occasions on the lessening of Wilson's dependence and warmth after the advent of Mrs. Galt (Smith, 359).
20. House diary, 11/26/15.
21. House diary, 12/8/15.
22. Thus, for example, in April, 1916, House noted in his diary that he and Mrs. Wilson had agreed that it would be most helpful to the President if his Secretary of the Navy, Josephus Daniels, and his private secretary, Joseph Tumulty, could be ousted. Mrs. Wilson undertook to see to Tumulty, and House agreed to find a way of getting rid of Daniels. In June, 1918, Mrs. Wilson wrote House expressing annoyance with another member of the President's circle and criticizing his political ambitions. House replied simulating sympathy with her point of view. Again, in January, 1917, House noted in his diary that Mrs. Wilson had criticized Admiral Grayson, the President's personal physician. House observed that it seemed the President's intimate circle had now dwindled down to just two, Mrs. Wilson and himself. (House

diary, 4/6/16 and 1/12/17; Mrs. E. B. Wilson to EMH, 6/14/18, and EMH to Mrs. E. B. Wilson, 6/23/18. See also diary entry for 3/3/17. For a documented account of the unsuccessful effort to oust Tumulty, see Blum, *op. cit.*, 118-22.)

23. Wilson, E. B., 155, 236-7.
24. *Loc. cit.* See also 251-2.
25. House diary, 4/2/16.
26. House diary, 6/10/16. See also entry for 11/18/16.
27. See EMH to Sidney Mezes, 3/1/15. Also EMH to Gordon Auchincloss, 5/25/15.
28. House diary, 9/8/18.
29. House diary, 12/14/16, 11/18/16, and 8/15/16. See also entry for 5/19/17.
30. House diary, 7/4/17 and 1/17/18. See also entry for 1/9/18.
31. House diary, 1/3/18. See also entry for 9/3/17 (cited in Chapter XI).
32. House diary, 8/15/17.
33. House diary, 3/4/16 and 12/20/16. A perceptive account of the effort by Wilson and Lansing to disarm Allied merchantmen is presented by Link, *WW&PE*, 205-10, in which he pointedly terms it "one of the most maladroit blunders in American diplomatic history."
34. See House diary, 8/23/17 and 12/18/17.
35. House diary, 7/21/17.
36. House diary, 4/2/17.
37. Seymour, III, 164.
38. House Papers.
39. House diary, 12/6/15.
40. Paderewski to EMH, 12/22/15.
41. House diary, 5/14/17.
42. See, for example, entries for 9/13/17, 6/14/18, 10/3/17, 11/11/17, 4/28/17, and 4/29/17.

## Chapter XI: WORLD LIBERATOR

Our main purpose is to show Wilson's personal involvement in peacemaking and the resulting distortion of his judgment in dealing with political forces both at home and at Paris.

Footnote citations reflect the major sources consulted in preparing the present chapter, which is largely a synthesis of facts assembled and reported by previous writers. The four addresses in which Wilson stated the Fourteen Points and his various supplementary points, which together comprised his peace program, are the addresses to Congress of 1/8/18 and 2/11/18; the address at Mount Vernon, 7/4/18; and the address in New York City of 9/27/18. They are printed in the *Public Papers, War & Peace*, I, 155-162, 177-84, 231-5, 253-61. The points themselves are conveniently quoted in Bailey, *Woodrow Wilson and the Lost Peace*, 333-6. Important background material on the formulation of the war aims addresses is to be found in Baker, VII and VIII; Seymour, III and IV; James R. Mock and Cedric Larson, *Words That Won the War* (Princeton: Princeton University Press, 1939).

Bailey's book provides a concise account of the mistakes made by Wilson in his preparations for the Peace Conference. For additional material on Wilson's selection of peace commissioners, see *Foreign Relations, U. S.*, I, 155-92; and Bailey, 87-105, 341-2. For Wilson's relations with peace commissioners other than House (both for this and the next two chapters), see Robert Lansing, *The Peace Negotiations* (Boston and New York: Houghton Mifflin Co., 1921); *The Big*

*Four and Others of The Peace Conference* (Boston and New York: Houghton Mifflin Co., 1921); and especially his unpublished diary in the Lansing Papers, The Library of Congress; Allan Nevins, *Henry White;* Frederick Palmer, *Bliss, Peacemaker: The Life and Letters of General Tasker Howard Bliss* (New York: Dodd, Mead & Co., 1934).

1. Harriman, Mrs. J. Borden, *From Pinafores to Politics* (New York: Henry Holt & Co., 1923), 280-1.
2. EMH to WW, 2/4/17, 2/10/17, 3/17/17, 3/29/17, Baker, VI, 498. Baker adds: "The thought that America could and should participate in, and in some measure dominate, the peace conference was indeed highly persuasive with Wilson."
3. Seymour, IV, 153.
4. Seymour, III, 282-3.
5. Oscar T. Crosby to R. S. Baker, Baker, VIII, 253; Baker, VIII, 505; WW to L. S. Rowe, 11/11/18, Baker, VIII, 593.
6. This exchange of cables between Wilson and House is to be found in *Foreign Relations, U. S.*, I, 129-31, 134-5 (quoted in part in Baker, VIII, 584-6, and Seymour, IV, 212-4).
7. House diary, 12/21/18.
8. It was this conversation, Lansing later noted (*The Peace Negotiations*, 22-4), which marked the beginning of the rupture between the two men.
9. Memorandum of Conversation with Vance McCormick, 7/15/28, Baker Papers, Series IB.
10. Kansas City *Star*, 11/26/18, quoted in Fleming, 56.
11. Bailey, 93.
12. Bartlett, Ruhl J., *The League to Enforce Peace* (Chapel Hill: University of North Carolina Press, 1944), 96-7, 127-8.
13. WW to EMH, 3/20/18, Baker, VIII, 38.
14. Seymour, IV, 4; Pringle, Henry F., *The Life and Times of William Howard Taft* (New York and Toronto: Farrar & Rinehart, Inc., 1939), II, 932-7.
15. Seymour, IV, 49-50.
16. *Ibid.*, 26, 52-3.
17. Baker, *WW&WS*, I, 214.
18. Nevins, 355.
19. Wilson's address to joint session of Congress, 12/2/18, *Public Papers, War & Peace,* I, 308-23.
20. Seymour, IV, 280-2. See also Baker, *WW&WS*, I, 11.
21. Hillman, William, *Mr. President* (New York: Farrar, Straus and Young, 1952), 230.
22. New York *Times*, 12/31/18; (second quotation) Seymour, IV, 255.
23. House diary, probably 12/30/18, Seymour, IV, 255.
24. See, for example, Wilson's address in Manchester, England, 12/30/18, which is generally regarded as containing Wilson's answer to Clemenceau's vote of confidence on the preceding day (*Public Papers, War & Peace*, I, 354).
25. Willert, Sir Arthur, *The Road to Safety: A Study In Anglo-American Relations* (New York: Frederick A. Praeger, 1953), 17.
26. Miller, II, 156, 158.
27. Seymour, IV, 251-2 (probably House diary, 12/14/18).
28. Lloyd George, I, 114, 115 (italics supplied).
29. Lloyd George, I, 89; House diary, 12/15/18, Seymour, IV, 252.
30. Henry White to Edith Bolling Wilson, 6/17/24, Baker Papers.
31. General Bliss to Mrs. Bliss, 12/18/18, Palmer, *Bliss, Peacemaker*, 359.

32. General Bliss to N. D. Baker, 1/11/19, Baker Papers, Series I.
33. Palmer, *op. cit.*, 363.
34. House diary, 3/28/19.

## CHAPTER XII: THE PARIS PEACE CONFERENCE

The account of the Peace Conference presented in this and in the next chapter is adapted from a more detailed study (unpublished) which we prepared in 1951 and which draws upon sources too numerous to list in full. Among the more important sources utilized mention should be made of the verbatim transcripts of the meetings of the Council of Ten, the Council of Four, and of other official proceedings at the Peace Conference contained in *Papers Relating to the Foreign Relations of the United States, Paris Peace Conference, 1919*, eleven volumes. (The account of the Council of Four discussions in this source is based on the minutes of Sir Maurice Hankey, of the British delegation; lack of time prevented us from exploiting the recent publication of parallel minutes of the same meetings taken by the official interpreter, Paul Mantoux.)

For personal materials on Wilson and House, we relied mostly on the House and Baker Papers; Baker, *Woodrow Wilson and World Settlement*, three volumes; E. B. Wilson, *My Memoir*; and Seymour, *The Intimate Papers of Colonel House*, IV.

Of the numerous interpretive studies of the Peace Conference, most useful for our purposes have been Thomas Bailey's *Woodrow Wilson and the Lost Peace* and Paul Birdsall's *Versailles Twenty Years After* (New York: Reynal & Hitchcock, 1941). Both are balanced and accurate, and we have used them to check our own reconstruction and interpretation of events. Birdsall presents more material than does Bailey on the House-Wilson relationship and on policy conflicts within the American delegation. His treatment of these matters is an important one, despite the fact that he did not have direct access to the full House diary. Bailey is more critical than Birdsall of Wilson as a negotiator.

For bibliographical essays on the development of historical scholarship on the Paris Peace Conference, see Robert C. Binkley, "Ten Years of Peace Conference History" and Paul Birdsall, "The Second Decade of Peace Conference History," *Journal of Modern History*, I (1929), 607-29; XI (1939), 362-78.

The following books have been especially useful: David Hunter Miller, *Drafting of the Covenant* (two volumes); James T. Shotwell, *At the Paris Peace Conference* (New York: The Macmillan Co., 1937); René Albrecht-Carrié, *Italy at the Peace Conference* (New York: Columbia University Press, 1938); Edward M. House and Charles Seymour (eds.), *What Really Happened at Paris* (New York: Charles Scribner's Sons, 1921); Harold W. V. Temperly (ed.), *A History of the Peace Conference of Paris* (6 vols., London: H. Frowde, and Hodder and Stoughton, 1920-24); Harold G. Nicolson, *Peacemaking, 1919* (New York: Harcourt, Brace & Co., 1939); Henry Wickham Steed, *Through Thirty Years, 1892-1922* (2 vols., Garden City, N. Y.: Doubleday, Page & Co., 1924); André Tardieu, *The Truth About the Treaty* (Indianapolis: The Bobbs-Merrill Co., 1921); David Hunter Miller, *My Diary at the Conference of Paris* (21 vols., New York, privately printed, 1924).

On Wilson's various difficulties with the Senate and domestic public opinion, in addition to Bailey's book, we found the books already referred to by Fleming, Pringle, Lodge, Garraty, and Tumulty particularly useful.

1. *Public Papers, War & Peace*, I, 398.
2. House diary, 1/21/19 and 1/22/19, Seymour, IV, 274.

3. Shotwell, *op. cit.*, 154.
4. Baker, Ray Stannard, *What Wilson Did at Paris* (Garden City, N. Y.: Doubleday, Page & Co., 1919), 27-8.
5. *Foreign Relations, U. S.*, III, 767.
6. Seymour, IV, 320.
7. Lloyd George, I, 185.
8. House diary, 12/20/19.
9. Fleming, 111.
10. House diary, 2/7/19, Seymour, IV, 312.
11. House diary, 2/3/19, Seymour, IV, 302.
12. House diary, 2/13/19, Seymour, IV, 315.
13. *Foreign Relations, U. S.*, III, 1003-4.
14. House diary, 2/14/19, Seymour, IV, 329-30.
15. *Loc. cit.*
16. Seymour, IV, facing p. 318.
17. House diary, 2/14/19, Seymour, IV, 318.
18. Lloyd George, I, 140-2.
19. Baker, *WW&WS*, II, 252.
20. House-Seymour Conversation, 5/12/22, House Papers.
21. House diary, 2/14/19, Seymour, IV, 315-6.
22. Quoted in Fleming, 54.
23. Pringle, *op. cit.*, II, 942, 944.
24. Fleming, 117.
25. *Ibid.*, 119.
26. *Loc. cit.*
27. EMH to WW, 2/18/19, *Foreign Relations, U. S.*, XI, 509.
28. *Public Papers, War & Peace*, I, 438.
29. Lodge, 100.
30. Bailey, 198-9; Fleming, 134.
31. Lodge, 246.
32. Tumulty, 378-9, 332-4. Bailey notes (354) that Wilson's speech to the Democratic National Committee on February 28, 1919, was presumably not intended for public consumption. but that some of it was reported in the press on the next day. It was published in full only in 1921, in Tumulty's book.
33. *Public Papers, War & Peace*, I, 444-55 (italics supplied).
34. Wilson, E. B., 245.

## Chapter XIII: THE "BREAK"

The major sources used in our account of the Peace Conference were indicated in the bibliographical note to the previous chapter.

In his later public comments, Colonel House minimized both the extent of the breach in his relationship with Wilson which developed at Paris and his insight into its underlying causes (see EMH to Charles Seymour, 4/20/28, Seymour, IV, 517-8; Viereck, *The Strangest Friendship in History*, 7, 21, 246-7, 265-7, 270, 274-5).

As our account indicates, however, his diary and some of his unpublished speculations show him to have had considerable insight, even at the time, as to the risks he was taking and the magnitude of the breach which developed at the Paris Peace Conference. It is understandable that House should have preferred not to attempt a frank public justification of those aspects of his behavior at the Peace Conference which contributed to the breach. To do so would have required him not only to disclose that he had knowingly jeopardized the relationship with Wilson but also, in justifying this course of action, he would have had to go much further than he desired in revealing his critical appraisal at the time of Wilson's abilities and his conduct of the negotiations.

In later years, House seems to have come to the view that the circle of persons around Wilson—Mrs. Wilson, Admiral Grayson and Bernard Baruch—were primarily responsible for the break and for preventing him from repairing it (Viereck, "Behind the House-Wilson Break," Chapter 12 of *The Inside Story*. While the account by Viereck must be used with caution, there are other indications as well that with the passing of time House oversimplified in his own mind the reasons for the break.

For an early criticism of Wilson's addiction to generalities and his lack of interest in detail, and the thesis that these played an important role in the failure to obtain a better peace, see the articles by Walter Lippmann, who was largely responsible for drafting the interpretive commentary to the Fourteen Points, in the *New Republic*, Vol. 20 (September 3 and 17, 1919), pp. 145-6, 194-7; Vol. 21 (December 13, 1919), p. 151. See also the perceptive analysis by John Dewey, "The Discrediting of Idealism," *New Republic*, Vol. 20 (October 8, 1919), pp. 285-7.

For additional material on the Allied negotiators' withholding for bargaining purposes their support of the League Covenant and, particularly, of the Monroe Doctrine amendment, see the following: *Foreign Relations, U. S.*, V, 248, 317-8, 325-6; Baker, *WW&WS*, I, 337; II, Chapter 28, esp. 64-7, 75-6, and Chapter 36, esp. 241, 257-8, 261-2, 266; Miller, I, 321, 337-8, 453-4, and Chapter 30; Lansing, *The Big Four*, 50-1; Nevins, 446 (White to William Phillips, 5/8/19); Birdsall, *Versailles Twenty Years After*, Chapters 4 and 5; Seymour, IV, 409, 415-31, 450-5.

1. Seymour, IV, 480.
2. Wilson, E. B., 245-6.
3. On the other hand, the possibility cannot be dismissed, especially if the conversation with Wilson had been unpleasant for House, that he did not record a full account of it in his diary. On at least one other important occasion on which House suffered personal humiliation, he did not refer to the matter in his diary. (This was the occasion, referred to in our text on pp. 260-1, when six American experts effectively opposed House's effort to arrange a compromise on the Fiume issue; for a full account see Birdsall, *op. cit.*, 280-3.)

   There are inaccuracies of minor detail in Mrs. Wilson's account which in themselves, however, need not cast doubt on her report of the substance of the conversation between her husband and House. She states that the meeting took place aboard the *George Washington* on the evening of March 13, 1919, and lasted until after midnight. According to House's diary (3/14/19, quoted in part in Seymour, IV, 385-6), however, he did not board the ship but waited for the President and Mrs. Wilson at the landing stage. Further, his diary states that he had little opportunity for a talk with the President that night because the French Ambassador, Jusserand, engaged Wilson's time. It was not until the next morning, according to House's account, that the President and he conferred at length.

   An Associated Press dispatch in the New York *Times*, March 14, 1919, reports the arrival of the *George Washington* at Brest at 7:45 p.m. on March 13. A party of officials boarded the ship to extend greetings to the President but, states the dispatch, "Colonel House met the President at the dock." At 11 p.m., a special train carrying the President, Mrs. Wilson and a party including Colonel House departed for Paris.

Apparently, therefore, Mrs. Wilson's account, written some years after the event, is inaccurate at least as to the place of the conference between Wilson and House, which would seem to have taken place on the President's train rather than aboard the *George Washington,* and possibly also as to the time it was held.

4. Wilson, E. B., 247.
5. Baker, *WW&WS,* I, 295-314. Baker's charges have to do in part with the fate of the initial plan adopted by the Conference (and favored at one time by Wilson) for a preliminary peace treaty. This complicated matter need not be dealt with here; the reader is referred to the sources cited in rebuttal of Baker (footnote 6 below).
6. Bailey, 211, 356; Binkley, Robert C., "Ten Years of Peace Conference History," *Journal of Modern History,* I (1929), 612-21; Miller, I, 92-100; Birdsall, *op. cit.,* 133-4, 155-8. See also Seymour, IV, Chapter X, especially the appendix to this chapter.
7. Seymour, IV, 363; *Foreign Relations, U. S.,* IV. Nonetheless, it is true, as we have noted (pp. 247, 259) that during Wilson's temporary absence from the Conference House, impressed with the need for making concessions to the Allies in order to complete the Treaty quickly, was exploring various compromise arrangements. That he was doing so could not have been a complete surprise to Wilson since House had informed him by cable of at least the more important proposals under consideration and Wilson had replied cautioning him to avoid any commitment, even of a preliminary character. It is possible, therefore, that even before he reached Brest, Wilson was already somewhat disturbed at House's readiness to make concessions and that House's report at their first meeting added to Wilson's distress. (This theme is developed in Birdsall, *op. cit.,* 199-207.) For the exchange of cables between House and Wilson during the President's temporary absence from the Conference, see *Foreign Relations, U. S.,* XI, 511, 512-4, 516-7, 518, 521; Seymour, IV, 332-6, 348-53, 354-5, 357-9; Birdsall, *op. cit.,* 200-1 and 204, quotes portions of Wilson's cables to House, from the House Papers, which were not reproduced in Seymour.)
8. House diary, 1/1/19, Seymour, IV, 256.
9. House-Seymour Conversation, 2/17/22, House Papers.

Some years after this conversation with Seymour, House professed to be less certain that it had been a mistake for him to have taken an official position on the Peace Commission. According to Viereck, House wrote as follows: "If I had been with him in Paris solely as an adviser—who could have seen the constant throng of people that it was necessary to see? Wilson would not have done it, and outside of myself there was no one who could or would speak with any degree of authority—not that I had the actual authority, but I assumed it, feeling certain that, as in the past, Wilson would confirm my decisions . . ." (Viereck, "Behind the House-Wilson Break," *The Inside Story,* 153).

House's reflection is interesting because it implicitly acknowledges that as Peace Commissioner in Paris he had attempted to assert authority and control over the negotiations in such a fashion as to risk Wilson's displeasure. Immediately after the passage quoted above, House writes: "I knew then, as I had known before, that I took my fortunes into my hands every time I did this, but I was never lacking in courage of this kind, and it was essential that I should act promptly and decisively if the work was to be efficiently done." This effort at self-justification obscures the fact that he was asserting himself at Paris in a way he never had before. He was knowingly taking risks—which he acknowledged in his diary at the time—he had not taken previously in their collaboration.

10. House diary, 12/19/18.
11. House diary, 3/7/19.
12. House diary, 12/20/19.
13. Wilson, E. B., 251-2. See also references to Auchincloss in the Lansing diary, entries for 12/9/19 and 10/14/21, Lansing Collection, Library of Congress.
14. House diary, 3/3/19, Seymour, IV, 362.
15. Seymour, IV, 361-2, 379, 389-90. For a detailed account and assessment of the differences in approach to compromise within the American delegation and, particularly, between House and Wilson, see Birdsall, *op. cit.*, especially 199-207, and Chapter 11.
16. House diary, 5/31/19. Also, Lansing diary, VI, 10/11/20; Library of Congress.
17. Lansing, *The Big Four*, 66.
18. Shotwell, *op. cit.*, 252-3.
19. See also entry for 4/26/19.
20. House diary, 3/22/19 and 4/2/19.
21. Baker, *WW&WS*, I, 328; Fleming, 183.
22. House diary, 3/18/19, Seymour, IV, 411.
23. Baker, *WW&WS*, I, 329 *ff*.
24. Nevins, 391.
25. *Ibid.*, 399, 401. See also the account of Lodge's debate with President Lowell of Harvard in Fleming, 194.
26. Remarks quoted in Seymour, IV, 396. See also Edward Mandell House and Charles Seymour (eds.), *What Really Happened at Paris*, 464-5.
27. Baker, *WW&WS*, II, 61.
28. Seymour, IV, 404.
29. Wilson. E. B., 249.
30. WW to EMH, 10/30/18, Baker, VIII, 533. Later, Wilson attempted to account for his failure at Paris to raise the principle of freedom of the seas by asserting that the creation of the League made a definition and guarantee of this principle unnecessary. But this explanation hardly bears scrutiny. Material for refuting Wilson's argument is to be found in the official American commentary on the Fourteen Points issued in October, 1918, and accepted at that time by Wilson (Seymour, IV, 153). Indeed, the question of freedom of the seas would not arise in the event of a general war entered into by the League. But the crux of the matter was that rights of neutral shipping and private property on the high seas would remain a problem in the event of limited wars in which the League did not take sides. If Wilson abandoned freedom of the seas at Paris, therefore, it was not because the issue could no longer arise after the League of Nations was established. Rather, Wilson seems to have quietly sacrificed this major point of his peace program in order to retain British support for the League.
31. EMH to Cecil, 4/9/19, Seymour, IV, 420-1. See also Miller, I, 421, House diary, 3/27/19, and Seymour, IV, 418-20.
32. See, for example, Bailey, 190, 206, 215-6.
33. See, for example, the article by Frank Simonds in the London *Times*, 3/15/19.
34. Bailey, 215.
35. Shotwell, *op. cit.*, 18-9, also 200-2.
36. Wilson, E. B., 250-1.
37. House diary, 3/12/24. See also Lawrence, 337-8.

38. On Wilson's "appeal" habit, see Bailey, 361.
39. Baker, *WW&WS*, II, 166, argues that Lloyd George and Clemenceau implicitly approved Wilson's decision to make a public statement and that it was Wilson's understanding they would make their position public too. But the record shows merely that Wilson announced his intention and that neither Lloyd George nor Clemenceau commented (*Foreign Relations, U. S.*, V, 150).
40. House felt, with some justification, that his effort to bring the Italians and the Yugoslavs to an agreement had been severely prejudiced by Wilson's refusal to permit him to bring any pressure at all upon the Yugoslavs while, at the same time, countenancing considerable pressure upon the Italians. (For House's postwar reflections on this issue see Viereck, *The Strangest Friendship in History*, 254-5).

    Birdsall, *op. cit.*, Chapter 11, gives a detailed account of the deterioration of relations between Wilson and House during the negotiation of the Italian claims. Both in this book and in his bibliographical article, "The Second Decade of Peace Conference History," *Journal of Modern History*, XI, 373, Birdsall warns against taking the personal incidents which occurred at the Conference out of their context and permitting them to obscure fundamental differences between Wilson and House in their approach to peacemaking and methods of negotiation.
41. A good case can be made for the thesis that the Fourteen Points were realized to an appreciable degree in the Versailles Treaty (see, for example, Bailey, 317-9, 367-9). Nonetheless, particularly because of the reparations and territorial settlements, the treaty did not square with the expectations aroused by Wilson's principles and did not satisfy many of his followers.
42. For an early criticism of Wilson's failure to develop a closer relationship with the British at the Peace Conference, see Walter Lippmann in the *New Republic*, XXI ( Dec. 31, 1919), 151: "Just as the threat against sea power was the central reason for our intervention, so a working partnership with sea power was the indispensable basis of a liberal peace. We should have played with Britain, instead of letting Mr. George bob back and forth between M. Clemenceau and the President."
43. For the Council of Four meeting of June 2, 1919, and Wilson's meetings of the following day with the American delegation, see *Foreign Relations, U. S.*, VI, 138-46; XI, 197-222. The minutes of the June 3rd meeting are also reproduced in Baker, *WW&WS*, III, 469-504.
44. *Foreign Relations, U. S.*, VI, 142. Compare with Wilson's attitude toward the Saar arrangement before he accepted it: on April 2, 1919, he had tried to get House to admit that it was inconsistent with the Fourteen Points (House diary, 4/2/19, Seymour, IV, 397).
45. Baker, *WW&WS*, II, Chapter XXX, especially 109-15. See also Baruch's recollection of his conversation with Lloyd George and of Wilson's comments at a subsequent meeting with Lloyd George, which Baruch had arranged (Philip Mason Burnett, *Reparation at the Paris Peace Conference*, [New York: Columbia University Press, 1940], I, 136, footnote 32).
46. The major American effort to secure modification of the Treaty at this time was directed to the reparations problem. The American effort to set German reparations at a fixed sum, however, went beyond what Lloyd George had in mind and remained unsuccessful (Baker, *WW&WS*, II, 114-5; Burnett, *op. cit.*, I, 137). For the discussion of the reparations problem in the Council of Four at this time, see *Foreign Relations, U. S.*, VI, 155-7, 240, 261-4, 272-80, 290-4, 301-3.
47. House diary, 5/31/19 (quoted in part in Seymour, IV, 472).

48. House diary, 6/10/19, Seymour, IV, 480.
49. House diary, 6/29/19, Seymour, IV, 487.

## Chapter XIV: BATTLE WITH THE SENATE

The best secondary sources for events covered in this chapter and the next are Fleming's *The United States and the League of Nations* and Bailey's *Woodrow Wilson and the Great Betrayal*. Fleming's book is copiously documented, which makes it invaluable to the student despite the author's tendency to be an apologist for Wilson. Bailey's book is excellently written and organized, and presents, on the whole, a balanced interpretation of the Treaty fight. On one important point, our interpretation runs counter to his. He implies (170-1) that Wilson's attitude toward "interpretive reservations" fluctuated in the course of the Treaty fight. We have found no evidence that Wilson ever wavered from the position he took upon his return home in July, namely, that interpretations not embodied in the resolution of ratification were acceptable, but that reservations which were part of the resolution of ratification were not. He never, so far as we have been able to discover, "stiffened" on the former, as Bailey suggests.

Lodge's posthumous account of the Treaty fight is highly revealing of his strategy for dealing with the Treaty and conveys something of the personal animosity he bore Wilson. The best biography of Lodge is by John Garraty, whose book is based upon Lodge's papers and who views his subject objectively.

For a chronological unfolding of events and much contemporary flavor, the New York *Times* is indispensable. Bartlett's *The League to Enforce Peace* is useful in showing the impact of Wilson's behavior on the organized supporters of the League. Taft's poignant position is ably presented by Pringle in *The Life and Times of William Howard Taft*, II, 926 *ff*.

1. Nevins, 455.
2. Lodge statement to press, 4/29/19, and Lodge speech in Senate, 5/23/19, Fleming, 196, 212-3.
3. Lodge to A. J. Beveridge, 12/3/18, Bartlett, *League to Enforce Peace*, 108.
4. Lodge to J. A. Beck, 3/22/20, Garraty, 390; James E. Watson, *As I Knew Them* (Indianapolis and New York: Bobbs-Merrill Co., 1936), 213.
5. New York *Times*, 11/21/20, quoted in Fleming, 487. On Lodge's satisfaction with the Senate's rejection of the Treaty, see also Lodge, 210, 214; statement by Lodge's daughter in New York *Herald Tribune*, 3/7/30, quoted in Fleming, 476; Lodge to A. J. Beveridge, 3/8/19 and 3/21/19, in Claude G. Bowers, *Beveridge and The Progressive Era* (Houghton Mifflin Co., The Riverside Press, Cambridge, 1932), 504; Lodge to L. A. Coolidge, 2/11/20, Garraty, 388; Alice Roosevelt Longworth, *Crowded Hours* (New York and London: Charles Scribner's Sons, 1933), 292.
6. *Congressional Record*, Vol. 51, 6456.
7. Nevins, 353.
8. Fleming, 199-203.
9. Garraty, 312.
10. Lodge, 220-1.
11. Bonsal, Stephen, *Unfinished Business* (Garden City, N. Y.: Doubleday, Doran and Company, Inc., 1944), 275.
12. See, for example, New York *Times*, 12/1/19; Lodge to Henry White, 7/2/19, Nevins, 455.
13. Lawrence, William, *Henry Cabot Lodge: A Biographical Sketch* (Boston and New York: Houghton Mifflin Co., 1925), 17-9.
14. Quoted in Garraty, 25.

15. Bailey, *WW&GB*, 9.
16. *Public Papers, War & Peace*, I, 537-52.
17. New York *Tribune*, 7/11/19.
18. Bailey, *WW&GB*, 10; Fleming, 165-71, 205; Bartlett, *op. cit.*, 130.
19. Garraty, 350.
20. *The Nation*, 9/27/19 and 10/4/19.
21. Bailey, *WW&GB*, 38.
22. Watson, *op. cit.*, 190.
23. Lodge, 226, 212-3, 218-9.
24. *Ibid.*, 146-8.
25. *Ibid.*, 151-2; David Bryn-Jones, *Frank B. Kellogg: A Biography* (New York: G. P. Putnam's Sons, 1937), 113-4.
26. Watson, *op. cit.*, 200-1.
27. Lodge, 226.
28. Baker, *WW&WS*, III, 181.
29. *Ibid.*, 184.
30. For Lodge's attitude on the Monroe Doctrine amendment, see Garraty, 364-5; Lodge speech to Senate, 6/6/19, Fleming, 213-4.
31. Baker, *WW&WS*, III, 176.
32. *Ibid.*, 179.
33. See, for example, speech by Senator Claude Swanson (D., Va.), 7/14/19, Fleming, 242-3.
34. Lodge, Henry Cabot, *War Addresses, 1915-1917* (Boston and New York: Houghton Mifflin Co., 1917), 41.
35. *Enforced Peace: Proceedings of the First Annual National Assembly of the League to Enforce Peace, Washington, May 26-27, 1916* (New York: League to Enforce Peace, date not given), 166. See also Lodge, 129-32; Fleming, 282.
36. See, for example, speech by Senator Smith (D., Ariz.), quoted in Fleming, 278.
37. Wilson statement to newsmen, 7/10/19, Bailey, *WW&GB*, 170.
38. See Wilson's response to suggestion of Senator McCumber, one of the mildest of the "reservationists," that a reservation be made to Article X, quoted in Lodge, 315-6.
39. Wilson statement to press, 7/10/19, and report of his conference with Republican Senators, 7/17/19, in New York *Tribune*, 7/18/19, quoted in Fleming, 237-8 and 292-3.
40. See exchange between Wilson and Senator Lodge and between Wilson and Senator Fall at the August 19th meeting between the President and the Senate Foreign Relations Committee, Lodge, 312-3, 317-9.
41. Fleming, 322.
42. Bailey, *WW&GB*, 8.
43. Lodge, 156.
44. Fleming, 294.
45. Bailey, *WW&GB*, 76-7.
46. New York *Times*, 8/1/19; New York *Herald*, 8/2/19.
47. New York *Times*, 8/1/19.
48. *Ibid.*, 8/16/19.
49. *Ibid.*, 8/27/19.
50. *Ibid.*, 7/19/19.
51. Hitchcock Papers, Library of Congress, Vol. I, correspondence.
52. New York *Times*, 7/25/19.
53. Fleming, 293; Garraty, 369-70.
54. New York *Times*, 8/20/19.
55. Bailey, *WW&GB*, 13.

## Chapter XV: DEFEAT

In addition to the sources noted for the preceding chapter, see the following for individual views concerning Wilson and the Treaty: Lee Meriwether, *Jim Reed* (Webster Groves, Mo.: International Mark Twain Society, 1948), 58-92; Claudius O. Johnson, *Borah of Idaho* (New York and Toronto: Longmans, Green and Co., 1936), 223-56; Watson, *As I Knew Them*, 184-206; Alice Roosevelt Longworth, *Crowded Hours*, 272-312; Johnson, *George Harvey*, 262-72.

The best single source on Wilson after he left the White House is an excellent memorandum by Katharine E. Brand based on the "S" Street files. This unpublished document is in the Baker Papers, Series IB. On Wilson's interest in a third term in 1920, see Bainbridge Colby to WW, 7/2/20 and 7/4/20, quoted in Homer Cummings' memorandum, 1/18/29, Baker Papers, Series I; Charles Stein, *The Third Term Tradition* (New York: Columbia University Press, 1943), 247-9; Rixey Smith and Norman Beasley, *Carter Glass* (New York and Toronto: Longmans, Green & Co., 1939), 205-6.

1. Bailey, *WW&GB*, 277.
2. WW address, Fall, 1909, Baker, II, 307.
3. Wilson, *Constitutional Government in the United States*, 139-40 (italics supplied).
4. Tumulty, 435, 439; E. B. Wilson, 273-4.
5. Fleming, 336.
6. Tumulty, 438.
7. For text of the list of interpretations which Wilson gave to Hitchcock, see Fleming, 493.
8. Compare, for example, Wilson's interpretation concerning Article X with that then being sponsored by the "mild reservationists":

*Wilson's interpretation*

"It understands that the advice of the Council of the League with regard to the employment of armed force contemplated in Article Ten of the Covenant of the League is to be regarded only as advice and leaves each member State free to exercise its own judgment as to whether it is wise or practicable to act upon that advice or not."
(Quoted by Fleming, 493.)

*"Mild Reservation" announced August 1 (New York Tribune, 8/2/19)*

"That the suggestions of the council of the league of nations as to the means of carrying the obligations of Article X into effect are only advisory, and that any undertaking under the provisions of Article X, the execution of which may require the use of American military or naval forces or economic measures, can under the Constitution be carried out only by the action of the Congress, and that the failure of the Congress to adopt the suggestions of the council of the league, or to provide such military or naval forces or economic measures, shall not constitute a violation of the treaty."

9. For a further indication that it was to the form of the "mild reservations" rather than to their substance that Wilson objected, see Wilson's reply to Senator McCumber's question about the desirability of a reservation to Article X during the August 19, 1919, meeting with the Senate Committee on Foreign Relations, quoted in Lodge, 315-6.

10. Tumulty, 439.
11. For an account of the trip, see Tumulty, 434-51; E. B. Wilson, 273-85; Fleming, 337-59.
12. For Wilson's speeches on behalf of the League, see *Public Papers, War & Peace*, I, 590-644; II, 1-416. Specific materials from these speeches in the following paragraphs of our text are from I, 615, 619, 622, 633, 641; II, 9, 26, 39 42, 63, 64, 144, 148-9, 155, 173, 212, 234, 280, 302, 345, 355, 356, 369, 400.
13. New York *Times*, 9/10/19 and 9/11/19.
14. Garraty, 371.
15. See Lodge, 165-77, for text of the majority report.
16. For Wilson's reaction to the Bullitt affair, see Tumulty, 442-3.
17. In this and the following paragraphs, the quotations from Wilson's speeches, in which he rejected the notion that his personal motivations were involved in the Treaty dispute, are from *Public Papers, War & Peace*, I, 604; II, 43, 410, 398, 399, respectively.
18. E. B. Wilson, 282-3.
19. Tumulty, 447-8.
20. E. B. Wilson, 284-5.
21. New York *Times*, 9/27/19.
22. *Ibid*., 10/3/19.
23. *Harvey's Weekly*, October 4, 1919, quoted in Fleming, 358.
24. New York *Times*, 9/28/19 and 10/9/19.
25. Wilson statement to House, House diary, 5/17/18.
26. See, for example, New York *Times*, 7/12/19.
27. Bailey, *WW&GB*, 148.
28. E. B. Wilson, 289-90.
29. See, for example, Bailey, *WW&GB*, 166 and 383-4, citing Taft, Hoover, Bliss, White and Miller; see also Fleming, 438.
30. Hitchcock Papers, Vol. III, undated address, "Wilson's Place in History."
31. E. B. Wilson, 296-7.
32. Fleming, 395; Bailey, *WW&GB*, 178.
33. W. H. Taft to Hitchcock, 11/15/19, Hitchcock Papers; also quoted by Pringle, *op. cit*., II, 948-9.
34. Fleming, 398.
35. *Congressional Record*, Vol. 58, 8779-80, 8786.
36. New York *Times*, 11/20/19.
37. EMH to WW, 7/14/19, 8/26/19, 9/15/19, 9/19/19, 9/30/19; WW to EMH, 8/28/19; House Papers.
38. House diary, 9/4/19, 9/21/19.
39. House diary, 9/24/18, 10/25/18, 5/10/19, 9/21/19, 9/30/19; House-Seymour Conversation, 3/31/22.

House did not testify before the Senate Foreign Relations Committee. On October 13, 1919, he wrote Lodge explaining that he was ill but placing himself at the Committee's disposal as soon as his health permitted. Lodge replied suggesting that House let him know when he felt able to appear. On October 31, Stephen Bonsal brought Lodge a message from House that he would be able to testify any time from a few days forth. Lodge told Bonsal that the hearings had ended and that he did not think House would be called. (Seymour, IV, 504-6.)

According to George Sylvester Viereck, House later felt that his letter of October 13 to Lodge was used against him by Mrs. Wilson, Grayson and Baruch to give Wilson the impression that he had been conspiring with

Lodge. House thought it was this letter which prompted Baruch to remark that House had broken Wilson's heart and had been disloyal. (Viereck, "Behind the House-Wilson Break," *The Inside Story*, 151.)

40. Mrs. E. B. Wilson to Mrs. House, 10/17/19; EMH to Mrs. Wilson, 10/22/19; Mrs. Wilson to EMH, 10/23/19. See also Mrs. Wilson to EMH, 11/18/19, informing him that she had told Wilson that House was ill, and that the President had expressed regret; she said, too, that she had not mentioned that House was back in the United States, so she fancied Wilson still thought he was in Paris. (All in House Papers.)

41. Stephen Bonsal claims that House made an attempt to effect a compromise between Wilson and Lodge before the November vote. At House's request, according to Bonsal (see his *Unfinished Business*, 271-6), he (Bonsal) conferred with Lodge in late October and secured from him a statement of his minimum demands in the form of a printed copy of the Covenant on which the Senator, in his own hand, made the changes and additions which he considered necessary. The alterations Lodge thus indicated seemed to Bonsal less objectionable than the reservations Lodge was publicly backing. As soon as he left Lodge's house, Bonsal rushed to the post office and mailed the emended Covenant to House. The Colonel, according to Bonsal, sent it on to Wilson but never had any acknowledgment of its receipt.

As to the nature of Lodge's "changes," Bonsal concedes that he could not "clearly recall" them, "except that they were few and unimportant." He did recall, however, that Lodge made some pencilled additions to Articles X and XVI; that he emphasized that no obligations under Article X should be assumed without Congressional approval; and that after the Senator had made his notations and had his say, Bonsal pointed out that there remained the drawback that any changes would have to be referred back to the other signatories for approval. In short, evidence is lacking that Lodge conceded anything either on Article X or the problem of resubmission of the Treaty to the other signatories—the two major points of contention between Wilson and the reservationists. Indeed, it seems hardly likely that Lodge would have chosen Bonsal as the channel for communicating concessions, had he desired to make any. Bonsal's hasty conclusion that the changes Lodge indicated would satisfy him were less objectionable than those he was publicly sponsoring cannot be uncritically accepted. Bonsal was a journalist, not an expert on international law. He had been abroad until shortly before his talk with Lodge. His comprehension of the niceties of the problem may have been inadequate.

Further, since Mrs. Wilson's letter to Colonel House on November 18 suggests that the President still thought House was in Paris, it seems improbable that he was aware of any effort by House to compose the difficulties with Lodge.

Until the document Bonsal obtained from Lodge is found and Lodge's notations independently evaluated, it seems to the writers that judgment concerning the significance of this episode must remain in abeyance.

42. EMH to WW, 11/24/19, 11/27/19, Seymour, IV, 509-11. EMH to Mrs. E. B. Wilson, 11/24/19, 11/27/19, House Papers. House-Seymour Conversation, 5/12/22.

43. House diary, 2/18/20; also 4/3/21.

44. New York *Times*, 12/15/19.

45. *Public Papers, War & Peace*, II, 455.

46. See the plea by W. J. Bryan that the Treaty be kept out of the 1920 campaign, New York *Times*, 7/9/20.

47. Bailey, *WW&GB*, 224.
48. *Ibid.*, 214-5, 399.
49. Mrs. E. B. Wilson to Hitchcock, 12/19/19, and Hitchcock to Mrs. Wilson, 1/5/20, Hitchcock Papers.
50. New York *Times*, 1/17/20.
51. Lodge, 194.
52. *Public Papers, War & Peace*, II, 460-1.
53. In his letter of January 26, 1920, to Hitchcock, Wilson explicitly accepted Hitchcock's "reservations." He had previously preferred to refer to them as "interpretations." There is no indication, however, that Wilson was willing to consent to embodying these reservations into the resolution of ratification. In his Jackson Day message earlier in the month, he had reiterated the position he had consistently taken, that "there can be no reasonable objection to interpretations accompanying the act of ratification itself." (*Public Papers, War & Peace*, II, 455.) Interpretations *accompanying*, not part of the resolution of ratification, be it noted. It seems highly improbable that Wilson's use of the word "reservations" in his letter of January 26 betokened a willingness to reverse himself on this issue. In any case, Hitchcock does not seem to have pursued the possibility and Wilson certainly gave no other sign of relenting.

    When Hitchcock had introduced his reservations into the Senate on November 13, 1919, he had sidestepped the problem of whether or not they were to be included in the resolution of ratification. He simply did not offer a resolving clause. (See *Congressional Record*, Vol. 58, 8433.)
54. Trevelyan, *Grey of Fallodon*, 397-400.
55. Quoted in Fleming, 412-3.
56. Bailey, *WW&GB*, 205, 241; Georges Clemenceau, *Grandeur and Misery of Victory* (New York: Harcourt, Brace and Co., 1930), 258-9.
57. Bailey, *WW&GB*, 239.
58. Quoted in Nicholas Murray Butler, *Across The Busy Years: Recollections and Reflections* (New York and London: Charles Scribner's Sons, 1939), II, 201.
59. Bailey, *WW&GB*, 256.
60. *Public Papers, War & Peace*, II, 311; I, 621-2, 626.
61. Bailey, *WW&GB*, 271, 266.
62. Hitchcock Papers, III, undated address, "Wilson's Place in History."
63. Lodge, 214.

# INDEX

## ABOUT THE AUTHORS

Alexander L. George is Graham H. Stuart Professor of International Relations and Professor of Political Science at Stanford University. He has been President of the International Studies Association, Head of the Social Science Department of the RAND Corporation, a Fellow at the Center for Advanced Study in the Behavioral Sciences, and is a member of the American Academy of Arts and Sciences. He has written extensively on political decision-making and U.S. foreign policy and won a Bancroft prize in 1975 as senior author of *Deterrence in American Foreign Policy*. From 1983–1988 he was a MacArthur Fellow.

Juliette L. George is a graduate of the University of California at Berkeley and Columbia University. She is a Senior Scholar at the Institute of International Studies at Stanford University.

The Georges' study of the application of psychodynamic theory to biographical research has been supported by a grant to Professor George by the Foundations' Fund for Research in Psychiatry. In 1972–73, as a Fellow of the National Institute of Mental Health, Professor George was attached to the Department of Psychiatry, Stanford University.

A CATALOG OF SELECTED

# DOVER BOOKS

IN ALL FIELDS OF INTEREST

# A CATALOG OF SELECTED DOVER BOOKS IN ALL FIELDS OF INTEREST

DRAWINGS OF REMBRANDT, edited by Seymour Slive. Updated Lippmann, Hofstede de Groot edition, with definitive scholarly apparatus. All portraits, biblical sketches, landscapes, nudes. Oriental figures, classical studies, together with selection of work by followers. 550 illustrations. Total of 630pp. 9⅛ × 12¼.
21485-0, 21486-9 Pa., Two-vol. set $25.00

GHOST AND HORROR STORIES OF AMBROSE BIERCE, Ambrose Bierce. 24 tales vividly imagined, strangely prophetic, and decades ahead of their time in technical skill: "The Damned Thing," "An Inhabitant of Carcosa," "The Eyes of the Panther," "Moxon's Master," and 20 more. 199pp. 5⅜ × 8½. 20767-6 Pa. $3.95

ETHICAL WRITINGS OF MAIMONIDES, Maimonides. Most significant ethical works of great medieval sage, newly translated for utmost precision, readability. Laws Concerning Character Traits, Eight Chapters, more. 192pp. 5⅜ × 8½.
24522-5 Pa. $4.50

THE EXPLORATION OF THE COLORADO RIVER AND ITS CANYONS, J. W. Powell. Full text of Powell's 1,000-mile expedition down the fabled Colorado in 1869. Superb account of terrain, geology, vegetation, Indians, famine, mutiny, treacherous rapids, mighty canyons, during exploration of last unknown part of continental U.S. 400pp. 5⅜ × 8½. 20094-9 Pa. $6.95

HISTORY OF PHILOSOPHY, Julián Marías. Clearest one-volume history on the market. Every major philosopher and dozens of others, to Existentialism and later. 505pp. 5⅜ × 8½. 21739-6 Pa. $8.50

ALL ABOUT LIGHTNING, Martin A. Uman. Highly readable non-technical survey of nature and causes of lightning, thunderstorms, ball lightning, St. Elmo's Fire, much more. Illustrated. 192pp. 5⅜ × 8½. 25237-X Pa. $5.95

SAILING ALONE AROUND THE WORLD, Captain Joshua Slocum. First man to sail around the world, alone, in small boat. One of great feats of seamanship told in delightful manner. 67 illustrations. 294pp. 5⅜ × 8½. 20326-3 Pa. $4.95

LETTERS AND NOTES ON THE MANNERS, CUSTOMS AND CONDITIONS OF THE NORTH AMERICAN INDIANS, George Catlin. Classic account of life among Plains Indians: ceremonies, hunt, warfare, etc. 312 plates. 572pp. of text. 6⅛ × 9¼. 22118-0, 22119-9 Pa. Two-vol. set $15.90

ALASKA: The Harriman Expedition, 1899, John Burroughs, John Muir, et al. Informative, engrossing accounts of two-month, 9,000-mile expedition. Native peoples, wildlife, forests, geography, salmon industry, glaciers, more. Profusely illustrated. 240 black-and-white line drawings. 124 black-and-white photographs. 3 maps. Index. 576pp. 5⅜ × 8½. 25109-8 Pa. $11.95

THE BOOK OF BEASTS: Being a Translation from a Latin Bestiary of the Twelfth Century, T. H. White. Wonderful catalog real and fanciful beasts: manticore, griffin, phoenix, amphivius, jaculus, many more. White's witty erudite commentary on scientific, historical aspects. Fascinating glimpse of medieval mind. Illustrated. 296pp. 5⅜ × 8¼. (Available in U.S. only) 24609-4 Pa. $5.95

FRANK LLOYD WRIGHT: ARCHITECTURE AND NATURE With 160 Illustrations, Donald Hoffmann. Profusely illustrated study of influence of nature—especially prairie—on Wright's designs for Fallingwater, Robie House, Guggenheim Museum, other masterpieces. 96pp. 9¼ × 10¾. 25098-9 Pa. $7.95

FRANK LLOYD WRIGHT'S FALLINGWATER, Donald Hoffmann. Wright's famous waterfall house: planning and construction of organic idea. History of site, owners, Wright's personal involvement. Photographs of various stages of building. Preface by Edgar Kaufmann, Jr. 100 illustrations. 112pp. 9¼ × 10. 23671-4 Pa. $7.95

YEARS WITH FRANK LLOYD WRIGHT: Apprentice to Genius, Edgar Tafel. Insightful memoir by a former apprentice presents a revealing portrait of Wright the man, the inspired teacher, the greatest American architect. 372 black-and-white illustrations. Preface. Index. vi + 228pp. 8¼ × 11. 24801-1 Pa. $9.95

THE STORY OF KING ARTHUR AND HIS KNIGHTS, Howard Pyle. Enchanting version of King Arthur fable has delighted generations with imaginative narratives of exciting adventures and unforgettable illustrations by the author. 41 illustrations. xviii + 313pp. 6⅛ × 9¼. 21445-1 Pa. $6.50

THE GODS OF THE EGYPTIANS, E. A. Wallis Budge. Thorough coverage of numerous gods of ancient Egypt by foremost Egyptologist. Information on evolution of cults, rites and gods; the cult of Osiris; the Book of the Dead and its rites; the sacred animals and birds; Heaven and Hell; and more. 956pp. 6⅛ × 9¼. 22055-9, 22056-7 Pa., Two-vol. set $20.00

A THEOLOGICO-POLITICAL TREATISE, Benedict Spinoza. Also contains unfinished *Political Treatise*. Great classic on religious liberty, theory of government on common consent. R. Elwes translation. Total of 421pp. 5⅜ × 8½. 20249-6 Pa. $6.95

INCIDENTS OF TRAVEL IN CENTRAL AMERICA, CHIAPAS, AND YUCATAN, John L. Stephens. Almost single-handed discovery of Maya culture; exploration of ruined cities, monuments, temples; customs of Indians. 115 drawings. 892pp. 5⅜ × 8½. 22404-X, 22405-8 Pa., Two-vol. set $15.90

LOS CAPRICHOS, Francisco Goya. 80 plates of wild, grotesque monsters and caricatures. Prado manuscript included. 183pp. 6⅝ × 9⅝. 22384-1 Pa. $4.95

AUTOBIOGRAPHY: The Story of My Experiments with Truth, Mohandas K. Gandhi. Not hagiography, but Gandhi in his own words. Boyhood, legal studies, purification, the growth of the Satyagraha (nonviolent protest) movement. Critical, inspiring work of the man who freed India. 480pp. 5⅜ × 8½. (Available in U.S. only) 24593-4 Pa. $6.95

ILLUSTRATED DICTIONARY OF HISTORIC ARCHITECTURE, edited by Cyril M. Harris. Extraordinary compendium of clear, concise definitions for over 5,000 important architectural terms complemented by over 2,000 line drawings. Covers full spectrum of architecture from ancient ruins to 20th-century Modernism. Preface. 592pp. 7½ × 9⅝. 24444-X Pa. $14.95

THE NIGHT BEFORE CHRISTMAS, Clement Moore. Full text, and woodcuts from original 1848 book. Also critical, historical material. 19 illustrations. 40pp. 4⅝ × 6. 22797-9 Pa. $2.25

THE LESSON OF JAPANESE ARCHITECTURE: 165 Photographs, Jiro Harada. Memorable gallery of 165 photographs taken in the 1930's of exquisite Japanese homes of the well-to-do and historic buildings. 13 line diagrams. 192pp. 8⅝ × 11¼. 24778-3 Pa. $8.95

THE AUTOBIOGRAPHY OF CHARLES DARWIN AND SELECTED LETTERS, edited by Francis Darwin. The fascinating life of eccentric genius composed of an intimate memoir by Darwin (intended for his children); commentary by his son, Francis; hundreds of fragments from notebooks, journals, papers; and letters to and from Lyell, Hooker, Huxley, Wallace and Henslow. xi + 365pp. 5⅜ × 8. 20479-0 Pa. $6.95

WONDERS OF THE SKY: Observing Rainbows, Comets, Eclipses, the Stars and Other Phenomena, Fred Schaaf. Charming, easy-to-read poetic guide to all manner of celestial events visible to the naked eye. Mock suns, glories, Belt of Venus, more. Illustrated. 299pp. 5¼ × 8¼. 24402-4 Pa. $7.95

BURNHAM'S CELESTIAL HANDBOOK, Robert Burnham, Jr. Thorough guide to the stars beyond our solar system. Exhaustive treatment. Alphabetical by constellation: Andromeda to Cetus in Vol. 1; Chamaeleon to Orion in Vol. 2; and Pavo to Vulpecula in Vol. 3. Hundreds of illustrations. Index in Vol. 3. 2,000pp. 6⅛ × 9¼. 23567-X, 23568-8, 23673-0 Pa., Three-vol. set $38.85

STAR NAMES: Their Lore and Meaning, Richard Hinckley Allen. Fascinating history of names various cultures have given to constellations and literary and folkloristic uses that have been made of stars. Indexes to subjects. Arabic and Greek names. Biblical references. Bibliography. 563pp. 5⅜ × 8½. 21079-0 Pa. $7.95

THIRTY YEARS THAT SHOOK PHYSICS: The Story of Quantum Theory, George Gamow. Lucid, accessible introduction to influential theory of energy and matter. Careful explanations of Dirac's anti-particles, Bohr's model of the atom, much more. 12 plates. Numerous drawings. 240pp. 5⅜ × 8½. 24895-X Pa. $4.95

CHINESE DOMESTIC FURNITURE IN PHOTOGRAPHS AND MEASURED DRAWINGS, Gustav Ecke. A rare volume, now affordably priced for antique collectors, furniture buffs and art historians. Detailed review of styles ranging from early Shang to late Ming. Unabridged republication. 161 black-and-white drawings, photos. Total of 224pp. 8⅜ × 11¼. (Available in U.S. only) 25171-3 Pa. $12.95

VINCENT VAN GOGH: A Biography, Julius Meier-Graefe. Dynamic, penetrating study of artist's life, relationship with brother, Theo, painting techniques, travels, more. Readable, engrossing. 160pp. 5⅜ × 8½. (Available in U.S. only) 25253-1 Pa. $3.95

HOW TO WRITE, Gertrude Stein. Gertrude Stein claimed anyone could understand her unconventional writing—here are clues to help. Fascinating improvisations, language experiments, explanations illuminate Stein's craft and the art of writing. Total of 414pp. 4⅝ × 6⅜. 23144-5 Pa. $5.95

ADVENTURES AT SEA IN THE GREAT AGE OF SAIL: Five Firsthand Narratives, edited by Elliot Snow. Rare true accounts of exploration, whaling, shipwreck, fierce natives, trade, shipboard life, more. 33 illustrations. Introduction. 353pp. 5⅜ × 8½. 25177-2 Pa. $7.95

THE HERBAL OR GENERAL HISTORY OF PLANTS, John Gerard. Classic descriptions of about 2,850 plants—with over 2,700 illustrations—includes Latin and English names, physical descriptions, varieties, time and place of growth, more. 2,706 illustrations. xlv + 1,678pp. 8½ × 12¼. 23147-X Cloth. $75.00

DOROTHY AND THE WIZARD IN OZ, L. Frank Baum. Dorothy and the Wizard visit the center of the Earth, where people are vegetables, glass houses grow and Oz characters reappear. Classic sequel to *Wizard of Oz.* 256pp. 5⅜ × 8.
24714-7 Pa. $4.95

SONGS OF EXPERIENCE: Facsimile Reproduction with 26 Plates in Full Color, William Blake. This facsimile of Blake's original "Illuminated Book" reproduces 26 full-color plates from a rare 1826 edition. Includes "The Tyger," "London," "Holy Thursday," and other immortal poems. 26 color plates. Printed text of poems. 48pp. 5¼ × 7. 24636-1 Pa. $3.50

SONGS OF INNOCENCE, William Blake. The first and most popular of Blake's famous "Illuminated Books," in a facsimile edition reproducing all 31 brightly colored plates. Additional printed text of each poem. 64pp. 5¼ × 7.
22764-2 Pa. $3.50

PRECIOUS STONES, Max Bauer. Classic, thorough study of diamonds, rubies, emeralds, garnets, etc.: physical character, occurrence, properties, use, similar topics. 20 plates, 8 in color. 94 figures. 659pp. 6⅛ × 9¼.
21910-0, 21911-9 Pa., Two-vol. set $15.90

ENCYCLOPEDIA OF VICTORIAN NEEDLEWORK, S. F. A. Caulfeild and Blanche Saward. Full, precise descriptions of stitches, techniques for dozens of needlecrafts—most exhaustive reference of its kind. Over 800 figures. Total of 679pp. 8⅛ × 11. Two volumes. Vol. 1 22800-2 Pa. $11.95
Vol. 2 22801-0 Pa. $11.95

THE MARVELOUS LAND OF OZ, L. Frank Baum. Second Oz book, the Scarecrow and Tin Woodman are back with hero named Tip, Oz magic. 136 illustrations. 287pp. 5⅜ × 8½. 20692-0 Pa. $5.95

WILD FOWL DECOYS, Joel Barber. Basic book on the subject, by foremost authority and collector. Reveals history of decoy making and rigging, place in American culture, different kinds of decoys, how to make them, and how to use them. 140 plates. 156pp. 7⅞ × 10¾. 20011-6 Pa. $8.95

HISTORY OF LACE, Mrs. Bury Palliser. Definitive, profusely illustrated chronicle of lace from earliest times to late 19th century. Laces of Italy, Greece, England, France, Belgium, etc. Landmark of needlework scholarship. 266 illustrations. 672pp. 6⅛ × 9¼. 24742-2 Pa. $14.95

ILLUSTRATED GUIDE TO SHAKER FURNITURE, Robert Meader. All furniture and appurtenances, with much on unknown local styles. 235 photos. 146pp. 9 × 12. 22819-3 Pa. $7.95

WHALE SHIPS AND WHALING: A Pictorial Survey, George Francis Dow. Over 200 vintage engravings, drawings, photographs of barks, brigs, cutters, other vessels. Also harpoons, lances, whaling guns, many other artifacts. Comprehensive text by foremost authority. 207 black-and-white illustrations. 288pp. 6 × 9. 24808-9 Pa. $8.95

THE BERTRAMS, Anthony Trollope. Powerful portrayal of blind self-will and thwarted ambition includes one of Trollope's most heartrending love stories. 497pp. 5⅜ × 8½. 25119-5 Pa. $8.95

ADVENTURES WITH A HAND LENS, Richard Headstrom. Clearly written guide to observing and studying flowers and grasses, fish scales, moth and insect wings, egg cases, buds, feathers, seeds, leaf scars, moss, molds, ferns, common crystals, etc.—all with an ordinary, inexpensive magnifying glass. 209 exact line drawings aid in your discoveries. 220pp. 5⅜ × 8½. 23330-8 Pa. $3.95

RODIN ON ART AND ARTISTS, Auguste Rodin. Great sculptor's candid, wide-ranging comments on meaning of art; great artists; relation of sculpture to poetry, painting, music; philosophy of life, more. 76 superb black-and-white illustrations of Rodin's sculpture, drawings and prints. 119pp. 8⅜ × 11¼. 24487-3 Pa. $6.95

FIFTY CLASSIC FRENCH FILMS, 1912–1982: A Pictorial Record, Anthony Slide. Memorable stills from Grand Illusion, Beauty and the Beast, Hiroshima, Mon Amour, many more. Credits, plot synopses, reviews, etc. 160pp. 8¼ × 11. 25256-6 Pa. $11.95

THE PRINCIPLES OF PSYCHOLOGY, William James. Famous long course complete, unabridged. Stream of thought, time perception, memory, experimental methods; great work decades ahead of its time. 94 figures. 1,391pp. 5⅜ × 8½. 20381-6, 20382-4 Pa., Two-vol. set $19.90

BODIES IN A BOOKSHOP, R. T. Campbell. Challenging mystery of blackmail and murder with ingenious plot and superbly drawn characters. In the best tradition of British suspense fiction. 192pp. 5⅜ × 8½. 24720-1 Pa. $3.95

CALLAS: PORTRAIT OF A PRIMA DONNA, George Jellinek. Renowned commentator on the musical scene chronicles incredible career and life of the most controversial, fascinating, influential operatic personality of our time. 64 black-and-white photographs. 416pp. 5⅜ × 8¼. 25047-4 Pa. $7.95

GEOMETRY, RELATIVITY AND THE FOURTH DIMENSION, Rudolph Rucker. Exposition of fourth dimension, concepts of relativity as Flatland characters continue adventures. Popular, easily followed yet accurate, profound. 141 illustrations. 133pp. 5⅜ × 8½. 23400-2 Pa. $3.95

HOUSEHOLD STORIES BY THE BROTHERS GRIMM, with pictures by Walter Crane. 53 classic stories—Rumpelstiltskin, Rapunzel, Hansel and Gretel, the Fisherman and his Wife, Snow White, Tom Thumb, Sleeping Beauty, Cinderella, and so much more—lavishly illustrated with original 19th century drawings. 114 illustrations. x + 269pp. 5⅜ × 8½. 21080-4 Pa. $4.50

SUNDIALS, Albert Waugh. Far and away the best, most thorough coverage of ideas, mathematics concerned, types, construction, adjusting anywhere. Over 100 illustrations. 230pp. 5⅜ × 8½. 22947-5 Pa. $4.50

PICTURE HISTORY OF THE NORMANDIE: With 190 Illustrations, Frank O. Braynard. Full story of legendary French ocean liner: Art Deco interiors, design innovations, furnishings, celebrities, maiden voyage, tragic fire, much more. Extensive text. 144pp. 8⅜ × 11¾. 25257-4 Pa. $9.95

THE FIRST AMERICAN COOKBOOK: A Facsimile of "American Cookery," 1796, Amelia Simmons. Facsimile of the first American-written cookbook published in the United States contains authentic recipes for colonial favorites—pumpkin pudding, winter squash pudding, spruce beer, Indian slapjacks, and more. Introductory Essay and Glossary of colonial cooking terms. 80pp. 5⅜ × 8½. 24710-4 Pa. $3.50

101 PUZZLES IN THOUGHT AND LOGIC, C. R. Wylie, Jr. Solve murders and robberies, find out which fishermen are liars, how a blind man could possibly identify a color—purely by your own reasoning! 107pp. 5⅜ × 8½. 20367-0 Pa. $2.50

THE BOOK OF WORLD-FAMOUS MUSIC—CLASSICAL, POPULAR AND FOLK, James J. Fuld. Revised and enlarged republication of landmark work in musico-bibliography. Full information about nearly 1,000 songs and compositions including first lines of music and lyrics. New supplement. Index. 800pp. 5⅜ × 8¼. 24857-7 Pa. $14.95

ANTHROPOLOGY AND MODERN LIFE, Franz Boas. Great anthropologist's classic treatise on race and culture. Introduction by Ruth Bunzel. Only inexpensive paperback edition. 255pp. 5⅜ × 8½. 25245-0 Pa. $5.95

THE TALE OF PETER RABBIT, Beatrix Potter. The inimitable Peter's terrifying adventure in Mr. McGregor's garden, with all 27 wonderful, full-color Potter illustrations. 55pp. 4¼ × 5½. (Available in U.S. only) 22827-4 Pa. $1.75

THREE PROPHETIC SCIENCE FICTION NOVELS, H. G. Wells. *When the Sleeper Wakes, A Story of the Days to Come* and *The Time Machine* (full version). 335pp. 5⅜ × 8½. (Available in U.S. only) 20605-X Pa. $5.95

APICIUS COOKERY AND DINING IN IMPERIAL ROME, edited and translated by Joseph Dommers Vehling. Oldest known cookbook in existence offers readers a clear picture of what foods Romans ate, how they prepared them, etc. 49 illustrations. 301pp. 6⅛ × 9¼. 23563-7 Pa. $6.50

SHAKESPEARE LEXICON AND QUOTATION DICTIONARY, Alexander Schmidt. Full definitions, locations, shades of meaning of every word in plays and poems. More than 50,000 exact quotations. 1,485pp. 6½ × 9¼. 22726-X, 22727-8 Pa., Two-vol. set $27.90

THE WORLD'S GREAT SPEECHES, edited by Lewis Copeland and Lawrence W. Lamm. Vast collection of 278 speeches from Greeks to 1970. Powerful and effective models; unique look at history. 842pp. 5⅜ × 8½. 20468-5 Pa. $11.95

THE BLUE FAIRY BOOK, Andrew Lang. The first, most famous collection, with many familiar tales: Little Red Riding Hood, Aladdin and the Wonderful Lamp, Puss in Boots, Sleeping Beauty, Hansel and Gretel, Rumpelstiltskin; 37 in all. 138 illustrations. 390pp. 5⅜ × 8½. 21437-0 Pa. $5.95

THE STORY OF THE CHAMPIONS OF THE ROUND TABLE, Howard Pyle. Sir Launcelot, Sir Tristram and Sir Percival in spirited adventures of love and triumph retold in Pyle's inimitable style. 50 drawings, 31 full-page. xviii + 329pp. 6½ × 9¼. 21883-X Pa. $6.95

AUDUBON AND HIS JOURNALS, Maria Audubon. Unmatched two-volume portrait of the great artist, naturalist and author contains his journals, an excellent biography by his granddaughter, expert annotations by the noted ornithologist, Dr. Elliott Coues, and 37 superb illustrations. Total of 1,200pp. 5⅜ × 8.
Vol. I 25143-8 Pa. $8.95
Vol. II 25144-6 Pa. $8.95

GREAT DINOSAUR HUNTERS AND THEIR DISCOVERIES, Edwin H. Colbert. Fascinating, lavishly illustrated chronicle of dinosaur research, 1820's to 1960. Achievements of Cope, Marsh, Brown, Buckland, Mantell, Huxley, many others. 384pp. 5¼ × 8¼. 24701-5 Pa. $6.95

THE TASTEMAKERS, Russell Lynes. Informal, illustrated social history of American taste 1850's–1950's. First popularized categories Highbrow, Lowbrow, Middlebrow. 129 illustrations. New (1979) afterword. 384pp. 6 × 9.
23993-4 Pa. $6.95

DOUBLE CROSS PURPOSES, Ronald A. Knox. A treasure hunt in the Scottish Highlands, an old map, unidentified corpse, surprise discoveries keep reader guessing in this cleverly intricate tale of financial skullduggery. 2 black-and-white maps. 320pp. 5⅜ × 8½. (Available in U.S. only) 25032-6 Pa. $5.95

AUTHENTIC VICTORIAN DECORATION AND ORNAMENTATION IN FULL COLOR: 46 Plates from "Studies in Design," Christopher Dresser. Superb full-color lithographs reproduced from rare original portfolio of a major Victorian designer. 48pp. 9¼ × 12¼. 25083-0 Pa. $7.95

PRIMITIVE ART, Franz Boas. Remains the best text ever prepared on subject, thoroughly discussing Indian, African, Asian, Australian, and, especially, Northern American primitive art. Over 950 illustrations show ceramics, masks, totem poles, weapons, textiles, paintings, much more. 376pp. 5⅜ × 8. 20025-6 Pa. $6.95

SIDELIGHTS ON RELATIVITY, Albert Einstein. Unabridged republication of two lectures delivered by the great physicist in 1920–21. *Ether and Relativity* and *Geometry and Experience.* Elegant ideas in non-mathematical form, accessible to intelligent layman. vi + 56pp. 5⅜ × 8½. 24511-X Pa. $2.95

THE WIT AND HUMOR OF OSCAR WILDE, edited by Alvin Redman. More than 1,000 ripostes, paradoxes, wisecracks: Work is the curse of the drinking classes, I can resist everything except temptation, etc. 258pp. 5⅜ × 8½. 20602-5 Pa. $4.50

ADVENTURES WITH A MICROSCOPE, Richard Headstrom. 59 adventures with clothing fibers, protozoa, ferns and lichens, roots and leaves, much more. 142 illustrations. 232pp. 5⅜ × 8½. 23471-1 Pa. $3.95

PLANTS OF THE BIBLE, Harold N. Moldenke and Alma L. Moldenke. Standard reference to all 230 plants mentioned in Scriptures. Latin name, biblical reference, uses, modern identity, much more. Unsurpassed encyclopedic resource for scholars, botanists, nature lovers, students of Bible. Bibliography. Indexes. 123 black-and-white illustrations. 384pp. 6 × 9. 25069-5 Pa. $8.95

FAMOUS AMERICAN WOMEN: A Biographical Dictionary from Colonial Times to the Present, Robert McHenry, ed. From Pocahontas to Rosa Parks, 1,035 distinguished American women documented in separate biographical entries. Accurate, up-to-date data, numerous categories, spans 400 years. Indices. 493pp. 6½ × 9¼. 24523-3 Pa. $9.95

THE FABULOUS INTERIORS OF THE GREAT OCEAN LINERS IN HISTORIC PHOTOGRAPHS, William H. Miller, Jr. Some 200 superb photographs capture exquisite interiors of world's great "floating palaces"—1890's to 1980's: *Titanic, Ile de France, Queen Elizabeth, United States, Europa,* more. Approx. 200 black-and-white photographs. Captions. Text. Introduction. 160pp. 8⅞ × 11¾. 24756-2 Pa. $9.95

THE GREAT LUXURY LINERS, 1927–1954: A Photographic Record, William H. Miller, Jr. Nostalgic tribute to heyday of ocean liners. 186 photos of Ile de France, Normandie, Leviathan, Queen Elizabeth, United States, many others. Interior and exterior views. Introduction. Captions. 160pp. 9 × 12. 24056-8 Pa. $9.95

A NATURAL HISTORY OF THE DUCKS, John Charles Phillips. Great landmark of ornithology offers complete detailed coverage of nearly 200 species and subspecies of ducks: gadwall, sheldrake, merganser, pintail, many more. 74 full-color plates, 102 black-and-white. Bibliography. Total of 1,920pp. 8⅝ × 11¼. 25141-1, 25142-X Cloth. Two-vol. set $100.00

THE SEAWEED HANDBOOK: An Illustrated Guide to Seaweeds from North Carolina to Canada, Thomas F. Lee. Concise reference covers 78 species. Scientific and common names, habitat, distribution, more. Finding keys for easy identification. 224pp. 5⅜ × 8½. 25215-9 Pa. $5.95

THE TEN BOOKS OF ARCHITECTURE: The 1755 Leoni Edition, Leon Battista Alberti. Rare classic helped introduce the glories of ancient architecture to the Renaissance. 68 black-and-white plates. 336pp. 8⅜ × 11¼. 25239-6 Pa. $14.95

MISS MACKENZIE, Anthony Trollope. Minor masterpieces by Victorian master unmasks many truths about life in 19th-century England. First inexpensive edition in years. 392pp. 5⅜ × 8½. 25201-9 Pa. $7.95

THE RIME OF THE ANCIENT MARINER, Gustave Doré, Samuel Taylor Coleridge. Dramatic engravings considered by many to be his greatest work. The terrifying space of the open sea, the storms and whirlpools of an unknown ocean, the ice of Antarctica, more—all rendered in a powerful, chilling manner. Full text. 38 plates. 77pp. 9¼ × 12. 22305-1 Pa. $4.95

THE EXPEDITIONS OF ZEBULON MONTGOMERY PIKE, Zebulon Montgomery Pike. Fascinating first-hand accounts (1805–6) of exploration of Mississippi River, Indian wars, capture by Spanish dragoons, much more. 1,088pp. 5⅜ × 8½. 25254-X, 25255-8 Pa. Two-vol. set $23.90

A CONCISE HISTORY OF PHOTOGRAPHY: Third Revised Edition, Helmut Gernsheim. Best one-volume history—camera obscura, photochemistry, daguerreotypes, evolution of cameras, film, more. Also artistic aspects—landscape, portraits, fine art, etc. 281 black-and-white photographs. 26 in color. 176pp. 8⅜ × 11¼. 25128-4 Pa. $12.95

THE DORÉ BIBLE ILLUSTRATIONS, Gustave Doré. 241 detailed plates from the Bible: the Creation scenes, Adam and Eve, Flood, Babylon, battle sequences, life of Jesus, etc. Each plate is accompanied by the verses from the King James version of the Bible. 241pp. 9 × 12. 23004-X Pa. $8.95

HUGGER-MUGGER IN THE LOUVRE, Elliot Paul. Second Homer Evans mystery-comedy. Theft at the Louvre involves sleuth in hilarious, madcap caper. "A knockout."—Books. 336pp. 5⅜ × 8½. 25185-3 Pa. $5.95

FLATLAND, E. A. Abbott. Intriguing and enormously popular science-fiction classic explores the complexities of trying to survive as a two-dimensional being in a three-dimensional world. Amusingly illustrated by the author. 16 illustrations. 103pp. 5⅜ × 8½. 20001-9 Pa. $2.25

THE HISTORY OF THE LEWIS AND CLARK EXPEDITION, Meriwether Lewis and William Clark, edited by Elliott Coues. Classic edition of Lewis and Clark's day-by-day journals that later became the basis for U.S. claims to Oregon and the West. Accurate and invaluable geographical, botanical, biological, meteorological and anthropological material. Total of 1,508pp. 5⅜ × 8½.
21268-8, 21269-6, 21270-X Pa. Three-vol. set $25.50

LANGUAGE, TRUTH AND LOGIC, Alfred J. Ayer. Famous, clear introduction to Vienna, Cambridge schools of Logical Positivism. Role of philosophy, elimination of metaphysics, nature of analysis, etc. 160pp. 5⅜ × 8½. (Available in U.S. and Canada only) 20010-8 Pa. $2.95

MATHEMATICS FOR THE NONMATHEMATICIAN, Morris Kline. Detailed, college-level treatment of mathematics in cultural and historical context, with numerous exercises. For liberal arts students. Preface. Recommended Reading Lists. Tables. Index. Numerous black-and-white figures. xvi + 641pp. 5⅜ × 8½.
24823-2 Pa. $11.95

28 SCIENCE FICTION STORIES, H. G. Wells. Novels, *Star Begotten* and *Men Like Gods,* plus 26 short stories: "Empire of the Ants," "A Story of the Stone Age," "The Stolen Bacillus," "In the Abyss," etc. 915pp. 5⅜ × 8½. (Available in U.S. only)
20265-8 Cloth. $10.95

HANDBOOK OF PICTORIAL SYMBOLS, Rudolph Modley. 3,250 signs and symbols, many systems in full; official or heavy commercial use. Arranged by subject. Most in Pictorial Archive series. 143pp. 8⅛ × 11. 23357-X Pa. $5.95

INCIDENTS OF TRAVEL IN YUCATAN, John L. Stephens. Classic (1843) exploration of jungles of Yucatan, looking for evidences of Maya civilization. Travel adventures, Mexican and Indian culture, etc. Total of 669pp. 5⅜ × 8½.
20926-1, 20927-X Pa., Two-vol. set $9.90

DEGAS: An Intimate Portrait, Ambroise Vollard. Charming, anecdotal memoir by famous art dealer of one of the greatest 19th-century French painters. 14 black-and-white illustrations. Introduction by Harold L. Van Doren. 96pp. 5⅜ × 8½. 25131-4 Pa. $3.95

PERSONAL NARRATIVE OF A PILGRIMAGE TO ALMANDINAH AND MECCAH, Richard Burton. Great travel classic by remarkably colorful personality. Burton, disguised as a Moroccan, visited sacred shrines of Islam, narrowly escaping death. 47 illustrations. 959pp. 5⅜ × 8½. 21217-3, 21218-1 Pa., Two-vol. set $19.90

PHRASE AND WORD ORIGINS, A. H. Holt. Entertaining, reliable, modern study of more than 1,200 colorful words, phrases, origins and histories. Much unexpected information. 254pp. 5⅜ × 8½. 20758-7 Pa. $4.95

THE RED THUMB MARK, R. Austin Freeman. In this first Dr. Thorndyke case, the great scientific detective draws fascinating conclusions from the nature of a single fingerprint. Exciting story, authentic science. 320pp. 5⅜ × 8½. (Available in U.S. only) 25210-8 Pa. $5.95

AN EGYPTIAN HIEROGLYPHIC DICTIONARY, E. A. Wallis Budge. Monumental work containing about 25,000 words or terms that occur in texts ranging from 3000 B.C. to 600 A.D. Each entry consists of a transliteration of the word, the word in hieroglyphs, and the meaning in English. 1,314pp. 6⅛ × 10. 23615-3, 23616-1 Pa., Two-vol. set $27.90

THE COMPLEAT STRATEGYST: Being a Primer on the Theory of Games of Strategy, J. D. Williams. Highly entertaining classic describes, with many illustrated examples, how to select best strategies in conflict situations. Prefaces. Appendices. xvi + 268pp. 5⅜ × 8½. 25101-2 Pa. $5.95

THE ROAD TO OZ, L. Frank Baum. Dorothy meets the Shaggy Man, little Button-Bright and the Rainbow's beautiful daughter in this delightful trip to the magical Land of Oz. 272pp. 5⅜ × 8. 25208-6 Pa. $4.95

POINT AND LINE TO PLANE, Wassily Kandinsky. Seminal exposition of role of point, line, other elements in non-objective painting. Essential to understanding 20th-century art. 127 illustrations. 192pp. 6½ × 9¼. 23808-3 Pa. $4.50

LADY ANNA, Anthony Trollope. Moving chronicle of Countess Lovel's bitter struggle to win for herself and daughter Anna their rightful rank and fortune—perhaps at cost of sanity itself. 384pp. 5⅜ × 8½. 24669-8 Pa. $6.95

EGYPTIAN MAGIC, E. A. Wallis Budge. Sums up all that is known about magic in Ancient Egypt: the role of magic in controlling the gods, powerful amulets that warded off evil spirits, scarabs of immortality, use of wax images, formulas and spells, the secret name, much more. 253pp. 5⅜ × 8½. 22681-6 Pa. $4.00

THE DANCE OF SIVA, Ananda Coomaraswamy. Preeminent authority unfolds the vast metaphysic of India: the revelation of her art, conception of the universe, social organization, etc. 27 reproductions of art masterpieces. 192pp. 5⅜ × 8½. 24817-8 Pa. $5.95

CHRISTMAS CUSTOMS AND TRADITIONS, Clement A. Miles. Origin, evolution, significance of religious, secular practices. Caroling, gifts, yule logs, much more. Full, scholarly yet fascinating; non-sectarian. 400pp. 5⅜ × 8½.
23354-5 Pa. $6.50

THE HUMAN FIGURE IN MOTION, Eadweard Muybridge. More than 4,500 stopped-action photos, in action series, showing undraped men, women, children jumping, lying down, throwing, sitting, wrestling, carrying, etc. 390pp. 7⅞ × 10⅝.
20204-6 Cloth. $21.95

THE MAN WHO WAS THURSDAY, Gilbert Keith Chesterton. Witty, fast-paced novel about a club of anarchists in turn-of-the-century London. Brilliant social, religious, philosophical speculations. 128pp. 5⅜ × 8½. 25121-7 Pa. $3.95

A CEZANNE SKETCHBOOK: Figures, Portraits, Landscapes and Still Lifes, Paul Cezanne. Great artist experiments with tonal effects, light, mass, other qualities in over 100 drawings. A revealing view of developing master painter, precursor of Cubism. 102 black-and-white illustrations. 144pp. 8¾ × 6⅜. 24790-2 Pa. $5.95

AN ENCYCLOPEDIA OF BATTLES: Accounts of Over 1,560 Battles from 1479 B.C. to the Present, David Eggenberger. Presents essential details of every major battle in recorded history, from the first battle of Megiddo in 1479 B.C. to Grenada in 1984. List of Battle Maps. New Appendix covering the years 1967–1984. Index. 99 illustrations. 544pp. 6½ × 9¼. 24913-1 Pa. $14.95

AN ETYMOLOGICAL DICTIONARY OF MODERN ENGLISH, Ernest Weekley. Richest, fullest work, by foremost British lexicographer. Detailed word histories. Inexhaustible. Total of 856pp. 6½ × 9¼.
21873-2, 21874-0 Pa., Two-vol. set $17.00

WEBSTER'S AMERICAN MILITARY BIOGRAPHIES, edited by Robert McHenry. Over 1,000 figures who shaped 3 centuries of American military history. Detailed biographies of Nathan Hale, Douglas MacArthur, Mary Hallaren, others. Chronologies of engagements, more. Introduction. Addenda. 1,033 entries in alphabetical order. xi + 548pp. 6½ × 9¼. (Available in U.S. only)
24758-9 Pa. $11.95

LIFE IN ANCIENT EGYPT, Adolf Erman. Detailed older account, with much not in more recent books: domestic life, religion, magic, medicine, commerce, and whatever else needed for complete picture. Many illustrations. 597pp. 5⅜ × 8½.
22632-8 Pa. $8.50

HISTORIC COSTUME IN PICTURES, Braun & Schneider. Over 1,450 costumed figures shown, covering a wide variety of peoples: kings, emperors, nobles, priests, servants, soldiers, scholars, townsfolk, peasants, merchants, courtiers, cavaliers, and more. 256pp. 8⅜ × 11¼. 23150-X Pa. $7.95

THE NOTEBOOKS OF LEONARDO DA VINCI, edited by J. P. Richter. Extracts from manuscripts reveal great genius; on painting, sculpture, anatomy, sciences, geography, etc. Both Italian and English. 186 ms. pages reproduced, plus 500 additional drawings, including studies for *Last Supper*, *Sforza* monument, etc. 860pp. 7⅞ × 10¾. (Available in U.S. only) 22572-0, 22573-9 Pa., Two-vol. set $25.90

THE ART NOUVEAU STYLE BOOK OF ALPHONSE MUCHA: All 72 Plates from "Documents Decoratifs" in Original Color, Alphonse Mucha. Rare copyright-free design portfolio by high priest of Art Nouveau. Jewelry, wallpaper, stained glass, furniture, figure studies, plant and animal motifs, etc. Only complete one-volume edition. 80pp. 9⅜ × 12¼. 24044-4 Pa. $8.95

ANIMALS: 1,419 COPYRIGHT-FREE ILLUSTRATIONS OF MAMMALS, BIRDS, FISH, INSECTS, ETC., edited by Jim Harter. Clear wood engravings present, in extremely lifelike poses, over 1,000 species of animals. One of the most extensive pictorial sourcebooks of its kind. Captions. Index. 284pp. 9 × 12. 23766-4 Pa. $9.95

OBELISTS FLY HIGH, C. Daly King. Masterpiece of American detective fiction, long out of print, involves murder on a 1935 transcontinental flight—"a very thrilling story"—NY Times. Unabridged and unaltered republication of the edition published by William Collins Sons & Co. Ltd., London, 1935. 288pp. 5⅜ × 8½. (Available in U.S. only) 25036-9 Pa. $4.95

VICTORIAN AND EDWARDIAN FASHION: A Photographic Survey, Alison Gernsheim. First fashion history completely illustrated by contemporary photographs. Full text plus 235 photos, 1840–1914, in which many celebrities appear. 240pp. 6½ × 9¼. 24205-6 Pa. $6.00

THE ART OF THE FRENCH ILLUSTRATED BOOK, 1700–1914, Gordon N. Ray. Over 630 superb book illustrations by Fragonard, Delacroix, Daumier, Doré, Grandville, Manet, Mucha, Steinlen, Toulouse-Lautrec and many others. Preface. Introduction. 633 halftones. Indices of artists, authors & titles, binders and provenances. Appendices. Bibliography. 608pp. 8⅜ × 11¼. 25086-5 Pa. $24.95

THE WONDERFUL WIZARD OF OZ, L. Frank Baum. Facsimile in full color of America's finest children's classic. 143 illustrations by W. W. Denslow. 267pp. 5⅜ × 8½. 20691-2 Pa. $5.95

FRONTIERS OF MODERN PHYSICS: New Perspectives on Cosmology, Relativity, Black Holes and Extraterrestrial Intelligence, Tony Rothman, et al. For the intelligent layman. Subjects include: cosmological models of the universe; black holes; the neutrino; the search for extraterrestrial intelligence. Introduction. 46 black-and-white illustrations. 192pp. 5⅜ × 8½. 24587-X Pa. $6.95

THE FRIENDLY STARS, Martha Evans Martin & Donald Howard Menzel. Classic text marshalls the stars together in an engaging, non-technical survey, presenting them as sources of beauty in night sky. 23 illustrations. Foreword. 2 star charts. Index. 147pp. 5⅜ × 8½. 21099-5 Pa. $3.50

FADS AND FALLACIES IN THE NAME OF SCIENCE, Martin Gardner. Fair, witty appraisal of cranks, quacks, and quackeries of science and pseudoscience: hollow earth, Velikovsky, orgone energy, Dianetics, flying saucers, Bridey Murphy, food and medical fads, etc. Revised, expanded In the Name of Science. "A very able and even-tempered presentation."—The New Yorker. 363pp. 5⅜ × 8. 20394-8 Pa. $6.50

ANCIENT EGYPT: ITS CULTURE AND HISTORY, J. E Manchip White. From pre-dynastics through Ptolemies: society, history, political structure, religion, daily life, literature, cultural heritage. 48 plates. 217pp. 5⅜ × 8½. 22548-8 Pa. $4.95

SIR HARRY HOTSPUR OF HUMBLETHWAITE, Anthony Trollope. Incisive, unconventional psychological study of a conflict between a wealthy baronet, his idealistic daughter, and their scapegrace cousin. The 1870 novel in its first inexpensive edition in years. 250pp. 5⅜ × 8½. 24953-0 Pa. $5.95

LASERS AND HOLOGRAPHY, Winston E. Kock. Sound introduction to burgeoning field, expanded (1981) for second edition. Wave patterns, coherence, lasers, diffraction, zone plates, properties of holograms, recent advances. 84 illustrations. 160pp. 5⅜ × 8¼. (Except in United Kingdom) 24041-X Pa. $3.50

INTRODUCTION TO ARTIFICIAL INTELLIGENCE: SECOND, ENLARGED EDITION, Philip C. Jackson, Jr. Comprehensive survey of artificial intelligence—the study of how machines (computers) can be made to act intelligently. Includes introductory and advanced material. Extensive notes updating the main text. 132 black-and-white illustrations. 512pp. 5⅜ × 8½. 24864-X Pa. $8.95

HISTORY OF INDIAN AND INDONESIAN ART, Ananda K. Coomaraswamy. Over 400 illustrations illuminate classic study of Indian art from earliest Harappa finds to early 20th century. Provides philosophical, religious and social insights. 304pp. 6⅝ × 9⅝. 25005-9 Pa. $8.95

THE GOLEM, Gustav Meyrink. Most famous supernatural novel in modern European literature, set in Ghetto of Old Prague around 1890. Compelling story of mystical experiences, strange transformations, profound terror. 13 black-and-white illustrations. 224pp. 5⅜ × 8½. (Available in U.S. only) 25025-3 Pa. $5.95

ARMADALE, Wilkie Collins. Third great mystery novel by the author of *The Woman in White* and *The Moonstone*. Original magazine version with 40 illustrations. 597pp. 5⅜ × 8½. 23429-0 Pa. $9.95

PICTORIAL ENCYCLOPEDIA OF HISTORIC ARCHITECTURAL PLANS, DETAILS AND ELEMENTS: With 1,880 Line Drawings of Arches, Domes, Doorways, Facades, Gables, Windows, etc., John Theodore Haneman. Sourcebook of inspiration for architects, designers, others. Bibliography. Captions. 141pp. 9 × 12. 24605-1 Pa. $6.95

BENCHLEY LOST AND FOUND, Robert Benchley. Finest humor from early 30's, about pet peeves, child psychologists, post office and others. Mostly unavailable elsewhere. 73 illustrations by Peter Arno and others. 183pp. 5⅜ × 8½. 22410-4 Pa. $3.95

ERTÉ GRAPHICS, Erté. Collection of striking color graphics: *Seasons, Alphabet, Numerals, Aces* and *Precious Stones*. 50 plates, including 4 on covers. 48pp. 9⅜ × 12¼. 23580-7 Pa. $6.95

THE JOURNAL OF HENRY D. THOREAU, edited by Bradford Torrey, F. H. Allen. Complete reprinting of 14 volumes, 1837–61, over two million words; the sourcebooks for *Walden*, etc. Definitive. All original sketches, plus 75 photographs. 1,804pp. 8½ × 12¼. 20312-3, 20313-1 Cloth., Two-vol. set $80.00

CASTLES: THEIR CONSTRUCTION AND HISTORY, Sidney Toy. Traces castle development from ancient roots. Nearly 200 photographs and drawings illustrate moats, keeps, baileys, many other features. Caernarvon, Dover Castles, Hadrian's Wall, Tower of London, dozens more. 256pp. 5⅜ × 8¼. 24898-4 Pa. $5.95

*CATALOG OF DOVER BOOKS*

AMERICAN CLIPPER SHIPS: 1833–1858, Octavius T. Howe & Frederick C. Matthews. Fully-illustrated, encyclopedic review of 352 clipper ships from the period of America's greatest maritime supremacy. Introduction. 109 halftones. 5 black-and-white line illustrations. Index. Total of 928pp. 5⅜ × 8½.
25115-2, 25116-0 Pa., Two-vol. set $17.90

TOWARDS A NEW ARCHITECTURE, Le Corbusier. Pioneering manifesto by great architect, near legendary founder of "International School." Technical and aesthetic theories, views on industry, economics, relation of form to function, "mass-production spirit," much more. Profusely illustrated. Unabridged translation of 13th French edition. Introduction by Frederick Etchells. 320pp. 6⅛ × 9¼. (Available in U.S. only) 25023-7 Pa. $8.95

THE BOOK OF KELLS, edited by Blanche Cirker. Inexpensive collection of 32 full-color, full-page plates from the greatest illuminated manuscript of the Middle Ages, painstakingly reproduced from rare facsimile edition. Publisher's Note. Captions. 32pp. 9⅜ × 12¼. 24345-1 Pa. $4.95

BEST SCIENCE FICTION STORIES OF H. G. WELLS, H. G. Wells. Full novel *The Invisible Man,* plus 17 short stories: "The Crystal Egg," "Aepyornis Island," "The Strange Orchid," etc. 303pp. 5⅜ × 8½. (Available in U.S. only)
21531-8 Pa. $4.95

AMERICAN SAILING SHIPS: Their Plans and History, Charles G. Davis. Photos, construction details of schooners, frigates, clippers, other sailcraft of 18th to early 20th centuries—plus entertaining discourse on design, rigging, nautical lore, much more. 137 black-and-white illustrations. 240pp. 6⅛ × 9¼.
24658-2 Pa. $5.95

ENTERTAINING MATHEMATICAL PUZZLES, Martin Gardner. Selection of author's favorite conundrums involving arithmetic, money, speed, etc., with lively commentary. Complete solutions. 112pp. 5⅜ × 8½. 25211-6 Pa. $2.95

THE WILL TO BELIEVE, HUMAN IMMORTALITY, William James. Two books bound together. Effect of irrational on logical, and arguments for human immortality. 402pp. 5⅜ × 8½. 20291-7 Pa. $7.50

THE HAUNTED MONASTERY and THE CHINESE MAZE MURDERS, Robert Van Gulik. 2 full novels by Van Gulik continue adventures of Judge Dee and his companions. An evil Taoist monastery, seemingly supernatural events; overgrown topiary maze that hides strange crimes. Set in 7th-century China. 27 illustrations. 328pp. 5⅜ × 8½. 23502-5 Pa. $5.95

CELEBRATED CASES OF JUDGE DEE (DEE GOONG AN), translated by Robert Van Gulik. Authentic 18th-century Chinese detective novel; Dee and associates solve three interlocked cases. Led to Van Gulik's own stories with same characters. Extensive introduction. 9 illustrations. 237pp. 5⅜ × 8½.
23337-5 Pa. $4.95

*Prices subject to change without notice.*

Available at your book dealer or write for free catalog to Dept. GI, Dover Publications, Inc., 31 East 2nd St., Mineola, N.Y. 11501. Dover publishes more than 175 books each year on science, elementary and advanced mathematics, biology, music, art, literary history, social sciences and other areas.